QUEBEC UNDER FREE TRADE

MAKING PUBLIC POLICY IN NORTH AMERICA

PRESSES DE L'UNIVERSITÉ DU QUÉBEC
2875, boul. Laurier, Sainte-Foy (Québec) G1V 2M3
Téléphone : (418) 657-4399
Télécopieur : (418) 657-2096
Catalogue sur internet : http://www.uquebec.ca/puq/puq.html

Distribution :

DISTRIBUTION DE LIVRES UNIVERS S.E.N.C.
845, rue Marie-Victorin, Saint-Nicolas (Québec) G0S 3L0
Téléphone : (418) 831-7474 / 1-800-859-7474
Télécopieur : (418) 831-4021

Europe :
ÉDITIONS ESKA
27, rue Dunois, 75013, Paris, France
Téléphone : (1) 45 83 62 02
Télécopieur : (1) 44 24 06 94

QUEBEC UNDER FREE TRADE

MAKING PUBLIC POLICY IN NORTH AMERICA

EDITED BY
GUY LACHAPELLE

FOREWORD BY
STEPHEN BLANK

Presses de l'Université du Québec

Canadian Cataloguing in Publication Data

Main entry under title :
   Quebec under free trade : making public policy in North America
   ISBN 2-7605-0874-9

   1. Free trade – Quebec (Province). 2. Quebec (Province) – Commerce – North America.
3. North America – Commercial treaties. 4. North America – Economic integration.
I. Lachapelle, Guy, 1955 -   .

HF1769.Q8Q82 1995   382'.71'09714   C95-941524-6

Révision linguistique : Robert Paré
Mise en pages : Info 1000 mots
Couverture : Caron & Gosselin communication graphique

Dépôt légal – 4ᵉ trimestre 1995
Bibliothèque nationale du Québec / Bibliothèque nationale du Canada
Imprimé au Canada

Contents

Foreword

Stephen Blank
Americas Society

For many years, one spoke of "North America" with great reluctance in Anglophone Canada. The term signaled an accommodation with the temptations of continentalism and the fatal elephantine embrace. For French Quebecers, however, the reemergence of national self-consciousness has also meant the rediscovery of Quebec's historic North American identity.

Just how deeply this sense of North America runs is open to question. The best educated and most sophisticated Quebecers of my generation are far more familiar with Paris and even the cities of the *Francophonie* than with New York or Chicago, not to speak of Mexico City or Monterrey. Yet of the many distinct strands that are braided together in the Quebec personality – *canadienne*, Canadian, French, British – North America is also one. It is this sense of a fundamental North American identity that leads Quebecers to insist, awkwardly at times, that they are not "immigrants".

Personality aside, Quebecers representing the entire array of political persuasions from ardent federalist to passionate sovereigntist have viewed the emergence of a North American economic space as a profoundly liberating prospect for Quebec, either within the context of a Canadian political community or as an independent North American nation. Turning Canadian economic nationalism on its head, they believe that integration into a continental economic system will enhance, not diminish, Quebec's distinctiveness and will widen, not narrow, its prospects for economic development.

This much needed book explores the emerging reality of Quebec in North America. The tone is not excessively optmistic. This book reminds us, for example, that barely a third of Quebecers supported NAFTA and that more than a majority opposed it. And yet, Quebec is deeply affected by the ongoing "spatial recomposition of North America" which is leading to higher levels of North American integration, an key element of which is a very substantial increase in Quebec–U.S. trade in liberalized sectors.

The volume brings together a group of scholars with varied perspectives on Quebec under free trade whose work has been rarely available in English. This introduction to these perspectives and colleagues is of great value in itself.

Quebec in the North American Economy:
Historical, Political, Social and Economic Dimensions

1

Quebec under Free Trade:
Between Interdependence and Transnationalism

Guy Lachapelle
Concordia University

This paper presents an overview of the central contentions made by a number of authors about the paradox between sovereignty and integration, and the resulting implications for Quebec's future economic relations with its North American partners. The central question that this essay addresses is: Would an autonomous political unit become engaged in a process in which the logical outcome will be the reduction and perhaps the complete elimination of its power and autonomy? The answer to this question raises several further questions about the strategy Quebec should adopt in the case of a 1995 or later vote in favour of political sovereignty. Several policy alternatives are proposed. Finally, since the most recent figures indicate an increase in trade between Quebec and the United States, we conclude that, whatever the outcome of the 1995 referendum, this pattern would continue.

Since Quebec's overwhelming support of the 1988 free trade agreement with the United States, the animosities between Canada's two nations have intensified. While English Canadians and English Quebecers expressed their adamant opposition to the Free Trade Agreement (FTA) prior to its endorsement, the majority of French Quebecers encouraged it. English Canadians claim that Quebecers were self-interested in supporting a deal that threatened the very existence of the Canadian state; and English Quebecers assert that free trade is a big step towards greater integration with the U.S. For their part, most French Quebecers maintain that the FTA and the North American Free Trade Agreement (NAFTA) will ensure Quebec's prosperity, and they are willing to succumb to a continental integration if that is what it will take to be an independent state.

According to many English Canadians, particularly those who subscribe to Georges Grant's basic view of a borderless North American society, the only way to counter full integration with the United States is to have a stronger centralized federal government (Grant, 1991: 54). Ottawa can formulate policies that will protect the Canadian identity, just as the Trudeau governments of the 1970s created the Foreign Investment Review Agency (FIRA) and established the National Energy Program (NEP) in 1973. However, federal policies such as these were challenged not only by the private sector but also by provincial governments, who considered them provincial matters. And the election of the Conservative Party of Brian Mulroney in 1984, with its new policy formulation, led Canadian nationalists to talk of the end of Canada as a "distinct nation and culture" from the United States.

English Canadians are suspiciously critical of Quebec's support of free trade, since they consider it a detriment to Canada's economic sovereignty and culture (Thomas, 1992-93: 182). This assumption demonstrates a clear misunderstanding of Quebec nationalism. Canadians must understand that Quebecers do not differentiate integration from sovereignty. Quebec's involvement in the FTA has allowed them to become a part of the global political system and has enabled them to develop their own identity. As a possible ensuing result, the FTA may even compel Quebec to accept some form of common interpendency with Canada, the United States and Mexico.

For those who share a "liberal" view of the world, it is difficult to see Quebec's idea of sovereignty as the only acceptable path towards greater autonomy (Lachapelle, 1978). The Canadian government and institutions have always prevented Quebec from participating in world affairs and refused to allow the Quebec government to establish a delegation in Washington D.C. The position adopted by the Canadian Ambassador to Washington D.C. during the 1994 ACQS meeting clearly showed that the Canadian Embassy is the only channel through which the Quebec government can meet with American officials and explain Canadian unwillingness to grant Quebec a "special status" that would recognize its distinctiveness within Canada. It seems highly plausible that Ottawa should want Quebecers to renounce their convictions and convert to universalism. The question is: Can the earnest voice of Quebec be heard in a world which neglects the cultural and political needs of smaller nations? As early as 1970, as Quebec remembers it, former Prime Minister Pierre E. Trudeau used coercion to stifle the growth of the sovereignist movement. Evidently, the problem with liberalism is that it leaves no room for maturing nations to prosper.

Contrary to what Grant's analysis may suggest and what Canadian nationalists assert, most Quebecers believe in the pursuit of progress while still advocating the preservation of their sovereignty. How could any autonomous political unit engage in a process that might eliminate its power and home rule? In Grant's view, economic integration and sovereignty are incompatible because one cancels out the other. But if Canada is able to strive for greater sovereignty to improve its world status and rank, would it not be possible for Quebec to do the same? If free trade speeds up the "homogenization of cultures," as author Ramsey Cook states in his book *The Maple Leaf Forever* (1971), then consequently, should not the economic relationship between Quebec and Canada bring the same impetus? And finally, since Quebec has flourished peacefully within the Canadian unit, would it not be safe to presume that it would succeed equally as well as a separate North American sovereign entity?

Despite many empirical analyses by the integration and transnational theorists, the paradox between integration and sovereignty still remains unresolved (Brams, 1976: 80; Legaré, 1992). The problem does not only encompass the economic and political relationship between nation-states, but also the state's relative autonomy in the decision-making process.

Most political students and devotees do not know the true meaning of a sovereign and/or autonomous state. This should not be too surprising. Even amongst scholars and political scientists, the true concept of "sovereign state" is ambiguous, and the search for a clear definition still provokes profound debates. However, the general understanding of the term "sovereign state" is a country where the power of decision remains in the hands of the leading political party or monarch, and where any autonomous organization within the system may influence political decisions. On its own, the term "sovereignty" is a more legal concept resulting in reorganization of political entities. It is important to mention that all states are autonomous to various degrees, depending on their association with other autonomous organizations within the state. The study of politics deals with the relationship between these different autonomous groups, inside and outside the state.

Quebec's predicament is interesting. The province's economic liaison with Canada has been the subject of several political conflicts in recent years, a plight that may very well lead to the disintegration of Canada if Quebec obtains its sovereignty in 1995 or later. If Quebec separates, it will be contrary to the views of many integrationists who preach for a united world. However, theorists such as Lindgren argue that a country's independence can remove all major barriers, effectively eliminating the sources of conflicts and alienation to enhance cooperation between two entities or countries (Lindgren, 1959; Etzioni, 1965: 185). The same argument was recently publicized by 1992 Nobel Economics Laureate, Gary S. Becker, who wrote:

> It is commonly believed that French-speaking Quebec will decline economically if it separates from the rest of Canada. That view ignores the role international trade plays in economic success. After perhaps a severe adjustment period, Quebec could find a prosperous place in the world economy in trading with

Canada, the U.S., and Mexico as well as the rest of Latin America. That separation could also help the economies of English-speaking Canada because it would reduce cultural battle and eliminate the confrontations with Quebec over the allocation of tax revenues and government expenditures (Becker, 1994).

Quebec is protective of its national sovereignty in the North American realm. But it is also ready to face the challenge and actively cooperate in NAFTA and in other continental organizations, such as NATO and the Organization of American States (OAS).

The main purpose of this chapter is to present a conceptual framework that may resolve the well-known paradox between government autonomy and policy effectiveness. Quebec's support of the North American Free Trade Agreement should not be underestimated; if Quebec becomes a sovereign country, the Parti Québécois government will be ready and willing to sign the treaty. This government's objective is also the smooth integration of Quebec's economy into the North American market. Bill 51, an act respecting the promotion of international trade agreements, follows this line. Nonetheless, the Canadian and Mexican governments have indicated that they are reluctant to see Quebec become a member of NAFTA. They have gone so far as to suggest that Quebec might have a tough time negotiating its entry – a view that the U.S. State Department does not seem to share. The Quebec government should therefore look for other alternatives and prepare itself for any possible scenario.

The second part of our chapter presents a discussion on three central arguments:

1. NAFTA does not and will not impede Quebec's government autonomy.

2. Under NAFTA, Quebec is identified as a "functional state" and, if sovereignty is achieved, it will become a "nation-state" pursuing global policy goals.

3. The Quebec government presently has full power to establish the principles of its economic association with its North American partners.

THE INTEGRATION AND TRANSNATIONAL APPROACHES

There are two ways of approaching the issue of the economic relationship between nations: first, through the *integrationists'* perspective, and second, by means of the *transnational* perspective. The conceptual discussion on the power and impact of decisions taken by a sovereign state remains a difficult topic for the integration theorists. It raises some ethical concerns as well, dealing, for instance, with the existence of a natural political order or the achievement of a world system. For many integration theorists, the nation-state cannot be politically sovereign because the pressures stemming from the international market are so forceful that they weaken the power of the state. To counter the effect, the peripheral states, sharing common political ideas and cultural background, impose economic barriers and create an economic union.

FIGURE 1

**The Dilemma between Government Autonomy
and Policy Effectiveness**

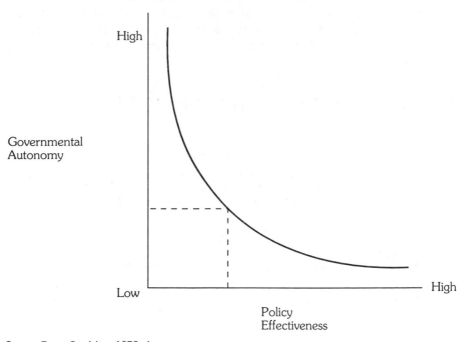

Source: Bengt Sundelius, 1978, 4.

On the other hand, the transnational theorists, such as John Kenneth Galbraith, argue that the power of multinational corporations (MNC) weakens the political sovereignty of the state. Galbraith writes that "standing astride of international boundaries, (it) is an assault on political sovereignty" (Galbraith, 1975: 160). Furthermore, economic barriers such as tariffs, quotas and embargoes place no major constraints on the power of multinational corporations. Because MNC dominate the national and global markets, the aim of international governments is to come to an arrangement whereby the autonomy or the sovereignty of the state is only slightly affected while its policies remain indubitably effective. As Bengt Sundelius once pointed out, this is the principal dilemma of most small countries or regional entities similar to Quebec. No research findings have ever truly established the relationship between policy effectiveness and government autonomy in a way that would indicate how a change in one variable relates to a change in another variable (Sundelius, 1978: 160).

In this respect, the transnational theorists consider that "the hard shell of national sovereignty appears less daunting" (Keohane and Nye Jr., 1972: ix-xxix). One of the greatest illusions of our time is the belief that a worldwide economy and modern technology have devaluaed the political sovereignty of the state. To go more deeply into this discussion, different schools of thought must be examined. We must see how each of these approaches defines the notions of sovereignty and autonomy in order to determine the impact of a sovereign Quebec as a member of NAFTA based on its economic relationships with the United States, Canada and Mexico.

PERSPECTIVES ON THE SOVEREIGN OR AUTONOMOUS STATE

After the Second World War, the *confederal* view rapidly became the main stream. Advanced by such well-known political leaders as Charles de Gaulle and Winston Churchill, this view represented an important step towards developing intergovernmental cooperation in Europe. It was promoted through the League of Nations, a permanent organization that believed profoundly in the sovereignty of the nation-state, as it sought to preserve the political independence of European states. Inis Claude wrote this in his book *Swords Into Plowshares – The Problem and Progress of International Organization*:

> The League was strongly imbued with the Wilsonian conviction that the nation is the natural and proper unit of world politics, and that the only sound and moral basis for international order is a settlement which enables peoples to achieve autonomous existence within a system dedicated to the preservation of the independence and sovereignty of nations. Sovereignty was not a naughty word for the League; it was a symbol of liberty in international relations comparable to democracy as a symbol of domestic freedom (Claude, 1956: 57-58).

According to the confederalists, the economic relationship between states and the creation of an economic union such as the Common Market cannot be used as substructures for a real federation since most states share their political identity and sovereignty.

From this standpoint, the Canadian example is enlightening. When four provinces, including Quebec, signed the British North American Act in 1867, they had formed a confederation, and many Canadians still describe Canada as such. A confederation is, by definition, an association of independent states that agree to confer a certain amount of authority upon the central government while still retaining their full individual sovereignty. Although there was much publicity surrounding the "Fathers of the Confederation" event during the 125th anniversary of Canada in 1992, in the post-war period the country has tried to evolve as a federation rather than a confederation. However, try as it may, Canada cannot seem to reap the benefits. Most political barriers, such as the search for regional identity and autonomy, have not been eliminated and have impeded the remodeling of the Canadian political system.

The Federalist and Pluralist Perspectives

Standard mechanisms used to achieve international equilibrium (i.e. diplomacy) have proven to be non-permanent and unreliable in maintaining peace and security. The *federalists* therefore believe that the state's autonomy must be controlled. A system that legitimizes the existence of a multitude of sovereign entities can only lead to conflicts and war. However, the *pluralists'* perspective takes the classical version of the federalist view into consideration and encourages the attainment of international order and national security by peaceful means. While the pluralist believes integration to be a legal process, the federalist sees it as a sociological development.

Sovereignty is a legal status. An entity is either sovereign or it is not. Since some federations have been created in the aftermath of revolutions, federalists postulate that an integration process will be successful only if different nations merge peacefully in order to establish a new political identity. The pluralists share this view. However, *sociological federalists* believe that a new political system emerges only when the legal expression of sovereignty and its political basis no longer exist in the new system.

In opposition to the pluralist view, federalists assume that the only way to resolve the paradox between sovereignty and interdependency is by enforcing coercive measures. Laureen S. McKinsey acknowledged this in her analysis of the integration process in Canada. In her opinion, "the emphasis of the supranational theorists upon peaceful change as the mark of integration must be rejected. In Canada, peaceful change could be associated with disintegration rather than integration" (McKinsey, 1976: 353). Simply put, McKinsey suggests that the only way for Canada to face the problem of the Quebec sovereignty-association or sovereignty issue is by persuasion and intimidation. However, it is comforting to know that countries such as Norway and Sweden managed to obtain their independence relatively peacefully.

Donald J. Puchala criticized the federal model by arguing that it tends to circumvent some crucial concerns. An example would be whether "participation in an international integration arrangement actually enhances rather than undermines national sovereignty" (Puchala, 1972: 271). And as Francis

Rosenstiel once pointed out, "at the same time as federalism integrates sovereignties, it integrates policies and, with these, problems... Federalism, being a technique, cannot be a result" (Rosenstiel, 1963: 133). In other words, integration processes are not necessarily successful.

Pluralists recognize that international political integration requires the reduction or elimination of a nation-state's sovereign power. However, if a nation is to accept limitations on its political self-determination, this could only be for two vital reasons: either to maintain peace, or to protect the lives of its people. The integration process is regarded as a choice between sovereignty/ autonomy and security (Deutsch, 1963: 202-229; Deutsch, 1966: 7). The ultimate result of this is the creation of what Karl W. Deutsch has identified as a "security-community," where several nations submit to constraints on their political autonomy in order to develop common political institutions. A pluralistic security-community retains the legal independence of separate governments, just as Quebec and Canada would if the former became sovereign.

Pluralists believe that, ideally, peace should be maintained in the international community by means of diplomatic meetings. This is where the decision-making power of the state is safeguarded; the nation-state is not only an important political player but also an analytical unit. Integration is only possible if the nation-state is preserved and if international peace and security together with the development of the nation as a political form are recognized and consistent in their terms (e.g., reinforcing national autonomy and international stability in the North American system). Pluralists assume that the process of integration does not provoke the demise of the nation-state, but rather the end of the "state of war" among nations (Pentland, 1973: 36). In short, they prefer an integration model because it does not compromise the essential power of the state (for example, its national security) and it maintains national sovereignty not merely as a legal function but also as a political, economic, military and technological reality (Deutsch, 1974).

The Supranational Perspective

The notion of "supranationality" is difficult to understand because it cannot be studied unless the state's sovereignty is recognized by the international community. In addition, there is a reasoning which maintains that the progress of history needs a larger unit than the nation-state. The federalists' definition of a supranational state therefore seems to be an unfortunate intellectual heritage from the Enlightenment period.

According to the *supranational* theorists, any political or economic union is an association of concurrent sovereignties and not the creation of just one. They hope the new state, a supranational actor, will soon become a unified entity. In such a system, part of the state's sovereignty is lost when a union such as NAFTA is created, since a state can only stay sovereign if it retains its power on residual issues. Francis Rosenstiel makes a distinction between the juridico-political apparatus of the state and what he calls its "sociological sovereignty," i.e. the behaviour of government officers who act as though Quebec were already an independent state (Rosenstiel, 1963: 129).

FIGURE 2

Approaches and Perspectives to the Study of State Autonomy

Approaches and perspectives	The integrationist approach (policy effectiveness)	The transnationalist approach (government autonomy)
Confederalism	Development of intergovernment cooperation	Shared political identity and sovereignty
Federalism	Creation of "new communities"	Undermines national sovereignty
	Use of coercion	State autonomy must be restrained and/or abolished
Pluralism	Diplomatic meeting and common political institutions	Preservation of the decision-making power of the state
	Cooperation + security/peace and autonomy	"Concordance system"
Functionalism/Neo-functionalism	Future global trade pattern	Erosion of national sovereignty
Supranationalism	One unified identity	Concurrent-sociological sovereignty
		Residual issues
Neo-Marxism	Dependency relationship	Constant erosion of state autonomy

The former Quebec Premier, Robert Bourassa, adopted the supranational position after the failure of the Meech Lake Accord. In his opinion, this outlook served Canada's best interests because it provided an outlet for addressing the Quebec sovereignty issue (particularly since both the Canadian and Quebec entities would maintain individual sovereign status). And although the nation-state never relinquishes its juridico-political power, the citizens of different states may become members of a new supra-community. This concept is clearly, in practice, more of an ethical ideology than a political one (Rosenstiel, 1963: 130).

For Quebec, Canada and the United States, a supranational stance is a source of considerable apprehension since it involves the creation of a supranational identity (i.e. we are all North Americans). But since the governments involved have not addressed the idea of supranational unification, it is highly unlikely that a real North American Common Market (NACM) will be formed in the near future. So far there has been no discussion of the creation of a North American Council, an institution which would essentially act as an inter-governmental association. The possibility of NAFTA and a common market actually instigating an economic union, or even a political union with supra-national bodies, certainly seems improbable at this stage and completely contrary to the aspirations of the American, Mexican, Canadian and Quebec governments.

Thus, nation-state sovereignty should remain an important factor in defin-ing the relationship between the Canadian-U.S.-Mexican partners, and the Quebec sovereignty issue should not change their standing. It is the strain of nationalism, the fierce demand that each nation be *sui juris*, free from political control, even though such control is based on equal membership in a jointly-constructed union, that will undermine the creation of a fully integrated North American market.

To unite all these controversial conceptual frameworks for economic inte-gration, Donald J. Puchala proposes a "concordance system." Here, conflicts between nations are resolved peacefully and the national governments main-tain their position as central actors. Puchala points out that this system is essen-tially based on the relationship between sovereign states and on separate peoples who adapt themselves at the subnational, national, transnational and supranational levels. The "concordance system" does not need to be assimi-lated into a supranational identity. Puchala recognizes the interdependency between national and international markets, but writes that the system does not negate a state's sovereignty. There are different procedures for each level, and:

> They are rather recognitions of modern economic and technological forces that transverse national frontiers, recognitions that states no longer relieve internal pressures by external imperialism, and indeed affirmations that nation-states can be preserved as distinct entities only through the international pooling of resources to confront problems that challenge their separate existence (Puchala, 1972: 282).

The Functional and Neo-Functional Perspectives

According to the *functionalists*, the push towards national autonomy is a major impediment to the development of a North American community – a vision prevalent in English Canada. The state's sovereignty would inevitably be worn away by successive fits of self-interested "absentmindedness." The outcome would be the formation of territorial units (nation-states), where protective atti-tudes of sovereignty abound, and of functional units (communities), where rationality and technocracy override the decisions of the nation-states. Charles

Pentland wrote, concerning the future of nation-states, that "the sociological, economic and technological base of national sovereignty is swiftly eroding, and the future global pattern becoming daily more evident and more necessary" (Pentland, 1973: 78).

Thus, the nation-state, with its supporting doctrines of sovereignty and non-intervention, is considered to be an obstacle to the resolution of economic difficulties. National sovereignty becomes the prerogative of people with irrational, dysfunctional and destructive emotions, while the amalgamation of states becomes the goal of the reasonable person. This suggests that Quebec should remain a community and that its search for nationhood is trifling. On the other hand, a sovereign Quebec may also be perceived as a nation pursuing rational objectives, and perhaps even a solution to Northern difficulties.

Neo-functionalists avoid this entanglement by dissolving the state system into an interdependent network of subnational political foci, seeking narrow interests across boundaries. Here, the state's sovereignty loses its impact: "The study of regional integration is concerned with tasks, transactions, perceptions, and learning, not with sovereignty, military capability, and balance of power" (Haas, 1971: 4). Neo-functionalists assume that there is sufficient *de facto* interdependency among nation-states for them to dismiss the state as a political actor and to analyze only the relationships between political leaders, governments and bureaucrats.

Neo-functionalists also try to explain political integration between countries by examining the arrangements under which nation-states cease to be autonomous decision-makers. Although the neo-functionalists are not primarily interested in state sovereignty, they are concerned with explaining "how and why states cease to be wholly sovereign, how and why they voluntarily mingle, merge, and mix with their neighbours so as to lose the factual attributes of sovereignty while acquiring new techniques for resolving conflicts between themselves" (Haas, 1971: 6). They also consider that any movement which reduces the decision-making power of the state, or which minimizes its political sovereignty, represents a wholesome development for world peace. From this perspective, Quebec's break from Canada may provoke friction and strife between both nations and beyond.

The functional/neo-functional approach lies at the centre of Faucher and Lamontagne's work (1973, 1971). These theorists presented a continental perspective in which natural resources and technology are considered to be the determinants of economic development. This in turn led to the concepts of centres and peripheries, providing the economic nucleus, the United States, with greater clout. In this approach, geo-economic factors and regional disparities become the fundamental motives for immigration and economic variations. Some critics, however, have argued in response that this perspective overestimates the role of national resources and technology and underestimates the importance of investment and labour. As Linteau, Durocher and Robert point out, Faucher wrote superficially of the cultural and social factors, which must be examined critically in order to comprehend the economic growth of a society (Linteau, Durocher and Robert, 1979).

In light of the overall positive negotiation of the FTA and NAFTA, and the unquestionable faith in the technological society, Gagnon and Montcalm reiterate the importance of Faucher and Lamontagne's hypothesis in their own work (1989). These authors argued that Quebec became economically marginalized primarily because of North American economic restructuring. Capital investments and decision-making powers were emphasized, they said, to the detriment of Quebec's economy. This was particularly true for the Greater Montreal area where, during the 1980s, a period of rapid de-industrialization was observed. The major criticism of the centre-periphery theory is its overall incapacity to explain the socio-political phenomenon; Gagnon and Montcalm even go so far as to suggest that the Quiet Revolution may never have happened at all. More significantly, the centre-periphery theory devalues the importance of the Quebec state's political autonomy.

In contrast, a document on Greater Montreal, prepared by the Quebec Liberal government during the Bourassa regime, suggests that the economic difficulties of the Quebec/Montreal regions appear to be based on the economic and sociological influences operating within Quebec's territory, and not on outside influences. The report examines, among other things, the sluggish renewal of the manufacturing industry, the economic policies of different levels of government, the financial sector's shift to Toronto, and the language issue as factors accounting for the Montreal region's economic decline (Quebec Government: 12-13).

The Neo-Marxist Perspective

With respect to the integrationist theorists' arguments, the *neo-Marxist* perspective takes the view that the state's base-level autonomy is constantly eroding. Researcher Raimo Vayrymen defines the base level as "the totality of productive forces and their interrelations across national boundaries as well as market mechanisms through which the exchange of commodities, financial flows, etc., takes place" (Vayrymen, 1974: 82). However, on a superstructural level, the nation-states can express their ideological solidarity by harmonizing their economic relationships and by having their sovereignty recognized by the international community. Usually, sovereignty recognition is the result of an economic dependency among nation-states.

Canadian unity is not based solely on the autonomous cooperation between Quebec and English Canada. Its intercourse is regulated by the economic and political forces within the U.S. as well, more so at the base level than at the superstructural level. Although Canada and Mexico are autonomous countries internally, they are dependent economically on the U.S. This in turn creates an "external dependent unity" between Quebec and Canada. In other words, a free trade system is a powerful factor which builds and maintains economic and political dependency between nations. The neo-Marxist approach is close to the transnational idea; the distinction is that government discussions on autonomy and/or sovereignty in the former is certainly more of an internal process than in the latter. Hence political autonomy can be eroded by MNCs. This process does not, however, explain the impact of external forces.

QUEBEC AND A NORTH AMERICAN INTEGRATION: SOME ALTERNATIVES TO RESOLVE THE PARADOX

Although Quebec wants to preserve its political and economic sovereignty within North America, it is difficult to ignore the lure from south of the border. Since the early 1960s, the United States has become an attractive economic force to be reckoned with, and it seems impossible for Quebec to avoid the U.S. market. If Quebec does become a sovereign state, it will definitely have some concerns over its authority in North America, and it will certainly voice its disagreement if its powers are taken away by yet another political force.

Although the United States is watching the situation, it does not want to get involved in what is obviously an internal matter in another sovereign state. However, given the clamour of the Quebec sovereignists, it would be difficult for the U.S. to ignore what is going on above its northern frontier for very long, particularly if it might affect trade in some way.

In all probability, the United States will play a major role in cementing the pieces of the fractured North American trading corporation back together. The fact that President Clinton made deals with almost every interest group to secure enough votes to get NAFTA through Congress suggests that Quebec's sovereignty may provide a good excuse for the U.S. authorities to reopen the debate over interdependency. What is important to the United States in the "future serviceability of the Canadian debt" is that Quebec's share of the bill be equal to its relative ability to service it (Wonnacott, 1991: 22). A sovereign Quebec could refuse to share part of the Canadian debt. Canada could also refuse to negotiate (which is unlikely); at the very least, it could determine the terms of reimbursement if negotiations over other issues cannot be resolved.

One such issue is, of course, the free trade agreement. Any re-negotiation between the members of NAFTA to include a sovereign Quebec would either be amicable or difficult to pull off. Canada would probably want major concessions from Quebec. Quebec would probably want to set a precedent, a guarantee that it will not be easily pushed around. Ronald Wonnacott wrote that "each part will have its own set of conflicting internal interests, which means that its negotiating position may change at any time because of a configuration of power among its domestic interest groups. Moreover, there will be a wide range of issues to negotiate, and the greater the number and complexity of issues to be resolved, the more likely that conflicts will arise" (Wonnacott, 1991: 28). As John Rawls points out in his *Theory of Justice*, it is up to the individuals and nations to elaborate the principles that will guide their associations. A framework will serve not only the spirit of justice but the spirit of freedom as well.

Three economic alternatives are proposed for a sovereign Quebec – notwithstanding the preferred expectation of signing the NAFTA agreement immediately after separation. These are: (1) Quebec should suggest the creation of a North American Committee on Cultural Cooperation; (2) Quebec should be ready to sign economic and cultural treaties with each partner; (3) a sovereign Quebec should not alter North American economic and trade patterns. Each of these options will help Quebec in its struggle with the sovereignty and economic cooperation issue, and will ease the transition period.

First Alternative: Quebec and NAFTA – The Creation of a North American Committee for Economic Cooperation (NACEC)

The Quebec government and its present leader, Jacques Parizeau, have always stated that the best option for Quebec is to sign the NAFTA agreement independently of Canada's pen mark. However, because some critics considered this option unrealistic, the Quebec government was obliged to explore alternative solutions, including the creation of a North American Committee for Economic Cooperation (NACEC). This committee proposes, first of all, to analyze the possibility of strengthening the economic relationships between Quebec, Canada, the United States and Mexico. If Quebec ever became a sovereign country, an expected ten-year transition period would probably be necessary before an economic union between the four countries could be fully achieved.

Because its economy is based on only a few products, a sovereign Quebec will certainly be reluctant to engage itself completely in NAFTA. On a short-term basis, an economic union may have negative effects on Quebec's economy; should this be the case, the free trade "relative advantage" theory will not apply. Even after Quebec becomes independent, Canada and the United States will continue to hold a "relative advantage" in fields such as agriculture and the industrial sectors. The question of whether Quebec should throw its doors open to free trade remains unanswered, particularly since a significant amount of restructuring is expected in some of its major economic sectors.

Quebec will certainly not be the only state wishing to form a North American economic union; subsequently, the other countries involved must try to cooperate. There is no doubt that the strain on Quebec's political integrity/ territoriality will be used as a way of attaining political unity. But the creation of a federation amongst the North American partners is unlikely. Once separated from the Canadian federal unit, Quebecers will certainly refuse other similar forms of government. And to keep its political strength, Quebec will have to deflate any member of the future North American council who attempts to increase its own power of decision at the expense of Quebec's. A North American economic committee should be established as a consultative organization rather than a legislative one.

It is obvious that the economic relations between the four states would have to be strengthened. Some assurances would be required to guarantee that each country could benefit from the cooperation. A joint North American committee would probably be necessary at the intergovernmental level, since the political autonomy of NAFTA members would most likely be questioned. No doubt the North American cooperation would also insist on a partial retention of each nation-state's sovereign power. In any case, a North American Committee for Economic Cooperation would be important in supervising future economic relations between NAFTA members, even if it had no decision power.

A North American Committee for Economic Cooperation (NACEC) could also lead to greater collaboration in certain fields and in the negotiation of some products and commodities. The Quebec members of the committee may even decide that some Quebec enterprises would need protection in areas such as furniture, heavy chemicals, textiles and agriculture.

The work of the committee would be regarded as the basis for all future discussions leading towards Quebec's full inclusion in NAFTA. Since its economic cooperation with other member-states would probably be strengthened, Quebec would certainly not want to lose its hard-won political autonomy, nor would it want to be dependent on another state – especially Canada. And all members, especially Canada and Mexico, would probably want to foster a closer economic cooperation amongst themselves so as to reduce the economic influence of the United States.

Second Alternative: The Signature of Economic and Cultural Agreements

The formation of an economic union between Canada, the United States and then Mexico has been a major issue since the early sixties. It has always been Quebec's belief that its membership of NAFTA would be approved without difficulty, since Quebecers voted in favour of the treaty during the 1988 Canadian election. Other governments, such as Chile and Brazil, have already expressed serious interest in joining NAFTA. In view of Quebec's situation, it is only fair that it would give its unequivocal support to other countries seeking inclusion in the agreement.

To prevent a breakup of the Quebec-Canada "community-security" of interests and deceleration of ongoing cooperations between present NAFTA members, a bilateral agreement on cooperation should be signed between Quebec and each individual partner. A proposal for cooperation should also be produced, in the hope that it may become a treaty for economic and cultural cooperation. In this document, Quebec must clearly state the ideology of the North American cooperation movement. To achieve the greatest possible freedom, a section on economic cooperation should also express the desire of Quebec and other countries to promote direct cooperation in which all barriers are removed.

The document or treaty should be considered to be a blueprint for future action. If not, its impact may be insignificant. It should also confirm the will of the Quebec government to participate fully in the formation of the North American community. Bill 51 was introduced into Quebec's National Assembly on January 26, 1995, for precisely this purpose (see Appendix 1).

Third Alternative: The Trade Pattern

In discussing the characteristics of a sovereign state, it is difficult to find any indicators that truly measure the autonomy of a nation-state. It also seems that the degree of autonomy is not the same between sovereign states and can be evaluated only by an inferential process rather than a descriptive one. The more effective the policy, the less autonomous the government. If we can measure the impact of NAFTA on the Quebec trade market, we will be able to establish the Quebec government's degree of autonomy. As the transnationalist view implies, the greater the impact of NAFTA on the trade pattern between Quebec, the United States and Mexico, the less government autonomy Quebec will possess over its economic field.

Conversely, traditional *integration* theorists argue that the greater the impact of NAFTA on Quebec's external trade, the greater the impact of the treaty on the integration process. The aim here is to see which region – Quebec or Canada – is economically more attractive for trade.

Karl W. Deutsch proposes an interesting hypothesis. First, he found that, the main factor needed for an integration is the level of arms transfer between countries; subsequently, the goal of each country is to consort with other countries in order to ensure security. He also suggests that the term "sovereignty" should be used as a mechanism for self-defense against outside aggression. It can be argued equally that the judicial apparatus, which includes the legal system and the army, reveals certain contradictions at the base level.

As the data in Table 1 shows, the FTA and NAFTA agreements have until now had a positive effect on Quebec's imports and exports to the United States. If Quebec votes for sovereignty in the 1995 referendum, it is assumed that the percentage of exports to the United States will not diminish. In the year following the 1977 election of the first Parti Québécois government and after the referendum of 1980, exports in fact increased. If by mischance sovereignty had a short-term negative impact on trade, this is more likely to be on Canada than on any other of Quebec's new-found economic partners.

The negative impact of the FTA in its early days was minimal and short-lived. Recent yearly data show that the growth rates of Quebec's exports and imports to the United States have been higher post-1988 than previously. This is due primarily to the higher degree of consultation and cooperation between the Quebec, Canadian and U.S. governments after 1984 (the year the Conservative government of Brian Mulroney took office). Second, since the endorsement of the Free Trade Agreement, Quebec has wanted to be a member of NAFTA separately from Canada, and it is expected that a majority of Quebecers will support such a deal. Third, since the political relationships between Quebec, Canada and the U.S. have become more significant in the last decade, the degree of economic interdependency since 1988 is also higher. The 1988 FTA agreement has thus strengthened the economic relationships between Quebec and its economic partners, contrary to what many have believed.

The United States is by far Quebec's largest trading partner in terms of both exports and imports. It is interesting to observe that, while the American share of Quebec's exports continues to increase, its share of imports fluctuates. In 1970, the United States received 58.2 % of Quebec's exports. The trend has been upward since the mid-1980s, and by 1993 the figure had reached 79.7 %. After 1976, United States exports to Quebec grew steadily to a high point of 53.1 % in 1983, and have decreased ever since. In 1993, American imports stood at 45.0 %. In this regard, Quebec's figures are much lower than Canada's, which have ranged from 70.1 % in 1980 to 68.7 % in 1987.

Although Quebec is economically less dependent on the United States than it has been at other times in the past thirty years, American investments are still significant for the prosperity of Quebec's economy, particularly in areas of natural resources (especially mining) and manufacturing. In the latter case, American investors control the most productive sectors.

TABLE 1
Quebec's Exports and Imports to the United States, 1976-1993

Year	Exports (% of total exports)	Imports (% of total imports)
1976	62.8	41.2
1977	65.0	43.5
1978	65.0	45.6
1979	63.8	51.3
1980	59.9	51.5
1981	65.0	46.4
1982	64.5	47.1
1983	69.6	53.1
1984	75.1	52.7
1985	75.8	50.5
1986	77.5	49.0
1987	77.3	47.5
1988	75.3	45.0
1989	72.8	45.3
1990	76.1	46.3
1991	73.4	44.1
1992	76.1	44.0
1993	79.7	45.0

Source: Ministère des Affaires internationales – Direction États-Unis

CONCLUSION

In order to understand the relationship between sovereignty and integration, it is important to examine the most salient issues and to discuss policy alternatives. What can be said about the sovereignty and/or autonomy of the Quebec state? And what will be the impact of the economic and political cooperation between Quebec and Canada on trade between Quebec and the United States-Mexico? These are some of the questions this book wants to answer. From a traditional integrationist point of view, NAFTA is a powerful integrative force. In others words, any economic treaty between Quebec and Canada would not alter their economic relationship.

Since Quebec governments have always been eager to form an economic union that will satisfy their need for productive cooperation and consultation, NAFTA is probably a crucial element from a strategic and military viewpoint. In fact, the creation of a North American economic zone is also the basis for a "security-community" in Quebec. The rationale is that the North American integration movement of the 1980s should be regarded positively as the basis for additional trade among partners. Over the past twenty years, Quebec has increased its international exports to the United States, while its sources of imports have become more diversified (though the U.S. still accounts for approximately 50 % of total imports).

The last Quebec referendum may have no trade impact in the long run because the trade pattern is not going to change drastically anyhow. The concern instead is with the short-term impact. The effect of the referendum will be psychological for the most part. A 'YES' response would end ten years of painful negotiations over Quebec's political status within Canada and could open discussions on the economic ties between Quebec, Canada, the United States and Mexico. A 'NO' response, on the other hand, would leave Quebec striving for its political and economic autonomy once again. Many authors have predicted a negative outcome in the upcoming referendum, but, as we have said, this is unlikely to endanger the present trade relationship between Quebec and the United States. A 'NO' response will also leave the Quebec society torn between two forceful passions: Quebec sovereignty and the North American reality. Whatever the outcome, Quebecers will not lose faith in the next challenge awaiting them.

REFERENCES

BALASSA, Bela, "Toward a Theory of Economic Integration," in M.S. Wionszek (ed.), *Latin American Economic Integration*, New York, 1966, pp. 21-31.

BARRERA, M., and HAAS, E.B., "The Operationalization of Some Variables Related to Regional Integration: A Research Note," *International Organization*, 23(1), Winter 1969, pp. 150-160.

BECKER, Gary S., "Why So Many Mice Are Roaring," *Business Week*, November 7, 1994, p. 20.

BRAMS, Steven J., *Paradoxes in Politics*, The Free Press, Collier Macmillan Publishers, London, 1976.

CLARK, Cal, and WELCH, Susan, "National Conditions as a Base for Supranational Integration: The Case of Trade Patterns," *Comparative Political Studies*, 8(3), October 1975, pp. 345-359.

CLAUDE, Inis L., *Swords Into Plowshares – The Problems and Progress of International Organization*, Random House, New York, 1956, p. 497.

COOK, Ramsay, *The Maple Leaf Forever*, Macmillan of Canada, Toronto, 1971.

DEUTSCH, Karl W., "Between Sovereignty and Integration," *Government and Opposition*, 9(1), Winter 1974, pp. 113-119.

DEUTSCH, Karl W., *The Nerves of Government*, New York, Free Press–Macmillan, 1963.

DEUTSCH, Karl W., "External Influences on the Internal Behaviour of States," in R. Barry Farrell (editor), *Approaches to Comparative and International Politics*, Evanston, Ill., Northwestern University Press, 1966.

ETZIONI, Amatai, "A Stable Union: The Nordic Associational Web – 1953-1964," in *Political Unification*, Holt, Rinehart and Winston Inc., 1965.

FAUCHER, Albert, *Québec en Amérique au XIXe siècle. Essai sur les caractères économiques de la Laurentie*, Montréal, Fides, 1973.

FAUCHER, Albert, and Maurice Lamontagne, "Histoire de l'industrialisation," René Durocher and Paul-André Linteau (eds.), *Le retard du Québec et l'infériorité économique des Canadiens français*, Boréal Express, Montreal, 1971, pp. 25-42.

GAGNON, Alain, and Mary Beth MONTCALM, *Quebec Beyond the Quiet Revolution*, Nelson, 1989.

GALBRAITH, John Kenneth, *Economics and the Public Purpose*, New American Library, Mentor Book, 1975, p. 321.

GOLD, Marc, and David LEYTON-BROWN, *Trade-Offs on Free Trade*, The Carswell Company Ltd., Agincourt, Ontario, 1988.

GRANT, George, *Lament for a Nation*, Carleton University Press, Ottawa, 1991.

HAAS, E.B., "Turbulent Fields and the Theory of Regional Integration," *International Organization*, 30(2), Spring 1976, pp. 173-212.

HASS, Ernest B., "The Study of Regional Integration: Reflections on the Joy and Anguish of Pretheorizing," in Leon L. Lindberg and Stuart B. Scheingold, *Regional Integration, Theory and Research*, Harvard University Press, Cambridge, Mass., 1971.

HANSEN, R.D., "Regional Integration: Reflections on a Decade of Theoretical Efforts," *World Politics*, 21(2), January 1969, pp. 242-271.

HVEEM, H., "Integration by Whom, for Whom, against Whom? On the Relationship Between Neo-Classical Integration Theory, Processes of Integration and Social Structure," *Cooperation and Conflict*, 9(4), 1974, pp. 263-284.

KEOHANE, Robert O., and NYE, Joseph S. Jr., *Transnational Relations and World Politics*, Harvard University Press, Cambridge, Mass., 1972, p. 428.

LACHAPELLE, Guy, "Du nationalisme à l'universalisme ou la recherche d'une identité," *Phi-Zéro – Revue d'études philosophiques*, 6(2), March 1978, pp. 53–73.

LEGARÉ, Anne, *La souveraineté est-elle dépassée?*, Boréal, Montreal, 1992.

LINDGREN, Raymond E., *Norway-Sweden: Union, Disunion and Scandinavian Integration*, Princeton University Press, Princeton, N.J., 1959, p. 298.

LINDBERG, Leon N., and SCHEINGOLD, Stuart A., *Regional Integration, Theory and Research*, Harvard University Press, Cambridge, Mass., 1971.

LINTEAU, Paul-André, René DUROCHER, and Jean-Claude ROBERT, *Histoire du Québec contemporain – De la Confédération à la crise (1867-1929)*, Boréal Express, Montreal, 1979.

MCKINSEY, Lauren S., "Dimensions of National Political Integration and Disintegration: The Case of Quebec Separatism – 1960-1975," *Comparative Political Studies*, 9(3), October 1976, pp. 335-360.

NYE, Joseph S., "Comparative Regional Integration: Concept and Measurement," *International Organization*, 22(4), Autumn 1968, pp. 855-880.

PENTLAND, Charles, *International Theory and European Integration*, Faber and Faber Limited, London, 1973.

PUCHALA, Donald J., "Of Blind Men, Elephants and International Integration," *Journal of Common Market Studies*, 10(3), March 1972, pp. 267-284.

PUCHALA, Donald J., "The Pattern of Contemporary Regional Integration," *International Studies Quarterly*, 12(1), March 1968, pp. 38-64.

Quebec Government, *Change Today for Tomorrow*, 1992.

RAWLS, John, *Théorie de la Justice*, Seuil, Paris, 1987.

ROSENSTIEL, Francis, "Reflections on the Notion of Supranationality," *Journal of Common Market Studies*, 2(2), November 1963, pp. 127-139.

SUNDELIUS, Bengt, *Managing Transnationalism in Northern Europe*, Westview Press, Boulder, Col., 1978.

THOMAS, Tim, "Georges Grant, the Free Trade Agreement, and Contemporary Quebec," *Journal of Canadian Studies*, 27 (1992-1993), pp. 180-195.

VAYRYMEN, Raimo, "Relations between the Nordic Countries and the European Community: An Analysis of Main Trends," *Instant Research on Peace and Violence*, 4(2), 1974, pp. 79-101.

WONNACOTT, Ronald J., "Reconstructing North American – Free Trade following Quebec's Separation: What Can Be Assumed?," in Gordon Ritchie et al., *Broken Links: Trade Relations after a Quebec Secession*, C.D. Howe Institute, Renouf Publishing Company Limited, Ottawa, 1991, pp. 20-44.

2

Quebec in North America:
Historical and Socio-Political Dimensions

Anne-Marie Cotter
Concordia University

This chapter will examine Quebec and its relationship with the United States and Canada over the centuries, from the 1700s until today. The author demonstrates that Quebec has sought through the years to forge its own identity, first within Canada and then alongside Canada on the international scene. While the relationship with Great Britain has never been a strong one, Quebec has turned to the United States, developing strong economic, political and social ties. Nationalism has moved Quebec away from Canada, to the point that it is now seeking a separate status, and continentalism, through foreign investment, trade and emigration, has moved Quebec closer to the United States to form international ties.

Nationalism is defined as an "ideological movement for the attainment and maintenance of autonomy, cohesion and individuality for a social group deemed by some of its members to constitute an actual or potential nation" (Smith, 1976: 1). A nation exists where a significant number of people consider themselves to be one and behave accordingly (Balthazar, 1993: 93). Anthony Smith has stated that "all the evidence suggests that we shall be witnessing many more ethnic upsurges and nationalist movements in the decades to come" (Smith, 1983: xxxvi). Quebec, like many other countries, is therefore following an international pattern, as it moves towards independence.

Quebec, in trying to forge an identity within North America and the world, has tried to emphasize its goals: Quebecers have been a distinct people in North America for over four centuries, and wish to be seen for themselves and not through the Canadian prism; Quebec is not a traditional society, but a modern industrial one with close ties to the United States; Quebecers cannot be compared with the groups of recent immigrants in the United States, since they have always spoken French and constitute a growing majority in the home society; the French language of Quebec occupies a role in international relations; and Quebecers are North Americans like all the others, adapted to their non-European society and sharing American mass culture and values (Thompson: 234).

FROM PRECONQUEST TO CONFEDERATION: THE DEVELOPMENT OF QUEBEC

Right from the early days, Quebec has been different from the rest of North America. The roots of what was once new France, and is now Quebec, were very different from those of the United States. Quebec was not formed by dissident groups seeking refuge, but was financed by ruling administrators of the French Court (Guindon, 1988: 5). The inhabitants were soldiers, businessmen in the fur trade and immigrants with their own elites comprising the colonial administrators and the clergy (Guindon: 5). "The system of social institutions traditional to French Canadians was built upon rural society, financed by its economics, controlled by its own ethnic elite with a cultural flavour of its own." (Guindon: 17.) The traditional elites were the commanding institutions in French Canadian society, and the clergy especially was powerful and exercised ascendancy over the political and commercial spheres (Guindon: 19).

During the American Revolution, the loyalties of the French Canadians and their clerical elite were pledged in exchange for political concessions, guaranteeing the preservation of the French language and the Catholic religion (Guindon: 45). Thus, the tradition of political guarantees for the cultural survival of French Canadians as a community was begun (Guindon: 45). The American severance provided the impetus that led the British Canadian nationalists to forge British North America (Guindon: 45). However, from the outset, French Canadians wanted their own separate identity.

From Conquest to Confederation, the British took over the political and economic institutions, and the country witnessed a massive exodus of the middle-class entrepreneurs and political administrators of New France, with only the farmers and priests remaining (Guindon: 52). The future Quebec was a rural society with a clerical elite concerned with ethnic and religious survival (Guindon: 52). Interaction with the English political elite was mediated by the French elite in self-sufficient rural parishes (Guindon: 53).

Quebec Nationalism

Nationalism initially served to establish Quebec and preserve its French language and Catholic religion. Canada had an autonomous relationship with Britain and was un-American (Oliver, 1991: 213). It wanted a separate identity, with little emphasis on ethnic or cultural ties. Contrary to the French-Canadian brand of nationalism, it wanted the preservation of the state rather than the nation (Oliver: 213). British North America's overstatement of a shared assumption between the two cultures led to deep divisions, and the lack of consensus encouraged the development of a strong provincialism in Quebec (Oliver: 215).

From the end of the French regime in 1759 to Confederation, nationalism led to deals between the "Canadiens" and the English in the hopes of building a democratic country for the French (Gougeon, 1994: 1). According to the Parti Patriote, the "Canadien" territory and nation were different from British America which was part of the British Empire (Gougeon: 18). Lower Canada, which later became Quebec, was a distinct society that respected the "Canadien" culture, ruled by a government mindful of language and religion. However, according to Jean-Paul Bernard, the British minority benefited from its links and business relationship with the imperial government, and its ascent threatened the development of the "Canadien" nation (Gougeon: 19). With the passage of the Act of Union of 1837-38, John Stuart Mill stated that the French were compelled to "consider themselves, not as a separate body, but an integral part of a larger body to merge their nationality of race in a nationality of country; instead of French Canadian...make them British American" (Gougeon: 20).

From 1840 onward, the roots of nationalism were defensive, aimed at getting rid of British American abuses by colonial administrators with the power to grant jobs and public lands, and replacing them with diversified economic development less dependent on large imperial commercial interests (Gougeon: 21). In 1850, the French language was considered to be the "gardienne de la foi" (the "defender of the faith") (Gougeon: 22).

The Rouge Party existed in Quebec from 1848 to 1867. It was against the plans for Confederation and believed that if the French Canadians disappeared into the larger richer universe of the United States, then their ties with America would be better than with English Canada (Gougeon: 25). The Rouge Party stood for liberalism, radicalism, nationalism and anti-clericalism (Bernard, 1971: 6). It called for universal suffrage, abolition of the temporal power of the Pope, independence before the clergy, religious freedom, hostility toward the English, and the acceptance of representation based on the population numbers (Bernard: 3). It pressed for a French Canada, mass education, the agricultural development of lands, decentralization of powers, a free press and equal rights for all citizens (Bernard: 49). More importantly, the Rouge Party advocated the independence of Canada from England and its annexation to the United States, in order for Quebecers to make their own laws and extend Quebec's industry beyond its borders (Bernard: 371). The "Rouges" considered the United States to be the only valid market, but were ahead of their time (Bernard: 372).

Foreign Investment and Trade

The staple approach sees staple exports to more advanced industrialized economies as the engine of growth for the Canadian economy (Watkins, 1989: 17). The commercial rather than industrial bias of the Canadian capitalist class and the dependent branch plant industrialization are a result of the unequal alliance with American foreign ownership and capital (Watkins: 17).

The war of 1812 brought an end to belief in American annexation of Canada. Instead, a commercial and economic rivalry emerged between the two countries (White, 1988: 37). In this period, Quebec prospered, with American products sold at the seaports of New England, taking the northern routes through Lake Champlain and Montreal (Jones, 1946: 42). The Quebec of 1851 shared the traditional North American government concepts of intervention and public enterprise in public navigation and railway works, but using British capital (Hamelin, 1971: xi). The national sentiment favored trade with the United States (Hamelin: xiv).

Quebec's agricultural enterprises specialized so as to be able to meet American demand during the Civil War, but ceded these activities to Ontario in the last part of the 19th century (Hamelin: xv). In 1840, the English abolished preferential tariffs (Hamelin: 369). The United States was not seen as the enemy but as a competitor, providing Quebec with the possibility of progressing and profiting from its strategic commercial position by supplying natural resources and cheap manpower (Hamelin: 371). However, there were also drawbacks caused by Quebec's small market, a declining agricultural sector, inadequate education for advancing technology, the push by the clergy for rural ideology, and foreign economic domination (Hamelin: 371).

The trade relationship between Quebec and the United States developed over several decades. Free trade is an economic benefit or association, first introduced in 1854. For Quebec, it implies a number of social, cultural and political considerations (Riggs, Velk, 1987: xi). The American Civil War influenced the economic development of the British North American provinces, as new markets opened up for Canadian exports in the United States (Easterbrook, Aitken, 1975: 361). At the end of the war, the removal of constraints on American settlement expansion west of the Mississippi jeopardized the security of the Canadian west and hastened Confederation (Easterbrook, Aitken: 361). The waterways became a uniting force (Easterbrook, Aitken: 362). Upper Canada businessmen were the first to seize the idea of reciprocity. However, immediate economic and political union with the United States would have meant the sacrifice of valued institutions, national identity and loyalty to Britain.

The first major trade law passed between the United States and Canada was the Elgin-Marcy Reciprocity Treaty of 1854 (Fry, 1987: 28). The Treaty of Reciprocity opened up the market to Quebec (Hamelin: 372). However, the

Civil War in 1857 ended all major investment, and the market finally closed down upon Confederation (Hamelin: 372). The Treaty had allowed for the free flow of natural products, but was abrogated by the United States in 1866 because of British support for the Confederacy during the Civil War and new tariffs imposed in Canada (Fry: 28).

Reciprocity was an attempt to create a single market area in North America covering several distinct political jurisdictions, where specific products were freely exchanged for a partial and limited economic union between British North America and the United States (Easterbrook, Aitken: 362). It was seen as the only feasible alternative to annexation. The South, with its plantations, wanted low tariffs to lower the price of imported goods and reduce the cost of production for exports of raw materials (Easterbrook, Aitken: 363). The North, with its small farms and factories, was protectionist (Easterbrook, Aitken: 363). Reciprocity generated little enthusiasm in the United States and was seen simply as a concession for the inclusion of fisheries, which were the immediate and urgent objective.

Canadian commercial policy upset the United States, and the Treaty was abrogated on March 17, 1866, because of its disastrous effects on timber and grain growing regions in the United States and resentment of Canadian competition by farming and lumber interests. Moreover, shipping and forwarding interests in Buffalo and Philadelphia were jealous of the St Lawrence Route. The Grand Trunk, with the completion of the Victoria Bridge in Montreal in 1860, enhanced competition, the manufacturing interests blamed Canadian tariffs for the decline in exports of furniture, stoves, clothing, boots and shoes (Masters, 1963: 69). All these elements joined together to call for the end of the Treaty (Masters: 69).

FROM CONFEDERATION TO 1960: THE DEVELOPMENT OF QUEBEC IN THE NATIONAL SPHERE

Nationalism

As a result of nationalism, Quebec has developed a common but separate identity from Canada. Nationalism acts as a unifying factor for shared history, identity, territory, language and religion (Linteau 1, 1989: 358). The nationalism of Quebec affects Canada since, according to Oliver, there can be no stable power in Canada without Quebec's support (Oliver, 1991: 16). Confederation was seen as an institution of the British Canadian Nationals (Guindon: 32). Ethnic cohabitation took the form of complete self-segregation in the institutions of education, religion, welfare and leisure, and the ethnies came together only for work and politics (Guindon: 33). Industrialization took place when Anglo-Saxon industry moved into a Quebec society that had a surplus population, political and religious elites, well-anchored rural institutions and technologically unskilled workers. Managerial and technical positions were filled by the incoming group with their own set of institutions serving their own nationals. Since the local elites were not challenged, the politicians and clergy mostly welcomed business transactions.

The period from Confederation to the 1950s saw ethnic accommodation, with the settling of the West and the industrialization of Quebec. English Canadians were concerned with political supremacy and sovereignty, depending on the military strength of Britain more than ever after the external threat of the successful secession of the United States (Guindon: 53). In Quebec, the assimilationist impulse from civil and industrial society was countered by kinship and religion (Guindon: 55). A pattern of mutually self-satisfying, self-segregated institutions was established (Guindon: 57).

English and French nationalism were very different. English nationalism was built on imperialism, distinguishing Canada from the United States (Linteau 1: 361). In a Canada born against the backdrop of the United States' revolution (Linteau 1: 362), history was stronger than geography. From the early days conflict arose between the forces of French Canadian nationalism and large-scale English language capitalism (Little, 1989: 205). The nationalism of the period 1867 to 1917 saw a French-speaking population who believed in a different Canada from their English-speaking compatriots, who saw the country merely as a branch of the British Empire (Gougeon: 27). In 1867, Canada was a bilingual, bicultural nation, with two equal, founding cultures bound, according to Réal Bélanger, by a pact of respect (Gougeon: 29). However, the French hoped for a provincial state, with an autonomous Quebec as a separate nation, with its own language, religion, culture, institutions and laws (Gougeon: 29). They wanted a peaceful conquest of the territory that was lost in 1760 (Gougeon: 30). As time went by, the French gradually became a minority, as more provinces were formed, and the centralist government was seen as doing nothing to stop the flow of French Canadian emigrants to the United States (Gougeon: 32).

Honoré Mercier was the father of Quebec's independence. He asked for economic development and government investment to modernize the agricultural society into a market economy (Gougeon: 39). He believed that the provinces had created the federal state, which was therefore subordinate to the Quebec state. The Quebec state should therefore be recognized internationally. However, he also believed that, since the Confederation respected Quebec, separation was not necessary as long as Canada remained separate from the Empire.

Henri Bourassa led a pan-Canadian nationalist movement opposed by English Canada (Gougeon: 39). He believed that "La Patrie c'est le Canada" and defended the idea of a bilingual, bicultural Canadian nation, without colonial ties, so that French Canadians could flourish in Canada and in Quebec (Gougeon: 40). This differed from English Canadian nationalism, which was unilingual and uniculturally British, Protestant, tolerant of French within but not outside Quebec, and close to the Empire (Gougeon: 41).

While the English were striving for industrialization, the French were still concerned with the survival of their language and religion (Balthazar: 95). Although there have been many forms of nationalism in Quebec, the central one – traditional nationalism – was predominantly cultural rather than political, unconcerned with economic dimensions, more religious, inward-looking, not open to newcomers but maintaining ethnic entity (Balthazar: 96).

Traditional nationalism looked to language, religion and the conservatism of family, parish and rural life (Linteau 2, 1989: 114). Initially, urbanism, state intervention and the United States were all seen as threats (Linteau 2: 114). In the 1920s, the traditional message was hard to defend with modern American culture permeating the cities, but the crash reactivated it (Linteau 2: 116). Foreign monopoly was seen as exploitative at the expense of the nationalist interests of language and religion (Linteau 2: 117).

Conscription during the two World Wars showed the French-speaking population that there was little to look forward to in Canada. This widened the gulf separating the two cultures and gave new life to nationalism. The new phase lasted from 1917 to 1960 (Gougeon: 47). According to Pierre Trépanier, Groulx sought national affirmation of French Canada, with the new elite and the state playing an important role in neutralizing the conquest (Gougeon: 56). He wanted an integral French state within the Confederation (Gougeon: 57). According to Robert Comeau, the Great Depression led to the radicalization of Quebec nationalism, independence rather than separation (Gougeon: 67). Amidst deteriorating social conditions, nationalism attacked the dictatorship of monopolies and foreign political economic domination, accusing the federal political elites of treason (Gougeon: 67). Conscription and English Canada's 80% vote released the government from its promise to Quebec not to introduce conscription, and this too fanned the flames (Gougeon: 77). With World War II and conscription, the anti-imperialist nationalism of the early 1900s returned. The traditional elites and a large part of the population turned to Quebec rather than the centralist federal state (Linteau 2: 125). World War II was a rallying point for French Canadian unity for quick industrialization and diversification, as opposed to conscription and in the push for provincial independence (Oliver: 196).

Nationalism further served to strengthen Quebec on the international scene, creating important ties with the United States. Opposition to traditional nationalism was expressed at the end of the 1940s, as people sought a more modern approach (Linteau 2: 349). After World War II, Canada became more interventionist, eroding provincial powers to build a stronger Canadian identity (Linteau 2: 350). In neo-nationalism, Quebec was seen as the victim of the federalist system (Linteau 2: 357). Economy, society and politics were emphasized instead of religion, with a shift from conservatism and survival to one of affirmation and modernity (Linteau 2: 358).

Continentalism

Continentalism has helped nationalism by bringing Quebec closer to the United States through emigration, foreign investment and trade. Faucher and Lamontagne reject specific cultural factors as an explanation for Quebec's economic lay, and believe instead that it was caused by geographical factors such as Quebec's location in the North American continent (Faucher, Lamontagne, 1953: 24). Compared to other regions, Quebec was slow in developing its industrial structure (Faucher, Lamontagne: 23). In the commercial era between 1866 and 1911, when wood and grain were the staples, Quebec was historically prominent in the development of Canadian economic life, since it was located strategically along the commercial route (Faucher, Lamontagne: 24). Quebec "did not have a behavior of its own. Its cities, like other North American seaboard centres, participated very actively in the prosperity brought about by commercialism" (Faucher, Lamontagne: 25).

However, times changed. Commercialism became industrialism, and steel replaced wood. Coal and iron became the primary factors in economic development, and the North American centre of economic gravity shifted (Faucher, Lamontagne: 25). The Canadian seaboard lost its geographical advantage and Quebec was deprived of its major importance as the land of lumber and shipbuilding (Faucher, Lamontagne: 26). In the United States and Canada, economic activity moved towards the geographical centre, Southern Ontario became the cheapest route to the West, wedged island-like alongside Pittsburgh and Cleveland. Therefore, according to Faucher and Lamontagne, Quebec's experience was not a regional phenomenon, but was reflected throughout the whole continent (Faucher, Lamontagne: 26).

With the new rules of the industrial game, Quebec was no longer in a position to develop its industrial economy (Faucher, Lamontagne: 27). At the end of the 19th century, the province was predominantly agricultural and its population was growing rapidly (Faucher, Lamontagne: 28). It was the "outstanding feature of the Quebec community at that time that it would so rapidly multiply with so little opportunity for commercial or industrial employment" (Faucher, Lamontagne: 28). This demographic factor brought with it some important economic implications. Agriculture became a tool of nationalism, but "the possibilities of agricultural expansion were much too limited to fill the gap between the rate of population growth and the rate of industrial development, so that large-scale emigration became a necessity" (Faucher, Lamontagne: 29).

Quebec's surplus population could not easily move to Ontario because it lacked technological knowledge of the steel industry. However, New England needed manpower because its labour force had moved to the East Central States (Faucher, Lamontagne: 29). Foreign investment was viewed positively, with imports of capital considered more important than exports of Quebecers (Linteau 1: 37). Faucher, in a continentalist approach, believes that geoeconomic and interregional disparities favour population displacement (Linteau 1: 38). The Franco-Americans provided a market for Quebec, and the exodus to the United States helped relieve demographic pressures (Linteau 1: 39).

Faucher and Lamontagne suggest that the economic evolution of Quebec during the 19th century was primarily conditioned by geographical and economic factors inherent in the North American system (Faucher, Lamontagne: 30). Quebec had developed a close association with New England, since both had experienced a similar economic fate. Both were leaders in commercialism, with labour-oriented rather than resource-oriented industries, until the advent of industrialization, when New England lost its economic predominance to the East Central States.

At the beginning of the 20th century, Quebec still had close ties to the North American continent, but its behaviour differed fundamentally from that of New England. During the era of commercialism, Quebec developed economically in parallel to the United States. However, during industrialization, Quebec had to fight for its survival against the economic influence of the East Central States. However, Quebec was past of the North American system, and its economic development was based on the overall continental resource pattern (Faucher, Lamontagne: 30). Its natural resources now fulfilled a definite function and met a specific need within North America, and the province was strongly favoured by the new industries (Faucher, Lamontagne: 31). It continued to lag behind Ontario, because of the previous period of stagnation and its less favourable geographic location outside the industrial belt (Faucher, Lamontagne: 32). Quebec and Ontario had experienced two separate phases of economic expansion, but were now moving in similar directions in response to the American impetus (Faucher, Lamontagne: 32).

Quebec's natural resources attracted widespread American investment and control and a strong incoming flow of capital (Faucher, Lamontagne: 36). Its economic development was financed, directed and controlled from outside (Faucher, Lamontagne: 36). Faucher and Lamontagne suggest that what happened in Quebec was a regional manifestation of overall economic developments in North America (Faucher, Lamontagne: 35). Quebec's industrial development was therefore North American, based on natural resources, and its expansion was characterized by large-scale monopolistic industries (Faucher, Lamontagne: 35).

Trade and Foreign Investment

In 1911, with the exception of Great Britain, Canada was the chief trading partner of the United States (Velk, Riggs, 1988: 93). President Taft negotiated full-scale reciprocity for better trade relations – the 3000 miles of joint border and the common interests of the two countries called for special arrangements (Stevens, 1987: 14). The 1911 agreement was similar to the 1854 pact. Most U.S. tariffs on manufacturing goods were reduced, while most Canadian manufacturing tariffs remained in place (Fry, 1987: 28). However, the agreement was defeated by a sentiment of "no truck or trade with the Yankees" (Brecher, 1987: 70).

The Quebec economy was dominated by foreign interests, especially American (Drache, 1972: 193). As a result of this, according to Drache, Quebec's resources have been used to colonize it and keep it under foreign control, with almost absolute American economic control through ownership by way of direct investment (Drache: 254).

From the outset, the trade pattern was to import manufactured goods and export staples (Watkins, 1989: 29). This led to overwhelming trade dependency on the United States (Watkins: 29). Canada and Quebec fell within the tight embrace of the American empire and occupied the space left open by the American capital (Watkins: 30). Canada became the exemplary client state (Watkins: 31).

Finally, it was foreign capital which transformed society from rural to urban, and the "population needed no persuasion, since it needed work" (Guindon: 19). The local power elite composed of the clergy and the political parties allowed the foreign capitalists to dictate the industrial rules of the game, seeking maximum yields with minimum involvement in the local game of politics, religion and urban development. The invading foreign capitalists brought money and industry, and provided structural relief to the traditional elites (Guindon: 19).

The Quebec state was caught between the English-speaking Canadian bourgeoisie and American imperialism (Drache: 17). Quebec needed foreign investment, especially from the United States, if it wished to develop (Drache: 21). In 1927, Taschereau said of American investment: "this capital is welcome, and I'm not afraid our people will be Americanized by the arrival of American capital. I'd rather import foreign capital than export our workers" (Drache: 21).

The liberal politicians promoted trade with the United States but wanted a stop to emigration (Roby, 1976: 208). With the 1929 crash, agriculture and fisheries suffered a tragic blow that caused prices to drop and incited more people to leave for the United States (Roby: 208). The liberal press encouraged agricultural production but wanted American capital, and it thought that the federal government should increase tariffs and force American companies wishing to do business to build plants in Quebec (Roby: 209).

The conservative press and the clerics, however, opposed American penetration of Quebec society (Roby: 211). In this period, Quebec underwent many changes in language, religion and traditional values as it became an independent economy (Roby: 212). The nationalist groups also opposed the rural exodus to the urban areas and to the United States, pushing for emancipation and a significant industrial role for the population (Roby: 216). Quebec was torn between two opposing currents of thought: development and conservation (Roby: 219).

Quebec was one of the first provinces to go through the Industrial Revolution, and by 1921 the majority of the population had become urban (Balthazar: 95). In 1871, 22.82% of the population was urban and 77.18% rural. By 1921, the figures had changed to 56.01% and 43.99% respectively (Roby: 12). The primary sectors of agriculture, fisheries, lumber and mines provided employment for 48.32% of the population in 1901 but only 42.36% in 1921 (Roby: 14). Employment in the secondary manufacturing and construction sector also decreased from 25.2% in 1901 to 21.77% in 1921. However, the tertiary sector (transportation, services and trade) increased from 26.48% in 1901 to 35.86% in 1921 (Roby: 14).

Great Britain was once Quebec's major investor. However, from 1930 onwards it was replaced by the United States (see Table 1) (Linteau 1: 443). Quebec shifted from dependency on the British to dependency on the Americans, and its economy was still controlled by foreigners (Linteau 1: 444).

TABLE 1
Ratio of Foreign Investment in Quebec

	Great Britain	**United States**	**Other**
1900	85%	14%	1%
1910	77%	19%	4%
1920	53%	44%	3%
1930	36%	61%	3%

(Linteau 1: 443).

The nature of foreign investment also changed. The British invested indirectly through shares and finance, while the Americans invested directly, usually through proprietory funding of production. The United States penetrated Quebec's economy by installing branch plants for American-made products (Linteau 1: 446). However, the majority of American investment went to Ontario; Quebec received only 16% of U.S. firms in 1931. The United States dominated the industrial sector, and their investment strategy led to virtual integration of Quebec into the United States Empire (Linteau 1: 446).

During the period 1918-1929, Quebec experienced economic development and made good progress in industrialization and urbanization (Roby: 3). In fact, this period became the most prosperous in the history of Quebec (Roby: 4). Hydroelectric and natural resources left the industrial centres under foreign control, mostly American. With the penetration of American capital came the integration of Quebec's industry into the North American economy. Tariffs and natural resources attracted American enterprises, and Quebec benefited from their capital, technological advancement and mass production. Some 36% of all American enterprises in Canada were established between 1920 and 1929 (Roby: 5).

Emigration

Emigration from Quebec became a natural adjustment response to the North American economic situation. Movements of capital and people reached their high point during the 19th-century economic revolution (Faucher, 1964: 279). The stronger economic zones became a point of attraction for the weaker ones (Faucher: 280). Quebec was considered part of North America but was often used as a transit point to the United States (Faucher: 281). People and capital circulated freely across the border (Faucher: 281). The exodus of Quebecers to the United States was curtailed only by strict control of immigration and an economic crisis (Lavoie 1981: 7).

Between 1871 and 1931, Canada received 6,500,000 immigrants, half of whom eventually moved to the United States (Lavoie: 77). In 1815, Canada had instituted a policy of excluding American settlers (Easterbrook, 1956: 272). However, emigration to Canada was later seen as a cure for unemployment, poverty, social unrest and rising taxes (Easterbrook: 272). Quebec received 700 immigrants in 1815, 12,600 in 1827, 28,000 in 1830 and more than 66,000 in 1832. Many, however, moved on to the United States (Easterbrook: 273). During this period, Quebec developed politically, while maintaining its participation in the expanding North American economy (White: 45).

Emigration from Quebec to the United States began with Quebecers who sympathized with France against England and Canada or who supported the concept of liberty and the forming of the United States (Little: 13). During the

1840s, many people moved to the United States to escape poor living conditions. This movement continued well into the second quarter of the 20th century (Lavoie: 13). During this period, the border between the United States and Canada was practically non-existent, with free circulation for the development of industry south of the 45th parallel (Lavoie: 13).

The exodus from Quebec began seasonally in 1820 and became permanent in 1845 (Hamelin: 3). In 1849, 3.4% of Quebecers (1 out of every 27, or 30,000 of the 800,000 population) emigrated to the United States (Lavoie: 14). Two-thirds of the emigrants came from the agricultural class and one-third from the working class (Lavoie: 17). Following the rebellions in Lower Canada of 1837 and 1838, more people were exiled to the United States (Roby, 1990: 14). New England became a favourite destination for Quebecers, receiving 8,700 immigrants in 1840, 19,380 in 1850 and 37,420 in 1860 (Roby: 18).

The exodus began in rural Quebec, as people moved first to the cities of Quebec and then crossed the border. Two areas of the United States were popular: the North-East and the Mid-West (Lavoie: 17). In the five years prior to 1857, 45,000 people left Quebec, and only a quarter of then would ever return (Lavoie: 21). The major causes of emigration were the lack of railways and bridges linking areas and the seasonal unemployment that seriously affected the agricultural industry in winter (Lavoie: 24). In addition, the United States could offer better salaries and more opportunities, and plenty of encouragement from the people who had already emigrated (Lavoie: 24).

Between 1860 and 1870, the number of migrants fell as a result of the poor conditions in the United States caused by the Civil War (Lavoie: 29). The people who did emigrate had to be willing to accept lower salaries. The period 1880-1890 saw the largest exodus, with some 200,000 emigrants. Young people accounted for 18% and families for 72% (Lavoie: 41). The flow began to decline in 1890; by 1910-1920, the figures had halved (Lavoie: 51). From 1930 onward, political restrictions limited entry into the United States (Lavoie: 51). Nevertheless, during the last three decades of the 19th century Quebec lost 10% of its population (see Table 2) (Linteau 1: 36).

Between 1871 and 1931, more people left Quebec than entered it (Linteau 1: 35). Curé Labelle called emigration "the cemetery of the race," and Raoul Blanchard compared it to a haemorrhage (Linteau 1: 35). Hamelin and Roby believe that agricultural modernization left workers with no option but to emigrate if they wanted to survive (Linteau 1: 37).

With the onset of World War I the French-speaking population began to resent British imperialism. Bloc Populaire leader Maxime Raymond said that "the immigration of our people to the United States since 1919, is the ransom of war... War... is the principle and real cause of the exodus of our people to the United States" (Oliver: 198).

TABLE 2
Emigration to the United States from Quebec

1840-50	35,000	5.4%
1850-60	70,000	7.8%
1860-70	–	–
1870-80	120,000	10.1%
1880-90	150,000	11.3%
1890-1900	140,000	9.6%
1900-10	100,000	6%
1910-20	80,000	4%
1920-30	130,000	5.6%
1930-40	–	–
1840-1940	900,000	–

(Lavoie: 53)

The French emigrants to the United States were referred to as "the Chinese of the Eastern States" (Lavoie: 46). They were considered to be "hyphenated Americans" (Roby: 290). Once in the United States, they found themselves isolated and assimilated (Lavoie: 58). They always dreamed of returning one day to Quebec (Lavoie: 36).

According to the 1970 United States census, two and a half million Americans have French as their mother tongue. The majority of these are immigrants from Quebec or descendants of 19th- and 20th-century immigrants (Lavoie: 9). Most settled in New England, which now has one million Franco-American citizens who have become anglicized over the years (Little: 9).

French-speaking emigrants to the United States can be divided into three main groups: Quebecers at the end of the 17th century and the first half of the 18th century, and Acadians in the latter half of the 18th century, now living in Louisiana, Texas, Mississippi and Alabama; Quebecers and Acadians who went to New England, including New York, and the upper Mid-West between 1830 and the Great Depression; and Quebecers settling after World War II in Florida, California and the South-West. Except for the last group, all these people have lost their language and been assimilated (Hero, 1988: 267). In 1976, 72.9% of native French-speakers in Louisiana, 77.1% in Northern New England, 92.4% in Southern New England and 86.4% elsewhere in the United States had adopted English as their principal language at home (Hero: 267). French was more predominant among older people; those aged 40 and older were three times more likely to speak French than those under 20 in Louisiana and New England. If the trend continues, the next generation of Franco-Americans will probably be English unilinguals.

FROM 1960 TO THE PRESENT: THE DEVELOPMENT OF QUEBEC IN THE INTERNATIONAL SPHERE

Nationalism

In the 1970s, language became a priority and Quebec nationalists began to push for the recognition of a distinct society (Linteau: 678). The structural conditions prerequisite to national liberation were in place. A newly-created native elite, highly educated and politically conscious, engineered the expectations of an alert, restless native population whose aspirations would be fulfilled by political independence (Guindon: 27). A significant new group appeared in the mid-20th century, the new middle class of white collar workers. The separatist leaders who emerged were better educated, younger, professional, salaried white collar workers, unhappy with real or imagined restrictions on occupational mobility (Guindon: 31). Their objective was to condemn the promotional practices of the federally-operated bureaucracies.

Lionel Groulx once said: "The only option now open to us in this: to become the masters of our own house, or resign ourselves forever to the fate of a nation of servants" (Guindon: 31). Groulx's views remained largely marginal and ineffectual until the new middle class gained access to political power. It brought with it a unifying ideology, a political cohesion ambivalent toward foreign capital and indignant about the handing-over of national resources to foreign investors. The middle class recognized the positive role of the state in economic affairs (Guindon: 32).

The post-war period was marked by ethnic tension and French Canadian social mobility, with neonationalism linked to social change for modernization (Guindon: 57). The new middle class extended in scope and size and improved its mobility (Guindon: 57). French Canada sought a new social convention of ethnic accommodation with English Canada, this time with competition and within an industrial bureaucracy (Guindon: 58).

The nationalism that emerged in the period 1960-1980 saw the state as a driving force in economic and nationalist self-assertion, along with the independence movement (Gougeon: 89). The Quiet Revolution brought about an overall change in values, elites and culture, and neologisms such as "Québécois" and "francophone" began to be heard (Gougeon: 89).

According to Richard Desrosiers, the 1980 Referendum was not only a major disappointment but also a rebirth. The new players were the businessmen (Gougeon: 95). Quebec felt stronger and able to survive without its federal big brother in Free Trade (Gougeon: 95). According to Balthazar, the nationalism of the 1960s was secular and outward-looking, convinced that the Canadian missions abroad did not adequately represent the interests of French

Canada (Gougeon: 108). The Quebec identity took precedence over a bilingual Canada (Gougeon: 111). The French minority in North America wanted to remind the majority of its rights and affirm its collective existence (Gougeon: 113). According to Balthazar, French Canadians live in Canada but their immediate sense of belonging and primary loyalty is to Quebec (Gougeon: 114).

The new form of nationalism was political, economic, secular, outward-looking and territorial, in favour of the continual preservation of the French-speaking nation (Balthazar: 97). The main protagonist of the new nationalism was the government (Balthazar: 99). Balthazar stated that "the more the state is present, powerful and interventionist, the more intense nationalism will be" (Balthazar: 99). The response by Quebec to Canadian nationalism was "the more you try to unite Canada, the more you unite Quebec. Quebec nationalism is the illegitimate child of Canadian nationalism" (Balthazar: 100).

Quebec was geared to the external market in a dependent development, and believed it could not generate from within the capital it needed to develop its natural resources (Lachapelle, 1993: 20). Through statism, the state played a fundamental role in the development of Quebec in the 1960s (Lachapelle: 23). According to Donald Smiley, Canadian duality prior to 1960 was characterized by a federal division of legislative powers with language and cultural issues left to Quebec, and by institutional self-segregation, cooperation among elites, traditional French distrust of the federal state, and the defense of historical prescriptive rights (Lachapelle: 38). However, the federal government began to encroach on the areas of health, welfare and education. Quebec further pressed for enhanced French participation in the traditional English areas, to maximize its presence both nationally and internationally (Lachapelle: 38).

Trade

The Free Trade Agreement and the subsequent North American Free Trade Agreement were the most important trade agreements ever reached, and Quebec now has its role to play on the international scene (Velk, Riggs, 1988: 3). NAFTA removes all tariffs and liberalizes nontariff barriers to trade (Ritchie, 1988: 9). It includes an agreement on regulation of the trade in services and a liberalization of investment, with a mechanism for binding dispute resolution unprecedented in any free trade area (Ritchie: 9). It provides an environment for investment, new production plants, economies of scale and specialization, better production performance, better and more secure jobs for the future, high productivity and low inflation, stronger economic growth and new wealth to finance social, cultural and environmental goals (Layton, 1987: 202).

The objectives of free trade are the removal of tariff and nontariff barriers for goods and services, the neutralizing of policies, practices and procedures of government trade, and the consistency of the Free Trade Agreement with

GATT to cover all trade (Laun, 1987: 208). Its long-term goals for Canada are to improve real income, wages and production, to increase the number of jobs, to reduce exposure to United States protectionism, to reduce competitive pressures from developing and newly-industrialized countries, to mitigate pressures from global macroeconomic imbalances, and to reduce tensions between provinces and the federal government, and among provinces (Harris, 1988: 52).

The United States had several objectives: to eliminate tariffs, to reduce nontariff barriers, to formulate rules governing trade in services, trucking, insurance, to improve protection of intellectual property, to introduce greater discipline over subsidies, and to create an open and secure environment for foreign investment (Laun, 1987: 209).

Quebec's own objectives for the North American Free Trade Agreement were: to maintain its previous advantages, to preserve its position on the American market, to take advantage of the trading potential offered with Canada, the United States and Mexico, to develop its comparative advantages so as to foster investment, and to adapt to stiffer competition from products from outside its borders (Government of Quebec, 1993: 14).

Quebec's conditions for NAFTA were maintenance of the current division of legislative powers, full respect for its unique social policy, language and culture, continuing flexibility to modernize and develop its economy, the provision of transitional periods for businesses in less competitive sectors, the creation of a dispute settlement mechanism, maintenance of its special status for agriculture and fisheries, and the protection of its right to decide on the Agreement in light of its interests (Government of Quebec: 17).

In 1993, the last full year for which statistics are available, Quebec's exports to the United States totalled $25,920,529,000, and its imports $13,668,216,000 (Ministère des Affaires internationales, de l'Immigration et des Communautés culturelles du Québec 1993-1994: 1). Quebec's economic relationship with the United States continues to grow every year.

Canada's policy in economic relations has always been to favour east-west relations (Dinsmore, 1975: 187). However, the natural tendencies have been north-south. Suggestions for the future include: completing the industrial transformation phase by attracting American enterprises selectively, and further developing local enterprises in energy and natural resources; integrating Francophones culturally into the economy and into American enterprises with francophone manpower; building the relationship between American and local enterprises; transforming industries on an international scale to compete on the market; and opening Quebec's industries to the North American international market in order to include Quebec's economy in the sectors where it has the most to gain, without risking its cultural identity.

International Developments

Several indicators show that Quebec has developed over the centuries into a strong society with national and international relations, especially with the United States. The Department of External Affairs was established in 1982 to deal with overseas trade issues, especially those related to the United States (Balthazar, 1984: 224).

Quebec now has several delegation offices in the United States. When the New York office was established in 1940, it initially served narrow commercial functions, as did subsequent offices elsewhere; but they were later transformed into more general bodies with broader functions and emphasis on economic relations with the United States (Balthazar: 224). Eventually, the delegates with cultural and educational expertise were replaced by others with business and engineering expertise. Over the years, the number of delegations has increased, and Quebec currently has offices in Atlanta, Boston, Chicago, Los Angeles, New York, and Washington, D.C. (Ministère des Affaires internationales, de l'Immigration et des Communautés culturelles, Répertoire des représentations du Québec à l'étranger, Quebec, 1994).

In 1974, Quebec joined the Conference of New England Governors and Atlantic Provinces Premiers, which then became the Conference of New England Governors and Eastern Canadian Premiers (Balthazar: 224). The Conference of six states and five provinces provides a forum for discussion. It meets once a year for pragmatic economic and functional collaboration (Balthazar: 240). The political influence of the Conference remains limited and indirect, but it is nevertheless a significant vehicle for Quebec. Quebec has three times the gross provincial product and twice the population of the four Maritime provinces combined. Quebec is New England's most lucrative customer by a ratio of eight to one, and is seen as less protectionist (Balthazar: 240). Therefore, Quebec plays a major role in the Conference.

Balthazar believes that if the French character of Quebec was seen to be secured, than nationalism would be satisfied and Quebec would be willing to pledge allegiance to Canada (Balthazar: 103). He explains that the rise in sovereignty occurs when Quebec is not recognized by the rest of Canada (Balthazar: 103). The 1980s brought a new orientation to nationalism with an important role for businessmen, the interpreters of contemporary world trends (Balthazar: 105). With a rise in economic interdependency in the global economy and an emphasis on Quebec nationalism, the focus has shifted from national to international recognition. The majority of Quebecers want an association with other states as part of an international dialogue on economic association.

Quebec, although protective of its identity, looks outward (Balthazar: 105). However, it is difficult for it to follow the pluralistic nation-building of the

United States, because of the complications of multiculturalism and ethnicity, and the dissolution of national cohesion south of the border (Balthazar: 106).

Nationalism has therefore been a permanent fixture in Quebec, moving from insular collectivism to functional statism to individual entrepreneurship (Lachapelle: 70). "Supporting free trade makes sense to Quebecers, as does the belief that it is the French language that will prevent individual francophones who engage in free exchange with Americans from the fate of assimilation" (Lachapelle: 70). The French language is seen as the only means left to ensure the survival of the culture (Lachapelle: 68). Quebec is more dependent than ever on the American market for exports (Lachapelle: 321). However, its political modernization has put the provincial state in competition with the federal government (Lachapelle: 401).

Canada has always been dependent on outside forces, and through continentalism for North American autonomy Quebec is dependent on the United States (Linteau 1: 225). As we have seen, Quebec has traversed the eras of industrialization, urbanization, technology, cultural development, nationalism and statism (Linteau 2: 805). From 1867 to 1896, it adjusted slowly, with its limited autonomy, to economic, social and political transformations (Linteau 2: 805). The period 1896 to 1929 brought expansion and development of natural resources, with political stability for Quebec (Linteau 2: 806). From 1930 to 1945, the province experienced political realignment and the vigor of nationalism was renewed (Linteau 2: 807). The years 1945 to 1960 offered prosperity, industrialization, urbanization and statism in a new nationalism, but also economic and cultural integration with the United States (Linteau 2: 808). From 1960 onward, Quebec was declericalized in favour of state intervention in education, health and society, in a bid to obtain power in Canada and internationally (Linteau 2: 808). Quebec has not been monolithic and unanimous, it has adapted to change, traditional society has evolved gradually, and nationalism has permeated all areas of society for French affirmation (Linteau 2: 811).

The social contract of Confederation was one of two solitudes (Guindon: 105). However, "Je me souviens" "links the past's painful memories and unfulfilled dreams to the broken promises of the uncertain present...proclamation of continuity that forever binds the future to the past" (Guindon: 164).

However, Quebec's society, to remain viable, requires political and economic lines of power with the rest of North America (Levesque: 11). Whatever its future path with Canada, the strong link forged over the years between Quebec and the United States will continue to play a major role in the politics of Quebec. As President John F. Kennedy said: "Geography has made us neighbors, history has made us friends, the economy has made us partners and necessity has made us allies" (Laun: 208).

Nationalism and continentalism have served important roles in the development of Quebec. Over the centuries, Quebec, like a child, was born, has grown up under the watchful eye of Canada, has struggled to carve out a separate identity, and is now ready, with its ties to the United States, to move out onto the world scene.

REFERENCES

BALTHAZAR, Louis, "Quebec's Policies Toward the United States," in Alfred O. Hero, Jr. and Marcel Daneau, *Problems and Opportunities in the United States and Quebec Relations*, Westview Special Studies in International Relations, 1984.

BALTHAZAR, Louis, *The Faces of Quebec Nationalism*, in David Taras, Beverly Rasporich, and Elis Mandel, *A Passion for Identity*, Nelson Canada, Scarborough, 1993.

BERNARD, Jean-Paul, *Les Rouges – Libéralisme, nationalisme et anticléricalisme au milieu du 19e Siècle*, Les Presses de l'Université du Québec, 1971.

BRECHER, Irving, *The Free Trade Initiative, On Course or Off*, in A.R. Riggs and Tom Velk, *Canadian-American Free Trade: Historical, Political and Economic Dimensions*, The Institute for Research on Public Policy, Montreal, 1987.

CHARTIER, Armand, "Franco-Americans and Quebec," in Alfred O. Hero, Jr. and Marcel Daneau, *Problems and Opportunities in the United States and Quebec Relations*, Westview Special Studies in International Relations, 1984.

CREIGHTON, Donald, *The Empire of the St. Lawrence*, Macmillan, Toronto, 1970.

D'AQUINO, Thomas, "Truck and Trade with the Yankees, The Case for a Canada-U.S. Comprehensive Trade Agreement," in A.R. Riggs and Tom Velk, *Canadian American Free Trade: Historical, Political and Economic Dimensions*, The Institution for Research on Public Policy, Montreal, 1987.

DAVENPORT, Paul, "L'économie politique du libre échange, un survol," in A.R. Riggs and Tom Velk, *Canadian American Free Trade: (The Sequel) Historical, Political and Economic Dimensions*, The Institution for Research on Public Policy, Montreal, 1988.

DINSMORE, John, "Éléments d'une position du Québec dans les relations économiques avec les États-Unis," in *Choix*, Centre québecois de relations internationales, Laval, 1975.

DION, Léon, *Nationalismes et politique au Québec*, Hurtubise HMH, Montreal, 1975.

DRACHE, Daniel, *Quebec Only the Beginning*, New Press, Toronto, 1972.

EASTERBROOK, W.T., and AITKEN, Hugh, *Canadian Economic History*, Macmillan, Toronto, 1976.

FAUCHER, Albert, "L'Émigration des Canadiens francais au XIXe siècle," in *Recherches sociographiques*, 5(3), 1961, p. 277.

FAUCHER, Albert, and LAMONTAGNE, Maurice, "The History of Industrial Development," in Jean-Claude Falardeau, *Essays on Contemporary Quebec*, Les Presses de l'Université Laval, Quebec, 1953.

FRY, Earl, "Trends in Canada-U.S. Free Trade Discussions," in A.R. Riggs and Tom Velk, *Canadian-American Free Trade: Historical, Political and Economic Dimensions*, The Institute for Research on Public Policy, Montreal, 1987.

GOUGEON, Gilles, *History of Quebec Nationalism*, James Lorimer & Co., Toronto, 1994.

GOVERNMENT OF QUEBEC, *Quebec and the North American Free Trade Agreement*, Ministère des Affaires internationales, Quebec, 1993.

GUINDON, Hubert, *Quebec Society: Tradition, Modernity, and Nationhood*, University of Toronto Press, Toronto, 1988.

HAMELIN, Jean, and ROBY, Yves, *Histoire économique du Québec 1851-1896*, Fides, Montreal, 1971.

HAMELIN, Jean, *Histoire du Québec*, Edisem, St-Hyacinthe, 1976.

HARRIS, Richard, "Some Observations on the Canada-U.S. Free Trade Deal," in A.R. Riggs and Tom Velk, *Canadian American Free Trade: (The Sequel) Historical, Political and Economic Dimensions*, The Institution for Research on Public Policy, Montreal, 1988.

HERO, Alfred, and BALTHAZAR, Louis, *Contemporary Quebec and the United States 1960-1985,* University Press of America, Boston, 1988.

JONES, Robert, "Agriculture in Lower Canada, 1792-1815," in *The Canadian Historical Review*, 27, 1946, p.33.

LACHAPELLE, Guy, BERNIER, Gérald, SALÉE, Daniel, and BERNIER, Luc. *The Quebec Democracy: Structures, Processes, and Policies*, McGraw-Hill Ryerson Ltd., Toronto, 1993.

LAUN, Louis, "U.S.-Canada Free Trade Negotiations: Historical Opportunities," in A.R. Riggs and Tom Velk, *Canadian-American Free Trade: Historical, Political and Economic Dimensions*, The Institute for Research on Public Policy, Montreal, 1987.

LAVOIE, Yolande, *L'Émigration des Québécois aux États-Unis de 1840-1930*, Éditeur officiel du Québec, 1981.

LAYTON, Robert, "Why Canada Needs Free Trade," in A.R. Riggs and Tom Velk, *Canadian-American Free Trade: Historical, Political and Economic Dimensions*, The Institute for Research on Public Policy, Montreal, 1987.

Le Mémorial du Québec – 1760-1838, Société des Éditions du Mémorial, Montreal.

LÉVESQUE, René, *An Option for Quebec*, McClelland & Stewart Ltd., Toronto, 1968.

LINTEAU, Paul André, DUROCHER, René, and ROBERT, Jean-Claude, *Histoire du Québec contemporain 1967-1929*, Boréal Express, Quebec, 1989.

LINTEAU, Paul André, DUROCHER, René, and ROBERT, Jean-Claude, *Histoire du Québec contemporain depuis 1930*, Boréal, Quebec, 1989.

LISÉE, Jean-Francois, *Dans l'œil de l'aigle*, Boréal, Quebec, 1990.

LITTLE, J.I., *Nationalism, Capitalism and Colonization*, McGill Queen's University Press, Kingston, 1989.

MARR, William, and PATERSON, Donald, *Canada: An Economic History*, Gage, Toronto, 1980.

MASTERS, Donald, *The Reciprocity Treaty of 1854*, McClelland & Stewart Ltd., London, 1963.

MINISTÈRE DES AFFAIRES INTERNATIONALES, DE L'IMMIGRATION ET DES COMMUNAUTÉS CULTURELLES DU QUÉBEC, *Commerce international du Québec, États-Unis, janvier-juin, 1993-1994*, Quebec, 1994.

MINISTÈRE DES AFFAIRES INTERNATIONALES, DE L'IMMIGRATION ET DES COMMUNAUTÉS CULTURELLES DU QUÉBEC, *Commerce international du Québec, États-Unis, 1992-1993*, Quebec, 1994.

MINISTÈRE DES AFFAIRES INTERNATIONALES, DE L'IMMIGRATION ET DES COMMUNAUTÉS CULTURELLES DU QUÉBEC, *Répertoire des représentations du Québec à l'étranger*, Quebec, 1994.

OLIVER, Michael, *The Passionate Debate*, Vehicule Press, Montreal, 1991.

RIGGS, A.R., and VELK, Tom, *Canadian-American Free Trade: Historical, Political and Economic Dimensions*, The Institute for Research on Public Policy, Montreal, 1987.

RIGGS, A.R., and VELK, Tom, *Canadian American Free Trade: (The Sequel) Historical, Political and Economic Dimensions*, The Institution for Research on Public Policy, Montreal, 1988.

RITCHIE, Gordon, "The Free Trade Agreement," in A.R. Riggs and Tom Velk, *Canadian American Free Trade: (The Sequel) Historical, Political and Economic Dimensions*, The Institution for Research on Public Policy, Montreal, 1988.

ROBY, Yves, *Les Franco-Américains de la Nouvelle-Angleterre 1776-1930*, Septentrion, Sillery, 1990.

ROBY, Yves, *Les Québécois et les investissements américains (1918-1929)*, Les Presses de l'Université Laval, Quebec, 1976.

SMITH, Anthony, *Nationalist Movements*, MacMillan, London, 1976.

SMITH, Anthony, *Theories of Nationalism*, Duckworth, London, 1983.

STEVENS, Paul, "Reciprocity 1911: The Canadian Perspective," in A.R. Riggs and Tom Velk, *Canadian American Free Trade: Historical, Political and Economic Dimensions*, The Institution for Research on Public Policy, Montreal, 1987.

STONE, Frank, "Removing Barriers to Canada," in A.R. Riggs and Tom Velk, *Canadian-American Free Trade: Historical, Political and Economic Dimensions*, The Institute for Research on Public Policy, Montreal, 1987.

SURREY, David, *Choice of Conscience – Vietnam Era and Draft Resisters in Canada*, Praeger, New York, 1982.

THOMPSON, Mark, "Le Syndicalisme québécois dans le contexte nord-américain," in *Choix*, Centre québécois de relations internationales, Laval, 1975.

VELK, Tom, RIGGS, A.R., "The Men that Corrupted Everyburg, American Farmers and the Free Trade Initiative 1911," in A.R. Riggs and Tom Velk, *Canadian American Free Trade: (The Sequel) Historical, Political and Economic Dimensions*, The Institution for Research on Public Policy, Montreal, 1988.

VELK, Tom, and RIGGS, A.R., "The Ongoing Debate Over Free Trade," in A.R. Riggs and Tom Velk, *Canadian American Free Trade: (The Sequel) Historical, Political and Economic Dimensions*, The Institution for Research on Public Policy, Montreal, 1988.

WATKINS, Mel, "The Political Economy of Growth," in Wallace Clement and Glen Williams, *The New Canadian Political Economy*, McGill-Queen's University Press, Kingston, 1989.

WHITE, Randall, *Fur Trade to Free Trade: Putting the Canada-U.S. Trade Agreement in Historical Perspective*, Dundurn Press, Toronto, 1988.

WIGLE, Randall, "The Received Wisdom of the Canada-U.S. Free Trade, Qualifications," in A.R. Riggs and Tom Velk, *Canadian-American Free Trade: Historical, Political and Economic Dimensions*, The Institute for Research on Public Policy, Montreal, 1987.

3

Quebec International Trade:
Trade with American Regions

Pierre-Paul Proulx
Université de Montréal

This paper presents a brief examination of Quebec's evolving trade flows and their relationship to urban and regional development patterns in the United States. One of the hypotheses is that a spatial recomposition of North America is underway and is already discernible in its effects on Quebec's trade flows. The study reflects ongoing work on the causes and effects of economic integration in North America.

Many thanks to Guylain Cauchy, graduate student in the Department of Economics at the Université de Montréal, for the preparation of the tables presented in this paper.

INTRODUCTION

Quebec's economic development and trade flows have evolved and will continue to evolve under the influence of many factors, including the technological and organizational changes which accompany the process of economic integration; trade liberalization agreements such as the General Agreement on Tariffs and Trade, the Canada – U.S. Free Trade Agreement, and now the North American Free Trade Agreement; the growing importance of service-information-based activities; government policies concerning defence expenditures; the environment; and many others.

These interrelated factors have a significant impact on the location of economic activity in a world of growing mobility of goods, services, information, capital and other production factors.

It is our contention that the location of economic activity, and hence development in different regions of North America, have already been and will continue to be profoundly modified by the growing economic integration in North America, the western hemisphere, and the world.

Much remains to be done before we are in a position to forecast the recomposition of economic activity in North America. Location decisions concerning the production of goods are not driven by the same determinants that affect service-information activities. On the goods side, production and consumption are easily separated. Producers can be located farther away from their markets as high-technology and high valued-added goods increase in relative importance, and as technological change continues to cut transportation costs. Agglomeration economies and the regrouping of goods producers in certain geographic areas, hence the growing importance of cities as international actors, are not incompatible with the phenomenon of growing distances in trade flows – quite the contrary.

On the services side, production and consumption are nearly simultaneous; the service cannot generally be traded separately from the person who produces it, hence the location of suppliers near customers. In part, this linkage is strong, especially for services to individuals and lower order services. Explaining the location of goods production is helpful in explaining the location of such services. However, telecommunications and foreign direct investment are making it increasingly possible to export and import higher order services, especially when companies have advantages that they can internalize.

Our examination of data in this chapter concerns flows of primary and secondary products. No attempt has been made to examine service sector flows, for which data are very limited. The patterns and trends at the urban and regional levels in the U.S., which we will briefly examine, do however reflect developments in the location of services and goods in an increasingly integrated North American economy (see Proulx, 1990a and 1994).

Understanding Quebec's current and future economic, social, and political development requires an understanding of these underlying forces which are giving cities, regions and sub-national governments a growing role in economic development. Analysis of trade and development at the sub-national level will therefore become increasingly important.

This chapter presents a brief examination of Quebec's evolving trade flows and their relationship to urban and regional development patterns in the U.S.[1] One of our hypotheses is that a spatial recomposition of North America is underway and is already discernible in its effects on Quebec's trade flows.

---

1.   See PROULX, P.P., MANZAGOL, C., and AMESSE, F., *L'espace économique du Québec et de trois de ses régions.... Rapport au Secrétariat à l'aménagement régional*, Ministère du Conseil exécutif, 1994, for a more detailed consideration of these issues.

Manufacturing activity in North America was initially concentrated in the northeast and Great Lakes region, gradually moving westward and southward. This trend is likely to continue as economic activity on the Pacific Rim continues to outstrip Atlantic Rim activity and as the effects of NAFTA and integration with Central and South America manifest themselves. An understanding of Quebec's trade flows calls for an understanding of these underlying factors (Krugman, 1991).

This chapter follows a fairly recent, more broadly focused paper which examined province-state trade between Canada's different provinces and U.S. states and regions (Proulx, 1990). The paper described the concentration of 75% of Canada's trade in the borderlands (i.e. trade between provinces and adjoining or proximate states). Two American regions which include Michigan, Ohio, New Jersey, New York and Pennsylvania are very important destinations for Canadian exports to the U.S., particularly those of Ontario (responsible for over 60% of Canadian exports to the U.S.). The predominance of Ontario is in part a result of history, location (transportation costs), the availability of high quality coal in adjoining states, the synergies of the Ontario Family Compact (Ontario Inc.), the Auto Pact of 1965, the concentration of American foreign direct investment in Ontario, and the importance of Toronto and Metropolitan Toronto as an international city.

The contents of this chapter reflect ongoing work on the causes and effects of economic integration in North America. The research has prompted the formulation of the hypothesis that is tested in part here, namely that the growing tertiary, service-based nature of our economies and the evolution of our manufacturing activities toward more high-tech and higher value-added activities are changing the economic space for our firms and institutions. A major outcome of the process is an increase in the distance involved in exports and imports. High-tech and high-value-added goods and services travel further afield. As a consequence, although geographic proximity has been and remains a fundamental determinant of economic development (it is one of the five building blocks in the economic development strategy proposed for Quebec by this author),[2] one implication is that Quebec's trade flows will continue to change from their east-west orientation (still the most important given the efforts of Canada to build an east-west common market) to a north-south orientation. The destinations of exports and the origins of imports have begun and will continue to involve states which are progressively more distant from Quebec.

From this perspective flows our interest in interregional-international trade, i.e. trade between different regions of North America, for example

---

2.   For the official development strategy of the Quebec Government, as elaborated by Industry Minister Gérald Tremblay, see: Gagné and Lefèvre.

between the Mexican maquiladoras (special processing zones for export markets) and Montreal.

This hypothesis explains our interest in urban and regional development patterns in the U.S. An understanding of these patterns is necessary to explain Quebec's trade in North America.

GENERAL FEATURES OF QUEBEC'S INTERNATIONAL, TRANSBORDER AND INTERPROVINCIAL TRADE[3]

In 1993 Quebec exported C$33.8 billion in goods to foreign markets, an increase of 49.9% over the 1988 total (see Table 1.1). North America receives 79.7% of the total, its share having increased from 75.3% in 1988 as a result of Quebec's significant participation in the positive effects of the FTA.

The European Union (Western Europe in Table 1.1) represents the second market in importance. Its relative importance declined over the 1988-1993 period, its share of total exports falling from 13.8% to 11.8%.

Japan and South-East Asia are neither important nor dynamic destinations for Quebec's total exports. They grew by 17.2% over the 1988-1993 period, while the growth rates to the U.S. and Western Europe were 58.7% and 12.2% respectively. Some dynamism is observable in exports to South-East Asia, but that destination does not have the same interest for Quebec as it has for provinces further west.

Also worthy of note is the minute importance of South America, Central America the Caribbean and Mexico, which accounted for 2.6% and 1.9% of total exports in 1988 and 1993 respectively. Integration patterns between Quebec and the U.S. on the one hand and Mexico and other Latin American countries which we are currently studying with for the Conseil des relations internationales de Montréal (CORIM) on the other suggest growing interest for Quebec in such markets which, for a variety of economic, political, strategic and other reasons, are of more interest as are European markets, than are South-East Asian markets generally. Quebec business and the Quebec Government consider Mexico to be a huge potential market. The Quebec Government has recently opened an office in Mexico City to expand the commercial and cultural ties with that country, and is the only Canadian province to have done so. Quebecers will seek out specific niches in different dynamic South-East Asian markets, but the orientation of their trade efforts is not relevant for other provinces in Canada. The "Greater China" Market (the People's Republic of China, Hong Kong and Taiwan) already ranks as Quebec's fifth-largest foreign market. (Proulx, 1993: 25).

---

3.   All data on Quebec trade flows have been adjusted for transshipment.

That Quebec's trade orientation is different from that of the rest of Canada can be inferred from analysis of the destinations of Canada's exports as reported by Statistics Canada in the *Daily* of October 19, 1994. The U.S. is the destination of 82% of Canada's total exports, Japan receives 4.5% and the European Union 4.98%. In comparison, Quebec's exports go less towards the U.S. and South-East Asia and more towards Europe.

Data reported in a recent article (Proulx, 1993: 26) indicated that Quebec exports to Francophone countries had grown by 12.96%, exports to the U.S. by 5.48%, and exports to other countries by 2.45% during the 1988- 1992 period, when total exports to all destinations grew by 4.91%.

On the import side (see Table 1.2), Quebec is more oriented towards Europe and less towards Asia and the U.S. than the rest of Canada. In 1993, 45% of Quebec's imports came from North America, 22.2% from Western Europe, and 17.2% from other Asian countries. Imports from South America fell while those from Central America, the Caribbean and Mexico rose from 2.4% to 2.9% of the total.

In comparison, 74% of Canadian imports in 1994 came from the U.S., 4.1% from Japan, and 8.4% from the European Union (*Statistics Canada Daily*, October 19, 1994.)

The export intensity of Quebec's economy has remained stable in recent years. That is, Quebec's exports as a share of total GDP remain at the 17-18% level. This reflects the trend seen in the leading OECD economies. In six of the Group of Seven (G7) countries (Canada, U.S., France, Germany, U.K., Italy, Japan), exports represented a higher percentage of GDP in the late 1980s compared with the early 1970s (only Japan remains unchanged). But a reversal took place in the second half of the 1980s, when the relative importance of exports for the G7 countries such as Canada, Italy, the U.K. and Japan declined, while the U.S. and France registering little change. Increasing export globalization has not been a hallmark of recent G7 trade, but has characterized a number of dynamic developing countries and smaller European traders (Christie, 1993: 12-13).

Quebec had an overall trade surplus of C$34 billion in 1993, and a deficit of C$22 billion in 1988 in its primary and secondary sector trade. Traditionally, Quebec's surplus with the U.S. has compensated for any deficit with the rest of the world (Proulx, 1993: 28). In 1993, it had a surplus with the Middle East and North America (see Table 1.3). During 1988-1993, its trade balance with other African, other Asian, Oceania and Central America, Caribbean and Mexico regions deteriorated, while the balance with other regions improved.

In the first eight months of 1994, Canada had trade surpluses with the U.S. and Japan, and deficits with all other regions (*Statistics Canada Daily*, October 19, 1994.

No attempt is made here to supplement the trade flow data with data on production under Quebec control in the U.S. and vice versa, which would be a necessary complement to more adequate understanding of the nature of integration in North America.

Regression analysis of Quebec's total exports to the U.S. at the total U.S. and regional levels, described in our recent report to the Ministère du Conseil exécutif du Québec, indicates that a model taking into consideration each country's GNP, the price of exports and the FTA "explains 97% of Quebec's exports. Exchange rates do not improve the regression results" (Proulx, 1994: Appendix I).[4]

Leading Quebec exports include a mix of high-tech products, metals, and semi-processed raw materials (Table 1.4). The share of high-tech products increased from 12.6% in 1978 to 27.0% in 1992; that of intermediate technology fell from 19.0% to 10.1%; that of low-tech products remained relatively stable at 15.4% and 16.4% and resource based products also remained stable at 39.8% and 39.3% according to estimates by the Ministère des Affaires Internationales, de l'Immigration et des Communautés culturelles (1994-p. 53).

Newsprint and aluminium, Quebec's first and second export products in 1989 (12.0% and 10.1% respectively), were in second and third place respectively in 1993, having been overtaken by other telecommunications equipment and materials as Quebec's first export product (9.0% of the total). Other fast-growing products in Quebec's exports are airplanes and motors, softwood lumber, tools and other materials, precious metals, clothing, printed materials and electricity. The presence of intrafirm-intraindustry trade is noticeable in these product sectors (Proulx, 1995). To report on our analysis of these is beyond the scope of this chapter.

"Special commercial transactions," autos and petroleum are Quebec's most important imports (see Table 1.5).

Inorganic chemical products and clothing imports grew rapidly during the 1989-1993 period although the totals remain unimportant. The same applies to the products imported in 1993 that were not imported in 1989 (see bottom of Table 1.5).

---

4.   We regressed the log of Quebec's total exports to the U.S. in millions of U.S. constant 1982 dollars from 1978 to 1992 against the U.S. GDP, a variable to take into consideration the FTA and the log of a Lasperes price index of Canadian exports to the U.S. All coefficients are significant. See Proulx, 1994.

TRADE WITH THE UNITED STATES

According to a recent study by Statistics Canada (1993), the Canadian share of the U.S. manufactured products market (no such estimate exists for Quebec) increased from 2.3% in 1981-1983 to 2.5% in 1989-1991. The American share of the Canadian manufacturing market increased from 26.2% at the beginning to 27.4% at the end of this period.

During 1988-1993, Quebec's total exports and imports to and from the U.S. increased by 58.2% and 17.1% respectively (see Tables 2.1 and 2.2).

Quebec's Primary and Secondary Exports to Different Regions of the U.S.

The effects of history and the role of primary products in Quebec's exports to the U.S. have led to a concentration of exports to the neighbouring regions of New England, the mid-Atlantic and the North-East. Our hypothesis is that these regions will decline in relative and perhaps absolute importance as export destinations as the recomposition of economic activity in North America proceeds.

The proportion of Quebec's exports to the Atlantic Region (New York, New Jersey and Pennsylvania) is declining steadily as anticipated. While an average of 40% of Quebec's exports went to that region during the 1976-1987 period (Proulx, 1990) the percentage share fell to 36.5% in 1984, 30.9% in 1988, 27.4% in 1991, and stood at just 26,7% in 1993. Proximity remains important in a higher-tech world, but not in the same way as in a more primary low-tech economy, as we shall observe later.

The second region in importance, New England (Connecticut, Massachusetts, Rhode Island, Maine, New Hampshire and Vermont) represented 18.9% of Quebec's exports to the U.S. in 1991 and 19.4% in 1993. This was considerably higher than the 1978 figure of 12.4%. Initial decline followed by growth in one state has made for stability in the share, which in 1993 stood at the average of 20% observed during the 1976-1987 period.

This stability of the entire region is the result of lower than average export growth rates to each of the states concerned, excluding Vermont, whose relative share of Quebec's total exports increased from 5.1% in 1988 to 10.5% in 1993, basically as a result of intrafirm-intraindustry trade between IBM plants in Bromont, Quebec and Burlington and Essex Junction in Vermont. Our hypothesis to the effect that trade with proximate states would decline in relative importance is not contradicted by these results because Quebec's exports to Vermont do not stay there! They are presumably incorporated in products shipped elsewhere in the U.S. and internationally, a hypothesis we could test with the Miser data base among others. If this part of our hypothesis is confirmed, the implication for export strategies is that greater attention should be paid to helping small and medium-sized Quebec firms to become "problem solving" suppliers to large firms. Note, however, that Canada and Quebec do not do too well, since intrafirm trade and deficits are correlated (Proulx, 1990b).

We will not examine the product composition of Quebec's exports in this paper. However, one of its characteristics is relevant to a test of the hypothesis we have formulated. As indicated in Table 2.4, the "other telecommunications material and equipment" category of products, which was fourth in importance in 1988, became Quebec's first export product in 1993. Its share of Quebec exports to the New England region increased from 13.9 per cent in 1988 to 29.3 per cent in 1991 (Proulx, 1993). The largest single component in this category of telecommunications exports is the intrafirm trade by IBM, reflecting shipments between its plant in Bromont, Quebec and Essex Junction, Vermont, where IBM operates its largest semiconductor manufacturing facility. Quebec's imports of products related to this large flow of intrafirm trade have grown significantly: imports of electronic tubes and semiconductors grew from C$608 million in 1984 to C$953 million in 1991; imports of other telecommunications material and equipment jumped from C$180 million in 1984 to C$479 in 1989 and increased further to C$554 in 1993.

As a result of trade in this sector, Vermont is the fifth most dynamic export destination for Quebec, as may be seen in Table 2.1 where it is indicated that total Quebec exports to Vermont increased by 229.1% over the 1988-1993 period, with the percentage increase to the U.S. being 58.2%.

Quebec's exports towards the Center North-East region (Michigan, Ohio, Illinois, Wisconsin, Indiana) account for a stable share of Quebec's total exports. The share of this region fell from 24% in 1984 to 17.5% in 1991, but rose again to 24% in 1993 as a result of dynamism in exports to Ohio and Wisconsin (see Table 2.1).

Quebec's Trade with Its Immediate Neighbours, Maine, New Hampshire, Vermont and New York

In 1988, Quebec exported C$4,590,282,000 to the neighbouring states of Maine, New Hampshire, Vermont and New York. This amount represented 27% of total exports. By 1993, exports to these proximate states was C$8,162,224, 30.9% of the total, representing a slight decline from the 1991 percentage share of 32.95%.

As indicated above, this global result is explained by the dynamism of exports of "other telecommunications material and equipment" to Vermont, a state whose share of Quebec's exports to the U.S. is increasing (5.1% of total U.S. exports in 1988 to 10.5% per cent in 1993, the share of other proximate states falling, i.e. from 19.21% to 17,9% for New York; from 1.2% to 0.80% for New Hampshire; and from 1.6% to 1.0% for Maine.

Quebec's imports from the proximate states increased from 16.54% of total imports from the U.S. in 1988 to 22.71% in 1992. Their share was 21.3% in 1993, at which time they totaled C$2,895,578. This increase in importance is manifest for each of the states involved, the Vermont share increasing from 5.2% in 1988 to 8.6% in 1993. A more detailed analysis of data would help to determine to what extent the Quebec-Vermont trade is intra-industry trade. In addition, examination of interprovincial trade data would help to indicate the extent of transshipment from these states through Quebec to other provinces in Canada.

Quebec has a positive trade balance with each of the transborder proximate states. In 1993, its surplus was C$95,138,000 with Maine, C$81,010,000 with New Hampshire, C$1,404,566 with Vermont and C$1,210,862 with New York (see Table 2.3). These surpluses are an important part of Quebec's primary and secondary sector trade surplus with the U.S. for they represent 49% of the total in 1988 and 1992, and 20.8% in 1993. Compared to surpluses in 1988, those of Maine and New Hampshire have declined, and those of Vermont and New York have increased. Since it is our interpretation that Vermont serves as a state of transit for Quebec exports, we maintain our conclusion that trade with proximate borderland states is declining and changing in its nature, hence the need for new export strategies to work with borderland states and beyond in the U.S. market.

A More Detailed Examination of Quebec's Exports by State: Transborder Trade in Decline

While Quebec's primary and secondary exports to the U.S. increased by 58.2% from 1988 to 1993, those of Maine increased by 14.9%, those to New Hampshire by 2.2%, those to Vermont by 229.3% and those to New York by 47.6%. Our hypothesis to the effect that exports to bordering states should grow by less than those to states further away holds because, as indicated above, Vermont is a transit state for Quebec exports.

Identification of American states to which Quebec's exports have been increasing most, and lagging, analysed alongside data on demographic and labor market change at the sub-national level in the U.S. (see below), provides interesting indications of the recomposition of economic activity in North America.

The following states are those to which Quebec exports increased most during the 1988-1993 period (the state's average share of total Quebec exports to the U.S. in 1993 is indicated in brackets).

States with the Fastest Growth for Quebec Exports, 1988-1993

	Total growth	Share of total exports (% 1993)
S. Dakota	425.2%	(0.1)
Nebraska	387.4%	(0.2%)
New Mexico	383.4%	(0.1)
Vermont	229.3%	(10.5%)
Arizona	223.7%	(0.4%)
Hawaii	193.9%	(0.0%)
Louisiana	187.3%	(0.3%)
Virginia	186.2%	(1.2%)
Delaware	163.1%	(0.4%)
Wisconsin	158.0%	(1.7%)

Except for Vermont, these states are not major destinations for Quebec exports. Nor are they close to Quebec, which suggests that our hypothesis may be valid. Needless to say, examination of exports to different states by product would be necessary to test our hypothesis, which is to the effect that these exports should be high-tech and high-value-added products.

The small shares of Quebec exports going to these states is such that the list of dynamic states varies from year to year. Examination of this question using average annual growth rates covering the period 1988-1992 reported in a recent article (Proulx 1993) saw Alaska, Puerto Rico, Montana, Wyoming and Colorado replacing Arizona, Louisiana, Virginia, Delaware and Wisconsin in the list of dynamic destinations. In both cases Vermont, the transit state, is the only state close to Quebec.

States to which Quebec exports declined or increased the least during the 1988-1993 period are: District of Columbia (–58.0%, 0.1% of Quebec's total exports in 1993), Rhode Island (–26.3%, 0.3%), Virginia (–24.9%, 1.4%), Alabama (–20.4%, 0.9%), Arkansas (–12.9%, 0.7%), Washington, (–11.8%, 1,3%), New Hampshire (2.2%, 0.8%), New Jersey (9.3%, 3.6%), Maine (14.9%,1.1%), Pennsylvania (26.1%, 5.2%). The states is this category of slow or declining markets over the 1988-1992 period were: Michigan, D.C., Virginia, New Hampshire, Washington, Rhode Island, New Jersey, Maine, Maryland and New York. Maine, New Hampshire and New York (1988-1992) are close to Quebec.

The states whose exports to Quebec grew the fastest over the 1988-1993 period are: Hawaii, North Dakota, New Mexico, Nebraska, Oklahoma, Montana, D.C., Colorado, South Carolina and Nevada. (See Table 2.2 for per cent increase and share of Quebec imports.) Six of these states were in the list of states with the fastest growth of exports to Quebec during the 1988-1992 period. That list, as reported in Proulx 1993, was: Wyoming, Hawaii, Utah, Oklahoma, New Mexico, Nebraska, District of Columbia, Montana, Alaska,

Virgin Islands. Note that these states are far from Quebec, a result in accordance with our basic hypothesis.

Three of these states (four for the 1988-1992 period) also appear on the dynamic destination list for Quebec exports. Analysis of the product composition of these flows will indicate whether we are observing intrafirm trade. We would, however, expect such intrafirm trade to occur between Quebec and states that are close by, with similiar incomes and foreign direct investment linkages.

The U.S. states with the worst performance (among states) in their exports to Quebec during the 1988-1993 period are: Idaho, Illinois, Washington, Delaware, Virginia, Alaska, Mississippi, Michigan, Maryland, and Iowa (see Table 2.2 for per cent increase and share of Quebec imports). States in this "slow exporters to Quebec" category established by examining the 1998-1992 growth rates (Proulx, 1993) were: Idaho, Illinois, Virginia, Maryland, Wisconsin, Delaware, Iowa, Michigan, California and Minnesota. Except for Michigan, these states are not close to Quebec.

That distant states should be among both the most dynamic and the slowest exporters to Quebec is a result which is only partly in accordance with our hypothesis. Analysis of the dynamics of trade by product and state could help to understand this result.

As a final introduction to this aspect of Quebec's trade flows in North America, let us examine the dynamics of its exports to its ten principal markets (see Table 2.1). The list of principal markets is identical for both the 1988-1992 and 1988-1993 periods, except that New Jersey is overtaken by Ohio, Texas and Illinois.

A comparison of the percent increase in Quebec's exports to each of its ten principal markets with the overall per cent increase (58.2%) indicates that growth was higher in three states (Vermont, Ohio, and Texas), and lower in seven states. New York and Michigan, the two largest markets, are close to Quebec, and Vermont, the third largest, is a "transit" state. Pennsylvania and Massachusetts are not very distant, nor is Connecticut, the tenth market in size. Growth rates are lower that the overall U.S. rate in close markets and higher in more distant ones, results which support our hypothesis.

Towards a Reorientation of Quebec's Trade: Market Dynamics at the Regional Level in the U.S.[5]

As mentioned above, three regions of the U.S.A – New England, the Atlantic states and the Great Lakes states (or Central North-East) – are major destinations for Quebec exports. They absorbed 76% of the exports in 1984,

---

5.   See Proulx, 1994, for a more detailed examination of the subjects examined in this section.

66% in 1991, and 70.1% in 1993, evidence of growing regional diversification in Quebec's exports to the U.S., in accordance with our basic hypothesis.

We will now briefly examine data on population and total incomes in these regions, for one would expect them to be related to Quebec's exports. As indicated in our 1993 article (Proulx, 1993: 33) since 1973 these three regions have experienced a population growth rate below the U.S. national average.

In terms of total revenues, the indicator is positive for each of the regions. The New England is more dynamic than for the other regions and the total U.S. We have noted above that Quebec exports to New England are reasonably steady, although they have declined in the other regions.

According to available forecasts (Terlecky, Coleman, 1991) population growth in the U.S. should continue to be strong in the South and West, especially in metropolitan areas. This confirms our theoretical expectations and explains of our concern with interregional-international and intercity analysis. The most dynamic regions for population growth would be: Southern Florida, Central Texas, California, the Pacific Northwest, and areas adjoining Washington and Atlanta. The old industrial centers of the north-east and midwest would see their populations increase, but at at rate lower than that in the South and West of the U.S.

In the South, the most marked increases would be in the South Atlantic (Maryland to Florida), followed by West South Central (which includes Texas and picks up some of the NAFTA effects). Population growth would be relatively small in the East South Central regions (Kentucky, Tennessee, Mississippi and Alabama).

In the west, the Mountain and Pacific states would witness significant increases in population according to the NPA forecasts. The share of Quebec's exports to these two regions has increased from 3.7% to 5.6% (Pacific) and from 2% to 6.9% (Mountain) during the 1984-1991 period (Proulx 1993: 34 and Figure 6).

Quebec's trade flows are slowly adapting to the spatial restructuring of North America. Forecasts indicate conflicting effects on the importance of proximate markets (population effects being negative and income effects being positive), an indication of the extent of the research which must be undertaken to clarify them. Data on trade in services would be of interest to generalize the analysis and test our hypothesis. General indications in this paper are, however, compatible with our hypothesis of a decline in borderlands trade.

Employment in Metropolitan Statistical Areas in the U.S.: Towards More Interregional-International Trade

A test of our basic hypothesis suggests particular interest in the dynamics of demographic, employment and income growth in urban agglomerations, where increasing numbers of the services and information activities that represent a growing share of GDP are located. The concentration of head offices in large cities and the growth of trade in services also underlie our interest in cities as locations where more of Quebec's international trade will be decided and with which it will be undertaken.[6]

In 1990, 81% of all employment and 78% of the U.S. population was located in Metropolitan Statistical Areas (MSAs). Between 1980 and 1990, the average annual rates of increase in population and employment in the U.S. were 0.4% and 1.3% in the non-metro areas, and 1.1% and 2.2% in metro areas. This is a reversal of the pattern observed in the 1970s.

According to National Planning Association forecasts, 85% of the increase in employment between 1990 and 2010, i.e. 31.4 million jobs, will occur in MSAs, hence a significant potential for interregional-international trade with Quebec (Terlecky, Coleman) The NPA forecast of employment focuses on the thirty MSAs with the largest projected employment in 2010.

The list includes MSAs that have been important for a long time. Among them are: New York (we have seen above that New York State is still the most important state for Quebec exports, although it is in decline), Los Angeles, Chicago, Boston, Detroit, Atlanta, San Francisco, Pittsburgh, Newark, Minneapolis, and Cleveland. Also included are MSAs adjacent to some of the above, i.e. Anaheim-Santa Anna; Nasau-Suffolk, Riverside-San Bernardino and San Jose. Among new MSAs in the largest MSAs are San Diego, Phoenix, Tampa, St. Petersburg, Sacramento and Orlando.

The NPA lists of the thirty MSAs with the largest projected increases in employment (in absolute numbers) between 1990 and 2010 and also of the thirty MSAs with the greatest employment growth over that period reveal one important fact: none of these MSAs are in regions to which Quebec exports significantly. One finds in the list large MSAs such as New York, Pittsburgh, Cleveland and Newark. The fastest growing ones are smaller and all located in the south and west of the U.S. Much remains to be done in terms of understanding the implications of these developments for Quebec's development and trade in North America.[7] The research, information and action network (North

---

6. See Proulx, 1990a and Proulx, 1995a for the development of the theory underlying these changes.

7. See Lamonde and Martineau, 1993 for an interesting analysis of development patterns of a number of these American studies and comparisons with Montreal, as well as an earlier effort by certain authors to compare eight North American cities (Fry and Soldatos, 1991).

American Cities International-NACI) which I am attempting to establish with Canadian, American and Mexican colleagues should help to pursue some of this research.

A Few Concluding Observations

Undestanding Quebec's place in North America, its trade patterns and its policy development calls for an understanding of the ongoing process of regional change in North America, now being influenced by military expenditure cutbacks (which in the past favored the coastal states at the expense of the Rust Belt), by the FTA, by NAFTA and integration processes in Latin America, as well as by some of the factors mentioned above. The result of these fundamental trends is a changing economic space of relevance to goods and service suppliers and purchasers from Quebec.

Another manifestation of the effects of the above-mentioned factors is the underlying trend towards a decline in relative importance of Quebec's trade within the Canadian common market in favour of its international trade with more distant regions in North America and the world. Recent research (based in this case on Statistics Canada data) has documented the extent to which interprovincial trade in Canada is predominantly Quebec-Ontario trade (Proulx, 1993; Proulx and Cauchy, 1991 and Proulx et al., 1995). In 1984, Ontario absorbed 60% of Quebec's interprovincial manufacturing shipments, i.e. 15% of Quebec's total shipments. In 1988 the Ontario share increased to 62% of shipments to all provinces, i.e. 16.4% of total shipments from Quebec. This reflects the strength of the now-spent expansion which was manifest particularly in Ontario. According to other estimates (Bureau de la Statistique du Québec) Quebec manufacturing shipments to other provinces increased from C$17,273,000 in 1984 to C$22,731,000 in 1988, while its international exports of manufactured goods increased from C$17,733,000 to C$22,581,000. Interprovincial shipments remained at approximately 50% of total interprovincial plus international shipments of goods over this period, a result which should change given the severe Ontario recession, the North American restructuring process (which is impacting Ontario much more negatively than Quebec, given the greater presence of American foreign direct investment there), and the underlying growing trend of Quebec – U.S. trade analyzed in this paper.

Statistics covering Quebec's total interprovincial activities (primary, secondary and tertiary), reported by Statistics Canada's input-output division, indicate that the ratio of Quebec's international exports of goods and services to GDP increased from 14.59% in 1974, to 20.80% in 1979, to 21.88% in 1984.

Between 1974 and 1984 Quebec's share of interprovincial shipments fell in each province to the west, and increased in the east, particularly in New Brunswick.

Proximity and history are still very much at work and evident in Quebec's trade flows in North America, but as indicated here, change is in the air.

Analysis of such patterns is essential to an understanding of the economic, social and political climate in Quebec and elsewhere in North America.

REFERENCES

CHRISTIE, Keith H., *Globalization and Public Policy in Canada: In Search of a Paradigm*, Department of External Affairs and International Trade Canada, Ottawa, Policy Planning Staff Paper 93-01, January 1993.

FRY, Earl, and SOLDATOS, P., eds. *New International Cities Era*, Brigham Young University Press, Provo, 1991.

KRUGMAN, Paul, *Geography and Trade*, MIT Press, Cambridge, 1991.

LAMONDE, P., and Y. MARTINEAU, *La désindustrialisation de Montréal.* Institut national de la recherche scientifique-Urbanisation, Montreal, 1993.

MINISTÈRE DES AFFAIRES INTERNATIONALES, DE L'IMMIGRATION ET DES COMMUNAUTÉS CULTURELLES DU QUÉBEC, *Partenaire d'affaires en Amérique*, Quebec, February, 1994.

PROULX, Pierre-Paul (1990a), "Cadre conceptuel pour la localisation des activités économiques, le cas des villes internationales", *Canadian Journal of Regional Science.* 14(2), Summer 1991.

PROULX, Pierre-Paul (1990b), "Primary and Secondary Trade between Canada and the United States: A National, Regional and Provincial Overview" Working paper, Université de Montréal, Département des sciences économiques.

PROULX, Pierre-Paul, and CAUCHY, G., "Un examen des échanges commerciaux du Québec avec les autres provinces canadiennes, les États-Unis et le reste du monde," in Commission sur l'avenir politique et constitutionnel du Québec, *Éléments d'analyse économique pertinents à la révision du statut politique et constitutionnel du Québec*, Working paper no. 1, Quebec, 1991.

PROULX, Pierre-Paul (1993a), "L'Aléna, le Québec et la mutation de son espace économique," in P. Drewe, D. Maillat and R. Ratti, *Les régions frontalières: un laboratoire de l'intégration européenne*, Association des sciences régionales de langue française, 1993.

PROULX Pierre-Paul, "Quebec in North America: From a Borderlands to a Borderless Economy," *Quebec Studies*, 16, pp. 23-37.

PROULX, Pierre-Paul, Report to the Ministère du Conseil exécutif du Québec (SAR), *L'espace économique extérieur du Québec et de trois de ses régions... Quebec*, October, 1994.

PROULX, Pierre-Paul et al., *Intégration économique et modèles d'associations économiques, Québec-Canada*, INRS-Urbanisation and Publication officielle du Québec, September 1995.

PROULX, Pierre-Paul, "The Determinants of Growth and Decline in cities," in Kreal, P. and Gapert, G., *North American Cities*, Sage, 1995.

STATISTICS CANADA, *Évolution du commerce: Canada–États-Unis, Les industries manufacturières 1981-1991*, Ottawa, March 1993.

TERLECKY N. E., and C. D. COLEMAN. *Regional Economic Growth in the U.S.: Projections for the 1992-2010 Period*, Report No. 91-R-1, National Planning Association Data Services, Washington, 1991.

Section 1
Quebec's Trade by Major Geographic Regions

TABLE 1.1
Total Exports from Quebec towards Principal Markets, 1988-1993
(thousands of dollars, percentage of total and variations)

	1988	% of total	1993	% of total	Variation 88/93
Western Europe	3,126,305	13.8	4,007,277	11.8	28.2%
Eastern Europe	100,626	0.4	112,882	0.3	12.2%
Middle East	248,139	1.1	425,285	1.3	71.4%
Other African countries	179,500	0.8	171,545	0.5	−4.4%
Other Asian countries	1,198,127	5.3	1,403,933	4.1	17.2%
Oceania	122,456	0.5	106,148	0.3	−13.3%
South America	317,539	1.4	364,891	1.1	14.9%
Central America, Caribbean, Mexico	280,947	1.2	272,309	0.8	−3.1%
North America	17,011,517	75.3	26,994,148	79.7	58.7%
Unspecified region	0	0.0	0	0.0	−
Total	**22,580,084**	**100.0**	**33,858,419**	**100.0**	**49.9%**

TABLE 1.2
Total Quebec Imports from Principal Markets, 1988-1993
(thousands of dollars, percentage of total and variations)

	1988	% of total	1993	% of total	Variation 88/93
Western Europe	6,427,790	25.9	6,747,596	22.2	5.0%
Eastern Europe	290,384	1.2	263,411	0.9	-9.3%
Middle East	110,574	0.4	262,104	0.9	137.0%
Other African countries	289,342	1.2	583,886	1.9	101.8%
Other Asian countries	4,211,369	17.0	5,248,792	17.2	24.6%
Oceania	223,044	0.9	535,748	1.8	140.2%
South America	839,673	3.4	611,542	2.0	-27.2%
Central America, Caribbean, Mexico	598,148	2.4	892,995	2.9	49.3%
North America	11,560,480	46.6	13,672,141	44.9	18.3%
Unspecified region	268,487	1.1	1,627,506	5.3	506.2%
Total	**24,807,031**	**100.0**	**30,445,721**	**100.0**	**22.7%**

TABLE 1.3
Balance of Quebec's Trade with its Principal Markets, 1988-1993
(Exports–Imports, thousands of dollars)

	1988	1993	Variation 93–88	Improvement
Western Europe	-3,301,485	-2,740;319	561,166	X
Eastern Europe	-189,759	-150,529	39,230	X
Middle East	137,565	163,181	25,616	X
Other African countries	-109,842	-412,341	-302,499	
Other Asian countries	-3,013,242	-3,844,859	-831,617	
Oceania	-100,588	-429,600	-329,012	
South America	-522,135	-246,651	275,484	X
Central America, Caribbean, Mexico	-317,201	-620,686	-303,485	
North America	5,451,036	13,322,007	7,870,971	X
Unspecified region	-268,487	-1,627,506	-1,359,019	
Total	**-2,226,946**	**3,412,698**	**5,639,644**	**X**

TABLE 1.4
Principal Products Exported from Quebec (1989-1993)
(thousands of dollars, percentage of total and variations)

Description of products	1989	% of total	1993	% of total	Variation 89/93
Other telecomm. equipment & materials	1,485,189	6.4	3,052,748	9.0	105.5%
Newsprint	2,786,256	12.0	2,898,334	8.6	4.0%
Aluminum, including alloids	2,344,398	10.1	2,778,826	8.2	18.5%
Personal vehicles and frames	1,825,494	7.8	2,672,188	7.9	46.4%
Special commercial transactions	379,187	1.6	1,877,771	5.5	395.2%
Airplanes and motors	497,928	2.1	1,326,021	3.9	166.3%
Airplane motors and parts	1,039,523	4.5	1,157,723	3.4	11.4%
Softwood lumber	547,922	2.4	978,202	2.9	78.5%
Wood pulp & similar pulp	742,540	3.5	691,884	2.0	−6.8%
Copper and alloys	647,793	2.8	656,276	1.9	1.3%
Office equipment	468,996	2.0	585,415	1.7	24.8%
Other equipment & tools	338,566	1.5	532,895	1.6	57.4%
Precious metals, including alloys	300,282	1.3	448,544	1.3	49.4%
Clothing and accessories	227,205	1.0	438,491	1.3	93.0%
Other med./opt. lab measuring instruments	399,945	1.7	433,542	1.3	8.4%
Metal frameworks	337,439	1.4	409,972	1.2	21.5%
Fresh, refrig. or frozen meat	365,915	1.6	406,359	1.2	11.1%
Printed materials	200,935	0.9	373,937	1.1	86.1%
Electricity	200,254	0.9	328,299	1.0	63.9%
Other paper & printing	225,186	1.0	326,532	1.0	45.0%
Crude asbestos	315,575	1.4	297,797	0.9	−5.6%

TABLE 1.4 (cont'd)

Among top 25 products in 89 only	1989	% of total	in 93 only	1993	% of total
Other waste & scrap materials	294,303	1.3	Other paper	362,432	1.1
Other motor vehicles	218,343	0.9	Other chem. products	316,922	0.9
Iron ore and concentrate	312,582	1.3	Toys, games & sporting goods	310,797	0.9
Zinc, including alloys	296,127	1.3	Tobacco	556,162	1.6
Top 10 products	**12,386,039**	**53.2**		**18,089,973**	**53.4**
Top 25 products	**16,797,882**	**72.1**		**24,218,068**	**71.5**
All products	**23,302,647**	**100.0**		**33,858,419**	**100.0**

TABLE 1.5
Principal Products Imported in Quebec (1989-1993)
(thousands of dollars, percentage of total and variations)

Description of products	1989	% of total	1993	% of total	Variation 89/93
Special commercial transactions	629,319	2.4	5,322,198	17.5	745.7%
Personal vehicles and frames	3251,891	12.2	3,375,399	11.1	3.8%
Crude petroleum	1229,340	4.6	2,115,238	6.9	72.0%
Other telecomm. equip. & mat.	749,801	2.8	834,488	2.7	11.3%
Inorganic chemical products	656,351	2.5	776,007	2.5	18.2%
Trucks, truck trailers and frames	564,666	2.1	638,331	2.1	13.0%
Organic chemical products	476,639	1.8	615,044	2.0	29..0%
Airplane motors & parts	532,526	2.0	490,764	1.6	–7.8%
Unknit top clothing	340,905	1.3	478,767	1.6	40.4%

TABLE 1.5 (cont'd)
Principal Products Imported in Quebec (1989-1993)
(thousands of dollars, percentage of total and variations)

Description of products	1989	% of total	1993	% of total	Variation 89/93
Airplane parts and motors	364,444	1.4	421,544	1.4	15.7%
Other oil & coal by-products	367,262	1.4	349,169	1.1	-4.9%
Electronic computers	485,358	1.8	327,221	1.1	-32.6%
Other ore, conc. and metal scrap	420,999	1.6	326,248	1.1	-22.5%
Paper and cardboard	278,426	1.0	290,020	1.0	4.2%
Other unedible refined products	342,541	1.3	282,057	0.9	-17.7%
Other lab, etc. measuring instruments	274,092	1.0	271,329	0.9	-1.0%
Other clothing & clothing acc.	260,023	1.0	259,020	0.9	-0.4%
TVs, radios and phonographs	334,021	1.3	255,655	0.8	-23.5%
Other transfer material	218,172	0.8	225,653	0.7	3.4%

Among top 25 products in 89 only	1989	% of total	in 93 only	1993	% of total
Elect. tubes & semiconductors	1,505,024	5.6	Dosed medicine & pharm. prod.	262,883	1.2
Compete planes, including motors	411,016	1.5	Other pers. effects & appliances	296,967	1.0
Fuel oil	397,682	1.5	Bulk plastic materials	286,608	0.9
Auto parts excl. motors	291,693	1.1	Knitted top clothing	260,257	0.9
Shoes	242,148	0.9	Other chemical products	238,836	0.8
Misc. equipment and tools	237,003	0.9	Fresh, refrig. or frozen meat	225,439	0.7
Top 10 products	10,081,015	37.7		15,067,780	49.5
Top 25 products	14,861,443	55.6		19,325,143	63.5
All products	**26,717,172**	**100.0**		**30,445,721**	**100.0**

Section 2
Quebec's Trade with the United States

TABLE 2.1
Total Quebec Exports to American States, 1988-1993
(thousands of dollars, percentage of total and variations)

States	1988	% of total	1993	% of total	Variation 88/93
New York	3,266,182	19.2	4,821,215	17.9	47.6%
Michigan	2,110,685	12.4	3,221,256	12.0	52.6%
Vermont	860,656	5.1	2,833,758	10.5	229.3%
Pennsylvania	1,108,108	6.5	1,397,589	5.2	26.1%
Massachusetts	873,127	5.1	1,178,552	4.4	35.0%
Ohio	573,566	3.4	1,170,736	4.4	104.1%
Texas	476,756	2.8	1,133,574	4.2	137.8%
Illinois	780,898	4.6	1,109,742	4.1	42.1%
New Jersey	887,090	5.2	969,186	3.6	9.3%
Connecticut	506,515	3.0	627,317	2.3	23.8%
California	355,293	2.1	617,851	2.3	73.9%
Florida	332,838	2.0	582,310	2.2	75.0%
Indiana	345,941	2.0	478,506	1.8	38.3%
Wisconsin	176,431	1.0	455,236	1.7	158.0%
Kentucky	275,293	1.6	450,078	1.7	63.5%
Tennessee	175,903	1.0	415,880	1.5	136.4%
Georgia	299,174	1.8	390,033	1.4	30.4%
Virginia	515,932	3.1	389,761	1.4	-24.9%
North Calorina	236,970	1.4	379,049	1.4	60.0%
Other states	80,772	0.5	371,776	1.4	360.3%
Washington	395,212	2.3	348,528	1.3	-11.8%
Maryland	242,313	1.4	315,556	1.2	30.2%
West Virginia	108,959	0.6	311,844	1.2	186.2%
Maine	264,314	1.6	303,655	1.1	14.9%
Kansas	131,836	0.8	261,897	1.0	98.7%
Alabama	300,589	1.8	239,404	0.9	-20.4%
Minnesota	90,410	0.5	213,784	0.8	136.5%
New Hampshire	199,133	1.2	203,596	0.8	2.2%
Arkansas	228,465	1.3	198,944	0.7	-12.9%

TABLE 2.1 (cont'd)
Total Quebec Exports to American States, 1988-1993
(thousands of dollars, percentage of total and variations)

States	1988	% of total	1993	% of total	Variation 88/93
Missouri	117,054	0.7	185,667	0.7	58.6%
Oregon	57,115	0.3	140,837	0.5	146.6%
Colorado	63,099	0.4	137,104	0.5	117.3%
South Carolina	83,772	0.5	129,461	0.5	54.5%
Delaware	45,289	0.3	119,149	0.4	163.1%
Arizona	35,623	0.2	115,323	0.4	223.7%
Iowa	58,377	0.3	103,905	0.4	78.0%
Mississippi	36,152	0.2	91,836	0.3	154.0%
Rhode Island	108,274	0.6	79,783	0.3	−26.3%
Louisiana	27,749	0.2	79,712	0.3	187.3%
Oklahoma	24,804	0.1	55,829	0.2	125.1%
Nebraska	10,138	0.1	49,411	0.2	387.4%
Utah	30,014	0.2	40,379	0.2	34.5%
Nevada	19,878	0.1	37,528	0.1	88.8%
South Dakota	6,477	0.0	34,017	0.1	425.2%
New Mexico	4,631	0.0	22,390	0.1	383.4%
Alaska	17,080	0.1	22,334	0.1	30.8%
Idaho	9,102	0.1	18,534	0.1	103.6%
North Dakota	5,247	0.0	18,164	0.1	246.2%
District of Columbia	27,651	0.2	11,262	0.0	−58.0%
Montana	4,121	0.0	8,055	0.0	96.2%
Hawaii	2,329	0.0	6,844	0.0	193.9%
Wyoming	3,165	0.0	4,935	0.0	55.9%
Total	**17,005,483**	**100.0**	**26,903,466**	**100.0**	**58.2%**

TABLE 2.2
Total Quebec Imports to American States 1988-1993
(thousands of dollars, percentage of total and variations)

States	1988	% of total	1993	% of total	Variation 88/93
New York	1,053,982	9.1	1,398,153	10.3	32.7%
Vermont	597,786	5.2	1,166,322	8.6	95.1%
Michigan	1,041,051	9.0	1,004,138	7.4	–3.5%
Ohio	645,057	5.6	814,814	6.0	26.3%
California	673,798	5.8	709,381	5.2	5.3%
Massachusetts	458,362	4.0	676,154	5.0	47.5%
New Jersey	516,167	4.5	660,647	4.9	28.0%
Texas	460,823	4.0	593,532	4.4	28.8%
Pennsylvania	405,941	3.5	536,052	4.0	32.1%
North Carolina	312,092	2.7	427,588	3.2	37.0%
Connecticut	315,103	2.7	421,498	3.1	33.8%
Illinois	834,226	7.2	404,094	3.0	–51.6%
Florida	265,651	2.3	368,533	2.7	38.7%
Missouri	330,532	2.9	311,972	2.3	–5.6%
Georgia	243,047	2.1	286,416	2.1	17.8%
Maryland	261,621	2.3	263,889	1.9	0.9%
Tennessee	130,305	1.1	247,036	1.8	89.6%
Washington	393,363	3.4	238,127	1.8	–39.5%
South Carolina	112,297	1.0	231,855	1.7	106.5%
Maine	161,548	1.4	208,517	1.5	29.1%
Other states	409,644	3.5	204,513	1.5	–50.1%
Wisconsin	243,957	2.1	199,471	1.5	–18.2%
Minnesota	171,142	1.5	187,221	1.4	9.4%
Kentucky	127,256	1.1	159,649	1.2	25.5%
Louisiana	111,088	1.0	159,348	1.2	43.4%
Indiana	136,130	1.2	158,669	1.2	16.6%
Virginia	195,193	1.7	152,574	1.1	–21.8%
Delaware	210,733	1.8	143,961	1.1	–31.7%
New Hampshire	98,514	0.9	122,586	0.9	24.4%
Colorado	48,120	0.4	116,465	0.9	142.0%
Alabama	74,180	0.6	113,022	0.8	52.4%
Oklahoma	32,083	0.3	110,939	0.8	245.8%

TABLE 2.2 (cont'd)
Total Quebec Imports to American States 1988-1993
(thousands of dollars, percentage of total and variations)

States	1988	% of total	1993	% of total	Variation 88/93
Kansas	65,659	0.6	109,764	0.8	67.2%
Rhode Island	63,802	0.6	104,873	0.8	64.4%
Arizona	57,347	0.5	95,412	0.7	66.4%
Iowa	76,800	0.7	77,915	0.6	1.5%
Utah	39,285	0.3	73,990	0.5	88.3%
Oregon	57,145	0.5	72,355	0.5	26.6%
Mississippi	20,967	0.2	36,526	0.3	74.2%
Arkansas	19,846	0.2	30,172	0.2	52.0%
Nebraska	7,285	0.1	25,585	0.2	251.2%
West Virginia	18,106	0.2	22,358	0.2	23.5%
Montana	6,060	0.1	20,584	0.2	239.6%
North Dakota	4,345	0.0	18,536	0.1	326.6%
Nevada	6,217	0.1	12,600	0.1	102.7%
Idaho	30,830	0.3	8,401	0.1	-72.8%
South Dakota	5,210	0.0	7,884	0.1	51.3%
Hawaii	561	0.0	7,011	0.1	1,150.7%
New Mexico	1,725	0.0	6,359	0.0	268.7%
Wyoming	2,283	0.0	3,693	0.0	61.8%
District of Columbia	602	0.0	1,596	0.0	165.2%
Alaska	880	0.0	802	0.0	-8.9%
Total	**11,560,462**	**100.0**	**13,533,552**	**100.0**	**17.1%**

TABLE 2.3
Balance of Quebec's Trade with American States 1988-1993
(Exports–Imports, thousands of dollars)

	1988	1993	Variation 93–88	Improvement
Vermont	262,870	1,667,436	1404,566	X
New York	2,212,200	3,423,062	1210,862	X
Michigan	1,069,633	2,217,118	1147,485	X
Illinois	−53,328	705,648	758,976	X
Texas	15,933	540,042	524,109	X
Other states	−328,872	167,263	496,135	X
Ohio	−71,491	355,922	427,413	X
Wisconsin	−67,256	255,765	323,291	X
California	−318,505	−91,530	226,975	X
West Virginia	90,852	289,486	198,634	X
Pennsylvania	702,168	861,537	159,369	X
Florida	67,187	213,777	146,590	X
Kentucky	148,038	290,249	142,391	X
Delaware	−165,444	−24,812	140,632	X
Tennessee	45,598	168,844	123,246	X
Indiana	209,811	319,837	110,026	X
Washington	1,849	110,401	108,552	X
Minnesota	−80,733	26,563	107,296	X
Massachusetts	414,765	502,398	87,633	X
Missouri	−213,478	−126,305	87,173	X
Kansas	66,177	152,133	85,956	X
Maryland	−19,309	51,667	70,976	X
Oregon	−30	68,482	68,512	X
Georgia	56,128	103,617	47,489	X
Iowa	−18,423	25,990	44,413	X
Arizona	−21,725	19,911	41,636	X
Mississippi	15,185	55,310	40,125	X
Idaho	−21,727	10,133	31,860	X
North Carolina	−75,122	−48,539	26,583	X
South Dakota	1,267	26,133	24,866	X
Nebraska	2,854	23,826	20,972	X
Connecticut	191,412	205,819	14,407	X

TABLE 2.3 (cont'd)
Balance of Quebec's Trade with American States 1988-1993
(Exports–Imports, thousands of dollars)

	1988	1993	Variation 93 – 88	Improve-ment
New Mexico	2907	16,031	13,124	X
Nevada	13,661	24,928	11,267	X
Colorado	14,979	20,639	5,660	X
Alaska	16,200	21,532	5,332	X
Louisiana	–83,338	–79,636	3,702	X
Wyoming	882	1,242	360	X
North Dakota	902	–372	–1,274	
Hawaii	1,768	–167	–1,935	
Maine	102,766	95,138	–7,628	
Montana	–1,940	–12,499	–10,559	
District of Columbia	27,049	10,030	–17,019	
New Hampshire	100,619	81,010	–19,609	
Utah	–9,271	–33,611	–24,340	
Arkansas	208,620	168,772	–39,848	
Oklahoma	–7,279	–55,110	–47,831	
New Jersey	370,922	308,539	–62,383	
Rhode Island	44,472	–25,090	–69,562	
South Carolina	–28,525	–102,394	–73,869	
Virginia	323,739	237,187	–86,552	
Alabama	226,410	126,382	–100,028	
Total	**5,445,022**	**13,369,914**	**7,924,892**	**X**

TABLE 2.4
Principal Products Exported from Quebec to the United States (1989-1993)
(thousands of dollars, percentage of total and variations)

Description of products	1989	% of total	1993	% of total	Variation 89/93
Other telecomm. equip. & materials	1,335,927	7.9	2,842,172	10.6	112.7%
Personal vehicles and frames	1,784,668	10.5	2,558,742	9.5	43.4%
Newsprint	2,434,529	14.4	2,542,177	9.4	4.4%
Aluminum, including alloys	1,842,725	10.9	2,113,892	7.9	14.7%
Special commercial transactions	253,389	1.5	1,522,883	5.7	501.0%
Softwood lumber	451,093	2.7	909,028	3.4	101.5%
Airplanes and motors	296,621	1.7	770,599	2.9	159.8%
Airplane motors and parts	564,880	3.3	651,652	2.4	15.4%
Office equipment	148,404	0.9	499,893	1.9	236.8%
Other equipment and tools	301,183	1.8	479,802	1.8	59.3%
Wood pulp & similar pulp	367,788	2.2	428,753	1.6	16.6%
Copper and alloys	374,698	2.2	396,737	1.5	5.9%
Clothing and accessories	182,146	1.1	391,560	1.5	115.0%
Metal frameworks	303,948	1.8	357,819	1.3	17.7%
Other paper	169,526	1.0	341,254	1.3	101.3%
Electricity	200,254	1.2	328,299	1.2	63.9%
Other paper and printing	182,872	1.1	319,583	1.2	74.8%
Printed materials	170,903	1.0	314,133	1.2	83.8%
Fresh, refrig. or frozen meat	248,577	1.5	261,530	1.0	5.2%
Auto parts, excl. motors	153,287	0.9	246,155	0.9	60.6%

TABLE 2.4 (cont'd)
Principal Products Exported from Quebec to the United States (1989-1993)
(thousands of dollars, percentage of total and variations)

Among top 25 products in 89 only	1989	% of total	in 93 only	1993	% of total
Zinc, incl. alloys	246,931	1.5	Tobacco	530,908	2.0
Other motor vehicles	200,331	1.2	Precious metals, incl. alloys	282,764	1.1
Other inorganic chem. products	182,962	1.1	Other chem. products	265,320	1.0
Trucks, truck trailers and frames	177,730	1.0	Toys, games & sporting goods	250,015	0.9
Other med./opt. lab measuring instr.	160,823	0.9	Ships, boats & parts	244,241	0.9
Top 10 products	9,761,440	57.6		14,941,946	55.5
Top 25 products	12,736,195	75.1		19,849,911	73.8
All products	16,954,467	100.0		26,903,466	100.0

TABLE 2.5
Principal Products Imported in Quebec from the United States
(1989-1993)
(thousands of dollars, percentage of total and variations)

Description of products	1989	% of total	1993	% of total	Variation 89/93
Special commercial transactions	281,577	2.3	2,296,398	17.0	715.5
Personal vehicles and frames	2,112,855	17.1	2,005,465	14.8	−5.1
Trucks, truck trailers and frames	488,287	4.0	571,405	4.2	17.0
Other telecomm. equipment & materials	479,353	3.9	554,152	4.1	15.6
Airplane motors and parts	338,672	3.1	389,109	2.9	1.4
Airplane parts, excl. motors	317,444	2.6	304,688	2.3	−4.0
Inorganic chemical products	389,934	3.2	270,183	2.0	−30.7
Organic chemical products	201,271	1.6	245,033	1.8	21.7
Bulk plastic materials	140,449	1.1	235,956	1.7	68.0
Electronic computers	315,824	2.6	213,451	1.6	−32.4
Paper and cardboard	159,136	1.3	184,340	1.4	15.8
Crude wood materials	131,821	1.1	183,760	1.4	39.4
Other lab. etc. measuring instr.	181,517	1.5	182,320	1.3	0.4
Airplanes and motors	210,660	1.7	181,033	1.3	−14.1
Other chemical products	111,790	0.9	178,190	1.3	59.4
Other ore and metal scrap	167,497	1.4	133,441	1.0	−20.3
Other unedible refined products	136,297	1.1	110,304	0.8	−19.1
Misc. measuring-regulating instr.	101,532	0.8	99,580	0.7	−1.9

TABLE 2.5 (cont'd)
Principal Products Imported in Quebec from the United States (1989-1993)
(thousands of dollars, percentage of total and variations)

Among top 25 products in 89 only	1989	% of total	in 93 only	1993	% of total
Elec. tubes and semiconductors	932,969	7.6	Dosed medicine & pharm. prod.	213,990	1.6
Fuel oil	136,039	1.1	Fresh, refrig. & frozen meat	127,704	0.9
Auto parts excl. motors	129,221	1.0	Other personal effects & appliances	125,005	0.9
TVs, radios and phonographs	127,427	1.0	Other non-metal mineral products	110,865	0.8
Artificial fibers	110,031	0.9	Containers and closings	108,247	0.8
Misc. materials and tools	98,516	0.8	Other lighting and distr. electric mat.	103,210	0.8
Petroleum and coal coke	97,091	0.8	Medical, ophthalm. & orthop. supplies	98,138	0.7
Top 10 products	5,912,575			7,086,380	52.4
Top 25 products	7,942,210			9,225,967	68.2
All products	12,323,452			13,533,552	100.0

4

Quebec and Its Canadian Partners:
Economic Relationships and Trade Barriers

Maryse Robert
Organization of American States

Because of the limited scope of Canada's common market clause, provinces have been able to erect trade barriers against each other. While some argue that the cost of these barriers is small, others suggest that it is quite high. In 1987, the Committee of Ministers on Internal Trade was created by the provinces and the federal government with the mandate to eliminate these barriers. Negotiations began in March 1993 and ended in July 1994 with the signature of the Agreement on Internal Trade.

Quebec is more dependent on the Canadian market for its export sales than on its exports to the rest of the world. Ontario is its main export market in Canada. In 1989, Quebec enjoyed a trade surplus in goods with all its Canadian partners and a deficit in services only with Manitoba and Ontario. Quebec's surplus comes essentially from its manufactured goods. Its leading interprovincial exports (textile and apparel, and food and beverages) show that the influence of the National Policy implemented in 1879 by the federal government is still at work. Quebec's interprovincial exports are concentrated in labour-intensive light manufactured goods. The province registers its largest trade deficits in sectors where Ontario has its largest surpluses. It is too early to analyze the impact of the Canada-U.S. FTA and NAFTA on interprovincial trade. However, since Quebec's interprovincial and international exports are very different, it is unlikely that NAFTA will affect interprovincial trade. The key issue is to what extent NAFTA will reduce Quebec's dependency on the rest of Canada.

INTRODUCTION

One month after the federal government had negotiated the Canada-U.S. Free Trade Agreement in October 1987, the Canadian provinces established the Committee of Ministers on Internal Trade (CMIT). This Committee was given the mandate to eliminate interprovincial trade barriers. Since the end of World War II Canada has participated in bilateral and multilateral trade negotiations aimed at reducing its trade barriers with the rest of the world, but the provinces have been unable, until recently, to tackle these same issues. However, a few months after Canada, the United States and Mexico signed NAFTA, the Canadian provinces embarked in March 1993 on a negotiation process to remove interprovincial trade barriers.

Before analyzing the Agreement on Internal Trade that was reached by the provinces in July 1994, the following section examines the different types of interprovincial barriers, their cost, and the failed attempts in the past 50 years to remove these impediments to trade. The next section is devoted to Quebec's trade within Canada. It addresses a number of questions: Is Quebec dependent on the Canadian market? Which province is Quebec's largest trading partner? Is Quebec a major market for the other provinces? What is Quebec's trade balance with the rest of Canada? What are the commodity products contributing to Quebec's trade surplus and deficit with its Canadian partners? The last section briefly assesses the impact of NAFTA on interprovincial trade and the strategies the Quebec government should favor with respect to internal trade.

TRADE BARRIERS WITHIN CANADA

Although interprovincial trade amounted to $146 billion in 1989, internal trade barriers have continued to impede the free flow of resources between the Canadian provinces. The existence of these barriers is the result of the "limited scope" of Canada's common-market clause (Partnership for Prosperity, 1991: 22). Section 121 of the Constitution Act, 1867, provides that "All Articles of the Growth, Produce, or Manufacture of any one of the Provinces shall, from and after the Union, be admitted free into each of the other Provinces." Therefore, Section 121 "applies only to the movements of goods, prohibits only the imposition of tariffs by one province on goods from another, and appears to constrain only provincial governments" (Partnership for Prosperity, 1991: 22).

Section 91(2) of the constitution, which grants exclusive authority to the federal government with regard to the regulation of trade and commerce, limits the creation of "direct barriers to interprovincial (but not necessarily intra-provincial) trade" (Flatters and Lipsey, 1983: 10). In its report, in 1985, the Royal Commission on the Economic Union and Development Prospects for

Canada, known as the MacDonald Commission, wrote that "the Supreme Court has recognized the provincial power to regulate some aspects of trade within the province, even in cases where the interprovincial flow of goods was affected by provincial production controls, marketing schemes, the creation of monopolies and the like" (1985: 114).

Types of Barriers

Internal trade barriers are usually classified in three general categories: impediments to mobility of goods and services, labour mobility, and capital mobility (Trebilcock et al., 1983; Milne, 1987; Economic Council of Canada, 1991). However, Schwanen (1992, 1994) has proposed a different approach.[1] He identifies three types of barriers. First, there are the "laws, regulations, or other kinds of policies in one province that discriminate against goods, services, people, or capital from other provinces on grounds of their origin" (Schwanen, 1994: 5). Examples of these barriers include government procurement policies which extend to municipalities, school boards and hospitals and which favor domestic bidders; farm marketing boards precluding the purchase of "farm products from the least-cost source within the country"; provincial liquor policies discriminating against out-of-province beer and wine; and labour laws that until recently prevented workers living in Ottawa, Ontario "from working across the river in Hull," Quebec (Schwanen, 1994: 5).

Administrative measures, regulations and standards constitute the second type of trade barrier in goods and services. These barriers encompass a number of examples. For instance, "the refusal by one province to recognize occupational and professional designations conferred by another" province, and regulations in "truck transportation, food packaging, dairy product substitutes or the delivery of financial services" (Schwanen, 1994: 5). The last type of barrier is aimed at attracting resources in the province by offering subsidies and tax incentives. Schwanen notes that each type of barrier has been imposed by both the provinces and the federal government.

Cost of Internal Trade Barriers

A few authors have attempted to estimate the cost of interprovincial trade barriers. Some argue that this cost is small (Whalley, 1983; Whalley and Trela, 1986; Norrie, Simeon and Krasnick, 1986) while others (Rutley, 1991; Falda,

---

1.   For an excellent survey of the provincial trade barriers in Canada in the mid-1980s, see TREBILCOCK, Michael J., WHALLEY, John, ROGERSON, Carol, and NESS, Ian, "Provincially Induced Barriers to Trade in Canada: A Survey," in *Federalism and the Canadian Economic Union*, Michael J. Trebilcock, J. Robert S. Pritchard, Thomas J. Courchene, and John Whalley (University of Toronto Press for the Ontario Economic Council, Toronto, 1983), pp. 243-351.

1994) suggest that the effects of Canada's internal barriers are large.[2] Whalley (1983: 191), for instance, has shown that welfare losses for 1974 could be as low as 0.11% of gross national product (GNP) or as high as 1.54% of GNP, and Falda (1994: xvi) has come up with a figure reaching $3,500 per year for the average Canadian family. However, none of these authors has calculated both the static and dynamic effects of removing these impediments to trade. The most serious studies (Whalley, 1983; Whalley and Trela, 1986; Norrie, Simeon and Krasnick, 1986) capture only the efficiency cost of trade barriers, i.e., the cost arising from the market distortions caused by these policies. Dynamic effects (e.g., economies of scale) are more difficult to measure and therefore are seldom estimated. Economists generally agree that trade barriers can have positive effects when government intervention is due to market failures, but they are quick to point out that trade policy is a second-best instrument.

One study by Todd Rutley of the Canadian Manufacturers' Association (CMA) suggests that the elimination of barriers would generate savings of over $6.5 billion. It has received wide coverage even though its methodology has been found to be seriously flawed in two of the three sectors it analyzes: agriculture and preferential government procurement (Copeland, 1993: 11). Failing to calculate the efficiency cost in these sectors, the CMA estimates to $1 billion the cost of interprovincial barriers in agriculture. Whalley and Trela (1986), on the other hand, have found that the impact of these internal barriers in supply-managed industries (e.g., milk, eggs, turkey and poultry) is low compared to the effects of international trade barriers. Interprovincial barriers "might contribute at most between $3 million and $5 million to economic inefficiency" (Copeland, 1993: 11).

In government procurement, the CMA argues that "on average governments pay 5% more for goods and services than they would have to if they bought from the least cost supplier" (Copeland, 1993: 12). After estimating the market for government procurement to be $100 billion, the CMA wrongly concludes that the inefficient allocation of resources in that sector amounts to $5 billion. Whalley and Trela have calculated an efficiency cost of $97 million for all provinces. In beer and wine, the CMA relies on a study by Irvine et al. (1990), where the authors found that trade barriers had an efficiency cost "between 11% and 14% of consumer expenditure on beer at market prices" (Copeland, 1993: 9).

---

2.   For a review of these studies (with the exception of Falda's) and others, see COPELAND, Brian R., "Interprovincial Barriers to Trade: A Review of the Empirical Evidence from a British Columbia Perspective," University of British Columbia, Vancouver, March 1993, mimeographed.

In addition to not calculating the efficiency cost in agriculture and government procurement, Copeland emphasizes that another shortcoming of the CMA study is that it does not include the cost of other types of barriers, such as trucking regulations and labour mobility restrictions (Copeland, 1993: 13).

Attempts to Remove Interprovincial Trade Barriers

In its recommendations published in 1940, the Royal Commission on Dominion-Provincial Relations (the Rowell-Sirois Commission) was the first to express concerns about internal trade barriers and to propose ways to prevent local protectionism. Following the increase in protective policies by municipalities and provinces in the 1930s, the report of the Commission emphasized the need for a Dominion-Provincial Conference where all legislatures would discuss how to address the removal of internal barriers.

Except for Quebec, which began to modernize itself and put more emphasis on its own economic development in the 1960s, it was in the 1970s that Canadian provinces shifted their objectives towards a "province-building" approach (Evenson and Simeon, 1978; Maxwell and Pestieau, 1980). The provinces offered incentives "to attract industry and to create jobs, and they began to use their own crown agencies to pursue economic development objectives" (Maxwell and Pestieau, 1980: 78).

The constitutional discussions in 1979 and 1980 led to proposals to strengthen the Canadian economic union. The Chrétien discussion paper (1980) "recommended entrenching mobility rights in the Constitution, strengthening Section 121 of the Constitution to cover services, as well as prohibiting nontariff barriers" (Economic Council of Canada, 1991: 55). It also proposed to expand the power of the federal government in Section 91 "in order to enable it to override provincially imposed barriers" (Economic Council of Canada, 1991: 55). None of these proposals were incorporated in the constitutional amendments of 1982. However, section 6 of the new Canadian Charter of Rights and Freedoms protects mobility rights for individuals, albeit with some limitations.

In the mid-1980s, the MacDonald Commission (1985) made its own recommendations on ways to reinforce the economic union. The Commission suggested changes to Section 121. It also argued for a "code of economic conduct" which would have identified "the policies and practices that are, and are not, acceptable in the Canadian union" (MacDonald Commission, 1985: 137).

In 1985, the federal and provincial ministers of economic development agreed to set up a task force that would study the impact of interprovincial barriers. In 1986, the First Ministers acquiesced to a moratorium on new barriers, and in November 1987 they established the Committee of Ministers on Internal Trade (CMIT) which was given the mandate "to take immediate steps to eliminate barriers to interprovincial trade" (Internal Trade Secretariat, 1994: 1). The CMIT focused its efforts in priority areas: government procurement, beer marketing, and wine and spirits. Two agreements were negotiated: the Intergovernmental Agreement on Beer Marketing Practices came into effect in January 1991 and the Intergovernmental Agreement on Goods Procurement concluded in November 1991 came into force in April 1992. But these agreements had a very limited coverage. For instance, the Beer Marketing Agreement eliminated discrimination against listing and pricing practices but did not deal with barriers in distribution.

During the constitutional discussions of 1991 and 1992, the federal government proposed to broaden Section 121 to include: 1) barriers related to goods, services, labour and capital; 2) tariff and non-tariff barriers; 3) barriers created by provinces and the federal government; and 4) "barriers arising from legislation, regulations and administrative practices" (Partnership for Prosperity, 1991: 23). The federal government also intended to create "a new constitutional power for Parliament that would allow it to pass legislation for the efficient functioning of the Canadian economic union in areas beyond its existing jurisdiction" (Partnership for Prosperity, 1991: 24). To become effective, legislation would have required the approval of two-thirds of the provinces representing at least 50% of the population of the country. Dissenting provinces could opt out of any federal law for a period of three years with the approval of 60% of the members of their legislatures (Partnership for Prosperity, 1991: 24). These proposals were, however, rejected by the provinces, which kept asking for exemptions.

In December 1992, the CMIT recommended the removal of internal trade barriers by June 30, 1994. The committee launched an accelerated and comprehensive negotiation process which started in March 1993 and ended in July 1994.

Agreement on Internal Trade

The agreement signed by First Ministers on July 18, 1994 is very limited.[3] It makes a number of exceptions. For instance, the agreement does not apply to aboriginal peoples (Article 1803) and does not cover national security (Article 1805). Quebec fought hard to exempt regional economic development programs (Article 1802); culture (Article 1804); taxation (Article 1806); financial institutions (Article 1807); and its Crown corporations.[4] Therefore, Hydro-

---

3.   The date of coming into force of the Agreement on Internal Trade is July 1, 1995.

4.   British Columbia and Saskatchewan also wanted to exempt their Crown corporations.

Quebec, the Société de développement de la Baie-James; the Société des alcools du Québec and other Quebec Crown corporations listed in Chapter 5, Annex 2 will be able to favour domestic suppliers. However, the agreement commits the Parties to "conclude negotiations no later than June 30, 1996, with a view to reducing, modifying or amending the list of entities listed in Annex 2, in order to achieve reciprocity, in particular, by including such entities in either Annex 1 or Annex 3" (Article 512.2).

The agreement provides for non-discriminatory treatment (Article 401); free movement across provincial boundaries (Article 402); prohibition of measures establishing obstacles to trade (Articles 403 and 404); reconciliation of regulations and standards-related measures (Article 405); and increased transparency with respect to laws, procedures, guidelines and administrative rulings of general application (Article 406). In addition, trade ministers have negotiated a dispute-settlement mechanism (Chapter 17) allowing governments and, in some cases, individuals to make complaints.

Chapter 5 covers procurement for government entities listed in Annex 1 for which the estimated procurement value is $25,000 or more for goods, and $100,000 or more for services and construction (Article 501(a)). The agreement also requires the parties to extend coverage of the chapter to the "MUSH sector," i.e. municipalities, municipal organizations, school boards and publicly-funded academic, health and social service entities (Article 501(d)).

The investment chapter prohibits the use of performance requirements (Article 606), local presence and residency requirements (Article 603). It allows for reciprocal non-discrimination (Article 602) and it contains a code of conduct restricting the measures a province can take to attract business from another province (Annex 607.3).

The labour mobility chapter limits the use of residency requirements (Article 705) and provides for recognition of occupational qualifications and reconciliation of occupational standards (Article 707 and Annex 707). Other sectors included in the agreement are natural resources processing, communications, transportation, and environmental protection. The agreement also requires the parties to complete an Energy Chapter by July 1, 1995.

Disappointing results were obtained in agriculture (Chapter 9) and in alcoholic beverages (Chapter 10), particularly in wine. Parties were unable to further liberalize these two sectors.

Bilateral agreements between Quebec and New Brunswick and Quebec and Ontario gave an impetus to the general talks on interprovincial trade barriers. Quebec and New Brunswick signed an agreement opening public procurement of goods and services in November 1993. Following a trade war in the construction sector between Ontario and Quebec because Quebec was imposing barriers against Ontario workers and firms while Quebec workers and firms were allowed to work in Ontario, the two provinces signed an Agreement on Public Procurement and Construction Labour Mobility in December 1993, and on May 3, 1994 they signed a two-part agreement: 1) the Mutual Recognition of Construction Workers' Qualifications, Skills and Work Experience, and 2) Opening Public Procurement for Ontario and Quebec.

QUEBEC'S TRADE WITHIN CANADA

The Role of the *National Policy*

Quebec's economic relationship with its Canadian partners has been shaped by the *National Policy* adopted by the federal government in 1879. This import-substitution policy "had three objectives: railway construction, development of the Canadian West, and growth of the manufacturing sector" (Nappi, 1978: 5). Tariff protection against the rest of the world helped foster the development of the manufacturing industries in both Quebec and Ontario.

Between 1880 and 1915, "Quebec's manufacturing sector ... was characterized by the production of leather goods, paper, textiles, clothing, and chemicals" (Nappi, 1978: 6). Sheltered by the protection of the *National Policy*, these industries flourished and "increased their shares of the province's total output" (Nappi, 1978: 6). Their products were exported to the rest of Canada, "except for paper, which was exported to the United States" (Nappi, 1978: 6).

The *National Policy* contributed to the specialization of the industrial base in Central Canada. Factor endowments, transportation costs and technological change also led Quebec to specialize in labour-intensive consumer goods "while ... industries with a higher value added were concentrated in Ontario" (Nappi, 1978: 6). Faucher and Lamontagne note that "the passage from a regime of mercantilism to a system of industrialism based upon coal, steel and steam" (Nappi, 1978: 6) benefited Southern Ontario which was "strategically located" to become part of the continental manufacturing belt. Faucher and Lamontagne also stress the importance of high customs duties in helping Ontario develop its manufacturing base (Nappi, 1978: 6). Proulx and Cauchy (1991: 56), on the other hand, emphasize the impact of clericalism and agriculture in slowing down Quebec's economic development between 1870 and 1940.

Nappi points out that "the main directions of Quebec's commercial activity became clear at the start of World War II" (Nappi, 1978: 8). Processed and raw materials were exported to other countries and "exports to the province's principal market – the rest of Canada – were concentrated in labour-intensive light manufactured goods, such as food and beverages, clothing, textiles, chemicals, and electrical appliances" (Nappi, 1978: 8).

Canada: An Important Market for Quebec

Interprovincial exports represented more than 50% of Quebec's total exports from 1984 to 1989.[5] While Newfoundland and British Columbia, Canada's easternmost and westernmost provinces, were selling respectively 75 and 65 percent of their products to other countries, Quebec, like Prince Edward Island, Nova Scotia, Manitoba and Alberta, was more dependent on the Canadian market for its export sales than on the rest of the world (Tables 1 and 3). The situation was reversed with respect to imports. Quebec and Ontario imported a larger portion of their goods from other countries than from other provinces (Tables 2 and 3). This is the result of "purchases of motor vehicle parts under the Canada-US Auto Pact" (Messinger, 1993b: 3.10).

Although statistical data are not comparable, Quebec's dependency on the Canadian market was also shown by Nappi. He found that in 1974 the province was exporting more of its manufactured goods to the rest of Canada than to other parts of the world (Nappi, 1978: 29). Moreau (1988: 67) reached similar conclusions for 1981.

TABLE 1
Trade with Other Provinces and Other Countries
Exports (in percentage)

	1984	1985	1986	1987	1988	1989
Newfoundland						
to other countries	72.92	72.01	75.49	70.84	76.11	74.66
to other provinces	27.08	27.99	24.51	29.16	23.89	25.34
Prince Edward Island						
to other countries	33.21	30.98	34.88	36.45	36.13	36.14
to other provinces	66.79	69.02	65.12	63.55	63.87	63.86
Nova Scotia						
to other countries	39.43	38.99	44.60	48.39	44.13	43.55
to other provinces	60.57	61.01	55.40	51.61	55.87	56.45
New Brunswick						
to other countries	52.58	50.85	52.28	54.12	52.00	48.19
to other provinces	47.42	49.15	47.72	45.88	48.00	50.81

---

5.   I wish to thank Hans Messinger, James Nightingale and Ronald Rioux of the Input-Output Division of Statistics Canada for their help in providing me with the data on interprovincial trade flows. I am also grateful to Marcel Dagenais of the Department of Economics of the Université de Montréal for more disaggregated data for 1989. At the time of writing, the data were only available for the 1984-1989 period.

TABLE 1 (cont'd)
Trade with Other Provinces and Other Countries
Exports (in percentage)

	1984	1985	1986	1987	1988	1989
Quebec						
to other countries	48.25	46.54	49.38	46.52	46.20	45.93
to other provinces	51.75	53.46	50.62	53.48	53.80	54.07
Ontario						
to other countries	58.17	58.72	59.08	56.93	55.63	55.31
to other provinces	41.83	41.28	40.92	43.07	44.37	44.69
Manitoba						
to other countries	40.72	38.03	37.49	40.30	41.07	38.25
to other provinces	59.28	61.97	62.51	59.70	58.93	61.75
Saskatchewan						
to other countries	62.50	57.75	54.99	57.59	55.53	52.71
to other provinces	37.50	42.25	45.01	42.41	44.47	47.29
Alberta						
to other countries	38.44	41.73	42.90	42.95	46.42	45.86
to other provinces	61.56	58.27	57.10	57.05	53.58	54.14
British Columbia						
to other countries	66.91	66.42	65.83	66.88	66.99	65.55
to other provinces	33.09	33.58	34.17	33.12	33.01	34.45

Source: Percentages computed by the author from data from Statistics Canada, Input-Output Division.

TABLE 2
Trade with Other Provinces and Other Countries
Imports (in percentage)

	1984	1985	1986	1987	1988	1989
Newfoundland						
from other countries	24.76	22.71	22.27	24.76	30.87	30.95
from other provinces	75.24	77.29	77.73	75.24	69.13	69.05
Prince Edward Island						
from other countries	17.93	18.76	19.80	17.83	18.68	17.19
from other provinces	82.07	81.24	80.20	82.17	81.32	82.81
Nova Scotia						
from other countries	38.73	41.81	38.02	38.18	36.77	36.89
from other provinces	61.27	58.19	61.98	61.82	63.23	63.11
New Brunswick						
from other countries	38.82	37.41	40.21	40.19	35.93	37.77
from other provinces	61.18	62.59	59.79	59.81	64.07	62.23

TABLE 2 (cont'd)
Trade with Other Provinces and Other Countries
Imports (in percentage)

	1984	1985	1986	1987	1988	1989
Quebec						
from other countries	49.20	51.25	51.45	51.43	51.01	51.86
from other provinces	50.80	48.75	48.55	48.57	48.99	48.14
Ontario						
from other countries	63.59	64.51	69.70	67.94	68.68	68.18
from other provinces	36.41	35.49	30.30	32.06	31.32	31.82
Manitoba						
from other countries	33.23	34.00	37.05	34.83	33.35	34.53
from other provinces	66.77	66.00	62.95	65.17	66.65	65.47
Saskatchewan						
from other countries	26.71	26.30	28.82	27.12	26.62	27.26
from other provinces	73.29	73.70	71.18	72.88	73.38	72.74
Alberta						
from other countries	38.65	37.69	38.29	36.49	35.39	35.04
from other provinces	61.35	62.31	61.71	63.51	64.61	64.96
British Columbia						
from other countries	40.93	41.47	45.59	44.43	45.30	45.38
from other provinces	59.07	58.53	54.41	55.57	54.70	54.62

Source: Percentages computed by the author from data from Statistics Canada, Input-Output Division.

TABLE 3
Quebec and Ontario's Exports and Imports
(in $ millions)

	1984	1985	1986	1987	1988	1989
Quebec						
exports to ROW	21,686	22,300	24,162	24,486	28,085	29,463
exports to ROC	23,262	25,619	24,770	28,154	32,703	34,680
imports from ROW	23,542	26,222	27,432	29,469	33,009	35,418
imports from ROC	24,311	24,940	25,886	27,825	31,705	32,872
Ontario						
exports to ROW	56,581	61,746	65,979	66,543	72,458	75,375
exports to ROC	40,682	43,399	45,702	50,352	57,784	60,891
imports from ROW	54,425	61,760	68,254	71,924	80,669	83,943
imports from ROC	31,160	33,978	29,672	33,937	36,794	39,183

ROW: Rest of the world.
ROC: Rest of Canada.
Source: Statistics Canada, Input-Output Division.

Ontario: Quebec's Largest Customer in Canada

Among all the Canadian provinces and territories, Ontario is overwhelmingly the most important market for Quebec. Over 60% of Quebec's exports to the rest of Canada were destined to Ontario during the 1984-1989 period (Tables 4 and 5). The other large provinces, British Columbia and Alberta, accounted for about 8% each while the Maritimes represented approximately 14%.

Table 6 also shows that Ontario is one of Quebec's largest customers in the world. Exports to Ontario made up over one-third of Quebec's total exports in the second half of the 1980s. The other Canadian provinces took a much smaller share. They accounted for less than 20% of Quebec's total exports in 1989.

TABLE 4
**Quebec's Exports to Other Provinces
as a Percentage of Quebec's Exports to the Rest of Canada**

	1984	**1985**	**1986**	**1987**	**1988**	**1989**
Newfoundland	3.54	3.51	3.76	3.22	3.20	2.98
Prince Edward Island	0.66	0.64	0.71	0.64	0.63	0.64
Nova Scotia	4.94	4.85	5.17	4.88	4.66	4.48
New Brunswick	5.96	5.80	5.79	5.51	5.21	5.27
Ontario	61.07	62.06	61.22	63.30	63.83	63.58
Manitoba	3.14	2.99	3.10	2.99	3.00	3.00
Saskatchewan	3.01	2.72	2.81	2.64	2.40	2.24
Alberta	8.69	8.71	8.62	8.28	8.07	8.09
British Columbia	8.15	7.99	8.03	7.81	8.35	8.99

Source: Percentages computed by the author from data from Statistics Canada, Input-Output Division.

TABLE 5
Quebec's Exports to Other Provinces
(in $ millions)

	1984	1985	1986	1987	1988	1989
Newfoundland	823.2	900.5	932.2	905.9	1,047.4	1,032.7
Prince Edward Island	154.5	163.3	175.6	180.4	206.3	223.2
Nova Scotia	1,148.6	1,243.7	1,279.6	1,374.2	1,523.9	1,553.7
New Brunswick	1,387.0	1,485.5	1,433.6	1,551.5	1,704.4	1,827.6
Ontario	14,205.2	15,899.2	15,163.4	17,822.0	20,875.0	22,047.7
Manitoba	729.8	766.1	767.2	843.0	979.6	1,041.2
Saskatchewan	699.3	696.5	696.5	742.5	784.3	776.4
Alberta	2,021.0	2,232.3	2,134.4	2,331.6	2,640.3	2,807.0
British Columbia	1,895.0	2,047.4	1,990.1	2,199.5	2,732.2	3,116.6

Source: Statistics Canada, Input-Output Division.

TABLE 6
Quebec's Exports to Other Provinces
as a Percentage of Quebec's Total Exports

	1984	1985	1986	1987	1988	1989
Newfoundland	1.83	1.88	1.91	1.72	1.72	1.61
Prince Edward Island	0.34	0.34	0.36	0.34	0.34	0.35
Nova Scotia	2.56	2.60	2.62	2.61	2.51	2.42
New Brunswick	3.09	3.10	2.93	2.95	2.80	2.85
Ontario	31.60	33.18	30.99	33.86	34.34	34.37
Manitoba	1.62	1.60	1.57	1.60	1.61	1.62
Saskatchewan	1.56	1.45	1.42	1.41	1.29	1.21
Alberta	4.50	4.66	4.36	4.43	4.34	4.38
British Columbia	4.22	4.27	4.07	4.18	4.49	4.86

Source: Percentages computed by the author from data from Statistics Canada, Input-Output Division.

Quebec: A Major Export Market
for Several Canadian Provinces

Quebec is a major export market for several Canadian provinces. It is, for instance, Ontario's largest trading partner. Over 40% of Ontario's exports to the rest of Canada go to Quebec (Tables 7 and 8). The figures for the Atlantic provinces are smaller but nonetheless significant: almost 30% of exports for New Brunswick and Newfoundland, less than 25% for Nova Scotia and approximately 20% for Prince Edward Island go to Quebec. Trade linkages with the Prairies and British Columbia are less important.

On a global scale, Ontario sells less than 20% of all its exports to Quebec (Table 9). New Brunswick comes next with 15%. Nova Scotia and Prince Edward Island follow with 14% and 13%.

The figures presented above suggest that Quebec is more dependent on Ontario's market than Ontario is on Quebec's market. However, the percentages do not tell the whole story because Ontario has a larger economy. The figures represent approximately the same dollar value (Messinger, 1993a: 3.6). In 1989, Quebec exported $15.59 billion of goods to Ontario and imported $15.47 billion. The situation is different in the services sector, where Quebec has registered a substantial trade deficit with Ontario over the years (Table 10).

TABLE 7

Other Provinces' Exports to Quebec as a Percentage of Their Exports to All Canadian Provinces

	1984	**1985**	**1986**	**1987**	**1988**	**1989**
Newfoundland	27.69	28.34	31.81	29.50	28.34	26.94
Prince Edward Island	17.13	17.21	17.17	18.79	19.66	20.31
Nova Scotia	19.56	20.92	24.76	23.75	24.82	23.96
New Brunswick	26.97	28.48	31.64	30.11	29.41	28.87
Ontario	41.63	40.75	41.76	41.56	42.47	42.13
Manitoba	15.96	15.32	17.50	14.46	13.74	12.63
Saskatchewan	24.58	19.69	17.47	15.75	15.13	14.34
Alberta	14.65	13.21	13.77	13.23	13.28	12.32
British Columbia	11.98	12.15	12.46	12.28	12.40	11.73

Source: Percentages computed by the author from data from Statistics Canada, Input-Output Division.

TABLE 8
Other Provinces' Exports to Quebec
(in $ millions)

	1984	1985	1986	1987	1988	1989
Newfoundland	178.4	187.8	198.4	220.4	220.7	217.1
Prince Edward Island	60.7	63.7	62.4	74.3	80.3	98.2
Nova Scotia	554.1	638.5	732.6	704.2	783.1	833.6
New Brunswick	630.3	711.4	860.6	904.9	973.5	1,051.6
Ontario	16,934.1	17,683.8	19,086.4	20,926.4	24,541.6	25,652.7
Manitoba	768.7	811.1	916.3	816.2	863.0	830.9
Saskatchewan	950.4	814.4	657.3	645.5	687.4	642.5
Alberta	3,324.9	3,016.9	2,346.5	2,406.0	2,279.2	2,250.5
British Columbia	802.5	923.0	1,002.9	1,101.6	1,249.0	1,270.5

Source: Statistics Canada, Input-Output Division.

TABLE 9
Other Provinces' Exports to Quebec
as a Percentage of Their Total Exports

	1984	1985	1986	1987	1988	1989
Newfoundland	7.50	7.93	7.80	8.60	6.77	6.83
Prince Edward Island	11.44	11.88	11.18	11.94	12.55	12.97
Nova Scotia	11.85	12.77	13.72	12.26	13.87	13.53
New Brunswick	12.79	14.00	15.10	13.82	14.12	14.67
Ontario	17.41	16.82	17.09	17.90	18.84	18.83
Manitoba	9.46	9.49	10.94	8.63	8.10	7.80
Saskatchewan	9.22	8.32	7.86	6.68	6.73	6.78
Alberta	9.02	7.70	7.86	7.55	7.12	6.67
British Columbia	3.96	4.08	4.26	4.07	4.09	4.04

Source: Percentages computed by the author from data from Statistics Canada, Input-Output Division.

Quebec: Trade Surplus with Other Provinces

Overall, in 1989, Quebec had a trade surplus in goods with all its Canadian partners and a trade deficit in services only with Manitoba in addition to Ontario (Table 10). Its largest trade surplus was with British Columbia. In both percentage and value terms, Quebec's exports to British Columbia were larger than

British Columbian exports to Quebec. Alberta's trade balance with Quebec, on the other hand, was adversely affected by "a sharp decline in petroleum prices in 1986" (Messinger, 1993a: 3.4). It moved from a surplus in 1984 to a deficit in both 1988 and 1989.

Quebec's trade balance shows that the province usually generates a modest trade surplus from its interprovincial trade (Table 10). This surplus comes essentially from its manufactured goods and is not large enough to compensate for the trade deficit with other countries (Table 11). In both primary goods and services, Quebec registered a trade deficit between 1984 and 1989. As mentioned earlier, the deficit in services was essentially with Ontario which "clearly dominated trade in services running large trade surpluses with each of the other provinces" (Messinger, 1993b: 3.13). Like Quebec, Ontario has a trade deficit in primary goods but its combined surpluses in manufactured goods and services have more than alleviated its deficit with the rest of the world.

TABLE 10
Quebec's Trade Balance with Other Provinces
(in $ millions)

	1984	1985	1986	1987	1988	1989
Newfoundland						
goods	444.2	427.7	465.0	410.2	492.8	527.9
services	200.6	285.2	269.4	275.2	333.9	287.7
Prince Edward Island						
goods	72.9	79.1	91.1	78.4	103.8	103.4
services	20.9	20.5	22.1	27.7	22.3	21.5
Nova Scotia						
goods	444.0	441.0	381.3	476.3	570.9	583.8
services	150.5	164.1	165.6	193.8	170.0	136.3
New Brunswick						
goods	521.5	549.4	354.3	370.7	440.2	481.4
services	235.2	224.7	218.7	276.0	290.7	294.7
Ontario						
goods	−1,070.8	−273.0	−1,411.0	−579.8	−143.1	120.6
services	−1,658.0	−1,511.6	−2,512.0	−2,524.6	−3,523.4	−3,725.6
Manitoba						
goods	35.4	37.3	−44.8	120.2	184.4	285.5
services	−74.3	−82.3	−104.3	−93.4	−68.0	−75.2
Saskatchewan						
goods	−206.7	−77.4	109.9	80.4	55.1	88.1
services	−44.3	−40.4	−70.7	16.6	41.8	45.9

TABLE 10 (cont'd)
Quebec's Trade Balance with Other Provinces
(in $ millions)

	1984	1985	1986	1987	1988	1989
Alberta						
goods	−1,477.1	−983.2	−193.0	−63.0	166.9	380.3
services	173.2	198.6	−19.1	−11.4	194.3	176.2
British Columbia						
goods	985.1	1,043.7	967.5	986.6	1,297.6	1,537.9
services	107.4	80.7	19.7	111.2	185.6	308.1

Source: Statistics Canada, Input-Output Division.

TABLE 11
Quebec's Trade Balance by Sector
(in $ millions)

	1984	1985	1986	1987	1988	1989
Primary Goods						
other countries	−1,610	−2,556	−190	−1,250	−1,261	−1,567
other provinces	−4,119	−3,201	−1,974	−2,140	−1,984	−1,488
total	−5,729	−5,757	−2,164	−3,391	−3,245	−3,056
Manufactured Goods						
other countries	−1,319	−2,202	−3,549	−4,057	−3,769	−4,650
other provinces	3,721	4,231	2,668	4,000	5,303	5,754
total	2,402	2,028	−881	−58	1,534	1,104
Goods (Total)						
other countries	−2,958	−4,825	−3,913	−5,346	−5,303	−6,479
other provinces	−235	1,280	831	1,984	3,273	4,235
total	−3,193	−3,545	−3,032	−3,362	−2,030	−2,244
Services						
other countries	1,102	903	643	364	379	525
other provinces	−814	−601	−1,947	−1,655	−2,275	−2,427
total	288	302	−1,304	−1,291	−1,896	−1,903
Goods and Services						
other countries	−1,856	−3,922	−3,269	−4,982	−4,924	−5,955
other provinces	−1,049	679	−1,116	329	998	1,808
total	−2,905	−3,243	−4,385	−4,653	−3,926	−4,147

Note: Numbers may not add up due to rounding.

Source: Statistics Canada, Input-Output Division.

Quebec's Total Supply and Demand

For Quebec and the other provinces, "the proportion of goods exported was significantly higher than services" for the 1984-1989 period (Messinger, 1993: 3.9). Quebec produces and consumes approximately 85% of its services (Tables 12 and 13), exports 10% of its supply to other provinces and imports 11 percent of its demand from its Canadian partners. In services, Ontario buys slightly over 50% of Quebec's exports to the rest of Canada while Quebec purchases more than 70% of its Canadian imports from Ontario. Messinger points out that "since goods are valued in producer ('factory gate') prices, a sizeable proportion (well over $20 billion) of interprovincial trade in services is directly linked to transporting and marketing goods" (Messinger, 1993: 3.8).

Primary goods is the only sector where Quebec exports more to the rest of the world than to other parts of Canada (Table 12). On the demand side, Alberta, Quebec's most important supplier until 1986, saw its share of Quebec's total demand in primary goods shrink following the drop in petroleum prices in the mid-1980s (Table 13).

In manufactured goods, Quebec's export share to both the rest of the world and to other Canadian provinces increased slightly between 1984 and 1989 (Table 12). Quebec was thus exporting more of its manufactured goods in both dollar value and percentage terms. The same remark also applies to the import share (Table 13).

TABLE 12
Quebec's Total Supply
(in percentage)

	1984	1985	1986	1987	1988	1989
Primary Goods						
own consumption	73.01	72.89	65.06	70.20	70.97	70.09
other countries	20.95	20.83	27.87	21.38	20.54	21.09
other provinces	6.04	6.28	7.06	8.42	8.48	8.82
Ontario	3.45	3.57	4.28	6.04	5.75	6.32
Manufactured Goods						
own consumption	47.62	46.41	46.36	46.23	44.49	43.64
other countries	25.94	25.97	27.24	25.81	26.83	27.23
other provinces	26.44	27.61	26.40	27.96	28.68	29.13
Ontario	16.69	17.70	16.57	18.25	18.78	18.88

TABLE 12 (cont'd)
Quebec's Total Supply
(in percentage)

	1984	1985	1986	1987	1988	1989
Goods (Total)						
own consumption	60.18	59.59	59.66	60.82	59.56	59.05
other countries	20.48	20.24	21.42	19.47	20.11	20.35
other provinces	19.34	20.17	18.92	19.70	20.33	20.60
Ontario	12.12	12.82	11.82	12.85	13.31	13.36
Services						
own consumption	84.66	84.99	86.57	86.37	85.45	85.41
other countries	5.90	5.34	5.00	4.99	5.19	5.10
other provinces	9.44	9.67	8.43	8.64	9.36	9.49
Ontario	5.40	5.65	4.90	5.07	5.62	5.76
Goods and Services						
own consumption	71.41	71.42	72.54	73.10	72.03	71.97
other countries	13.79	13.30	13.56	12.51	12.92	12.87
other provinces	14.79	15.28	13.90	14.39	15.04	15.15
Ontario	9.03	9.48	8.51	9.11	9.60	9.63

Note: Numbers may not add up to 100 due to rounding.

Source: Percentages computed by the author from data from Statistics Canada, Input-Output Division.

TABLE 13
Quebec's Total Demand
(in percentage)

	1984	1985	1986	1987	1988	1989
Primary Goods						
own production	41.74	41.12	51.75	50.09	51.92	52.68
other countries	24.00	31.10	23.97	25.82	25.46	28.59
other provinces	34.25	27.78	24.28	24.09	22.62	18.73
Alberta	17.26	14.29	10.44	8.70	7.37	6.20
Ontario	9.40	6.79	6.52	9.20	8.65	7.93
Manufactured Goods						
own production	49.62	47.97	45.72	46.19	45.40	44.25
other countries	29.34	30.49	32.38	31.72	32.37	33.56
other provinces	21.04	21.54	21.90	22.09	22.23	22.18
Ontario	17.74	17.96	18.19	18.35	18.66	18.53
Goods (Total)						
own production	58.00	57.33	57.75	58.87	58.50	57.94
other countries	23.09	24.65	24.81	23.94	24.38	25.42
other provinces	18.90	18.03	17.44	17.18	17.12	16.65
Ontario	12.89	12.63	12.91	12.99	13.20	13.01

TABLE 13 (cont'd)
Quebec's Total Demand
(in percentage)

	1984	1985	1986	1987	1988	1989
Services						
own production	85.00	85.32	85.27	85.20	83.93	83.98
other countries	4.39	4.20	4.18	4.54	4.74	4.55
other provinces	10.61	10.48	10.56	10.26	11.33	11.46
Ontario	7.72	7.61	7.73	7.65	8.82	8.93
Goods and Services						
own production	70.12	70.06	70.80	71.40	70.76	70.69
other countries	14.70	15.34	15.02	14.71	14.92	15.20
other provinces	15.18	14.59	14.18	13.89	14.33	14.11
Ontario	10.57	10.35	10.45	10.45	11.09	11.01

Note: Numbers may not add up to 100 due to rounding.

Source: Percentages computed by the author from data from Statistics Canada, Input-Output Division.

Commodity Products Contributing to Quebec's Trade Surplus and Deficit

Quebec enjoys its largest trade surpluses in textile and clothing, and in paper. Moreover, chemicals are always among the five most important commodity products with respect to the trade surplus. The province generally runs its largest deficits in finance, insurance, real estate; mineral fuels; fruits, vegetables, feed and miscellaneous food products; business services; and wholesale margins. Except for mineral fuels, commodity groupings contributing to Ontario's largest trade surpluses mirror those causing Quebec's largest trade deficits. Other important products on the positive side for Ontario include autos, trucks and other transportation equipment; electronic and communications products; and chemicals. It is in mineral fuels; transportation and storage; lumber; and clothing that Ontario registers its largest trade deficits with its Canadian partners.

Quebec's Leading Interprovincial Exports and Imports

Table 15 lists the main interprovincial exports and imports for Quebec in 1989. The data show that the influence of the *National Policy* is still at work. Textile and apparel; food and beverages (especially dairy products); and chemicals are among Quebec's leading exports along with wholesale margins and transportation, while its international exports are dominated by autos, trucks, other transportation equipment; primary metal products; paper; and electronic and communications products.

As emphasized earlier, Quebec's leading imports from other provinces are essentially Ontario's major interprovincial exports: wholesale margins; other finance, insurance and real estate; food and beverages; and business services (Table 15). Autos, trucks, other transportation equipment as well as machinery and equipment; electronic and communications products; and chemicals are Quebec's main imports from the rest of the world.

TABLE 15

Quebec's Leading Interprovincial Exports and Imports (Yr=1989)

(in $ millions)

Quebec

Exports

1)	Textile, clothing and knitted products	3,365.1
2)	Food & beverages	2,834.2
3)	Wholesale margins	2,790.6
4)	Transportation & storage	2,582.3
5)	Chemicals & chemical products	2,524.0
6)	Business services	2,107.2
7)	Paper & paper products	1,989.4
8)	Autos, trucks, other transportation equipment	1,748.6
9)	Metal fabricated products	1,732.5
10)	Primary metal products	1,588.0
11)	Elec. & communications products	1,497.8
12)	Other finance, insurance, real estate	1,316.7
13)	Communications services	989.1
14)	Rubber, leather, plastic fab. products	877.5
15)	Machinery & equipment	798.8

Imports

1)	Wholesale margins	3,324.5
2)	Food & beverages	3,172.2
3)	Other finance, insurance, real estate	2,817.5
4)	Business services	2,662.7
5)	Transportation & storage	2,365.3
6)	Autos, trucks, other transportation equipment	1,928.4
7)	Chemicals & chemical products	1,893.9
8)	Textile, clothing & knitted products	1,268.8
9)	Electronic & communications products	1,268.4
10)	Primary metal products	1,244.1
11)	Metal fabricated products	1,121.6
12)	Paper and paper products	1,107.1
13)	Communication services	1,097.9
14)	Machinery & equipment	877.6
15)	Mineral fuels	846.9

Source: Statistics Canada, Input-Output Division.

CONCLUSION

Since the data are not available, it is too early to assess the direct impact of the Canada-U.S. Free Trade Agreement and NAFTA on Quebec's interprovincial trade.[6] Will the removal of tariff and nontariff barriers with the United States and Mexico lead to less interprovincial trade or simply more international trade? It is unlikely that NAFTA will have a major negative impact on Quebec's interprovincial trade. The province's leading international exports (autos, trucks, other transportation equipment; primary metal products; and paper and paper products) are not the same as its main interprovincial exports (textile, clothing and knitted products; food and beverages; and wholesale margins). The same remark applies to imports. Services (wholesale margins; finance, insurance, real estate; and business services), with food and beverages, top the list of Quebec's imports from the rest of Canada while auto, trucks, other transportation equipment; machinery and equipment; and electronic and communications products are Quebec's leading international imports. However, the real issue is: to what extent will NAFTA reduce Quebec's dependency vis-à-vis its Canadian partners? Up to 1989, Quebec was still exporting more to the rest of Canada than to other parts of the world. Without data, it is for now impossible to analyze the impact of NAFTA on interprovincial trade, but further research should focus on this issue.

Although the government of Quebec has been one of the most fervent proponents of free trade with the United States, it has been rather timid in its efforts to remove internal trade barriers. As mentioned earlier, Quebec fought hard to exclude some of its Crown corporations from the rules of the July Agreement on Internal Trade requiring provincial governments not to discriminate against out-of-province suppliers. Moreover, it took a "trade war" with Ontario before Quebec agreed to liberalize its labour laws to allow workers living in that province to work in Quebec. However, Quebec is not the only province to blame for its weak commitment with regard to free trade within Canada. Other provinces such as Ontario in wine have also been reluctant to open up their markets to their Canadian neighbours.

Finally, as Quebec does most of its trade with Ontario, does it mean that it should not pay attention to its other Canadian partners? The answer is no. It is with these other provinces that Quebec registers a trade surplus in both goods and services. Therefore, even if as a group they are less important than Ontario in terms of percentage and dollar value, they still represent an important market for Quebec.

---

6.   The Canada-U.S. FTA entered into force in January 1989 while NAFTA came into force in January 1994.

REFERENCES

CANADA. ROYAL COMMISSION ON DOMINION-PROVINCIAL RELATIONS (Rowell-Sirois). 1940. *Report.* Book II. Ottawa: King's Printer.

CANADA. ROYAL COMMISSION ON THE ECONOMIC UNION AND DEVELOPMENT PROSPECTS FOR CANADA (MacDonald Commission). 1985. *Report.* Volume Three. Ottawa: Minister of Supply and Services Canada.

CANADA. PARTNERSHIP FOR PROSPERITY. 1991. *Canadian Federalism and Economic Union.* Ottawa: Minister of Supply and Services.

CHRÉTIEN, Jean. 1980. *Securing the Canadian Economic Union in the Constitution.* Ottawa: Minister of Supply and Services.

COPELAND, Brian R. 1993. "Interprovincial Barriers to Trade: A Review of the Empirical Evidence from a British Columbia Perspective," Vancouver: University of British Columbia, mimeographed.

EVENSON, Jeff, and Richard SIMEON. 1979. "The Roots of Discontent," in *Proceedings of the Workshop on the Political Economy of Confederation, November 8-10, 1978*, Institute of Intergovernmental Relations and Economic Council of Canada. Ottawa.

FALDA, Filip. 1994. "Why Canada Must Rid Itself of Interprovincial Trade Barriers," in *Provincial Trade Wars: Why the Blockade Must End*, ed. Filip Falda. Vancouver: The Fraser Institute.

FAUCHER, Albert, and Maurice LAMONTAGNE. 1953. "Historical of Industrial Development," in *Essays on Contemporary Quebec*, ed. Jean-Charles Falardeau. Quebec: Les Presses de l'Université Laval.

ECONOMIC COUNCIL OF CANADA. 1991. *A Joint-Venture: The Economics of Constitutional Options.* Twenty-Eighth Annual Review. Ottawa: Minister of Supply and Services Canada.

FLATTERS, F.R., and R.G. LIPSEY. 1983. *Common Ground for the Canadian Common Market.* Montreal: Institute for Research on Public Policy.

INTERNAL TRADE SECRETARIAT. 1994. "Brief History of Efforts to Enhance Internal Trade in Canada," Ottawa: Internal Trade Secretariat.

IRVINE, I.J., W.A. SIMS, and A. ANASTASOPOULOS. 1990. "Interprovincial Versus International Free Trade: The Brewing Industry," *Canadian Journal of Economics* 23: 332-47.

MAXWELL, Judith, and Caroline PESTIEAU. 1980. *Economic Realities of Contemporary Confederation.* Accent Quebec Series. Montreal: C.D. Howe Research Institute.

MESSINGER, Hans. 1993a. "Canada's Interprovincial Trade Flows of Goods, 1984-1988," *Canadian Economic Observer*, January. Ottawa: Statistics Canada, Catalogue 11-010.

MESSINGER, Hans. 1993b. "Interprovincial Trade Flows of Goods and Services," *Canadian Economic Observer*, October. Ottawa: Statistics Canada, Catalogue 11-010.

MILNE, William J. 1987. *Interprovincial Trade Barriers: A Survey and Assessment.* Ottawa: Purchasing Management Association.

MOREAU, François. 1988. *Le commerce extérieur du Québec.* Hull, Quebec: Les éditions Asticou/Les éditions Critiques.

NAPPI, Carmine. 1978. *The Structure of Quebec's Exports.* Accent Quebec Series. Montreal: C.D. Howe Research Institute.

NORRIE, Kenneth, Richard SIMEON, and Mark KRASNICK. 1986. *Federalism and Economic Union in Canada.* Volume 59 in the series of studies commissioned by the Royal Commission on the Economic Union and Development Prospects for Canada. Toronto: University of Toronto Press.

PROULX, Pierre-Paul, and Guilain CAUCHY. 1991. "Un examen des échanges commerciaux du Québec avec les autres provinces canadiennes, les États-Unis et le reste du monde," in *Éléments d'analyse économique pertinents à la révision du statut politique et constitutionnel du Québec*, Commission sur l'avenir politique et constitutionnel du Québec. Québec: Commission sur l'avenir politique et constitutionnel du Québec.

RUTLEY, Todd. 1991. *"Canada 1993": A Plan for the Creation of a Single Economic Market in Canada.* Toronto: Canadian Manufacturers' Association.

SCHWANEN, Daniel. 1992. "Open Exchange: Freeing the Trade of Goods and Services within the Canadian Economic Union," in *Free to Move: Strengthening the Canadian Economic Union*, ed. David M. Brown, Fred Lazar, and Daniel Schwanen. Toronto: C.D. Howe Institute.

SCHWANEN, Daniel. 1994. *One Market, Many Opportunities: The Last Stage in Removing Obstacles to Interprovincial Trade.* Commentary 60. Toronto: C.D. Howe Institute.

TREBILCOCK, Michael J., John WHALLEY, Carol ROGERSON, and Ian NESS. 1983. "Provincially Induced Barriers to Trade in Canada: A Survey," in *Federalism and the Canadian Economic Union*, ed. Michael J. Trebilcock, J. Robert S. Prichard, Thomas J. Courchene, and John Whalley. Toronto: University of Toronto Press for the Ontario Economic Council.

WHALLEY, John. 1983. "Induced Distortions of Interprovincial Activity: An Overview of Issues," In *Federalism and the Canadian Economic Union*, ed. Michael J. Trebilcock, J. Robert S. Prichard, Thomas J. Courchene, and John Whalley. Toronto: University of Toronto Press for the Ontario Economic Council.

WHALLEY, John, and Irene TRELA. 1986. *Regional Aspects of Confederation.* Volume 68 in the series of studies commissioned by the Royal Commission on the Economic Union and Development Prospects for Canada. Toronto: University of Toronto Press.

5

Quebec-Mexico Relationships:
A New Partner

María Isabel Studer
and **Jean-François Prud'homme**
Centro de Investigacíon y Docencia Económicas

This article examines the relations between Mexico and Quebec in the context of NAFTA. The objective is to explore the different future scenarios for such relations, to be determined, on the one hand, by the future shape of the North American region and, on the other, by domestic developments both in Quebec – the prospects for becoming an independent nation-state – and in Mexico – the transition to democracy. The aim is to explore how the different potential scenarios will alter the way Mexico and Quebec have traditionally interacted, particularly at the government level, and to identify the potential gains offered by the different post-NAFTA scenarios for the different non-government actors in both Quebec and Mexico, whose contacts have already multiplied. The article examines four issues: (a) the nature of Quebec as an international actor and how this peculiarity has shaped the temper of Quebec's relations with Mexico; (b) the growing internationalization of domestic politics in North America and future scenarios as to the emergence of different types of community in North America – a European model or a restrictive trade-investment association; (c) the potential for forging broader and more solid economic links between Quebec and Mexico, given that both the Quebec and the Mexican economies face the overwhelming weight of the U.S. economy; (d) the social and cultural dimension, how Quebec and Mexico have approached similar or potentially similar issues such as Indian revolts and linguistic policies.

INTRODUCTION

The North American Free Trade Agreement has brought a new dynamic to the international relations of North America. One of the most significant changes is the entry of Mexico as a North American partner. Another significant factor that will certainly modify the nature of the continent's international relations is the transformation of Quebec into an independent nation-state. Although it is difficult to say whether or not this will happen, expectations have already been created in Mexico and the United States by the pledge made by the recently-elected Parti Québécois government to hold a referendum on sovereignty in 1995.

The existing deadlock between Quebec and the rest Canada on negotiations for a constitutional reform, as evidenced by the failure of the Meech Lake and Charlottetown agreements, and the support for the sovereignist project from the 54 Bloc Québécois M.P.s are factors that may lead to the success of the project. However, opinion polls in September 1994 show that a majority of Quebecers – 56% – would have voted against independence if a referendum had been held at time. Only 30% said they would vote in favour of it (*Financial Times*, 1994). In addition, according to some analysts, in last September's elections in Quebec, Quebecers voted for the Parti Québécois because "they wanted a new government, not a new country." This explains why that party captured only 77 of the 125 seats in the provincial legislature and gained only 44.7% of total votes, compared with 44.4% for the Quebec Liberal Party (Chipello and Urquhart, 1994).

Whether or not Quebec becomes independent, the possibility alone has attracted attention in the other North American partner countries. Despite the fact that, in 1994, Mexico and Canada celebrated their 50th year of bilateral relations, their interest in enhancing mutual understanding has grown considerably since the Mexican government proposed the signing of a free trade agreement with the United States, back in the fall of 1990. This interest has already spurred a growing number of formal and informal contacts in academic, business, non-governmental and government circles in both countries. Notwithstanding this and the diplomatic rhetoric, a true partnership between Mexico and Canada as North American partners has yet to be forged.

The purpose of this chapter is to discuss Quebec-Mexico relations in the new context of NAFTA and, particularly, in the event of an independent Quebec. An important element in the understanding of Quebec-Mexico relations is naturally their asymmetrical character. For this reason, a first section of the chapter is devoted to explaining the peculiar role of Quebec as an international actor. While it may seem obvious for a Quebec audience, this section will surely give the Mexican audience, particularly foreign policy makers, information that will help them think of innovative ways to look at the cooperative links already established with the government of Quebec. An overview of Quebec-Mexico relations is then presented in a second section. It contains an overall description of the most salient aspects of such relations, emphasizing the factors of continuity and change in light of the transition of Mexico from Latin American partner to North American partner.

The prospects for Quebec-Mexico relations in the new North American context, and especially in the event of an independent Quebec, are presented in a third section. The implications of Quebec sovereignty on its relations with Mexico in different areas are discussed on the basis of two possible scenarios: full independence and sovereignty-association. A reflection on how relations might develop if the status quo prevails is made in a final section of concluding remarks.

QUEBEC AS AN INTERNATIONAL ACTOR

During the last thirty years, Quebec has maintained an active presence on the international scene. For some, the international participation of sub-units of government has become a natural outcome of the globalization process. However, in the case of Quebec, international participation is not new nor does it result solely from the globalization process. Other factors explain the peculiarity of Quebec's international affairs, including the nature of the Canadian federal system and the particularities of Quebec's society. A brief analysis of these factors is presented in the following paragraphs.

Increasing economic interdependency and the resulting increase in economic competition have made it imperative for sub-units of government to participate in the promotion of their own interests, particularly their economic interests. Canadian provinces have a long and active tradition in this regard (Nossal, 1985: 194-195). They have established provincial offices abroad to promote immigration, trade and other economic interests. In fact, by the early 1980s, seven provinces were operating more than 35 agencies on three continents (Nossal, 1985: 196).[1] Regional disparities in Canada make it difficult for the federal government to design general policies that respond to very different provincial needs. In addition, Canada's geographic proximity to the U.S. and provincial jurisdiction over such issues as forest fire-fighting, waterways, highways and bridge management have also encouraged a variety of contacts between provincial governments and neighbouring American states. From this perspective, provincial participation in transnational relations is easily understood.

---

1. In one of the few references to jurisdiction on foreign policy – section 92.A – the Canadian Constitution Act allows the establishment of provincial offices abroad with the chief objective of promoting immigration, expansion and trade.

The international involvement of Quebec and the other provinces is also largely explained by the fact that the British North America Act of 1867 and the subsequent Constitution Act of 1982 both fail to assign federal and provincial government jurisdiction in foreign policy and to prohibit provincial involvement in international affairs. In general, federal systems pose a dilemma for the principle of sovereignty as it is understood in international law. While the latter assumes the indivisibility of the sovereign authority of states,[2] the former implies the existence of a divided sovereignty. Most federations have solved this dilemma by giving the central authority exclusive power over foreign policy (Nossal, 1985: 189). As suggested above, the Canadian Constitution is an exception to this norm,[3] an exception that is explained partly by the peculiar way in which Canada obtained its status as an independent state.[4]

In addition, the Constitution Acts of 1867 and 1982 provide provincial governments with broad powers: the authority to borrow money and legislative power over a number of economic issues (Section 92); control over natural resources (Section 92A and 109); exclusive jurisdiction over education (Section 93); and shared authority for agriculture and immigration for both levels of government (Section 95). All these areas of jurisdiction are likely to include some type of international activity. In this context, provincial involvement in foreign affairs appears to be a natural extension of the dynamics of federalism in Canada. It is explained by the provincial governments' concern with protecting their constitutional, economic and functional interests. As discussed in further detail below, Quebec has been particularly vehement in demanding greater power over foreign policy from the federal government, to promote and protect its interests abroad.

Although Ottawa has shown some reluctance to accept involvement by the provincial governments in foreign affairs, the legality of such involvement was confirmed by a resolution of the Judicial Committee, in 1937. Referring to the Labour Conventions Case, the Committee established that "the federal government could not enact legislation in an area explicitly given to the provinces under section 92, even if it was designed to fulfil obligations under an

---

2.   As Nossal argues, the exercise of sovereignty in international affairs is "assumed to be zero-sum: other arrangements – such as a condominium, where two sovereign states share the powers of statehood – cannot be considered sovereignty" (Nossal, 1985: 188).

3.   Probably the only other case is the former Union of Soviet Socialist Republics. Each republic was granted the right to exercise all the powers of a sovereign state. In fact, the Ukrainian and the Byelorussian republics are full members of the Charter of the United Nations (Nossal, 1985: 189).

4.   It was only in 1931, with the Statute of Westminster, which put an end to the British Empire, that Canada gained full autonomy to conduct its foreign affairs. The British North America Act assumed that authority over foreign policy emanated from the British Empire (Section 132). The failure to explicitly assign authority over any level of government was not, however, amended in the Constitution Act of 1982 (Nossal, 1985: 190-191).

international treaty" (Nossal, 1985: 193; Balthazar et al., 1993: 14-15).[5] Notwithstanding this, the federal and provincial governments have agreed that any international agreement signed by a province requires explicit or implicit approval by the Secretary of State for External Affairs. In the view of the international community, it is Ottawa that gives legal status to agreements entered into by provincial and foreign governments. In less broad cooperative or exchange agreements, Ottawa usually does not intervene formally, although it is assumed that it would at least be informed (Balthazar et al., 1993: 366).

Quebec's special status

Like other provinces, a large part of Quebec's external contacts are with neighbouring American states – that is, equal levels of government (Balthazar et al., 1993: 368-372). Quebec, however, stands as a special case in terms of provincial participation in international affairs. To begin with, and compared to other provinces, Quebec has had a more active foreign policy. This is reflected by the number and type of its offices abroad[6] and its more institutionalized bureaucratic system in support of its foreign activities (Nossal, 1985: 198).[7] The Direction générale des Affaires internationales of the Department of Intergovernmental Affairs of Quebec (1967), later the Department of International Affairs (1988), is the equivalent of the foreign office of any other sovereign state.[8]

Most importantly, Quebec has managed to exercise at least two of the basic international rights reserved for sovereign states – sending diplomatic missions and negotiating legally binding treaties or agreements with other sovereign states (Brossard et al., 1967: 12). Quebec was the first Canadian province to establish foreign representation. At about the same time that the Canadian federal government opened the High Commission for Canada in London, the first ever Canadian representation abroad (1880), Quebec opened its Commissaire Général in Paris, in 1882. In the mid-1960s, Quebec established

---

5. This resolution referred to a federal attempt to implement International Labour Organization agreements to impose federal legislation pertaining to labour issues on provincial governments. Two precedents in the areas of civil aviation (Aeronautics case, 1932) and broadcasting (The Radio Case, 1932) had given the federal government jurisdiction over the regulation of civil aviation and radio broadcasting following ratification by the British Empire in the first case, and Ottawa in the second, of international agreements on those issues.

6. Quebec has five general delegations abroad and more than 20 touristic, cultural, commercial and immigration offices in 19 different countries.

7. Ontario and Alberta also have well-developed structures to support their international activities.

8. The institutions had geographical divisions – France, Europe, U.S., Africa, Latin America, Asia, and Oceania – as well as functional bureaux – Economic Affairs, Educational and Cultural Affairs, and Social and Institutional Affairs. The Deaprtment of International Affairs was created in 1988 from the merger of the Department of Foreign Trade (1983) and the General Directorate of International Affairs (Nossal, 1985: 198).

a meaningful relationship with France and other members of "La Francophonie." These formal contacts with sovereign states place Quebec in a unique position because, unlike the other provinces, its international activity has become a means of nation-building.[9]

A brief reflection on Quebec-France relations will help explain both the limits of Quebec's international participation and the framework of its relations with Mexico. Throughout the 1960s and 1970s, France undertook a series of actions that gave the Quebec government a symbolic legitimacy in pursuing its goal of greater foreign relations autonomy vis-a-vis Ottawa. Quebec's first international agreements were signed with the French government in 1965, in the areas of education and culture. Also, upon the recommendation of France in early 1968, Gabon invited the government of Quebec to a conference on education without informing Ottawa. Ottawa objected to all these actions, claiming that Quebec had no authority to sign international agreements nor to participate as a full member in any kind of international activity without Ottawa's consent. Paul Gérin-Lajoie, Quebec's Minister of Education at the time, replied that Quebec had "a right to conclude sovereign agreements on issues under [constitutional] provincial jurisdiction, and to participate as an actor in its own right in international conferences on issues such as education and culture." This is now known as the Gérin-Lajoie Doctrine (Nossal, 1985: 201; Balthazar et al., 1993: 222).

These and other incidents severed relationships between Canada and the French government. One of the most notorious incidents was President De Gaulle's Montreal speech in 1967, in which he proclaimed "Vive le Québec libre, vive le Canada français, vive la France" ("long live Free Quebec, long live French Canada, long live France"), and compared English-speaking Canada with the Nazis.[10] The incident caused Canada's Prime Minister, Lester Pearson, to declare the French President *persona non grata*. After the demise of De Gaulle and the failure of the 1980 referendum on sovereignty, the French government stopped directly supporting Quebec's nationalist aspirations and tried to avoid taking sides between the Canadian and Quebec governments (Gibbens, 1994). Aware of these limitations, from the early eighties on, Quebec focused on strengthening the economic aspects of its special relationship with France.

---

9.   It is no coincidence that the foundations of Quebec's active international participation were laid during the years when Quebec's society experienced important transformations in what has been termed Quiet Revolution, and that led to a gradual process of nationalist assertion. If the Quiet Revolution signalled the beginning of Quebec's active participation in the world as a distinct actor, the arrival of the Parti québécois to power represented the adoption in Quebec of a more aggressive foreign policy.

10.   What De Gaulle actually said was: "throughout my route, I found myself in an atmosphere similar to that of the Liberation [of France from the Nazis]" (quoted on Nossal, 1985: 205).

This brief account of Quebec's relationship with France illustrates the limits of Quebec's ability to exercise the type of international rights that are exclusive to sovereign states. The limits are largely influenced by the willingness of foreign interlocutors to pay the cost of breaching international principles and creating diplomatic conflicts with Ottawa.

QUEBEC-MEXICO RELATIONSHIP

Mexico's place in the International Activities of Quebec

From Quebec's perspective, Mexico has a double status as an international partner. It has become a North American partner but it was formely considered a Latin American partner. To understand the place of Mexico in the international activities of Quebec, a brief review of the evolution of Quebec's international affairs is needed. Special attention is paid to the aspects that make Quebec's relations with its other North American partner, the U.S., different from those with Latin American countries. This comparison will be useful in understanding the present context of Quebec-Mexico relations and for reflection on their future.

In their evaluation of a thirty-year period, Balthazar, Bélanger and Mace conclude that Quebec's international activities have been growing steadily since the 1960s. This is particularly true of the 1980s, when there was a clear desire to diversify relations with the world. Economics, education and culture have been the principal focus areas of such activity. The U.S., France and Europe have had priority in Quebec's international objectives, in terms of official visits and agreements signed.

Latin America has traditionally represented a very small fraction of all the province's total international activity, coming fifth after the U.S., France, Europe and even Asia. In its relations with Latin America, Quebec has focused mainly on those areas in which it has constitutional jurisdiction, such as education.[11] Agreements on educational exchanges, most often scholarships, constitute more than 50% of all agreements between Quebec and the Latin American countries – 14 out of 23 between 1960 and 1990. But even in this field, Latin America falls behind Africa, with which Quebec made 32 agreements on education and culture (Balthazar et al., 1993: 359).

The first Parti québécois government under René Lévesque (1976-1981) was interested in diversifying Quebec's international contacts, and started to pay more attention to South America. The number of representatives and official

---

11. In fact, more than half Quebec's international agreements with sovereign states, 230 in all, are on education and culture.

visits increased in the late 1970s.[12] An Office for Latin America and the Caribbean was also established within the Department of Intergovernmental Affairs, then in charge of Quebec's foreign affairs. For the reasons stated below, it should be noted that Quebec's interest in Latin America coincided with parallel interest on the part of the Canadian government under Pierre Trudeau, a result of his Third Option policy, to intensify Canada's Latin American contacts.

Although the Lévesque government was also very active in promoting investment and commercial links with Latin America (Balthazar et al., 1993: 286), these attempts were obstructed by the recession of 1982 and the debt crisis by which most Latin American countries were submerged for a decade. Quebec was thus prevented from taking full advantage of the potential opportunities offered by the region.[13]

Another aspect of the evolution of Quebec's foreign policy that is relevant in a discussion of Quebec-Mexico relations is the gradual but firm shift of Quebec's focus towards the U.S. on the one hand, and the growing prominence of economic issues on Quebec's international agenda on the other. Most of the province's relationship with the U.S. is conducted at the level of government sub-units and focuses on economic, environmental, and border issues such as transportation.[14] Of the 230 international agreements signed by the Quebec government, only one has been reached with the U.S. federal government. Instead, more than half of the agreements with non-sovereign states were signed with U.S. state governments.[15] A number of factors combine to explain this situation: geographical proximity, the changing international environment characterized by the globalization of economies and the spread of transnational contacts among societies, the decentralized nature of the U.S. federal system that grants states relative autonomy to participate in international affairs, and most importantly, Washington's reluctance to agree to formal diplomatic contacts with the Quebec government (Balthazar et al., 1993: 70).[16]

12.   Quebec opened several new offices in Latin America, Haiti (1974), Caracas (1979), and a General Delegation in Mexico (1980).

13.   As Balthazar et al. show, in this period Asia received more attention than Latin America, including Mexico. Between 1985 and 1989 Quebec's governmental activity in Latin America declined, its exports to the region dropped from 5.1% to 2.6%, and its imports dropped from 14.2% to 4.5% (Balthazar et al.: 226).

14.   Thirty U.S. states have entered into some kind of agreement with Quebec; 38 on commercial or economic issues, eight on environmental issues (Balthazar et al., 1993).

15.   Quebec participates in a series of institutions involving state governments, such as the Conference of Governors from New England, with Massachusetts, Connecticut, Rhode Island, Maine, Vermont, the Maritime provinces, and Newfoundland. Through its representatives in Parliament, Quebec participates in the National Conference of State Legislatures and the Council of State Governments. It is also an observer on the Council of Great Lakes Governors (Balthazar et al.: 86-87).

16.   Quebec has made efforts to establish political contacts in Washington. This was especially true in 1979-1980, with the prospects of a victory on sovereignty in the 1980 referendum. However, Washington has always been reluctant to respond to Quebec's requests.

It is interesting to note that the Lévesque government was interested in cultivating a special relationship with the U.S.[17] The common view is that this was related to its goal of securing independence for Quebec and recognition of its sovereign status. Balthazar et al. contradict this by pointing out that the interest stemmed more from the realization that a new open relationship with the U.S. was a way of compensating for the failure of the independence project. In fact, it was in the aftermath of the 1980 referendum that Quebec's relations with the U.S. intensified. It became another way of expressing Quebec's "reluctance to 'canadianization'" (Balthazar et al., 1993: 70).[18] The economic recession of the early 1980s amplified the need for Quebec to focus on the economic aspects of its international activities, and especially on its relationship with the U.S. (Ministère des Affaires internationales: 1992). This emphasized the **transnational** nature of Quebec's contacts abroad. In addition, as Balthazar et al. suggest, in the last decade the governments of Quebec have also realized that Quebec is part of a North American economic, environmental and cultural system (Balthazar et al., 1993: 100-103).

To conclude, the governments of the U.S. and Latin America prefer to establish relations with Quebec through Ottawa. There is, however, a basic difference in the type of relationship that Quebec has established with the U.S. and with Latin America. The difference is largely explained by geographic considerations, but also by the distinct nature of the political systems of those countries. The proximity of the U.S. and its decentralized federation determine the more transnational aspect of its relations with Quebec, whereas the remoteness and federally centralized or unitary nature of Latin American political systems seem to be the reason for the focus on education and culture in their contacts with Quebec. The changes in Quebec-Mexico relations in the last two or three years are similar to the difference between Quebec's relations with the U.S. and Latin America. It is a matter of speculation as to whether the North American dynamic will bring Quebec's relations with Mexico into line with its relations with the U.S. However, as a North American partner, Mexico will be certainly more subject to the pressures imposed by the dynamic of integration. Like Quebec, Mexico has also accepted that it is part of a North American economic and social system. The following sections will show how Mexico's recently-acquired status as a North American partner is already transforming its relationship with Quebec.

---

17. Lévesque's interest derived not only from his personal sympathy for the U.S. or the importance of assuring the U.S. that an independent Quebec would pose no threat to U.S. security. Rather, and as all Quebec governments have realized, Levésque understood the tremendous economic importance of the U.S. for Quebec.

18. According to some analysts, English and French Canadians "differ sharply in their rapport with the United States. Quebecers tend to identify more with the giant to the South. They feel less threatened by American culture than do English Canadians. Nathalie Petrowski, cultural reporter of *La Presse*, stressed that "Quebec has its own cultural identity and so we do not have to be so afraid of Americans taking us over" (Farnsworth).

Mexico as a Latin American Partner

Mexico has long been Quebec's major Latin American partner. Quebec's General Delegation in Mexico, which opened in 1980, is the largest in Latin America and one of the five largest in the world. Of all the Latin American countries, Mexico is the most visited by public officials from Quebec (Balthazar et al., 1993: 359). The majority of Quebec-Mexico relations centre on education and cultural exchanges. Like many federal states, the Mexican government supports the idea that foreign relations fall under the exclusive jurisdiction of central governments.

Mexico has jealously defended the principles of non-intervention and self-determination of nation-states. The history of foreign interventions, particularly by the U.S., in Mexico and other Latin American countries prompted Mexico to launch its well-known Doctrina Estrada in 1930. According to this doctrine, every government should abstain from making statements of recognition of another country's government since by doing so it infringes upon the sovereignty of that country. Mexico, particularly in the first decades of this century, suffered from a common practice among the U.S. and some European governments to use recognition as a way of gaining concessions from Latin American governments. They would make pronouncements about the legitimacy of certain regimes, questioning the legal capacity of an established or emerging government, as a way of forcing debt payments or other economic or political concessions. Mexico, in compliance with the Doctrina Estrada, has firmly opposed any official pronouncements that might violate the principle of non-intervention.

Given Mexico's centralized federation, the history of foreign interventions in Mexican affairs, and Mexico's defense of the principles of non-intervention and self-determination, it is not unreasonable to expect a certain uneasiness on the part of Mexican federal officials in dealing directly with non-sovereign states like Quebec. Although there are few public records to document this attitude, the position of the Mexican government appears clear in the diplomatic notes exchanged by the Secretariat of External Relations of Mexico (SRE) and Canada's Department of External Affairs with reference to the opening of the Quebec Delegation in Mexico. The SRE recognizes the Canadian Embassy as "the only channel of official communication between Mexican authorities and the Canadian provinces" (Medina, 1994: footnote no. 4). This, of course, has not prevented the governments of Quebec and Mexico from making exchanges and even formal agreements, although not without Ottawa's involvement. In fact, all agreements of cooperation between the governments of Quebec and of Mexico fall within the broader framework agreements between Canada and Mexico. This also explains why the level of Quebec's interest in Mexico parallels that of the Canadian federal government.

Until recently, and in line with the pattern of Quebec's relations with other Latin American countries, the majority of exchanges between Quebec and Mexico have focused on the areas of education and culture. Since 1979, the government of Quebec offered a "unilateral" program of scholarships for Mexicans studying in Quebec. Up to February 1993, a total of 450 Mexican students had benefited from the program (Medina, 1994). Also, the working group Mexico-Quebec, established in 1980, has held six meetings concerned mainly with fostering closer cultural and educational exchanges. Recently it has moved to fulfil its objectives through more institutional Mexican channels, via the Secretariat of Public Education (SEP) and the National Council on Science and Technology (CONACYT). Quebec's unilateral scholarship mechanism for Mexican students was replaced by a bilateral agreement on educational exchanges, which involves the participation of Quebec's Department of International Affairs and SRE, SEP, and CONACYT on the Mexican side.[19]

A number of cooperative arrangements exist between Mexican and Quebec universities. Participants include the Université de Montréal, Université Laval, the Université du Québec à Montréal, McGill University, the Universidad Nacional Autónoma de Mexico, the Universidad Autónoma del Estado de Mexico, the Universidad de Guanajuato, the Universidad Autónoma de Puebla, and the Instituto Tecnológico de Estudios Superiores. Quebec's presence in Mexico's cultural life has also increased and diversified.

Some other exchanges have taken place in agriculture, an area of joint responsibility for Canada's provincial and federal governments. In 1981, Quebec's Department of Agriculture signed a cooperation agreement with the Secretariat of Agriculture and Hydraulic Resources (SARH) to facilitate the exchange of technical information on agriculture. Another agreement on forestry assistance was reached in 1986 between Quebec's Department of Transports and the SARH. In the area of environment, a number of Quebec companies now assist the Environmental Commission of the Secretariat of Social Development (SEDESOL) in the implementation of environmental rules and standards.

A Canada-Mexico Program of Temporary Agricultural Workers was established in 1974. In 1992, 39% of foreign workers temporarily in Canada came from Mexico. Quebec took part in the program by hosting 15% of the total of 4,778 workers received in Canada in 1992 (Verea, 1994: 536). Agreements on coordination of fiscal policies and assistance in judicial matters are also the focus of mutual cooperation between Mexico and Quebec.

---

19. Personal interview with an SRE official.

Mexico as a North American Partner

Quebec's relationship with Mexico acquired a new dimension with the signing of the North American Free Trade Agreement. Under NAFTA, contacts between Mexico and Quebec have broadened to include other areas than education or culture. Although Quebec remains interested in access to the Mexican market, its main interest in NAFTA, like Canada as a whole, was to consolidate the benefits already achieved by the 1988 Canada-U.S. Free Trade Agreement. It is also important to mention that Quebec is one of the provinces that most enthusiastically supported free trade. According to some Quebec officials, their provincial advocacy for free trade was truly instrumental in Canada's approval of NAFTA. In their view, considering the level of opposition in English Canada, NAFTA would not have been approved in Canada without Quebec's support.

The specific weight of the U.S. in the economies of Quebec and Mexico constitutes a latent obstacle to the forging of stronger economic ties between Quebec and Mexico. The U.S. is the most important trading partner for both Quebec and Mexico. In the 1980s, 80% of Quebec's exports and 75% of Mexican exports went to the U.S. (Smith, 1993: 253). The U.S. is involved in 40% of Quebec's direct foreign investment and 63% of Mexico's (Balthazar et al., 1993: 222; Cameron et al., 1993: 310). Trade between Canada and Mexico totals only 1% of trade between Canada and the U.S. In 1991, 1.8% of Quebec's imports came from Mexico and less than 0.5% of its exports went to Mexico. However, trade between Quebec and Mexico started to increase even before NAFTA was approved (see Table 1).

Thus, notwithstanding the weight of the U.S. in the economic foreign relations of both Quebec and Mexico, the potential for increasing trade links is significant. In 1992, trade between the two partners amounted to $108 million, a figure that was exceeded during the first three months of 1993 ($130 million). This last figure represented 16% of total trade between Mexico and Canada in the same period. Although Mexico still maintains a surplus in its trade with Quebec (approximately $50 million), Quebec exports have been growing; they increased by 175% during the first semester of 1994. In fact, in 1994, Mexico became Quebec's leading customer in Latin America, overtaking Brazil (*El Financiero*).

Mexican exports to Quebec have traditionally included automobiles, trucks, auto parts and oil products. In 1992 these goods constituted almost 80% of total Mexican exports to Quebec. Quebec exports to Mexico consist of aircraft materials, minerals and everday products (Ministère des Affaires internationales, 1993: 7). Quebec and Mexico will also profit by improving their direct trade links, since the U.S. re-exports almost $100 million of Quebec goods to Mexico (Méndez Lugo, 1994: 6).

TABLE 1
Quebec's Trade with Mexico, 1987-1992
(millions of Canadian dollars)

	Quebec exports	Quebec imports	Trade Balance
1987	68	240	-172
1988	45	199	-154
1989	110	171	-61
1990	149	227	-78
1991	88	440	-352
1992*	58	312	-254

* first 8 months

Source: Ministère des Affaires internationales du Québec, 1993.

Also, Quebec and Mexico have complementary rather than competitive economies, which increases the potential for trade exchanges. Mexico is competitive in products that are labour intensive and Quebec, like Canada, is competitive in products that require more capital than labour. Some areas where Quebec is already increasing its investment participation in Mexico are telecommunications, computer information, transportation, environmental assistance, hydroelectricity and financial services.

In fact, it is in these areas that Quebec companies have increased their investments or services in Mexico. Bombardier invested $71 million in its purchase of Constructora Nacional de Carros de Ferrocarril. It also bought Gráficas Monte Albán. In the textile sector, ten investment projects totalling $33.5 million have also been implemented (Arnulfo R. Gómez in Méndez Lugo, 1994: 9). Quebecor, the Caisse de Dépôt, and Cambior y Sotel are among other Quebec companies that have investment projects in Mexico. The Mouvement Desjardins has entered into agreements with SEDESOL to create a hundred savings co-operatives. In addition, Northern Telecom, SLR Telecom, Compositro and SNC-Lavalin, among others, have obtained contracts to serve Mexican companies. At the institutional level, in October 1992 Nacional Financiera announced its participation of $15 million in a $60 million Mexico-Quebec investment fund.

An area of potential cooperation between Quebec and Mexico is government support of small and medium-sized firms to encourage joint investment or trade projects. Between 1990 and 1993, 87 Quebec companies had invested a total of $430 million in Mexico. Many of these were small and medium-sized companies. In both Mexico and Quebec, small and medium-sized firms constitute the core of the industrial structures. Contrary to the situation prevailing in provinces such as Ontario, small and medium-sized firms in Quebec are not dependent on transnational corporations to any significant extent. In general, however, alliances between Mexican firms and transnational corporations prevent the former from absorbing new technology or technical experience. In contrast, Quebec's small and medium-sized firms, with their strong export orientation and their ready access to technology, provide their Mexican counterparts with the possibility of new business opportunities and more equal alliances with foreign investors (Méndez Lugo: 2-3). Quebec's Department of International Affairs has already said that its objective for the 1990s will be to bolster exports and joint-venture activities by small and medium-sized firms (Ministère des Affaires internationales, 1992: 12).

At the end of 1992, the Department of International Affairs took a concrete step in this direction when it launched a Quebec-Mexico Action Plan aimed at granting specific support to Quebec's businesses and institutions willing to increase their presence in Mexico. The plan covers four areas of activity: information on Mexico, through organization of events, publication of documents and videos and the creation of a direct phone line providing specific information about NAFTA and Mexican markets; promotion of Quebec products and services in the Mexican political, institutional and business environments, including the Mexican states; and technical and economic support to help Quebec's enterprises to adapt to the Mexican market. Finally, institutional and government relations will provide a framework for building technical, commercial and scientific alliances between Quebec and Mexican companies (Ministère des Affaires internationales, 1993: 77-78).

In the future, Mexico could join forces with Canada and Quebec to exert pressure on the U.S. to agree upon a North American code of subsidies and countervailing duties to help protect against the U.S.'s so-called "unfair trade practices." A likely area of disagreement between Quebec and Mexico is the former's proposal to establish a formal mechanism for provincial participation in the administration of NAFTA and in the dispute resolution mechanism, in particular for the areas of provincial jurisdiction. This proposal may create problems for the highly centralized Mexican federation.

The new reality, not only in North America but in the rest of the hemisphere, has prompted Quebec to view Mexico as a "privileged partner" (Ministère des Affaires internationales, 1992). The Enterprise of the Americas initiative, for example, obliges Quebec to turn its attention towards Latin America, especially in trade and investment. In this regard, Mexico's trade agreements with other Latin American partners is welcomed by Quebec because they enable it to use Mexico as a gateway to those markets.

Quebec's desire to establish transnational contacts is noteworthy as a result of some recent events in Quebec-Mexico relations. A majority of Quebec's international agreements in the last three decades have been concluded with non-sovereign states. As mentioned before, nearly 30 U.S. states have signed some type of agreement with Quebec, most of them on economic, commercial and transportation issues. This aspect of Quebec's foreign activities is beginning to emerge in Mexico. Although all formal relations take place with or through the Mexican federal government, in recent years the Quebec government has established cooperative exchanges and technical assistance on agriculture and livestock with a number of Mexican states, including Veracruz, Aguascalientes, Hidalgo, Puebla, Querétaro and Zacatecas (Méndez Lugo: 4). All this, of course, with the full consent of the Mexican federal government.

The context of greater economic integration in North America may well unleash pressures towards the fragmentation of nation-states. The process of political reform in Mexico that has led to the emergence of state governments in the hands of opposition political parties (for example, Baja California Norte and Chihuahua, which are Northern states bordering with the U.S.) might well reinforce that trend. However, it will take time for a more decentralized Mexican federation to permit the transnational aspect of Quebec's international activities to dominate in its relations with Mexico.

In addition to the impact of the integration dynamic in North America in terms of strenghtening the links between Quebec and Mexico, the possibility of a successful referendum on Quebec's sovereignty in 1995 or later is good reason to reflect on the consequences that such an event might have on the future of Quebec-Mexico relations. The following section attempts to do this.

TWO SCENARIOS FOR THE FUTURE OF QUEBEC-MEXICO RELATIONS

This section presents two scenarios for the future of Quebec-Mexico relations in the event that a change occurs in the international status of Quebec. They represent the two traditionally discussed options for an independent Quebec: full independence and sovereignty-association. A brief reference to the status-quo is made in the concluding remarks. The main and general features of each presumed international status are outlined to assess their effect on the bilateral relation with Mexico.

For the sake of the argument below, it is important to stress that the complexity of the matter compels us to make some assumptions. Each of the options described here would come after resolution of Quebec's situation within the Canadian federation. No considerations are made here with regard to the transition period that would naturally follow Quebec's decision to declare sovereignty. The discussion below assumes that the level of conflict and cooperation in the aftermath of separation would vary according to the transition period. In general, the assumption is made that full independence would mean a lower level of cooperation between Quebec and the rest of Canada, while sovereignty-association would mean a higher level.

Full Independence

In this scenario, the main assumption is that efforts by Quebec to negotiate with the rest of Canada would fail, and therefore Quebec would make a unilateral declaration of independence. A certain degree of cooperation with the rest of Canada would be possible through the signature of limited agreements on topics of mutual interest, such as transit of goods and people from West to East Canada, for example, but the creation of supranational institutions would be excluded.

The immediate benefit for Quebec would be total recovery of the powers actually held by or shared with the federal government.[20] In its newly-acquired areas of jurisdiction, the new sovereign state would have full authority to enter into agreements with other sovereign states. Quebec's new status would oblige its government to re-negotiate Canada's existing bilateral and multilateral treaties and apply for admission to international organizations. Independence would obviously mean full autonomy in the area of foreign policy and a broadening of Quebec's state authority.

In a scenario of full independence, the Mexican government's attitude would be very similar to that which the U.S. has said it would follow (Lemco, 1992: 123-134). First, in accordance with the Doctrina Estrada (see above), it would adopt a very cautious stand. Then, following international recognition by major powers, it would proceed to grant recognition to the new state. Once the new independent country is recognized, the future of Mexico-Quebec relations will depend, like any other bilateral relationship, on how much the two governments would be able to capitalize on areas of potential cooperation and minimize the negative effect of issues that may be problematic.

Social, Cultural and Language Issues

Despite the fact that Quebec already has exclusive authority and control over most social and cultural policies, the majority of its foreign partners seem very cautious about establishing direct formal contacts, even France. As already mentioned, this is particularly true in the case of Mexico. Mexican officials at different levels and from different ministries are especially wary of acting in a way that could be seen as intruding in another country's domestic affairs.[21] If Quebec gains formal independence, these barriers would naturally disappear.

---

20. We refer here essentially to the powers included in article 91 of the Constitution Act of 1982, including regulation of Trade and Commerce, Currency and Coinage, Interest, Banking, Defence, Fisheries and Navigation, Unemployment Insurance, Indians and Lands reserved for Indians, Naturalization and Aliens and Criminal Law. Immigration, agriculture and some social services are areas of shared power. (These are the most relevant for the purposes of this exercise.)

21. Interview with a civil servant from the Quebec Delegation in Mexico City.

Should this happen, the Quebec government could be expected to adopt a much more aggressive policy on cultural and social cooperation with Mexico.

As it has done with "La Francophonie," Quebec would probably turn to its distinctive culture to foster the creation of special arrangements in Latin America, including an association of non-Anglo-Saxon countries. In fact, in approaching the Latin American governments, Quebec has already used the term "latinidad" to stress the cultural affinities of countries speaking Roman languages – French and Spanish. Although this may provide a way of gaining a presence in Latin America, "latinidad" is not "francophonie." It is not cen-tred around the defence and promotion of a language. Speaking a Roman language is not the essential condition for belonging to the Latin American community. Many other factors are involved, including geographic continuity and common history. Language protection may be a concern for some Latin American governments, but it certainly does not have the same priority for them as it does for Quebec.

In contrast to "La Francophonie," Quebec's association with Latin America will not automatically translate into recognition of Quebec as a full member of the Latin American construct. On the one hand, a large number of Latin American organizations endorse goals that go far beyond culture or lan-guage. On the other hand, Mexico may not welcome Quebec acting as a bridge between Latin America and North America, since it may wish to reserve that role for itself. Thus, Quebec may discover that the concept of "latinidad" would not help it to extablish a "distinct" relationship or special alliances with Latin American countries. It could, however, be conducive to building very fruitful cultural and other types of exchanges. A closer relationship with Mexico would also help Quebec to consolidate its presence in the southern hemisphere.

Closer cultural cooperation between Quebec and Mexico in North America may also bring mutual benefits. It is well-known that the U.S. has a vast community of legal and illegal Mexican immigrants, especially if U.S. citi-zens of Mexican origin are taken into account. Today Mexico maintains a close relationship with that community, even though it has restricted its active sup-port to demanding protection of the human rights of its citizens living in the U.S.[22] If Mexico decides to extend its actions to protect the Spanish language and the Mexican culture outside its own borders, this may lead to closer coop-eration with, or at least better understanding of, a sovereign Quebec regarding the survival of cultural minorities. From this perspective, it is not impossible that Mexico would ally itself with a sovereign Quebec to create a non-Anglo-Saxon front for the defence of language and other minority rights. They could

---

22. This refers mainly to the defence of the rights of illegal immigrants, as in the case of oppo-sition to California's 187 Proposal and the Mexican government's condemnation of the death penalty for its nationals in the U.S.

even push for the creation of a North American mechanism to protect these rights.

The possibility of Mexico seeking cooperation from Quebec on these issues may not be restricted to Mexico's relations with the U.S., but may also extend to the design of specific policies within its own borders. For almost 30 years, Mexico has given special attention to its northern borderland.[23] Federal policies have been aimed at protecting Mexican culture in the area. The natural flow of goods and people across the border has facilitated, among other things, a slow but persistent penetration of the English language into the northern states of Mexico. It is feasible that in the near future Mexico would confront the need to adopt regulatory measures to protect the Spanish language in that region. Despite the difference of circumstances, Quebec's experience in protecting culture and language might become very useful to Mexico.

Full sovereignty for Quebec would also mean recovering total control over immigration. The migrant workers agreement between Canada and Mexico has been highly successful and it signals a likely area of future bilateral cooperation. This contrasts with the problems existing between the U.S. and Mexico on the issue. An independent Quebec would want to maintain this area of cooperation with the Mexican government, but it might need to sign a new agreement.

Under the provisions of Article 91 of the British North America Act, "Indians, and Indian Affairs" fall under the sole jurisdiction of the federal government. Full sovereignty in Quebec would exacerbate the existing tensions with the aboriginal communities. Quebec's claim to self-determination on the basis of being a distinct people would be echoed by Native communities,[24] whose demands for self-determination could not legitimately be disregarded. Most northern Indians speak English and might decide to remain part of Canada. This would add to the complexity of defining borders between Quebec and Canada (McNeil, 1992; Lemco: 65). Quebec's aboriginal communities may try to take their case before international or American human rights authorities, as they did with the Great Whale issue (Balthazar et al., 1993: 104).

Canada and Quebec are not the only ones facing the challenge of redefining their relations with their aboriginal communities. Since January 1994, a major portion of the Mexican state of Chiapas has been controlled militarily by the mostly Indian Ejército Zapatista de Liberación Nacional. The Mexican government is therefore likely to sympathize with Quebec's defence of its own territorial integrity. Collaboration between Quebec and Mexico would not be

---

23.   Since the mid-sixties, a multipurpose policy program known as the "Programa fronterizo" has been operating in the northern fringe of the country. It covers aspects of industrial development, migration, social welfare and the defence of Mexican culture.

24.   For a good illustration of the First Nations's position, see Turpel, 1992.

restricted to the defence of territorial integrity. It may also extend to the creation of schemes providing positive solutions to the demands of Indian communities, be it in terms of environmental protection or more general social development.

Finally, in Quebec the state has historically played a key role in fostering economic and social development. Quebec's position in the Canada-U.S. Free Trade Agreement and in NAFTA was to provide governments with sufficient freedom of action to fulfil their goals of modernization and development (Quebec: 15). Although a subsidies code was not included in either the FTA or NAFTA, it is likely to become an issue of future negotiation in the North American context. The U.S. is likely to increase pressure for its partners to accept its views regarding subsidies, or else to continue unilaterally with its unfair trade practices, as the softwood lumber and Honda cases show (Lazar, 1992: 143).

Under Quebec's present status as a province of Canada, government intervention in the economy is relatively well-protected from direct U.S. pressures. However, this will change with independence. Quebec might be forced to re-negotiate its terms of entry to NAFTA, and its negotiating position would thus be reduced. A good indicator of Quebec's vulnerability vis-a-vis the U.S. is the latter's opposition to the James Bay II power project, on the basis that it represents subsidized electricity exports to the U.S. An alliance between an independent Quebec and Canada on this issue would not be automatic. Although it is possible to think that Quebec, Canada and Mexico might form a common front to negotiate an advantageous subsidies code with the U.S. – one that would permit government intervention to implement industrial policies – and exclusion from Section 301 of the 1974 U.S. Trade Act, which extends the concept of extraterritoriality of U.S. legislation beyond U.S. corporations (Lazar, 1992). Quebec might also discover a natural ally in Mexico in its efforts to prevent the U.S. from using environmental protection as a barrier to free trade.

Economic and Trade Issues

In this scenario, full independence would mean that Quebec would recover all powers related to trade and finance. However, in the context of North American integration, it is hard to imagine how Quebec could gain more room to manoeuvre on monetary policy, even if a reform of the Bank of Canada were implemented.[25]

---

25. If Quebec decides to have its own currency and its own central bank, it will have to ensure that its exchange rate is close to par with Canada's to minimize its obligations on the debt market. It could avoid that problem by choosing to keep the Canadian dollar, but it would not then have any independence on monetary policy. A reformed Bank of Canada may give Quebec a say in monetary policy decisions. The problem here is to obtain the agreement of the other provinces for such unequal representation in favour of Quebec (Chorney: 163).

In terms of economic policy, apart from the issues of certainty and confidence referred to above, there would be very little change from the present situation. A common argument put forward frequently by Quebec nationalists is that an independent or associated Quebec would have more resources for the promotion of Quebec's economic interests abroad. With full responsibility for the promotion of its own interests, Quebec would achieve its foreign policy goals more efficiently than the federal government. Quebec would not have to spend time trying to get Ottawa's approval for international agreements, for example.[26] But at the same time, a new independent Quebec would probably have to dedicate more resources to more urgent priorities. The creation of even a small army, for example, would initially cost Quebec approximately $6 to $10 billion, plus an annual maintemamce cost of $6 billion (Lemco, 1992: 91). Also, spending on international activities may will be restricted by the urgent need to clean up its public finances (Quebec has one of the highest debt burdens of all Canada's provinces) (Chipello and Urquart, 1994).

On the trade front, Quebec may encounter additional problems with its new North American partner. A few days after the September 1994 victory of the Parti québécois in the provincial elections, the Mexican Ambassador to Ottawa declared that an independent Quebec would not automatically be admitted to NAFTA. Ambassador Fuentes-Beráin justified his remarks by saying that "there is an accession clause for new countries into NAFTA. So a new country that wanted to be included would have to do like any other country and meet the procedures that are established for those countries" (*The Gazette*, 1994). Some Quebec officials were outraged by these declarations, which they describe as ingratitude in the face of Quebec's unwavering support for NAFTA. Quebec, according to some, was the most important ally of NAFTA, with Mexico. Fuentes' declarations may not have been a very diplomatic gesture towards Quebec nationalists, but they reflect a reality that surpasses diplomatic forms and even sympathies or courtesies towards the federal government in Canada.

Mexico may have good reasons for not opening NAFTA to other members, at least for the time being. NAFTA is a select club whose privileges are enjoyed only by members. Many countries have expressed a wish to join the club, but Mexico is not anxious for that to happen. Instead, in the last couple of years, and taking advantage of its participation in NAFTA, Mexico's strategy has been to establish free trade arrangements with a number of Latin American partners. It thus projects the image of a country trying to become a

---

26. According to some Quebec officials, the reluctance of the Mexican authorities to deal directly with the government of Quebec is an obstacle that delays the signing of some agreements – for example, the agreement on educational exchanges which took from March of 1993, when MAIICC presented its proposal to SRE, to October 1994.

broker between its Latin American and North American partners.[27] The present situation gives Mexico the benefits of "exclusive membership" in NAFTA, a membership that also allows it to flex its potential influence over the admission of other partners. Mexico would not want to lose those benefits.

Mexico's opposition to Quebec's automatic admission to NAFTA is based on the precedent that this would set for accepting other members. One way of avoiding this would be to put Quebec on the waiting list, probably after Chile. Mexico would then defend its position by arguing that it is acting strictly in accordance with NAFTA's rules of accession.

Finally, Mexico, like the other two present members of NAFTA, could be expected to try to take advantage of the weaker bargaining position of an independent Quebec to impose stricter entry conditions.[28]

Outside the North American context, it is interesting to note the prospects for an independent Quebec within the Organization of American States (O.A.S.). Without any doubt, Mexico is shifting towards a more open political system, although at a fairly slow pace. Notwithstanding this, it has become relatively isolated in organizations like the O.A.S. on the basis of human rights and democracy issues. By defending the principles of non-intervention and self-determination, Mexico has opposed resolutions aimed at allowing O.A.S. participation in enhancing the democratic processes of Latin America. In the event that an independent Quebec became a member of the O.A.S., it is almost certain that it would adopt a very similar position to that maintained by Canada today.[29] This could become a source of tension between Quebec and Mexico, unless of course the Mexican government modified its own position.

Sovereignty-association for Quebec

Although it is difficult to know exactly what the term "sovereignty-association" means (Lemco, 1992: 58-67), for the purposes of this paper it is defined as including the existence of some form of institutional cooperation between Quebec and the rest of Canada. It certainly requires the rest of Canada to

---

27. It is widely accepted that the United States does not need a broker in its relation with Latin American countries. However, it is in Mexico's interest to take advantage of its privileged access to the North American market and to gain influence in the southern part of the continent.

28. As stated by John Ciaccia, Quebec's Minister of International Affairs, NAFTA fulfils all the basic demands and expectations of the government of Quebec (Ministère des Affaires internationales, 1993: 13).

29. An example of this is Canada's support of the O.A.S. resolution in Nassau, in May of 1992, which proposes the expulsion of any member that, according to the O.A.S. Secretary General, does not show full respect for democratic institutions.

speak with one voice and remain willing to negotiate with Quebec on a one-to-one basis. In contrast to full independence, sovereignty-association would require an independent Quebec to share common institutions with the rest of Canada in policy areas such as banking, international trade, assets and debt, and defence. Most likely, these supranational institutions would be under the supervision of a Parliament or Council with equal representation for both Quebec and Canada.

From this point of view, sovereignty-association brings more benefits for Quebec. Quebec would fulfil its goal of political autonomy while keeping the advantages of an economic association with Canada. Quebec and Canada would have, on the one hand, the right to veto economic policies now under federal jurisdiction (customs, tariffs, monetary policy, taxation, etc.) and, on the other, Quebec would maintain enough autonomy to pursue an independent foreign policy in all non-economic areas. Consequently, it could seek to become a full member of all non-economic multilateral international organizations. It is less certain how representation within economic organizations such as the GATT would be managed. The dynamic of two voices, two vetoes complicates this latter issue, especially since in many international organizations there are no clear-cut differences between their economic and non-economic orientations.

This double representation would make the sovereignty-association scenario more unstable than full independence from the point of view of other countries. The double veto on economic matters, including international issues, which demands permanent negotiation between Quebec and Canada, would create a lack of confidence on the part of negotiating partners. If Canada and Quebec were to share the same trade policy, making decisions via common institutions but acknowledging separation of powers in areas such as labour and the environment, Quebec could, for example, demand full sovereign participation in the North American Environmental and Labour Commissions and not in the Free Trade Commission. It is hard to see why Mexico should agree to Canada and Quebec having separate voices in some NAFTA commissions and not in others. Mexico would also be reluctant to accept a situation that would introduce an asymmetrical element into the new power configuration of North America and set a precedent in terms of international representation that may not be in accordance with Mexico's centralized federation.

One foreseeable benefit for Mexico in a sovereignty-association scenario would be the possibility of obtaining support against trade sanctions based on environmental protection issues. The vulnerability of Quebec's hydroelectric projects would find an echo in Mexico's border observance of environmental regulations. Even in this situation, the grounds for a mutually beneficial alliance are thin, given the growing consensus in the international community regarding environmental protection.

In other aspects of bilateral relations with Mexico, it is to be expected that sovereignty-association would present a similar situation to the full independence scenario. The main difference would stem from the impact on Mexican perceptions of the fact that it would be dealing with a country holding a peculiar and probably unclear status rather than a fully independent country or provincial government. An associated Quebec might not be able to project itself with as much autonomy and effectiveness as an independent Quebec. Earlier, we speculated about the possibility of an alliance of non-Anglo-Saxon North American countries (Quebec and Mexico) on cultural and language issues. In sovereignty-association, that possibility would not emerge so clearly. The cultural change in the North American landscape prompted by full sovereignty, which would mean four countries and three languages, would not be as strong in the sovereignty-association scenario. However, this distinction is a matter of degree, because Quebec's ability to continue to project its distinctiveness through specific projects with Mexico would depend on Mexico's perceptions of Quebec. In a sovereignty-association scenario, Mexico might perceive Quebec as an inherent part of the Canadian entity rather than a separate and potential ally on cultural issues.

CONCLUSION

As mentioned in the introduction to this chapter, the prospects of an independent Quebec remain uncertain. The scenarios here described are merely speculations as to how the Quebec-Mexico relationship might develop in the event of independence or sovereignty-association. The dynamic of greater integration in North America is already changing the nature of international relations. Even without the prospects of sovereignty, relations between Quebec and Mexico will certainly intensify in the years to come. Naturally, greater autonomy for Quebec in foreign policy areas would intensify the pace and diversify the type of such relations. If Quebec remains within Canada, exchanges between Quebec and Mexico will continue to focus on education and culture, but more particularly on the economic domain.

A better understanding in Mexico of the peculiar status of Quebec might help to overcome some barriers that, in the past, have prevented more innovative handling of the relationship between the two partners. This would not necessarily mean a direct confrontation with the Canadian federal government. Other factors helping to optimize the relationship between Quebec and Mexico will emerge from changes in the Mexican context, although this may not take place in the short term. Such changes include a new Mexican stand on foreign policy with regard to non-intervention, leading to a more flexible interpretation of that principle; progress towards a more democratic political system; and a further reduction of the centralized nature of the Mexican federation.

BIBLIOGRAPHY

Books, Articles, and Official Documents

BALTHAZAR, Louis, Louis BÉLANGER, Gordon MACE et al., *Trente ans de politique extérieure du Québec. 1960-1990* (Quebec: Centre québécois de relations internationales, Les éditions du Septentrion, 1993).

BROSSARD, Jacques, André PARTY and Elisabeth WEISER, *Les pouvoirs extérieurs du Québec* (Montréal: Les Presses de l'Université de Montréal, 1967).

CAMERON, Maxwell A., Lorraine EDEN and Maureen APPEL MOLOT, "El libre comercio en América del Norte: cooperación y conflicto en las relaciones México-Canadá," in Gustavo Vega Cánovas, ed., *Mexico, Estados Unidos, Canadá. 1991-1992* (Mexico: El Colegio de Mexico, 1993, pp. 303-326).

CHORNEY, Harold, "Dividing the Debt: More than Bean Counting," in Daniel Drache and Roberto Perin, eds., *Negotiating with a Sovereign Quebec* (Toronto: James Lorimer & Co., Publishers, 1992, pp. 156-170).

LAZAR, Fred, "The Case for a Common Trade Strategy with a Sovereign Quebec," in Daniel Drache and Roberto Perin, eds., *Negotiating with a Sovereign Quebec* (Toronto: James Lorimer & Co., Publishers, 1992, pp. 139-155).

LEMCO, Johathan, *Turmoil in the Peaceable Kingdom: The Quebec Sovereignty Movement and Its Implications for Canada and the United States* (Canada-U.S. Outlook Series, vol. 3, no. 1/2, Washington, National Planning Association, 1992).

MCNEIL, Kent, "Aboriginal Nations and Quebec's Boundaries: Canada Couldn't Give What It Didn't Have," in Daniel Drache and Roberto Perin, eds., *Negotiating with a Sovereign Quebec* (Toronto: James Lorimer & Co., Publishers, 1992, pp. 107-124).

MEDINA XOCHICHUA, Oscar J., "Las relaciones México-Quebec frente al Acuerdo de Libre Comercio de Norteamérica," *Norteamérica: Relaciones políticas, espacio y sociedad*, Mexico: Coordinación de Posgrado de la ENEP-Acatlán/UNAM, forthcoming.

MÉNDEZ LUGO, Bernardo, "Alianzas estratégicas entre industrias pequeñas y medianas de Mexico y Canadá: el caso de la provincia de Quebec," Conference Document presented at "Canadá-Mexico: a 50 anos de relaciones diplomaticas," Mexico: UNAM, April 29th, 1994.

MINISTÈRE DES AFFAIRES INTERNATIONALES DU QUÉBEC, *Québec y el Tratado de Libre Comercio de América del Norte* (Quebec: Gouvernement du Québec: 1993).

MINISTÈRE DES AFFAIRES INTERNATIONALES DU QUÉBEC, *Le Québec et l'interdépendance, le monde pour horizon* (Quebec: Gouvernement du Québec, 1992).

NOSSAL, Kim Richard, *The Politics of Canadian Foreign Policy* (Ontario: Prentice Hall Canada Inc., 1985).

SMITH, Clint E., "Mexico y Estados Unidos: hacia una alianza económica," in Gustavo Vega Cánovas, ed., *Mexico, Estados Unidos, Canadá. 1991-1992* (Mexico: El Colegio de Mexico, 1993, 249-286).

TURPEL, Mary Ellen, "Does the Road to Quebec Sovereignty Run through Aboriginal Territory?," in Daniel Drache and Roberto Perin, eds., *Negotiating with a Sovereign Quebec* (Toronto: James Lorimer & Co., Publishers, 1992, pp. 93-106).

VEREA CAMPOS, Mónica, "La política migratoria canadiense," in Mónica Verea C. and Teresa Gutiérrez H., eds., *Canadá en Transición* (Mexico: Centro de Investigaciones sobre América del Norte, UNAM, 1994)

Newspaper Articles

CHIPPELLO, Christopher and John URQUHART, "Parti Québécois's Slim Margin of Victory In Quebec Election Signals Rocky Times," *The Wall Street Journal*, September 14th, 1994.

El Financiero, Editorial Note, September 21st, 1994.

FARNSWORTH, Clyde H., "Yoked in Twin Solitudes: Canada's Two Cultures," *New York Times*, September 18th, 1994.

GIBBENS, Robert, "Quebec Business Warns against Splitting," *Financial Times*, September 14th, 1994.

The Gazette, September 20th, 1994.

The Impact of NAFTA on Quebec Economy and Society

6

The Impact of the Free Trade Agreement on Bilateral Trade between Quebec and the United States

Gilles Duruflé and **Benoît Tétrault**
Caisse de dépôt et placement du Québec

This study was inspired by a previous study carried out by Daniel Schwanen and published by the C.D. Howe Institute which provided an in-depth analysis of the changes in bilateral trade between Canada and the United States since the implementation of the Free Trade Agreement on January 1, 1989. Two major conclusions of Mr. Schwanen's study were, first, that there has been a definite increase in bilateral trade between Canada and the United States in products liberalized under the Free Trade Agreement, be they exports or imports; and second, that the liberalized products which have benefited the most from the increase in exports to the United States are high-value-added products, and the sectors which stand to suffer the most from the increase in imports are the traditional sectors. In comparison with the economics of Canada and, in particular, Ontario, Quebec is over-represented in the traditional sectors and under-represented in the high-value-added sectors. This may mean that Quebec will find itself very much at a disadvantage as a result of the implementation of the Free Trade Agreement. In their study, Duruflé and Tétrault tried to verify this assumption by reproducing Mr. Schwanen's study and extending it to include sectorial trade balances and shipments.

One of their main conclusions confirms for Quebec the main conclusion of the Canadian study, namely a very substantial increase in bilateral trade in liberalized products from 1988 to 1992. Another important conclusion is that, for each liberalized sector, the bilateral balances have improved both for high-value-added sectors and the traditional or "soft" sectors.

*This last finding contradicts one of the conclusions of the study on Canada, which identified an **inter-sectorial** differentiation between the high-value-added sectors and the traditional sectors. The present study shows, instead, that all liberalized sectors seem to have taken advantage of liberalized trade. All statistics point to strong **intra-sectorial** discrimination between companies which were able to take advantage of the increase in exports to the United States and those which were confined to a sluggish domestic market and forced to compete with the increase in imports from the U.S. following implementation of the Agreement.*

INTRODUCTION

A recent study made by Daniel Schwanen and published by the C.D. Howe Institute provides an in-depth analysis of changes in bilateral trade between Canada and the United States since the Free Trade Agreement was implemented on January 1, 1989. It divides the products traded into two main categories:

- liberalized products, in other words those on which customs tariffs have been lowered under the Free Trade Agreement;[1]

- non-liberalized products, which are the other products, with the exception of petroleum products, automotive products and "special transactions,"[2] whose behaviour is different and which are dealt with separately.

---

1. The study does not take into account the other forms of liberalization that may result from dropping or eliminating non-tariff barriers.

   The appendix contains the list of liberalized products using the classification adopted by SEG (Summary of Exports Groupings) and SIG (Summary of Imports Groupings) at the five-digit level (see note 4). The list was drawn up by D. Schwanen, using various measurements set out in the Free Trade Agreement, on a product-by-product basis. The measurements are expressed according to customs classification, often on a more detailed level than five digits. Thus the correspondence is not perfect. Still, it is possible to determine trends whose convergence appears significant. Another limitation of the study is that it does not take into account differences in tariff-reduction scope and speed according to product. This field is open to other researchers who would like to take up the torch.

2. Exceptional transactions whose content is not disclosed.

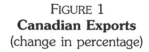

FIGURE 1
Canadian Exports
(change in percentage)

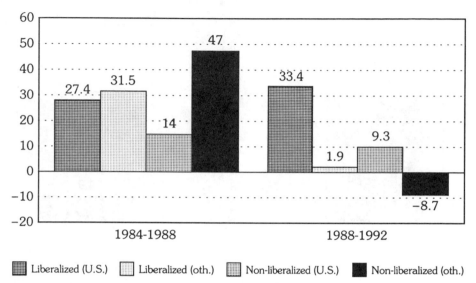

Source: D. Schwanen, "A Growing Success: Canada's Performance under Free Trade," 1993

On the basis of this analysis, the study by D. Schwanen draws the following conclusions, which are summarized in Figures 1 and 2:

– A comparison of the figures for the period from 1984 to 1988 and the period from 1988 to 1992 shows that in both cases there was a definite increase in bilateral trade between Canada and the United States in products liberalized under the Free Trade Agreement, be they imports or exports;

– Bilateral trade in non-liberalized products did not increase. In fact, it decreased;

– Nor did trade in liberalized products with the rest of the world increase; rather, it too decreased;

– The increase cannot be explained by macro-economic variables, such as growth in the domestic demand of the recipient country or exchange rate variations, since domestic demand, both in the United States and in Canada, was clearly weaker from 1988 to 1992 than from 1984 to

FIGURE 2
Canadian Imports
(change in percentage)

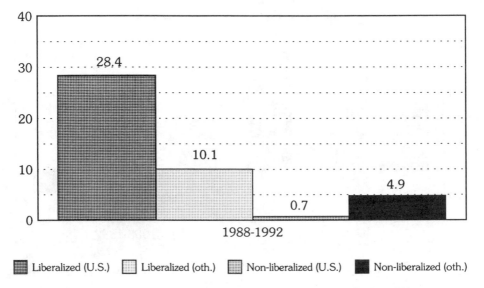

| | Liberalized (U.S.) | | Liberalized (oth.) | | Non-liberalized (U.S.) | | Non-liberalized (oth.) |

Source: D. Schwanen, "A Growing Success: Canada's Performance under Free Trade," 1993

1988 (Figure 3) and the average exchange rate for the Canadian dollar was at comparable levels in 1984 and 1988 and slightly higher in 1992 (Figure 4).[3]

- Thus it appears justifiable to attribute the increase mainly to the liberalization of trade in these products introduced by the Free Trade Agreement;

- D. Schwanen pursues his study on a sectorial level, stressing that the liberalized products that benefited the most from the increase in exports to the United States are high-value-added products (office and tele-communications equipment, industrial machinery, etc.), whereas the sectors that suffered the most from the increase in imports are the traditional sectors (furniture, textiles, clothing and food).

---

3. Taking into account that exchange rate fluctuations affect bilateral trade only after a certain period has elapsed (usually estimated at eight quarters in the case of Canada), the fact that the external value of the Canadian dollar, expressed in U.S. dollars, was on average substantially lower from 1985 to 1988 than from 1989 to 1992 should have stimulated Canadian exports to the United States during the first period and hindered them during the second. But, for liberalized products, the growth of exports was definitely more sustained during the second period than during the first.

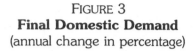

FIGURE 3
Final Domestic Demand
(annual change in percentage)

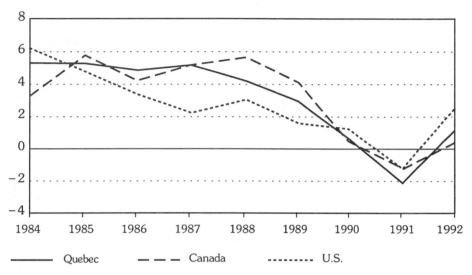

Source: Statistics Canada

Presented as such, the last conclusion has troublesome implications for Quebec's economy. In relation to the economy of Canada as a whole, and particularly in relation to Ontario's economy, Quebec has historically been over-represented in traditional sectors (furniture, textiles, clothing and food) and under-represented in high-value-added sectors (office and telecommunications equipment and industrial machinery (Table 1). The conclusion that D. Schwanen draws in his study therefore appears to suggest that application of the Free Trade Agreement could place Quebec's economy at a significant disadvantage.

To verify this assumption, we have reproduced the study made by the C.D. Howe Institute for Quebec, using the same methodology,[4] and we have pursued the sectorial analysis by studying changes in trade balances for certain sectors and by comparing changes in foreign trade with changes in manufacturing shipments.

---

4. To do so, we used data from the Bureau de la statistique du Québec (BSQ), which uses the same foreign trade classification as D. Schwanen. The SEG and SIG classification has the advantage of reflecting real trade flows in a fairly precise fashion. Still, the export classification differs slightly from the import classification and both differ from the industrial classification used for shipments. These differences introduce a certain element of imprecision with respect to trade balances. Still, one can obtain certain approximations whose changes over time are significant.

   The study by the C.D. Howe Institute also provides a few indications regarding trade in services. Unfortunately, this type of statistical information, drawn from the balance of payments, does not exist for Quebec.

FIGURE 4
External Value of the Canadian Dollar
(quarterly data in $U.S.)

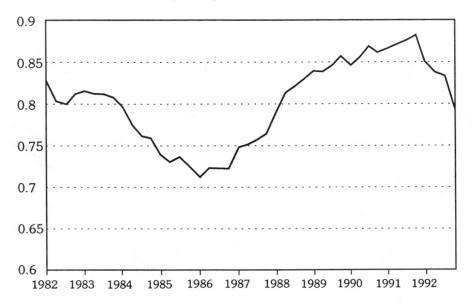

Source: Statistics Canada

TABLE 1
Structure of Manufacturing Sector Based on 1990 GDP

Sector	Canada	Ontario	Quebec
Total manufacturing sector	100%	100%	100%
Furniture	1.9%	2.0%	2.4%
Textiles	2.2%	1.8%	3.8%
Clothing	2.8%	1.5%	6.0%
Food and beverages	13.6%	12.2%	13.5%
Electrical and electronic products	7.9%	9.6%	7.5%
Industrial machinery	4.3%	4.7%	3.1%

Source: Statistics Canada

As we shall see, contrary to expectations, it appears that the increase in bilateral trade in the liberalized sectors is even more pronounced in Quebec than in Canada, principally with respect to exports, and that its impact is broadly positive for Quebec, even more so than for Canada as a whole, both overall and for each sector. Still, this does not exclude the fact that, within each sector, there is an increasing differentiation between the "winners," which were able to take advantage of the increase in exports, and the "losers," which were confined to a domestic market characterized by slow growth and increasing competition from imports.

GENERAL CHARACTERISTICS OF QUEBEC'S FOREIGN TRADE

In 1992, Quebec's GDP was 22.9% of Canada's, while its exports and imports totalled 17.7% and 19.5%, respectively, of their Canadian equivalents. Quebec's under-representation, especially in exports, is due mainly to automotive-related exports and imports and to oil and gas exports, which are concentrated in Ontario and the West. If liberalized products alone are taken into account, and they are the focus of this study, then Quebec's share is 22.9% of exports and 18.0% of imports.

As for the origin or the destination of trade, in 1992 76.9% of all Canada's exports went to the United States, as opposed to 76.3% of Quebec's. If liberalized products alone are taken into account, these shares are, respectively, 69.3% for Canada and 77.9% for Quebec. The concentration on the United States is therefore higher in Quebec, so that Quebec's share of Canadian exports of liberalized products to the United States is 25.7%.

For imports, however, the United States' share of total imports is 65.2% for Canada and 44.5% for Quebec. For liberalized products alone, these proportions are 63.0% and 39.5%, respectively. The concentration on the United States is therefore much weaker in Quebec than in the rest of Canada, and Quebec's share of Canadian imports of liberalized products from the United States is 11.3%.

Similarly, in 1992 liberalized products represented 61.5% of Quebec's exports to the United States, as opposed to 41.8% for Canada, and 48.8% of Quebec's imports from the United States, as opposed to 57.6% for Canada. As a result, the trade balance for liberalized products showed a surplus for Quebec ($2.9 billion in 1988 and $6.5 billion in 1992), whereas Canada as a whole had a deficit of $6.1 billion in 1988 and $5.9 billion in 1992 (Tables 2 to 5 and Appendices A to D).

Finally, in 1992 Quebec's total trade balance showed a deficit of $1.6 billion, whereas Canada had a surplus of $6.3 billion. Still, with the United States, as a result of the differentiated concentration phenomena that we have just described, Quebec had a trade surplus of $7.9 billion and Canada, $22.1 billion. Quebec's surplus with the United States thus represented 36% of the Canadian total (Appendices A and B).

TABLE 2
Quebec – Total Products
(dollars in millions)

	Change from 1984 to 1988	Change from 1988 to 1992	Proportion based on destination in 1992 (%)
Total trade			
exports	29.9%	20.7%	100
imports	28.6%	16.3%	100
trade balance[5]	$(316)	$620	
United States			
exports	30.5%	22.2%	76.3
imports	13.1%	11.1%	44.5
trade balance	$2,639	$2,498	
Other countries			
exports	28.2%	15.9%	23.7
imports	46.2%	20.9%	55.5
trade balance	$(2,955)	$(1,879)	

Source: Appendix A

TABLE 3
Canada – Total Products
(dollars in millions)

	Change from 1984 to 1988	Change from 1988 to 1992	Proportion based on destination in 1992 (%)
Total trade			
exports	23.2%	14.4%	100
imports	—	12.8%	100
trade balance	—	$2,627	
United States			
exports	18.7%	20.7%	76.9
imports	—	11.9%	65.2
trade balance	—	$10,126	
Other countries			
exports	37.4%	−2.5%	23.1
imports	—	14.6%	34.8
trade balance	—	$(7,500)	

Source: Appendix B

---

5.   Difference between the balance for the final year and that for the initial year.

TABLE 4
Quebec – Total Liberalized Products
(dollars in millions)

	Change from 1984 to 1988	Change from 1988 to 1992	Proportion based on destination in 1992 (%)
Total trade			
exports	32.0%	37.6%	100
imports	44.7%	6.4%	100
trade balance	$(1,696)	$3,532	
United States			
exports	36.4%	43.3%	77.9
imports	25.2%	3.9%	39.5
trade balance	$1,162	$3,628	
Other countries			
exports	20.3%	20.7%	22.1
imports	61.5%	8.1%	60.5
trade balance	$(2,858)	$(95)	

Source: Appendix C

TABLE 5
Canada – Total Liberalized Products
(dollars in millions)

	Change from 1984 to 1988	Change from 1988 to 1992	Proportion based on destination in 1992 (%)
Total trade			
exports	28.9%	21.8%	100
imports	–	20.9%	100
trade balance	–	$(2,432)	
United States			
exports	27.4%	33.4%	69.3
imports	–	28.4%	63.0
trade balance	–	$155	
Other countries			
exports	31.5%	1.9%	30.7
imports	–	10.1%	37.0
trade balance	–	$(2,587)	

Source: Appendix D

These simple structural data indicate that the impact of liberalized bilateral trade with the United States should, *a priori*, be more favourable to Quebec than to Canada as a whole.

THE INCREASE IN BILATERAL TRADE IN LIBERALIZED PRODUCTS BETWEEN QUEBEC AND THE UNITED STATES

Exports

Figure 5, which compares changes in Quebec's exports for 1984-1988 and 1988-1992, shows that they are very similar to those for Canadian exports (Figure 1):

- exports of liberalized products to the United States increased during the two periods, while U.S. domestic demand decreased;
- exports of non-liberalized products to the United States fell;
- the growth rate for exports of liberalized products to the rest of the world remained stable, whereas domestic demand was stronger than in the United States.

FIGURE 5
Quebec Exports
(change in percentage)

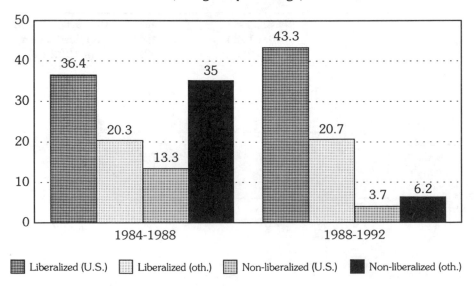

Source: Bureau de la statistique du Québec

From 1988 to 1992, the increase in exports of liberalized products to the United States was 43.3% in Quebec, compared with 33.4% in Canada.

Finally, Figure 6 shows that the increase during the period 1988-1992 is not the result of one exceptional year; rather, it is due to a gradual progression and an increasing discrepancy between the behaviour of liberalized products and that of non-liberalized products.

Thus in Quebec, as in Canada, there was an increase in exports of liberalized products to the United States, due essentially to the effects of the implementation of the Free Trade Agreement. This increase is slightly stronger in Quebec than in Canada.

FIGURE 6
Quebec Exports to the U.S.
(cumulative annual change in percentage)

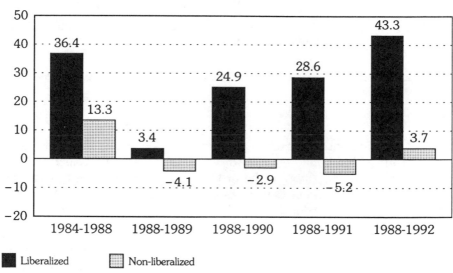

Source: Bureau de la statistique du Québec

Imports

As for imports (Figure 7), the effects of the Free Trade Agreement have also made themselves felt, although against the background of a very sharp decrease in imports; in other words imports of liberalized products from the United States fell over the two periods, but far less than imports of non-liberalized products from the United States or imports of liberalized and non-liberalized products from the rest of the world.

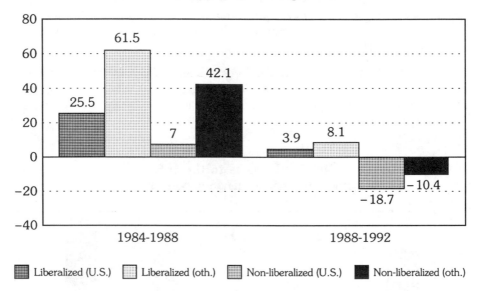

FIGURE 7
Quebec Imports
(change in percentage)

Source: Bureau de la statistique du Québec

Overall, imports of liberalized products from the United States increased by 3.9% in Quebec during the period, whereas in Canada the increase was 28.4% (Figure 2). The drop in the growth rate for imports was more pronounced in Quebec than in Canada as a whole, partly because of the larger drop in domestic demand in Quebec during the recession (Figure 3).

Figure 8, which presents the cumulative variations for Quebec, shows that this result is due to the very clear drop in Quebec's imports beginning in 1991 as a result of the recession. This drop was definitely more pronounced than in the rest of Canada.

Trade Balance

As a result, Quebec's trade balance for liberalized products with the United States improved by $3.6 billion (Table 4), whereas Canada's improved by only $155 million (Table 5).

This different evolution of the trade balance for liberalized products is due to the fact that:

- the growth of exports was stronger in Quebec (43.3% compared with 33.4%);

- the growth of imports was weaker in Quebec (3.9% compared with 28.4%);
- Quebec began with a trade surplus, which amplifies the positive effect on the balance when the growth rate for exports is greater than that for imports, whereas Canada began with a trade deficit, which produced the opposite effect.

It should also be noted that Quebec's trade balance with the rest of the world for the same products deteriorated by $95 million and that of Canada by $2.6 billion.

FIGURE 8
Quebec Imports from the U.S.
(cumulative annual change in percentage)

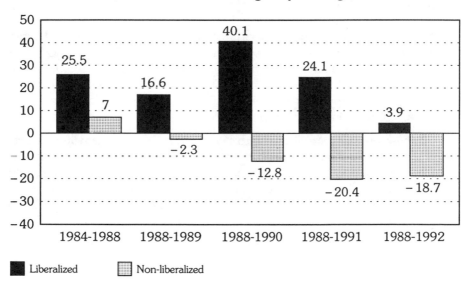

Source: Bureau de la statistique du Québec

Conclusions Regarding Bilateral Trade in Liberalized Products

In Quebec, as in Canada, application of the Free Trade Agreement accelerated bilateral trade in liberalized products, be they exports or imports.

The impact on exports was slightly more pronounced in Quebec than in Canada.

The impact on imports was offset in Quebec by a definite decrease in imports, beginning in 1991. This was due partly to the decrease in domestic demand which, during the recession, was greater in Quebec than in Canada as a whole.

The result in terms of the trade balance is clearly positive for Quebec, whereas it is almost neutral for Canada. Still, one must bear in mind that this positive result for Quebec is due partly to the pronounced weakness of domestic demand, which is anything but a positive phenomenon.

LIBERALIZED PRODUCTS: ANALYSIS BY PRODUCT

Resource-based Products and High-value-added Products

Appendix E presents Quebec's exports of liberalized products to the United States, arranging them in descending order of growth rate for the period from 1988 to 1992. The figures range from 180% for office and telecommunications equipment to –7% for chemicals. Still, the overwhelming majority of the rates are positive. Appendix F, drawn from the study by D. Schwanen, provides the equivalent information for Canada.

If these products are divided into two main categories, namely products based directly or indirectly on natural resources (wood products and paper, metallurgical and iron and steel products, chemicals, food and beverages), and other products (office and telecommunications equipment, precision equipment, machinery and tools), which are high-value-added products, the results are as follows (Table 6):

- in 1992 non-resource-based products represented 45% of Quebec's exports of liberalized products to the United States, compared with 35% of Canada's;
- the concentration of exports of these products to the United States was slightly greater in Quebec (82%) than in Canada (79%);
- the increase in exports of non-resource-based liberalized products to the United States from 1988 to 1992 was much greater in Quebec (90%) than in Canada (49%), whereas for resource-based products, the growth rate was greater in Canada (25%) than in Quebec (18%).

Thus the sectors producing liberalized high-value-added products in Quebec benefited greatly from liberalized trade with the United States. The increase in the exports of these products was much greater than for resource-based products, and it was definitely more sustained in Quebec than in the rest of Canada.

TABLE 6
Breakdown of Liberalized Products

	% of products liberalized in 1992		% exports to the U.S. in 1992		Change in exports to the U.S. 1988-1992	
	Canada	Quebec	Canada	Quebec	Canada	Quebec
Resource-based	65%	55%	64%	75%	25%	18%
Non-resource-based	35%	45%	79%	82%	49%	90%

Sources: Appendices E and F

Appendix G presents the same breakdown for Quebec's imports of liberalized products from the United States. The table shows that the growth rates are lower, since they range from 139.1% for meat and dairy products to −47.3% for office and telecommunications equipment. The traditional sectors, such as food, clothing and furniture, lead the way, whereas equipment and machinery recorded the lowest rates.

A more detailed analysis by product enables us to assess the impact of these changes in terms of trade balance and impact on production. For each of the products, the following indicators will be examined:

- the United States' share of Quebec exports and imports of the product;
- the growth rate for exports during the period 1988-1992: total, United States, other countries;
- the growth rate for imports during the period 1988-1992: total, United States, other countries;
- changes in the trade balance for the product during the period 1988-1992: total, United States, other countries;
- changes in shipments for this group of products during the period 1988-1990.[6] They can be broken down into deliveries by manufacturers that export outside Quebec and non-exporters.

---

6. The BSQ statistics on shipments per sector use SIC 80 industrial classification, which is not the case of export and import statistics. Thus the comparisons made in this study between these two types of data are to serve as illustrations and cannot constitute a direct measurement of a cause-and-effect link. Moreover, when this study was made, data on shipments were available only up to 1990.

Textiles

With a concentration on the United States of 66.7% for exports and 40.7% for imports (Table 7), this group of products is below the average for exports of liberalized products (77.9%) and similar to the average for imports (39.5%).

During the period from 1988 to 1992, exports to the United States increased by 165.1%, as opposed to −8.6% for the other countries and 62.4% overall. As for the United States, the increase in comparison with the previous period (1984-1988) is spectacular (165.1% compared with 64.8%).

Imports from the United States increased by 28.2%, compared with −14.5% for the other countries and −1.1% overall. As with exports, imports from the United States increased substantially compared with the previous period (28.2% as opposed to −2.4%).

The trade balance with the United States, which showed a large deficit at the beginning of the period, improved by $46 million and that with the other countries by $104 million.

In conclusion, the following trade phenomena are noted:

- a very large increase in bilateral trade with the United States, mainly in exports, but also in imports, whereas trade with the rest of the world fell;

- a $46-million improvement in the bilateral trade balance.

Shipments[7] decreased by 6.6% (−$218 million) from 1988 to 1990, whereas exports increased during the same period by 21% ($47 million), and imports remained relatively stable (−$8 million) (Appendix H).

These data on trade and shipments suggest that, contrary to a widely held opinion and the expectations created by D. Schwanen's study as a result of his comments on the traditional sectors, Quebec's textile sector, considered as a whole, seems to have benefited from liberalized trade with the United States (increased exports and improved trade balance). The big winners seem to have been companies able to take advantage of the increase in exports to the United States. If there were losers, they were those companies that served the domestic market exclusively. They saw their shipments fall as a result of this stagnating market and the increase in imports from the United States.

---

7. It should be recalled that the classification used in the data on shipments (CTI 80) differs from the foreign trade classification used in this study. The comparison that is made here between two types of data is therefore only an illustration of certain trends. It should also be recalled that the data available for shipments cover only the period from 1988 to 1990 and not the entire period from 1988 to 1992.

Still, it should be noted that the breakdown of shipments between Quebec's exporting and non-exporting manufacturers does not directly confirm the last part of this conclusion, since both categories saw their shipments fall at about the same rate. This is probably due to the fact that exports to the United States represent only a small portion of shipments (less than 5%) and that a large majority of the shipments were by manufacturers that consider themselves exporters, even though exports represent a very small portion of their output. The businesses that took advantage of the strength of exports to the United States are therefore lost in the mass.

TABLE 7
Quebec – Textiles
(dollars in millions)

	Change from 1984 to 1988	Change from 1988 to 1992	Proportion based on destination in 1992 (%)
Total trade			
exports	55.0%	62.4%	100
imports	22.2%	−1.1%	100
trade balance	$(133)	$150	
United States			
exports	64.8%	165.1%	66.7
imports	−2.4%	28.2%	40.7
trade balance	$44	$46	
Other countries			
exports	48.9%	−8.6%	33.3
imports	38.2%	−14.5%	59.3
trade balance	$(177)	$104	
Shipments*			
total manufacturers	19.8%	−6.6%	
export manufacturers	2.9%	−7.0%	
non-export manufacturers	154.0%	−5.4%	

* Figures on changes from 1988 to 1992 actually cover the years 1988 to 1990.
Source: Appendix H

Clothing

The concentration of clothing exports to the United States (88.6%) is greater than the average for liberalized products. However, the share of imports from the United States (8.2%) is very low (Table 8).

During the period from 1988 to 1992, clothing exports to the United States increased by 32.7%, whereas exports to the other countries fell by 25.1%, for an overall increase of 22.0%. Still, it should be noted that the level of exports to the other countries is low.

During the same period, imports from the United States increased by 111.2%, from an initially low level, compared with 13.6% for imports from other countries and 18.1% overall.

The balance with the United States improved by $31 million during the period, compared with decreases of $140 million for the other countries and $109 million overall.

The changes are therefore very similar to those recorded for textiles:

- rapid growth of bilateral trade, in both imports and exports, despite weak domestic demand on both sides of the border;

- improvement in the bilateral trade balance, whereas the balance with the other countries deteriorated.

TABLE 8
Quebec – Clothing
(dollars in millions)

	Change from 1984 to 1988	Change from 1988 to 1992	Proportion based on destination in 1992 (%)
Total trade			
exports	55.4%	22.0%	100
imports	41.8%	18.1%	100
trade balance	$(179)	$(109)	
United States			
exports	58.7%	32.7%	88.6
imports	3.7%	111.2%	8.2
trade balance	$89	$31	
Other countries			
exports	42.4%	−25.1%	11.4
imports	44.4%	13.6%	91.8
trade balance	$(268)	$(140)	
Shipments*			
total manufacturers	28.1%	5.2%	
export manufacturers	4.1%	10.4%	
non-export manufacturers	98.2%	−2.8%	

* Figures on changes from 1988 to 1992 actually cover the years 1988 to 1990.

Source: Appendix I

Shipments increased by 5.2% from 1988 to 1990.

Once again, as a whole, this typically "soft" sector benefited from liberalized trade with the United States. The winners are the companies that were able to take advantage of the increase in exports to the United States, whereas the losers are those that aimed exclusively at the domestic market and saw their output drop, while imports from the United States and the other countries increased.

The breakdown of shipments between exporters and non-exporters confirms this interpretation, since the former saw their shipments increase by 10.4% from 1988 to 1990, while the latter saw theirs decrease by 2.4%.

Chemicals

The concentration of exports to the United States (81.0%) is close to the average for all liberalized products, whereas for imports (52.5%) it is higher (Table 9).

During the period from 1988 to 1992, exports of chemicals to the United States increased by 51.0%, compared with −14.3% for the other countries and 31.9% overall; during the previous period, exports to the United States increased by only 40.5%.

Imports from the United States increased by 21.8%, compared with 3.9% for imports from the other countries and 12.6% overall.

As a result, the balance with the United States improved by $115 million, compared with $49 million overall and a deterioration of $66 million with the other countries.

The conclusions regarding trade are similar to those for the two preceding sectors:

- sustained growth of bilateral trade, particularly in exports, rather than imports;
- improvement in the bilateral trade balance, which more than offset the deterioration in the balance with the other countries.

Shipments increased by 27% from 1988 to 1990.

Again, overall the sector appears to be a winner in terms of trade. Moreover, unlike the previous sectors, total shipments also made strides at the beginning of the period. The main winners were exporters; the losers were companies that concentrated exclusively on the domestic market and thus faced competition from the increase in imports.

The breakdown of shipments between exporters (+37%) and non-exporters (−28%) confirms this conclusion. It should also be noted that the overwhelming majority of manufacturers in this sector consider themselves exporters, which, given the strength of exports to the United States, explains to a considerable degree the strong overall increase in shipments.

TABLE 9
Quebec – Chemicals
(dollars in millions)

	Change from 1984 to 1988	Change from 1988 to 1992	Proportion based on destination in 1992 (%)
Total trade			
exports	19.3%	31.9%	100
imports	79.3%	12.6%	100
trade balance	$(598)	$49	
United States			
exports	40.5%	51.0%	81.0
imports	49.5%	21.8%	52.5
trade balance	$(101)	$115	
Other countries			
exports	−12.6%	−14.3%	19.0
imports	120.8%	3.9%	47.5
trade balance	$(497)	$(66)	
Shipments*			
total manufacturers	31.9%	26.6%	
export manufacturers	11.6%	37.2%	
non-export manufacturers	1,765.0%	−27.7%	

* Figures on changes from 1988 to 1992 actually cover the years 1988 to 1990.

Source: Appendix J

Food

The concentration of trade with the United States, in terms of exports (67.3%) and imports (33.6%), is slightly lower than the average for liberalized products (Table 10).

During the period from 1988 to 1992, exports to the United States increased by 22.3%, compared with −3.2% for the other countries and 12.6% overall. During the previous period, exports to the United States decreased by 8.6%.

Imports from the United States increased by 10.3%, compared with 3.3% for the other countries and 5.5% overall. During the previous period, imports from the United States decreased by 6.2%.

As a result, the balance with the United States improved by $86 million, compared with $42 million overall and a deterioration of $44 million for the other countries.

The conclusions regarding foreign trade are similar to those for the preceding sectors:

- increase in bilateral trade with the United States, in both imports and exports;
- improvement in the bilateral trade balance, which more than offset the deterioration of the balance with the other countries.

TABLE 10
Quebec – Food
(dollars in millions)

	Change from 1984 to 1988	Change from 1988 to 1992	Proportion based on destination in 1992 (%)
Total trade			
exports	−7.8%	12.6%	100
imports	4.5%	5.5%	100
trade balance	$(144)	$42	
United States			
exports	−8.6%	22.3%	67.3
imports	−6.2%	10.3%	33.6
trade balance	$(26)	$86	
Other countries			
exports	−6.6%	−3.2%	32.7
imports	10.4%	3.3%	66.4
trade balance	$(119)	$(44)	
Shipments*			
total manufacturers	10.9%	4.4%	
export manufacturers	−5.6%	9.1%	
non-export manufacturers	60.4%	−3.8%	

* Figures on changes from 1988 to 1992 actually cover the years 1988 to 1990.
Source: Appendix K

Shipments increased by 4.4% from 1988 to 1990.

Once again, the sector appears overall to be a winner in terms of trade. The breakdown of shipments between exporters (+9.1%) and non-exporters

(−3.8%) confirms, at least for the period from 1988 to 1990, that the winners were the companies that took advantage of the strength of exports, whereas the losers were the ones that restricted themselves to the domestic market.

Office and Telecommunications Equipment

The concentration of exports to the United States (89.8%) is above average, whereas the concentration of imports (29.8%) is below average (Table 11).

For the period from 1988 to 1992, the increase in exports to the United States was 179.8%, compared with −28.1% for the other countries and 116.0% overall. During the previous period, exports to the United States increased by only 21.6%.

Imports from the United States fell by 47.3% (the drop occurred mainly in 1991 and 1992), whereas they rose 135.2% for the other countries and 15.8% overall.

As a result, the trade balance with the United States improved by $2.9 billion, compared with $1.6 billion overall and a deterioration of $1.3 billion with the other countries.

Thus the changes in trade in this sector present striking contrasts. One notes:

- an increase in exports to the United States, but also a drop in imports from the United States, whereas imports from the other countries increased;

- a spectacular increase in bilateral trade balance with the United States, which was partially cancelled out by the deterioration of the trade balance with the other countries.

Although for most of the liberalized products, the bilateral trade balance also improved for Quebec from 1988 to 1992, the office and telecommunications equipment sector is responsible for the largest portion of the overall improvement in the bilateral balance for liberalized products. It is mainly because of this sector that the main winners in the liberalization of trade with the United States are the high-value-added sectors, although the traditional sectors were not losers.

For reasons of statistical secrecy, data on Quebec shipments of office and telecommunications equipment are not available. If we turn to the larger electrical and electronic sector, which includes office and telecommunications equipment, the growth of shipments by manufacturing exporters from 1988 to 1990 (+9.6%) is again far higher than that for shipments by non-exporting manufacturers, which is strongly negative (−32.0%). In this case, however, the comparison, which again illustrates the fact that exporting companies are the main beneficiaries of liberalization, should be interpreted with care because the correspondence between data on international trade and shipments is weaker than for the other sectors covered by this study.

TABLE 11
Quebec – Office and Telecommunications Equipment
(dollars in millions)

	Change from 1984 to 1988	**Change from 1988 to 1992**	**Proportion based on destination in 1992 (%)**
Total trade			
exports	22.6%	116.0%	100
imports	46.3%	15.8%	100
trade balance	$(451)	$1,578	
United States			
exports	21.6%	179.8%	89.8
imports	28.7%	–47.3%	29.8
trade balance	$(144)	$2,850	
Other countries			
exports	24.9%	–28.1%	10.2
imports	97.4%	135.2%	70.2
trade balance	$(308)	$(1,272)	
Shipments*			
total manufacturers	61.8%	0.5%	
export manufacturers	40.0%	9.6%	
non-export manufacturers	264.6%	–32.0%	

*   Figures on changes from 1988 to 1992 actually cover the years 1988 to 1990 and relate to electrical and electronic products.

Source: Appendix L

Industrial Machinery

At 69.6%, the share of exports to the United States is significantly lower than the average for liberalized products, whereas for imports, the United States' share, at 52.9%, is decidedly higher than the average (Table 12).

In terms of variations, exports to the United States rose by 22.3% from 1988 to 1992, compared with an increase of 28.0% to the other countries, for a total of 24.0%. The higher result for exports to the other countries is due to the 1990 exports, which increased by 65.5% over the previous year. During the same period, imports from the United States fell by 12.0%, whereas imports from the other countries dropped by 50.2%, for a total of −35.3%. The purchase of equipment for aluminum smelters in 1991 by European consortiums may explain the large increase (18.2%) of imports of machinery from the other countries.

As a result of the double impact of the increase in exports and the decrease in imports, the trade balance improved by $750 million from 1988 to 1992. A large portion of this is due to the trade balance with the other countries ($578 million), the balance with the United States having improved by $172 million.

Shipments increased by 23% from 1988 to 1990, with exporters (+37%) outpacing non-exporters (+1.9%) by far.

TABLE 12
Quebec – Industrial Machinery
(dollars in millions)

	Change from 1984 to 1988	**Change from 1988 to 1992**	**Proportion based on destination in 1992 (%)**
Total trade			
exports	25.9%	24.0%	100.0
imports	94.9%	−35.3%	100.0
trade balance	$(724)	$750	
United States			
exports	56.5%	22.3%	69.6
imports	46.4%	−12.0%	52.9
trade balance	$(67)	$172	
Other countries			
exports	−14.2%	28.0%	30.4
imports	147.0%	−50.2%	47.1
trade balance	$(657)	$578	
Shipments*			
total manufacturers	63.5%	22.7%	
export manufacturers	20.7%	37.3%	
non-export manufacturers	230.1%	1.9%	

* Figures on changes from 1988 to 1992 actually cover the years 1988 to 1990.

Source: Appendix M

CONCLUSIONS

- Our study confirms for Quebec the main conclusion of the Canadian study, **namely a very substantial increase in bilateral trade in liberalized products from 1988 to 1992** despite the recession on both sides of the border. This increase is not explained by any other macro-economic variable and therefore must essentially be attributed to application of the Free Trade Agreement.

- The increase in exports of liberalized products to the United States was even more substantial in Quebec than in Canada as a whole. The growth of imports of liberalized products from the United States was, however, far weaker in Quebec than in Canada.

- As a result of the differences in the growth rates and the initial structural differences between Canada/United States bilateral trade and Quebec/United States bilateral trade, the impact on the bilateral trade balance for liberalized products was extremely positive in Quebec (+$3.6 billion), whereas it was almost neutral for Canada as a whole (+$155 million).

- In Quebec, as in Canada, high-value-added sectors are the ones that benefited the most from the increase in exports to the United States. This increase was much stronger in Quebec (+90%) than in Canada as a whole (+49%) from 1988 to 1992.

- For each sector comprising liberalized products, the bilateral trade balances improved both for high-value-added sectors, such as office and telecommunications equipment and industrial machinery, and the traditional, or "soft," sectors, such as textiles, clothing and food.

  Contrary to one of the conclusions of the study on Canada, this finding runs counter to an **inter-sectorial** differentiation between high-value-added sectors, which are assumed to have benefited from liberalization, and traditional sectors, which are assumed to have suffered from the increase in imports.

  However, all the statistics point to strong **intra-sectorial** discrimination between companies that were able to take advantage of the increase in exports to the United States and those that were confined to a sluggish domestic market and had to compete with the increase in U.S. imports resulting from implementation of the Free Trade Agreement.

  The information available on changes in shipments at the beginning of the period (1988-1990) generally confirms this conclusion.

- The data for 1993 indicate a substantial increase in Quebec's exports to the United States that is greater than the increase in exports to the

United States for Canada as a whole (Figure 9). In addition to the impacts of the Free Trade Agreement, which have been analyzed in this study, this increase is due to a drop in the value of the Canadian dollar, the greater competitiveness of Canadian products and the increase in the level of activity in the United States.[8]

In addition, imports from the United States also increased, although not as much as exports. The increase was more pronounced for Canadian imports than for Quebec imports (Figure 10) and was due mainly to the recovery in Canada.

It is quite likely that, overall, these changes have accentuated the trends described in this study with respect to liberalized products: increased bilateral trade, an improved trade balance – in Quebec more than in Canada – and intra-sectorial differentiation between companies able to take advantage of the increase in exports and those unable to do so.

The forecasts for 1994 and 1995,[9] which predict continued sustained growth of exports, indicate that these trends will continue in the quarters to come.

FIGURE 9
Exports to the U.S.
(annual change in percentage)

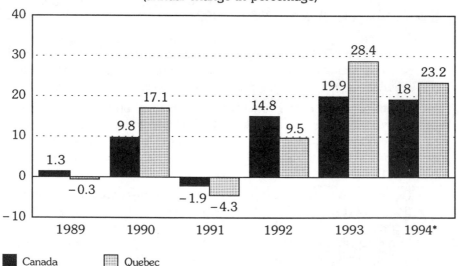

■ Canada   ▦ Quebec

* Figures cumulative to June 30.

Source: Bureau de la statistique du Québec

---

8.   See *Cycles et tendances*, December 1993, p. 20 and p. 33.
9.   Ibid.

FIGURE 10
Imports from the U.S.
(annual change in percentage)

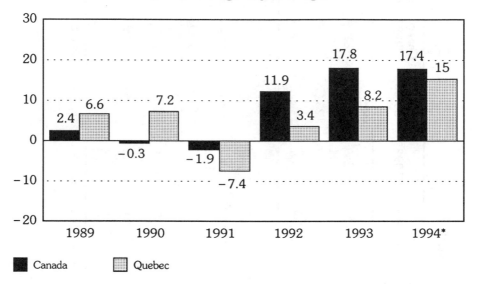

■ Canada   ▦ Quebec

* Figures cumulative to June 30.

Source: Bureau de la statistique du Québec

APPENDIX "A"
Quebec – Total Products

	1984	1988	1989	1990	1991	1992	Change 84-88	Change 88-92	Based on 1992 destination
			Value and annual change (in millions of dollars)						
Total trade									
exports	17,377	22,581	23,303	26,086	25,879	27,249	29.9%	20.7%	100.0
	–	6.8%	3.2%	11.9%	-0.8%	5.3%			
imports	19,279	24,799	26,718	28,494	27,686	28,848	28.6%	16.3%	100.0
	–	6.5%	7.7%	6.6%	-2.8%	4.2%			
trade balance	(1,902)	(2,218)	(3,415)	(2,409)	(1,807)	(1,599)	(316)	620	
United States									
exports	13,024	16,999	16,954	19,855	19,004	20,780	30.5%	22.2%	76.3
	–	6.9%	-0.3%	17.1%	-4.3%	9.3%			
imports	10,220	11,556	12,323	13,205	12,222	12,838	13.1%	11.1%	44.5
	–	3.1%	6.6%	7.2%	-7.4%	5.0%			
trade balance	2,804	5,443	4,631	6,650	6,782	7,942	2,639	2,498	
Other countries									
exports	4,353	5,581	6,349	6,231	6,875	6,469	28.2%	15.9%	23.7
	–	6.4%	13.7%	-1.9%	10.3%	-5.9%			
imports	9,060	13,243	14,394	15,289	15,464	16,009	46.2%	20.9%	55.5
	–	10.0%	8.7%	6.2%	1.1%	3.5%			
trade balance	(4,707)	(7,662)	(8,046)	(9,058)	(8,589)	(9,540)	(2,955)	(1,879)	

Note: Total products include certain products that are not comprised in either of the two sub-categories: oil, natural gas, cars, tobacco.

APPENDIX "B"
Canada – Total Products

	1984	1988	1992	Change 84-88	Change 88-92	Based on destination 1992
	(in millions of dollars)					
Total trade						
exports	109,437	134,853	154,302	23.2%	14.4%	100.0
imports	N/A	131,172	147,995	–	12.8%	100.0
trade balance	N/A	3,681	6,308	–	2,627	
United States						
exports	82,836	98,304	118,677	18.7%	20.7%	76.9
imports	N/A	88,268	95,515	–	11.9%	65.2
trade balance	N/A	12,036	22,163	–	10,126	
Other countries						
exports	26,601	36,549	35,625	37.4%	–2.5%	23.1
imports	N/A	44,904	51,480	–	14.6%	34.8
trade balance	N/A	(8,355)	(15,855)	–	(7,500)	

Note: Total products include certain products that are not comprised in either on the two subcategories: oil, natural gas, cars, tobacco.

APPENDIX "C"
Quebec – Total Liberalized Products

	1984	1988	1989	1990	1991	1992	Change 84-88	Change 88-92	Based on destination 1992
		Value and annual change (in millions of dollars)							
Total trade									
exports	9,033	11,923 7.2%	12,740 6.9%	14,572 14.4%	15,312 5.1%	16,405 7.1%	32.0%	37.6%	100.0
imports	10,256	14,843 9.7%	16,505 11.2%	17,831 8.0%	17,108 -4.1%	15,793 -7.7%	44.7%	6.4%	100.0
trade balance	(1,224)	(2,920)	(3,765)	(3,259)	(1,796)	612	(1,696)	3,532	
United States									
exports	6,538	8,922 8.1%	9,224 3.4%	11,141 20.8%	11,476 3.0%	12,784 11.4%	36.45	43.3%	77.9
imports	4,787	6,096 5.8%	7,005 16.6%	8,416 20.1%	7,456 -11.4%	6,243 -16.3%	25.5%	3.9%	39.5
trade balance	1,751	2,913	2,219	2,725	4,020	6,541	1,162	3,628	
Other countries									
exports	2,494	3,001 4.7%	3,516 17.1%	3,431 -2.4%	3,836 11.8%	3,621 -5.6%	20.3%	20.7%	22.1
imports	5,469	8,834 12.7%	9,500 7.5%	9,415 -0.9%	9,652 2.5%	9,549 -1.1%	61.5%	8.1%	60.5
trade balance	(2,975)	(5,833)	(5,985)	(5,984)	(5,816)	(5,928)	(2,858)	(95)	

APPENDIX "D"
Canada – Total Liberalized Products

	1984	1988	1992	Change 84-88	Change 88-92	Based on destination 1992
		(in millions of dollars)				
Total trade						
exports	45,663	58,855	71,697	28.9%	21.8%	100.0
imports	N/A	72,914	88,189	–	20.9%	100.0
trade balance	N/A	(14,059)	(16,491)	–	(2,432)	
United States						
exports	29,216	37,227	49,662	27.4%	33.4%	69.3
imports	N/A	43,289	55,569	–	28.4%	63.0
trade balance	N/A	(6,062)	(5,907)	–	155	
Other countries						
exports	16,447	21,627	22,036	31.5%	1.9%	30.7
imports	N/A	29,624	32,620	–	10.1%	37.0
trade balance	N/A	(7,997)	(10,584)	–	(2,587)	

APPENDIX "E"
Changes in Quebec Exports of Products Liberalized by FTA, 1988-1992

	Value of exports in 1992 ($000)	Exports to the U.S. in 1992 (%)	Change in exports to the U.S. (%)	Change in exports to other countries (%)
* Office, Telecommunications equipment	3,648,625	89.8	179.8	(28.1)
Textiles	186,592	61.9	158.6	(11.2)
Chemicals	620,562	83.8	153.0	(35.2)
Paper, excluding newsprint	854,263	90.4	103.7	4.3
Other raw materials	253,335	89.4	102.0	(59.0)
* Precision equipment	571,123	53.9	75.8	54.5
Wood products	253,216	90.6	59.1	28.8
* Other finished goods	1,324,560	77.9	50.9	9.8
Other food and feed	346,852	79.9	50.7	(18.5)
Beverages	122,978	87.1	25.4	198.2
* Other tools and equipment	1,079,794	82.7	22.6	36.5
* Industrial machinery	715,462	69.6	22.3	28.0
Meat and dairy products	528,493	57.1	12.5	13.8
Iron and steel	418,692	80.6	9.3	(30.4)
Fish	119,319	61.0	7.2	(42.4)
Other base products	4,925,519	70.7	(3.2)	86.3
Chemical elements	435,742	77.0	(7.1)	26.8
Total	**16,405,127**	**77.9**	**43.3**	**20.7**
of which:				
resource-based	9,065,563	74.8	17.7	31.6
* non-resource-based	7,339,564	81.8	89.8	5.6

APPENDIX "F"
Changes in Canadian Exports of Products Liberalized by FTA, 1988-1992

	Value of exports in 1992 ($ in millions)	Exports to the U.S. in 1992 (%)	Change in exports to the U.S. (%)	Change in exports to other countries (%)
Other raw materials	3,832	35	112.8	(11.7)
Paper, excluding newsprint	2,504	80	96.1	35.4
Textiles	817	74	92.2	0.0
* Office, telecommunications and precision equipment	10,187	80	85.0	16.9
Other food and feed	7,737	27	74.6	4.2
Chemicals	3,421	79	63.9	(15.8)
Meat and dairy products	2,672	79	63.7	8.5
Beverages	773	91	62.9	5.0
* Other finished goods	4,316	74	41.1	(5.5)
* Other tools and equipment	6,068	87	37.1	14.7
Wood products	1,360	87	30.8	(0.8)
Iron and steel	2,952	83	16.1	56.9
* Industrial machinery	4,352	74	14.7	44.4
Other basic products	15,582	72	3.9	2.4
Chemical elements	3,200	73	1.7	(33.5)
Fish	1,926	55	(13.3)	(6.6)
Total	**71,699**	**69**	**24.8**	**(1.6)**
of which:				
resource-based	46,775	64	24.8	(1.6)
* non-resource-based	24,922	79	48.9	15.4

Source: Schwanen, Daniel, "A Growing Succes: Canada's Performance Under Free Trade," *C.D. Howe Institute Commentary*, No. 52 September 1993, page 7.

APPENDIX "G"
Changes in Quebec Imports of Products Liberalized by FTA, 1988-1992

	Value of exports in 1992 ($000)	Exports to the U.S. in 1992 (%)	Change in exports to the U.S. (%)	Change in exports to other countries (%)
Meat and dairy products	265,853	50.2	139.1	22.5
Clothing	1,145,762	8.2	111.2	13.6
Processed food and beverages	686,523	21.3	66.8	(6.2)
Furniture and furnishing articles	321,794	32.5	64.5	(16.8)
Other finished goods	1,053,669	50.2	56.2	6.2
Other household products	769,171	24.1	55.4	25.8
Petroleum products	660,610	38.5	47.9	(18.8)
Transportation equipment, excluding cars	442,166	47.7	36.0	1.2
Textiles	1,047,064	38.3	33.8	(13.6)
Other fabricated materials	1,081,110	55.7	27.5	(17.8)
Chemical products and elements	1,851,506	52.5	21.8	3.9
Other equipment	1,364,958	55.7	14.4	12.3
Metal products	402,541	54.1	11.3	2.9
Selected raw materials	100,665	60.5	(3.4)	5.8
Steel	287,300	22.8	(12.3)	(60.9)
Fresh fruit and vegetables	371,365	45.8	(13.5)	34.8
Other industrial machinery	1,150,216	43.9	(20.0)	(18.8)
Office, telecommunications equipment	2,790,381	29.8	(47.3)	135.2
Total	**15,792,654**	**39.5**	**3.9**	**8.1**

APPENDIX "H"

Quebec – Liberalized Products – Textiles

	1984	Value and annual change (in millions of dollars)									Change 84-88	Change 88-92	Based on destination 1992
		1988		1989		1990		1991		1992			
Total trade													
exports	142	220	11.6%	248	12.6%	267	8.0%	279	4.5%	357	27.9%	55.0%	62.4%	100.0
imports	949	1,159	5.1%	1,240	7.0%	1,151	-7.2%	1,137	-1.2%	1,147	0.8%	22.2%	-1.1%	100.0
trade balance	(807)	(939)		(993)		(884)		(858)		(789)		(133)	150	
United States													
exports	55	90	13.3%	107	19.3%	112	4.0%	151	35.2%	238	58.0%	64.8%	165.1%	66.7
imports	373	364	-0.6%	421	15.6%	417	-1.1%	443	6.3%	467	5.4%	-2.4%	28.2%	40.7
trade balance	(319)	(274)		(314)		(305)		(292)		(229)		44	46	
Other countries													
exports	87	130	10.5%	140	7.9%	156	11.0%	128	-17.5%	119	-7.5%	48.9%	-8.6%	33.3
imports	575	795	8.4%	819	3.0%	735	-10.3%	694	-5.5%	680	-2.1%	38.2%	-14.5%	59.3
trade balance	(488)	(665)		(679)		(579)		(566)		(561)		(177)	104	
Shipments													
total manufacturers	2,743	3,286	4.6%	3,271	-0.5%	3,068	-6.2%	N/A	–	N/A	–	19.8%	-6.6%*	
export manufacturers	2,436	2,506	0.7%	2,515	0.4%	2,330	-7.4%	N/A	–	N/A	–	2.9%	-7.0%*	
non-export manufacturers	307	780	26.2%	756	-3.1%	738	-2.4%	N/A	–	N/A	–	154.0%	-5.4%*	

* Figures on changes from 1988 to 1992 actually cover the years 1988 to 1990.

APPENDIX "I"
Quebec – Liberalized Products – Clothing

	1984	1988	1989	1990	1991	1992	Change 84-88	Change 88-92	Based on destination 1992
			Value and annual change (in millions of dollars)						
Total trade									
exports	194	301	244	255	311	367	55.4%	22.0%	100.0
	–	11.7%	-18.9%	4.4%	22.1%	18.1%			
imports	684	970	1,053	1,131	1,028	1,146	41.8%	18.1%	100.0
	–	9.1%	8.5%	7.4%	-9.1%	11.5%			
trade balance	(490)	(669)	(808)	(876)	(716)	(778)	(179)	(109)	
United States									
exports	154	245	198	219	262	325	58.7%	32.7%	88.6
	–	12.2%	-19.3%	10.7%	19.6%	24.2%			
imports	43	44	61	72	73	94	3.7%	111.2%	8.2
	–	0.9%	37.4%	17.7%	2.5%	27.5%			
trade balance	112	201	137	147	189	232	89	31	
Other countries									
exports	39	56	46	36	49	42	42.4%	-25.1%	11.4
	–	9.2%	-17.2%	-22.8%	37.1%	-14.5%			
imports	641	926	992	1,059	954	1,052	44.4%	13.6%	91.8
	–	9.6%	7.1%	6.8%	-9.9%	10.3%			
trade balance	(602)	(870)	(945)	(1,023)	(905)	(1,010)	(268)	(140)	
Shipments									
total manufacturers	3,170	4,060	4,151	4,270	N/A	N/A	28.1%	5.2%*	
	–	6.4%	2.3%	2.9%	–	–			
export manufacturers	2,363	2,460	2,787	2,716	N/A	N/A	4.1%	10.4%*	
	–	1.0%	13.3%	-2.5%	–	–			
non-export manufacturers	807	1,599	1,364	1,554	N/A	N/A	98.2%	-2.8%*	
	–	18.7%	-14.7%	13.9%	–	–			

* Figures on changes from 1988 to 1992 actually cover the years 1988 to 1990.

APPENDIX "J"
Quebec – Liberalized Products – Chemicals

	1984	1988	Value and annual change 1989 (in millions of dollars)	1990	1991	1992	Change 84-88	Change 88-92	Based on destination 1992
Total trade									
exports	672	801 / 4.5%	783 / -2.3%	884 / 13.0%	901 / 1.9%	1,056 / 17.3%	19.3%	31.9%	100.0
imports	917	1,645 / 15.7%	1,784 / 8.5%	1,718 / -3.7%	1,776 / 3.4%	1,852 / 4.3%	79.3%	12.6%	100.0
trade balance	(246)	(844)	(1,002)	(834)	(875)	(795)	(598)	49	
United States									
exports	403	566 / 8.9%	595 / 5.0%	640 / 7.5%	719 / 12.4%	855 / 18.9%	40.5%	51.0%	81.0
imports	534	799 / 10.6%	1,033 / 29.3%	999 / -3.2%	1,057 / 5.8%	972 / -8.0%	49.5%	21.8%	52.5
trade balance	(131)	(232)	(438)	(360)	(338)	(117)	(101)	115	
Other countries									
exports	268	235 / -3.3%	188 / -20.0%	244 / 30.1%	182 / -25.6%	201 / 10.8%	-12.6%	-14.3%	19.0
imports	383	846 / 21.9%	752 / -11.2%	719 / -4.4%	719 / -0.0%	879 / 22.3%	120.8%	3.9%	47.5
trade balance	(115)	(612)	(564)	(474)	(537)	(678)	(497)	(66)	
Shipments									
total manufacturers	872	1,149 / 7.2%	1,278 / 11.2%	1,455 / 13.8%	N/A	N/A	31.9%	26.6%*	
export manufacturers	862	962 / 2.8%	1,205 / 25.3%	1,319 / 9.5%	N/A	N/A	11.6%	37.2%*	
non-export manufacturers	10	188 / 107.8%	74 / -60.8%	136 / 84.4%	N/A	N/A	1765.0%	-27.7%*	

* Figures on changes from 1988 to 1992 actually cover the years 1988 to 1990.

APPENDIX "K"
Quebec – Liberalized Products – Food

	1984	Value and annual change (in millions of dollars)					Change 84-88	Change 88-92	Based on destination 1992
		1988	1989	1990	1991	1992			
Total trade									
exports	1,051	969 -2.0%	959 -1.0%	1,020 6.4%	1,032 1.1%	1,091 5.7%	-7.8%	12.6%	100.0
imports	1,388	1,450 1.1%	1,459 0.6%	1,472 0.9%	1,503 2.1%	1,530 1.8%	4.5%	5.5%	100.0
trade balance	(337)	(481)	(500)	(452)	(471)	(439)	(144)	42	
United States									
exports	657	601 -2.2%	579 -3.6%	680 17.5%	697 2.4%	734 5.4%	-8.6%	22.3%	67.3
imports	497	466 -1.6%	446 -4.2%	433 -3.0%	465 7.3%	514 10.6%	-6.2%	10.3%	33.6
trade balance	160	135	132	247	232	220	(26)	86	
Other countries									
exports	395	369 -1.7%	380 3.2%	340 -10.6%	335 -1.4%	357 6.5%	-6.6%	-3.2%	32.7
imports	891	984 2.5%	1,013 2.9%	1,039 2.6%	1,038 -0.1%	1,016 -2.1%	10.4%	3.3%	66.4
trade balance	(497)	(616)	(632)	(699)	(703)	(659)	(119)	(44)	
Shipments									
total manufacturers	9,651	10,699 2.6%	10,887 1.8%	11,173 2.6%	N/A –	N/A –	10.9%	4.4%*	
export manufacturers	7,247	6,844 -1.4%	7,112 3.9%	7,464 4.9%	N/A –	N/A –	-5.6%	9.1%*	
non-export manufacturers	2,404	3,855 12.5%	3,775 -2.1%	3,709 -1.7%	N/A –	N/A –	60.4%	-3.8%*	

* Figures on changes from 1988 to 1992 actually cover the years 1988 to 1990.

Note: The food industry includes all foods and beverages, except tobacco.

APPENDIX "L"
Quebec – Liberalized Products – Office and Telecommunications Equipment

	1984	1988	1989	1990	1991	1992	Change 84-88	Change 88-92	Based on destination 1992
			Value and annual change (in millions of dollars)						
Total trade									
exports	1,378	1,689 5.2%	1,969 16.6%	3,340 69.6%	3,798 13.7%	3,649 -3.9%	22.6%	116.0%	100.0
imports	1,646	2,409 10.0%	3,153 30.9%	4,411 39.9%	4,639 5.2%	2,790 -39.8%	46.3%	15.8%	100.0
trade balance	(268)	(720)	(1,184)	(1,071)	(840)	858	(451)	1,578	
United States									
exports	963	1,171 5.0%	1,491 27.4%	2,876 92.9%	3,250 13.0%	3,276 0.8%	21.6%	179.8%	89.8
imports	1,224	1,576 6.5%	1,882 19.4%	3,025 60.8%	2,364 -21.9%	831 -64.8%	28.7%	-47.3%	29.8
trade balance	(261)	(405)	(391)	(149)	886	2,445	(144)	2,850	
Other countries									
exports	415	518 5.7%	478 -7.8%	464 -3.0%	549 18.3%	373 -32.1%	24.9%	-28.1%	10.2
imports	422	833 18.5%	1,271 52.6%	1,385 9.0%	2,275 64.3%	1,959 -13.9%	97.4%	135.2%	70.2
trade balance	(7)	(315)	(793)	(921)	(1,727)	(1,587)	(308)	(1,272)	
Shipments									
total manufacturers	2,975	4,814 12.8%	5,203 8.1%	4,837 -7.0%	N/A –	N/A –	61.8%	0.5%*	
export manufacturers	2,687	3,762 8.8%	3,924 4.3%	4,122 5.0%	N/A –	N/A –	40.0%	9.6%*	
non-export manufacturers	288	1,052 38.2%	1,279 21.6%	715 -44.1%	N/A –	N/A –	264.6%	-32.0%*	

* Figures on changes from 1988 to 1992 actually cover the years 1988 to 1990.

Note: shipments above are for electrical and electronic products, a sector that is much larger than the office and telecommunications equipment sector.

APPENDIX "M"

Quebec – Liberalized Products – Industrial Machinery

	1984	1988	1989	1990	1991	1992	Change 84-88	Change 88-92	Based on destination 1992
			Value and annual change (in millions of dollars)						
Total trade									
exports	458	577	622	738	744	715	25.9%	24.0%	100.0
	–	5.9%	7.8%	18.6%	0.8%	-3.8%			
imports	888	1,731	1,770	1,549	1,474	1,119	94.9%	-35.3%	100.0
	–	18.2%	2.2%	-12.5%	-4.8%	-24.1%			
trade balance	(430)	(1,154)	(1,147)	(810)	(730)	(404)	(724)	750	
United States									
exports	260	407	442	440	464	498	56.5%	22.3%	69.6
	–	11.8%	8.7%	-0.5%	5.4%	7.3%			
imports	460	674	371	616	371	593	46.4%	-12.0%	52.9
	–	10.0%	-45.0%	66.1%	-39.8%	59.8%			
trade balance	(200)	(267)	72	(175)	93	(95)	(67)	172	
Other countries									
exports	198	170	180	298	280	218	-14.2%	28.0%	30.4
	–	-3.8%	5.8%	65.5%	-6.1%	-22.2%			
imports	428	1,057	1,399	933	1,103	527	147.0%	-50.2%	47.1
	–	25.4%	32.3%	-33.3%	18.2%	-52.3%			
trade balance	(230)	(887)	(1,219)	(635)	(823)	(309)	(657)	578	
Shipments									
total manufacturers	1,020	1,667	2,026	2,045	N/A	N/A	63.5%	22.7%*	
	–	13.1%	21.6%	0.9%	–	–			
export manufacturers	811	979	1,173	1,344	N/A	N/A	20.7%	37.3%*	
	–	4.8%	19.8%	14.6%	–	–			
non-export manufacturers	208	688	853	701	N/A	N/A	230.1%	1.9%*	
	–	34.8%	24.0%	-17.9%	–	–			

* Figures on changes from 1988 to 1992 actually cover the years 1988 to 1990.

Note: exports and imports do not balance exactly due to a discrepancy between liberalized export products and liberalized import products.

APPENDIX "N"
Export Products Classification

Non-liberalized products	Codes
Ships, aircraft and parts	51210, 51310, 51311, 51319
Other finished goods	50261, 54110, 54220, 60010
Wood	40011, 40019
Agricultural machinery	50310, 50321, 50329, 50330
Wood pulp and newsprint	40310, 40321
Other unfinished products	20110, 30010, 30020, 30411, 30419, 30420, 30450, 30481, 30139, 30210, 30220, 30290, 30610, 30621, 30689, 30690
Other energy products, excluding oil	30599, 41810
Fertilizers	41110
Natural gas	30521

Liberalized products	Codes
Office, telecommunications equipment	52220, 51510, 51520
Textiles	40410, 40420, 40430, 40490
Chemicals	41120, 41130, 41190
Paper, excluding newsprint	40329, 40330, 40390
Other unfinished products	20810, 30430, 30440, 30460, 30470, 30489, 30090, 30110, 30121, 30131, 30190, 30310
Precision equipment	52211, 52119
Wood products	40121, 40129, 40210, 40220, 40290
Other finished goods	53010, 53020, 53110, 53190, 54010, 54020, 54120, 54210, 54230, 54290
Other food and feed	20311, 20312, 20319, 20320, 20329, 20390, 20410, 20490, 20510, 20590, 20610, 20620, 20690
Beverages	20710, 20799
Other tools and equipment	50340, 51010, 51131, 51420, 52010, 52020, 52030, 52210, 52290
Industrial machinery	50010, 50020, 50090, 50190, 50210, 50220, 50230, 50241, 50251, 50299
Meat and dairy products	10000, 20010, 20090, 20210
Iron and steel	41310, 41320, 41330, 41410, 41420, 41429, 41499
Fish	20120, 20130, 20140, 20150
Other basic products	41510, 41520, 41530, 41540, 41610, 41620, 41630, 40010, 40510, 41210, 41690, 41710, 41720, 41990
Chemical elements	41010, 41020, 41090

Sources: Schwanen, D., "A Growing Success: Canada's Performance under Free Trade,"
C.D. Howe Institute Commentary, No. 52, September 1993, 16 pages.
Commerce international du Québec, Bureau de la statistique du Québec

APPENDIX "O"
Import Products Classification

Non-liberalized products	Codes
Selected food and feed	10000, 20110, 20211, 20230, 20310, 20470, 20610, 20690
Other unfinished goods	30010, 30111, 30119, 30130, 30210, 30230, 30250, 30311, 30330, 30390, 30410, 30439, 30450, 30461, 30490, 30990
Selected fabricated materials	40080, 40110, 40210, 40910, 40960, 41210, 41230, 41240, 41250, 41740, 41810
Selected industrial machinery	51011, 51061, 51211, 51215, 51219, 51299, 51341, 51349
Agricultural machinery	51410, 51413, 51419, 51490, 51511, 51513, 51517
Aircraft	52160, 52170, 52180
Medical and security equipment	54160, 54210
Printed material	59040, 59050
Other transactions	59210, 60010

Liberalized products	Codes
Meat and dairy products	20010, 20090, 20120
Fresh fruit and vegetables	20151, 20214, 20216, 20219, 20321, 20329, 20411
Processed food and beverages	20190, 20241, 20249, 20260, 20290, 20390, 20419, 20430, 20450, 20460, 20710, 20790, 20810, 20590
Selected unfinished goods	30090, 30190, 30270, 30290, 30313
Textiles	40410, 40430, 40490, 40510, 40530, 40550, 40570, 40580, 40590, 40610, 40690
Chemical products and elements	40810, 40860, 40920, 40930, 40940, 40950, 40970, 40980, 40990
Petroleum products	41010, 41020, 41030, 41090
Steel	41110, 41120, 41130, 41140, 41150, 41190
Metal products	41311, 41319, 41510, 41611, 41615, 41690
Other fabricated materials	40010, 40060, 40120, 40190, 40310, 40170, 40790, 41220, 41290, 41710, 41721, 41729, 41730, 41790, 41890
Other industrial machinery	51212, 51019, 51020, 51031, 51039, 51040, 51050, 51090, 51110, 51120, 51130, 51140, 51190, 51213, 51310, 51311, 51313, 51314, 51318, 51320, 51331, 51339, 51350, 51361, 51390
Transportation equipment, excluding cars	52010, 52090, 52130, 52150, 52290
Office, telecommunications equipment	52311, 52320, 52330, 52390, 54261, 54269
Other equipment	54010, 54020, 54030, 54041, 54090, 54110, 54120, 54150, 54171, 54190, 54230, 54250, 54290

APPENDIX "O" (cont'd)
Import Products Classification

Liberalized products	Codes
Clothing	56010, 56020, 56090, 56110
Furniture and furnishing articles	54240, 56150
Other household products	56120, 56130, 56140, 56180, 56190
Other finished goods	59010, 59030, 59090, 59110, 59120, 59190, 59290

Sources: Schwanen, D., "A Growing Success: Canada's Performance under Free Trade,"
C.D. Howe Institute Commentary, No. 52, September 1993, 16 pages.
Commerce international du Québec, Bureau de la statistique du Québec

APPENDIX "P"
Sectors Classification

Exports	Codes
Textiles	30310, 40410, 40420, 40430, 40490
Clothing	53010, 53020
Chemicals	41010, 41020, 41090, 41110, 41130, 41190
Food	20010, 20090, 20110, 20120, 20130, 20140, 20150, 20311, 20312, 20319, 20320, 20329, 20390, 20210, 20410, 20490, 20510, 20590, 20610, 20620, 20690, 20710, 20799
Office, telecommunications equipment	52220, 51510, 51520
Industrial machinery	50010, 50020, 50090, 50190, 50210, 50220, 50230, 50241, 50251, 50299

Imports	Codes
Textiles	30230, 30250, 30270, 30290, 40410, 40430, 40490, 40510, 40530, 40550, 40570, 40580, 40590, 40610, 40690
Clothing	56010, 56020, 56090, 56110
Chemicals	40810, 40860, 40920, 40930, 40940, 40950, 40970, 40980, 40990
Food	20010, 20090, 20110, 20211, 20214, 20216, 20219, 20230, 20241, 20249, 20260, 20290, 20310, 20321, 20329, 20390, 20120, 20151, 20190, 20411, 20419, 20430, 20450, 20460, 20470, 20590, 20610, 20690, 20710, 20790
Office, telecommunications equipment	52311, 52320, 52330, 52390, 54261, 54269
Industrial machinery	51212, 51019, 51020, 51031, 51039, 51040, 51050, 51090, 51110, 51120, 51130, 51140, 51190, 51213, 51310, 51311, 51313, 51314, 51318, 51320, 51331, 51339, 51350, 51361, 51390

Sources: Schwanen, D., "A Growing Success: Canada's Performance under Free Trade,"
C.D. Howe Institute Commentary, No. 52, September 1993, 16 pages.
Commerce international du Québec, Bureau de la statistique du Québec

Notes: The food industry includes the following categories: other food and feed, beverages, meat and dairy products, fish, but excludes tobacco (tobacco was excluded from this study).

The chemicals industry includes the following categories: chemical products and chemical elements.

The clothing industry is included in other finished goods for exports (cf. appendix N).

7

United States/Canada Free Trade Agreement and Quebec Small Business Behaviour*

Pierre-André Julien
Université du Québec à Trois-Rivières

The term "globalization of the economy" has become very fashionable over the last few years, in particular to explain the development of supranational firms and increasing international trade in goods and services, capital and labour. However, very little research has been done to examine empirically the effect of globalization on small businesses. The research presented here is based on an in-depth survey of a large sample of SMEs directly affected by the USA-Canada Free Trade Agreement in three small regions of Quebec. It attempts to answer many questions concerning the behaviour of this type of firm when faced with the opening up of frontiers. The behavior of these firms after signature of the Agreement was measured. The results show that a high proportion have developed or are developing policies not just to respond to the impact of the FTA, but to face up to economic globalization, by modernizing their production, developing specificities and directing their strategy towards this new trend.

Very little research has been done to examine the effects of globalization of the economy on small businesses, except those situated in border regions (Jeanneret, 1985; Ratti, 1986; Maillat, 1990). The problem of small exporting firms has

*   This research was funded by the Office de planification et de développement du Québec. An earlier version of the text was presented to the 38th World Conference of the International Council for Small Business, Las Vegas, June 20-23, 1993. Another version has been published with colleagues André Joyal and Laurent Deshaies in the *Journal of Small Business Management* (Vol. 32, No. 3, 1994, pp. 52-64). The authors thank Richard Lachance and Martin Morin for their work in the field and in compiling the data.

been analysed on a number of occasions (for example, Nelson, 1984; Miesenbrock, 1988; Kathawala et al., 1989; Léo, Monneyer and Philippe, 1990; Chenier and Michael, 1990). However, researchers have only recently begun to pay closer attention to the effects of the opening up of national borders on regions (Lesage and De la Rochefordière, 1988; Laurencin and Rougier, 1990) and on small business (Lefebvre and Lefebvre, 1988; Rugttaman and Verbeke, 1989; Filion, 1990; OECD, 1991). These latter authors have shown that, compared to most larger firms, SMEs are generally less well-equipped to face increases in international trade. As a result of their lower productivity, many have found it difficult to defend themselves. Also, given their limited resources, they have found it more difficult to take advantage of the removal of tariff barriers.

The aim of the research described in this chapter was to examine the impact of globalization on SMEs (less than 250 employees) in three small regions of Quebec, using as a starting point their behaviour with respect to the Free Trade Agreement between Canada and the United States. More specifically, our aim was to discover how small firms in small regions viewed the opening up of the borders. Special attention was paid to how the SMEs reacted, either to face up to the increase in potential competition or to take advantage of reduced customs duties. The methodology used was an in-depth survey of small manufacturing firms in sectors seriously affected by the reduction of tariff barriers between Canada and the United States.

The results, initially, were surprising: only a small number of firms knew of and had taken concrete steps to counter or take advantage of the agreement. However, further analysis revealed that different actions had been taken within the wider framework of economic globalization. In other words, more SMEs had taken steps to reinforce their competitive position in terms of general international trade, whether with the United States or elsewhere. A later study of the diffusion of new technologies in small manufacturing firms in Quebec supported this observation, confirming that the reduction of tariff barriers is just one consideration in small business strategy for survival and development. The main purpose is to adapt to world competition. In other words, this research reveals that many more SMEs than might be thought have begun to build up their defences or seek to take advantage of market globalization, positioning themselves differently on markets. The differences lie mainly in (1) some product specificities, (2) the use of new technologies, (3) with, often, the addition of personalized innovations, (4) the creation of marketing and distribution forms and (5) changes in organization. All these elements help develop a specific market with this set of differences.[1]

This chapter will look, first, at the potential consequences of free trade for SMEs. The methodology used to verify the extent of these consequences in

---

1.   This differenciating behaviour holds true for big business too, as Amit and Shoemaker (1993) point out.

three regions of Quebec will then be described. This will be followed by a presentation of the results concerning SME behaviour, first with respect to the Free Trade Agreement, and second with respect to global competitiveness. Finally, the overall research procedure will be discussed and links made with other studies, in particular our own recent study of the diffusion of new technologies in SMEs in a poor overall economic context.

FREE TRADE, REGIONAL ECONOMY AND SMALL BUSINESS

The trend towards easing market restrictions can be explained *grosso modo* by the advantages, identified in neo-classical theory, of increased competition and subsequent price reductions. It should enable the resources freed to be used for other productive purposes, thus raising collective wealth (Cecchini, 1988). The assumption is that the pressure generated by wider competition will force more firms to ensure their own survival by systematically improving their competitiveness and differentiating their products. In return, the opening up of national borders will provide firms with new foreign market opportunities, thus allowing them to grow and, consequently, enjoy the benefits of economies of scale.

As far as the effects on SMEs are concerned, we already know that there are plenty of restrictions on this and on the increase of international trade. For example, there are distance barriers, the small size of some markets, cultural differences, and a number of "invisible" barriers, both regional and national, created by policies aimed at protecting national production. However, the opening up of borders can, for many regions, become an important factor in explaining differences in regional growth, as Maurice Catin (1989) has shown for the region of Baden-Württemberg in Germany or Rhône-Alpes in France. These differences may result from the presence of large foreign firms or new foreign investments. But what about small local firms, in particular those whose market is purely regional? Are they affected to the same extent, or could they, too, take advantage of the new open markets?

For those small businesses operating in open markets and unable to face worldwide competition because of low productivity, the increasing trend towards elimination of tariff barriers will lead to closure. Others will have to relocate to escape the new competitive pressures. As a result, regions such as Lille in France or Wallonie in Belgium, due to their increasing inability to adapt, will stagnate or even decline. On the other hand, other regions such as Lombardia in Italy, with more new resources, may experience spatial restructuring, for example as a result of new trade flows and the creation of new transportation channels or cores. This could encourage new manufacturing and service firms to move to the region, thus multiplying the exchange of commercial, competitive and technological information. It could reinforce the synergic networks which foster diffusion of new technologies and innovation. All this will result in the development of a new competitive capacity, and may enable SMEs already exporting to increase their exports, or help those wishing to start exporting. This may indirectly favour firms working as subcontractors for medium-sized or large exporters (Moini, 1992).

Finally, the restructuring of regional space may also lead to new relations with urban centres for advanced services, attract new resources to the employment market and stimulate training to produce a more qualified workforce. It may even, in some cases, increase regional specialization or change productive vocations.

RESEARCH METHODOLOGY

Following the creation of the North American free trade zone, we decided to assess the influence of all these elements on small businesses in three small regions in Quebec: the Laurentides region, to the north of Montreal; the Lanaudière region to the east of Montreal; and the Mauricie-Bois-Francs region in the centre of Quebec.[2] In 1990, these three semi-rural, semi-urban regions were home to 65 manufacturing firms with more than 250 employees and 3,837 SMEs. In the Bois-Francs (the southern section of the Mauricie-Bois-Francs region), small business has developed a remarkable dynamism over the last ten years, with the creation of dozens of small units.

The initial assumption was that only those firms directly affected by the Agreement, i.e., those offering products on which both Canadian and American customs duties would be eliminated within ten years, would have taken specific steps to counter or take advantage of the Agreement. Those firms already operating in sectors with no tariff barriers would not be directly influenced. The clauses of the Agreement (Government of Canada, 1988) taking effect in the period 1989 to 1999 were studied closely. We selected 21 sectors[3] that were seriously affected by the reduction of tariff barriers, and which

---

2. The choice of these regions was made by the research sponsor as representative of Quebec's industrialized regions without big cities.

3. The 21 sectors (three dots, with the Standard Industrial Codification) are: (101) Meat and poultry, (104) Dairy products, (107) Bakery products, (243) Men's and boy's clothing, (244) Women's clothing, (245) Children's clothing, (249) Other clothing, (251) Sawmills, planing mills and shingle mills, (252) Veneer and plywood, (254) Sash, doors and other millwood industries, (259) Wood (other), (261) Household furniture, (264) Office furniture, (269) Furniture and fixtures, (273) Paper box and bag industries, (279) Other converted paper products industries, (281) Commercial printing, (311) Agricultural implements, (312) Commercial refrigeration and cooling equipment, (319) Other machinery and equipment industries (except electrical), (328) Boat building and repair industry. For this paper and to simplify, we have grouped these into nine major sectors, as shown in Table 3.

accounted for a large proportion of SMEs and jobs in at least one of the three regions studied.

The questionnaire test was carried out by a direct preliminary session of approximately one-and-a-half hours with 25 firms selected by development agents in the regions and spread over the sectors. The questionnaire was then "personalized" by firm and by sector.[4] The questions were, to a large extent, closed and divided into four sections: the firm's attributes, the level of its equipment, scanning and R&D policies, its perception of and strategies for free trade and international competition, and its use of the milieu's various resources (Huberman and Miles, 1984). The inquiry was carried out at the end of spring 1991, when questionnaires were mailed to the entire population of 879 firms in the 21 sectors.[5] One reminder was sent, and a second made personally by telephone by the development agents in the regions concerned. A total of 242 firms or 27.5% of the population responded. Table 1 shows the attributes of the sample with respect to the population as a whole. The sample is representative of the population in terms of size, region and industries.[6]

TABLE 1
Some Characteristics of the Population and the Sample Studied

Regions	Population Number	Sample	No. of employees			
			1-19	**20-49**	**50-99**	**100-250**
Laurentides	223	57 (25.6%)	43	10	2	2
		100%	75.5%	17.5%	3.5%	3.5%
Lanaudière	211	47 (22.3%)	35	7	4	1
		100%	74.4%	14.9%	8.5%	2.1%
Mauricie Bois-Francs	445	138 (31.0%)	80	33	14	11
		100%	58.0%	23.9%	10.1%	8.0%
Total	879	242 (27.5%)	158	50	20	14
		100%	65.3%	20.7%	8.3%	5.8%

The results show that 84% of respondents were independent, the others being either subsidiaries or branches. The average number of employees was 27.5, of whom 81.4% were employed in production. The average growth in the total number of jobs since 1987 was 31.7% (the workforce of 70% of the

---

4. Each questionnaire sent out was identified in advance using information provided by the enterprise data bank at Quebec's Industrial Research Centre (name and address, number of employees, name(s) of owner-manager(s), main products, exports, etc.). The clauses of the Agreement affecting their products (under information obtained) were added.

5. The list came from the Centre de recherche industrielle du Québec's annual survey.

6. Chi-square test, p = 0.05%.

respondent firms had increased during that period). The average growth in profits for the same period was 20.4% in nominal value. In addition, the firms had invested an average of $9,700 per employee in equipment or fixed assets since 1989. One quarter of respondents (27%) said they carried out R&D on a fairly regular basis. Some 34% carried out commercial scanning, just over half of them formally. In addition, 40% carried out technological scanning, 60% of them regularly. Finally, 48% said they contracted out 16.7% of their production. There were almost as many subcontractors (44%), for whom subcontracting represented an average of 40.1% of their total production.

INFORMATION, PERCEPTION, EVALUATION AND REACTIONS WITH RESPECT TO THE FREE TRADE AGREEMENT

Despite the basis on which the sectors were selected, the products of one-quarter (23.6%) of respondent firms were sufficiently specialized or typical to avoid being influenced by the new Free Trade Agreement rules. However, whatever their situation, the firms were questioned on their level of understanding of the Agreement, their position before it began to be applied and, finally, the steps they had taken or planned to take to counter or take advantage of it.

Table 2 sets out information levels. Generally speaking, the firms seemed poorly informed. Only 26.4% considered they were fully or sufficiently informed. Surprisingly, the firms not affected by the Agreement were a little better informed than the others. Among the 625 references to information sources, the media in its various forms accounted for 169 (27%), the federal government 124 (19.8%) and specialized publications 104 (16.6%). Other sources included sectorial associations and the Quebec government, but to a lesser extent, with, respectively, 9% and 8% of the mentions.

TABLE 2
Quality of Information According to Effect of FTA

	Insufficient	Incomplete	Acceptable	Sufficient	Complete	Total
Firms not affected by FTA (23.6%)	7	13	14	15	2	51
	13.7%	25.5%	27.5%	29.4%	3.9%	23.6%
Firms affected by FTA (76.4%)	42	36	47	37	3	165
	25.5%	21.8%	28.5%	22.4%	1.8%	76.4%
Total of firms (100%)	49	49	61	52	5	216
	22.7%	22.7%	28.2%	24.1%	2.3%	100.0%

It was not surprising that 44% of respondents said they were in favour of the FTA during the debate preceding its adoption by the Canadian government, while 23% opposed it. One-third were indifferent. This division is substantially the same in the United States (Moini, 1992). However, after 1987, and especially as a result of the hard recession of 1991-1992, there was a slight shift in opinions, with 6% of those previously favourable becoming opposed. In 1991, when the Agreement was extended to include Mexico, fears ran higher, with 49% of respondents opposing the extension. As might have been expected, firms that exported or planned to do so were generally more favourable to the Agreement than the others.

Among the 47 firms that viewed the Agreement's effects favourably, half (25) mentioned (in various ways) access to new markets, one-quarter (12) spoke of lower prices for raw materials, and slightly over 20% (10) said that the new situation would force them to become more competitive, which they did not see as being a bad thing. In contrast, of the 68 that opposed the Agreement, the vast majority (90%) thought that increased competition and pressures resulting from the arrival of new American products had already caused or would cause them to lose customers. They did not have the time or resources to adjust their productivity to take account of the new competition due to lower salaries and raw material costs in the United States. Some firms also thought that their American competitors were not complying with the Agreement's rules, and that dumping had actually increased.

Three questions concerning reactions to the Agreement were then asked to see if respondent firms had taken or were planning to take any actions to benefit from the Agreement's positive effects or to counter its negative effects, and if so, what these steps were. *Only 70 (29%)* of the 242 respondent firms said they had taken or planned to take such steps. In all, 24 firms (10%) had taken steps to take advantage of the new situation, and 44 (18%) had acted to protect themselves from eventual negative consequences. In addition, 53 firms (22%) planned to take actions either to protect themselves or to take advantage of the Agreement.

The three questions concerning the action taken by these 70 firms were open questions. A total of 120 types of action were mentioned by respondents, and were grouped together under four headings: product-related action, productivity-related action, export-related action and structure-related action. Most of the action taken is of type 2 (international marketing-related) or type 3 (productivity increases). Both types received 46 mentions each, or 38.3% of the total. Next, in order, came product-related action (19 mentions or 15.8%) and structure-related action (9 mentions or 7.5%).

INCREASED SME COMPETITIVENESS

It may seem surprising that so few firms (just 29%) had taken action, despite the fact that 76.4% of SMEs in the sample were directly affected by the FTA. One reason for this emerged from the responses to question 27, which required owner-managers to assess the external variables having the most impact on the firm. First in order of importance was the economic recession, and second the high interest rates in force at the time. The third, fourth and fifth variables were the new sales taxes, the growth of the industry and the overvaluation of the Canadian dollar. The Free Trade Agreement came much further down the list, or was just one of the factors affecting the national and international economic environment. Is this because the SMEs are not very concerned or interested by the opening up of borders?

To answer this question, we had to pursue the inquiry in order to understand better the strategy of SMEs in the face of the new international situation. For that, the SMEs were classified, first, in terms of their exposure to free trade and, second, in terms of the various actions taken or to be taken to improve their overall competitiveness. The first measure gave what we call the level of "awareness" with respect to the opening up of international borders. The different actions taken to increase productivity and to become differentiated on markets provided the level of "dynamism." These two measures illustrating the firms' capacity to face up to the new situation gave a general measure of their "exposure." In other words, the "level of exposure" was measured by the extent of the firms' production affected by the reduction of Canadian customs duties within the new free trade framework (Lesage and De la Rochefordière, 1990). The more its products were affected by the Agreement, the greater the proportion of its total production composed of such products or the more it exported such products, the greater the firm's "exposure" to the new open international situation.

"Dynamism" was measured on the basis of five variable groups. The first group included the number of specific actions taken (as mentioned above) to counter or take advantage of the FTA ("product-related or production-related action," "a shift in operations to respond to the needs of the American market," etc.), giving a maximum of six possibilities (measure: 0 to 6 actions). The second group was concerned with the firm's integration in its environment, that is, its use of resources from the milieu, such as membership of an information network or professional association or recent use of government programs. The scale ran from 0 to a maximum of 4 kinds of relation with the milieu. The third variable was concerned with strategic attitudes measured on a Likert-type scale of 0 to 7, from reactive to active and even proactive attitudes.[7] Responses

---

7. For example, the firm was asked if it usually waited for other firms to try out new equipment before following suit, or whether it tried to beat them to it, etc. This question included four types of statement.

were averaged to place the firms in quintiles and rank them from 0 to 4. The fourth group was concerned with the firm's behaviour in terms of commercial scanning and technological and R&D watch. Respondents were required to qualify their internal policies ("absent due to lack of resources," "absent because the firm did not see the need for it," "spontaneous or contingent procedures," "systematic and formal procedures," etc.). Each firm was classified from 0 to 4 (4 being the greatest number of policies effected on a formal basis). The last group was concerned with investments made over the last three years and planned for the coming three years. The total amount of these investments was expressed per employee, and each firm was classified from 0 to 4 (0: no investment, 4: major investment).

These groupings led to the construction of a *composite dynamism indicator* on a theoretical scale of 0 to 22,[8] but in fact the minimum realised was 1 and the maximum 17 or, in percentage terms, 0 to 100%. A factorial analysis helped establish the variables used in the dynamism measure. Finally, Kendall tests were carried out, revealing a strong correlation between ranks over the five groups (Huberman and Miles, 1984). The calculations show that, on average, each variable adds new information and strengthens the dynamism measurement.

Figure 1 takes up the exposure factor (x axis) and the dynamism factor (reversed for easier reading) (y axis). The further a firm is located towards the bottom-left corner of the graph, the more steps it has taken to improve its ability to face national and international competition, even though not forced to do so by the reduction of customs duties between Canada and the U.S. Such firms seem less threatened by the new international competition resulting in part from the FTA. Conversely, the further a firm is located towards the upper-right corner of the graph, the greater the effects of free trade on its production, although it remains relatively passive as a result of ignorance, lack of resources, despondency or other reasons. Such firms therefore appear to be highly vulnerable to the new international situation.

Also located in the less threatened area (lower-left corner) are craft-type firms operating in relatively protected markets. These very small firms produce tailor-made products to order, operate in small, specific or highly localized markets, or achieve differentiation by adding specific services to their products. In all, 38 firms of this type were identified during the analysis of responses. The analysis covered product and market types and the position of the firm with respect to its competitors.

---

8. Or, as we said: 7 (0 to 6 actions with respect to FTA) + 5 (0 to 4 relations with the milieu) + 5 (0 to 4 quintiles) + 5 (0 to 5 levels of investment) = 22. These differents methods of calculation are well explained in Huberman and Miles (1984).

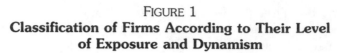

FIGURE 1
**Classification of Firms According to Their Level
of Exposure and Dynamism**

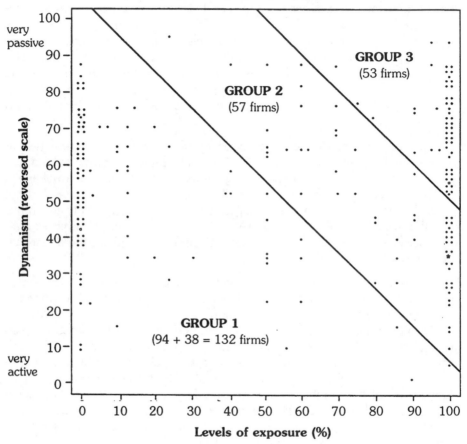

FIGURE 1
**Classification of Firms According to Their Level
of Exposure and Dynamism**

Key: . : firms on open markets

Note: Firms with specialized production or operating on local market (38 in all) were transferred to group 1, and have not therefore been shown in their initial placings.

The vulnerability of firms on open markets was measured by their level of passivity and the extent to which their production was affected by the reduction of tariff walls. Clearly, all those firms located in the upper-right corner of the graph operate on open markets.

One question remained unanswered: is the threat as great for a firm that is highly affected but also highly dynamic (lower-right corner) as for a firm that is only slightly affected but passive (upper-left corner)? In other words, should the level of dynamism increase in proportion to the level of exposure for a firm to be considered as vulnerable as another?

After running a number of computer simulations which did not provide better solutions,[9] we gave these two components an equal value for classification purposes, shown by a straight oblique line in the figure. Thus, in this figure, two firms on the same line were considered to be equally threatened whether they were highly affected and highly dynamic (lower-right corner) or moderately affected and moderately dynamic (centre). In this way, of the 204 SMEs operating in open markets[10] a first group of 94 were found to be more *dynamic but not threatened*. As mentioned above, the 38 very small firms operating on closed markets were added to this group, which, as a result, gives a total of 132 firms, or 54.5% of the respondents. The central area of the graph groups together 57 *vulnerable* firms (23.6% of respondents) that were either highly affected and highly dynamic, or moderately aware and less dynamic. The third group includes 53 *very vulnerable* firms (21.9% of respondents) that were found to be passive and highly affected.

Table 3 contains a grouping of respondents by industry. It shows that the most vulnerable industrial sector is the clothing sector, with 50% of the firms directly affected by free trade but having taken few or no steps to improve their competitiveness. Conversely, the machinery, commercial printing, sash, door and wood, and food industries have reacted well or fairly well to the opening up of the market; between 53% and 97% of firms in these industries have products that are less affected by the FTA or have taken extensive action to improve their competitiveness, or both. Between these two groups are SMEs in the boat building and paper industries, which are either vulnerable or highly vulnerable, with 60% and 40% of firms in the first case, and 50% and 30% in the second.

The second structure-related attribute is the size of the firm, and here again a difference emerges. Medium-sized firms, in particular those with between 100 and 250 employees, are vulnerable or more vulnerable.[11] In addition, 60% of firms with between 50 and 99 employees are either vulnerable or highly vulnerable. However, one-third of the smaller enterprises (with between 10 and 19 employees) also fall into the highly vulnerable group. The smallest firms, those with less than 10 employees, have products or operate in niches that are too specialized or specific to be vulnerable, and 80% of those with 20 to 49 employees seem to be holding their own in the new open markets.

---

9. This classification was compared to others, in which the proportional importance of the two components differed. A discriminant analysis produced the same set of predictor variables, but the chosen classification was the most effective in terms of correctly classifying cases. For a more detailed discussion on this, see Julien, Joyal and Deshaies (1992).

10. 242 SMEs less 38 craft-type firms.

11. But here, the very low number of firms may not ensure representativity.

TABLE 3
Vulnerability of Firms by Grouped Industrial Sector

Industry (CTI)	Group 1 No threat or slight threat	Group 2 Vulnerable	Group 3 Highly vulnerable	Total
Food (101, 104, 107)	16 55%	6 21%	7 24%	29
Clothing (243, 244, 245, 249)	7 22%	9 28%	**16** **50%**	32
Wood (251, 252, 259)	17 53%	8 25%	7 22%	32
Sash, door and other millwood (254)	26 60%	8 19%	9 21%	43
Furniture and fixtures (261, 264, 269)	17 44%	**15** **38%**	7 18%	39
Paper and allied products (273, 279)	2 20%	**5** **50%**	3 30%	10
Commercial printing (281)	**14** **78%**	2 11%	2 11%	18
Machinery (except electrical) (311, 319)	**33** **97%**	1 3%	0 0%	34
Boat building and repair industry (328)	0 0%	**3** **60%**	**2** **40%**	5
All industries studied	132 54%	57 24%	53 22%	242 100%

Other calculations show that exporting firms (18 % of the sample[12]) fall mainly into Group 2, that is, into the group that is moderately vulnerable, but are almost completely absent from the highly vulnerable group. These firms are often bigger than average and operate in the four moderately or highly threatened sectors (clothing, furniture, paper and boat building). In addition, investments in the last three years or planned for the next three years average only $9,700 per employee in firms in the most vulnerable group. This figure rises to $19,500 for firms in the first group and $18,500 for those in the second group. Use of resources from the milieu is much higher among the firms that are slightly or moderately vulnerable. The other variables, including debt levels, profitability, increases in manpower and, to a lesser degree, growth of sales and respondents' opinions of the FTA, were not significantly discrimina-

---

12.   On the specific behaviour of the exporting firms or other SMEs which want to export, see Joyal, Julien and Deshaies (1993).

tory between the three groups. The firm's location (rural or urban and in terms of region) had no effect on the level of vulnerability.

A further discriminant analysis enabled some other variables to be added to the list. For example, limited regional sales accompanied by insufficient product differentiation tended to increase vulnerability, as did a low level of use of new technologies or R&D: as we said earlier, only 6% of the firms in Group 3 carried out R&D. In contrast, Group 1 firms were more aggressive in terms of competition, and daring initiatives were more common in this group. Table 4 contains a summary of the different variables identified.

TABLE 4
Main Attributes Distinguishing the SMEs Studied with Respect to Free Trade

Attributes	**Group 1** **No threat or** **small threat**	**Group 2** **Vulnerable**	**Group 3** **Highly** **vulnerable**
Classification of sectors	Machinery (311, 319), commercial printing (281)	Furniture and fixtures (261, 264, 269), paper and (279) boat	Clothing (244, 245 and 249), allied products (273), building (328)
	Food (101, 104, 107) Wood (251, 252, 259) and Sash and door (254)		
Size (production employees)	1-9 20-49	10-19	
	50-99	100-250	
Situation vis-à-vis exporting		Exporters	No or few exports
Past or planned investments	19 500 $	18 500 $	9 700 $
Opinion vis-a-vis the FTA	in favour or indifferent		against almost
Regional sales	considerable	average	low
Product differentiation	high	average	none or small
Use of resources from milieu, use of new technols, R&D	Substantial	Substantial	Slight

GLOBALIZATION AND SME DIFFERENTIATION

By broadening the notion of competitiveness to include national and international markets, a total of 189 firms (78.1%) were found to have reacted to the opening up of markets, a substantial increase over the initial figure of 70

(28.9%). This suggests that, to measure the capacity of SMEs to act as a result of or react to the removal of international barriers, the initial approach, which considered only trade between two countries, was insufficient. Increasing numbers of SMEs are realizing the new challenges created by market globalization.

In the case of the study described here, this new exposure is concerned not only with the United States, but with the entire world. The free trade agreement with the United States is just one element in the new international structure. The challenge of market globalization is not limited to the United States, but includes the Common Market countries, Japan and the new industrialized countries too.

SMEs have developed different ways of facing up to this challenge. One is the use of new production technologies. A recent study of the level of computerization of SMEs (5 to 250 employees) showed that the number using at least three technologies had increased threefold in the period 1989-1992, from 5.7% to 16.7% (Carrière and Julien, 1992). More than 50% of the firms studied having at least 5 employees used at least one computer-controlled machine or CAD system. This research shows again that, compared to other countries, the proportion of Quebec's SMEs using at least one advanced technology has almost caught up with the American figure, exceeds the Ontarian figure and is not far from the Italian Piedmontais area (Julien, 1992; Stat-Can, 1992). Other studies have also shown that SMEs are particularly effective in terms of innovation to create differentiation on national or international markets (Acs and Audretsch, 1990). Current research in our research centre is tending to show the same thing: that more and more SMEs agree that international competitiveness depends as much on product differentiation (often by ad hoc innovation) as on the use of new production technologies or differences in distribution and specific markets.

However, this does not mean that all SMEs want or are able to face the resulting new international competition. As we said earlier, some SMEs do not need to change much, since they are protected in specific markets. On the other hand, others operating in more open markets are delaying adaptation or refusing to adapt to the new international environment. They will not be able to survive, and this will have a weakening impact on those regions in which they are present in large numbers.

Much research is still needed to measure the impact of market globalization in more detail not only on existing SMEs, but on new SMEs too, including those in new sectors. Most economists have focused too much attention on the "wave of globalization" and the opening up of borders, both of which are likely to give a second wind to big business. By doing this, they tend to forget the massive rise of SMEs, the new relationships with big business and, especially, their particular capacity to fight globalization in new and original ways.

REFERENCES

ACS, Z., and AUDRESTCH, D.B. (1990), *Innovation and Small Firms*, Cambridge, Mass.: MIT Press.

AMIT, R., and SCHOEMAKER, P.J.H. (1993), "Strategic assets and Organizational Rent," *Strategic Management Journal*, 14 (1), January, 33-46.

CANADIAN GOVERNMENT (1988), "An Act Respecting the Implementation of the Free Trade Agreement between Canada and the United States," Volume 3, Appendix Part B, "Tariffs and Trade," and Volume 4, Part B.

CARRIÈRE, J.B., and JULIEN, P.A. (1992), "Profil technologique de la PME manufacturière québécoise. Rapport final," Quebec Manufacturing Association, September.

CATIN, M. (1989), "Exportations, productivité et dynamique des industries régionales," Working Paper No. 107, 1989/9, Centre d'économie régionale, Université d'Aix-Marseille II.

CECCHINI Report (1988), "'1992': The New European Economy," Brussels: European Economic Commission, pp.17 and sq.

CHENIER, J.A., and MICHAEL, J.P. (1990), "Aid for Small Business Exporting Firms: the Role of Goverments and Information Networks," Halifax: The Institute of Research on Public Policy.

FILION, L.J. (1990), "Free Trade. The Need for a Definition of Small Business," *Journal of Small Business and Entrepreneurship*, 7 (2), January-March, 31-45.

HUBERMAN, A.B., and MILES, M.B. (1984), *Qualitative Data Analysis: A Sourcebook of New Methods*, Beverly Cliffs (Cal.): Sage.

JEANNERET, P. (1985), *Régions et frontières internationales*, Neuchatel: EDES.

JOYAL, A., JULIEN, P.A., and DESHAIES, L. (1993), "Les PME exportatrices et l'Accord de libre-échange," *Revue internationale PME*, 6 (1).

JULIEN, P.A. (1992), «Petites et moyennes entreprises manufacturières et nouvelles technologies: la situation au Québec», *Revue internationale de gestion*, 17 (2), November, 29-33.

JULIEN, P.A. (1993), "Small Businesses as a Research Subject: Some Reflexions on Knowledge of Small Businesses and Its Effects on Economic Theory," *Small Business Economics*, 5 (2), 157-166.

JULIEN, P.A., JOYAL, A., and DESHAIES, L. (1992), *La PME manufacturière en région et le libre-échange avec les États-Unis*, Quebec, OPDQ, and Trois-Rivières, GREPME, March, 172 pages.

KATHAWALA, Y., JUDD, R., MONIPALLIL, M., and WEIRRICH, M. (1989), "Exporting Practices and Problems of Illinois Firms," *Journal of Small Business Management*, 27 (1), January, 53-59.

LAURENCIN, J.P., and ROUSIER, N. (1990), "Une approche territoriale de l'économie régionale dans la perspective 1992. Le cas de la région Rhône-Alpes," *Revue d'économie régionale et urbaine*, No. 1, 79-104.

LESAGE, A., and DE LA ROCHEFORDIÈRE, Ch. (1990), "Sensibilités régionales à l'achèvement du Grand Marché Européen. Méthodologies et études de cas," *Revue d'économie régionale et urbaine*, No. 1, 59-78.

LEFEBVRE, L.A., and LEFEBVRE, E. (1988), "Technologie et libre-échange, une complicité souhaitable," *L'Actualité économique*, 64 (4), December, 616-629.

LÉO, P.Y., MONNEYER-LONGÉ, M.C., and PHILIPPE, J. (1990), *La PME: Stratégies internationales*, Paris: Economica.

MAILLAT, D. (1990), "Régions transfrontalières et Marché européen unique. Le cas de la région Franche-Comté/Suisse romande," *Revue d'économie régionale et urbaine*, No. 1, 117-136.

MIESENBROCK, K.J. (1988), "Small Exporting: A Literature Review," *International Small Business Journal*, 6 (2), January/March, 42-61.

MOINI, A.H. (1992), "Europe 1992: A Challenge to Small Exporters," *Journal of Small Business Management*, 30 (1), January, 11-20.

NELSON, C.A. (1984), "The Relationship of Export Obstacles to the Export Trading Company Act of 1982," *Dissertation Abstracts International*, Vol. 45/03-A, p. 904.

OECD (1991), "L'internationalisation des petites entreprises," *Cahiers ILE*, No. 14, January.

RATTI, E. (1986), "Théories du développement des régions frontières et mutations technologiques," Symposium of the Association des sciences régionales de langue française, Paris.

RUGMAN, A.M., and VERBEKE, A. (1989), "The Impact of Free Trade on Small Business in Canada," *Journal of Small Business and Entrepreneurship*, 6 (3), Spring, 51-56.

STATISTICS CANADA (1989), "Survey of Manufacturing Technology – The Characteristics of the Plants," Science Statistics, Catalogue 88-001, October.

8

Adjusting to NAFTA:
State Enterprises and Privatization in Quebec in Light of the Mexican and American Experiences[1]

Luc Bernier
École nationale d'administration publique

Privatization policy in Quebec is explained using a comparative perspective. Quebec and Mexico both extended their privatization efforts to reduce their vulnerability to trade disputes with their American partner. In Quebec, a new wave of privatization was launched while, in Mexico, some of the largest state enterprises were sold off. From interventionist traditions, the privatizations have brought Quebec and Mexico closer to the dominant American model.

STATE ENTERPRISES IN THE 1990s

In most industrial and developing countries since 1945, the state has moved beyond regulation and has become an investor, a trader and a producer. Initially, state enterprises were involved in declining industries or subsidized services, but many are now active in competitive and profitable sectors of the economy, sometimes on international markets (Laux and Molot, 1988: 3). In Canada, the federal and provincial governments have used state enterprises as a pragmatic response to market failures to foster economic development. Hundreds of these public enterprises have been created by the federal and all provincial governments mostly after 1960 (Prichard, 1983: ch. 4 & 5). By

---

1. This chapter is part of a larger research program on state enterprises in Quebec established with the financial help of the FCAR. In this chapter, state enterprise is used as a generic term for state-owned enterprise or public enterprise, i.e., an enterprise owned or controlled by the state and involved in commercial activities.

creating state enterprises, officials in Canada were following what Europeans have also been doing for a number of years, often on a greater scale (Laux and Molot, 1988). State enterprises are (or were) more important in Canada than in Switzerland or Japan but modest in comparison with France, Italy, the United Kingdom or Austria.

Comparisons have more often been drawn with the American neighbour, Canada's and Quebec's most important economic partner. Such comparisons have opposed the American private enterprise model and Canadian state interventionism.[2] The interest for such comparisons has been rejuvenated with the entry of Mexico into the North American free trade zone. Like Canada, the third member of the North American Free Trade Agreement (NAFTA), Mexico, also has an interventionist tradition.

Confronted in the past with very different economic realities, governments in the three countries developed adapted economic policy instruments. NAFTA now forces them to play according to the same rules and limits the capacity of governments to use some of their traditional instruments. Article 1503-1 of NAFTA specifies that "Nothing in this Agreement shall be construed to prevent a Party from maintaining or establishing a state enterprise." But article 1503-2 adds that "Each Party shall ensure... that any state enterprise... acts in a manner that is not inconsistent with Party's obligations under Chapters Eleven (Investment) and Fourteen (Financial Services)..." Finally, 1503-3 imposes non-discriminatory treatment to investors of another Party. If the wording of the treaty has not done so, trade disputes resulting from NAFTA have definitely reduced the capacity of governments to intervene in the economy by means of state enterprises. Decisions made by state enterprises that were of little interest outside national borders have become international issues. Hydro-Quebec, which was little known in the United States outside New York financial circles twenty years ago, is now under constant scrutiny for its handling of Native rights in the James Bay area and for "secret" contracts with a few companies in Quebec that are exporting on the US market (for example Norsk-Hydro's magnesium).

More than other policy instruments such as subsidies and regulation, state enterprises have been created to achieve discriminatory objectives: for example, to keep a plant operating or to do research in a specific mining area, etc. The use of this instrument was further limited over the last decade as governments decided to privatize some of these enterprises and rationalize their investments. Initiated during Mrs. Thatcher's first government for ideological reasons developed in reaction to the rather unique (dis)functionning of the British economy, privatization became popular around the world during the 1980s. In Canada, the British example was used by various governments,

---

2.   For an overview of the importance of state enterprises in Canada, see Stanbury (1994: 167-169).

although the strength of trade unions, the labour-management relations and the productivity records were in no way comparable to the British experience. The Quebec government used the British example out of context to justify its own privatization drive. Governments decided to privatize because of ideological pressures and also because they were running out of money to finance state enterprises.

The Quebec case constitutes an interesting paradox. On the one hand, in Quebec more than in any other Canadian province since the early 1960s, the bid for a relatively independent economy was placed in the hands of state enterprises (Bernier, 1989, ch. 4). The creation of Hydro-Quebec was the only issue of the 1962 provincial general election. After the beginning of the Quiet Revolution, the state of Quebec pursued two primary strategies: the creation of state enterprises and the strengthening of Quebec-based private enterprises (McRoberts, 1993: 132). Second, Quebec was the province most in favour of the free trade agreement. Its strong support made it possible for the Canadian Conservative party to fight and win the 1988 federal general election on this issue. Nevertheless, some of Quebec's major industries have been caught in trade disputes: beer, wood, magnesium, steel, etc. Several of its state enterprises have some kind of involvement in the trade disputes: Hydro-Quebec, Sidbec, Rexfor, the Société des alcools du Québec. International economic transformations and the "essoufflement" of the model developed during Quebec's Quiet Revolution forced a transformation of the state enterprise sector. In order to compete on the North American market, some state enterprises had to be privatized, others had to be rejuvenated.

Regardless of whether Quebec becomes an independent country in the coming year, the study of its state enterprises provides an understanding of how a sub-national government can adapt to a transforming world economy, a necessity also understood by the Mexican government. This chapter aims to situate Quebec's state enterprises and privatization policy in the context of the evolution of the NAFTA partners. The Mexican government has decided to open its border to foreign investment, and, to do this, to "normalize" its economic practices. Privatization is thus part of a more general process in Mexico. In the dominant economic partner country, the United States, state enterprises were practically unknown and this has set the norm for its free trade partners. In Mexico as in Quebec, privatization helps adjust to the American way of doing business. The role played by state enterprises and by the provinces themselves was obviously neglected when NAFTA was signed. In trade disputes, however, the role of provincial state enterprises has been discussed frequently. Foreign state enterprises have often been presented as a menace in the literature on the future of American economic development. In 1979, Lamont wrote that foreign state enterprises were a threat to American business. For Vernon (1988), their privatization constitutes a challenge for American foreign policy.

As discussed in the second section of this chapter, the privatization drive had ended in Quebec by the time the first free trade agreement was reached in 1988. In 1992, NAFTA forced both the Quebec and Mexican governments to move further along the road to privatization. In Quebec, the government initiated a second wave of privatization. In Mexico, as discussed in the third section of the chapter, the same government that had initially sold off its smallest state enterprises went further by privatizing the largest ones. Both governments did so to play the economic game according to American rules. The primary interest of both Quebec and Mexico in NAFTA was to secure access to the American market. In order to do so, state enterprises had to be privatized. In Mexico, privatizations were carried out prior to entering NAFTA. In Quebec, several trade disputes with American companies and the U.S. government were needed to trigger them.

THE QUEBEC CASE[3]

For Quebec, which does not control monetary policy and shares control over regulation, subsidies and fiscal instruments with Ottawa, what could be achieved through state enterprises is of vital importance (Bernier, 1988). Economic development over the last thirty years has relied heavily on Hydro-Quebec, the Caisse de dépôt et placement and other smaller state enterprises. Hydro-Quebec is certainly the best known state enterprise.[4] The electricity company is one of the very few state enterprises that have not seriously been considered for privatization, with the Caisse de dépôt et placement. In Quebec, the network of state enterprises has been reduced but still exists, as Table 1 illustrates. Quebec's state enterprises fulfill the roles of bankers, traders, investors and producers. They compete with private enterprises in finance, forest products, steel, mining, oil and gas, manufacturing, television broadcasting, and agriculture. Some of them have been very useful instruments of policy implementation, but successive governments have been unable to control many of them. In 1985, at the beginning of the privatization drive, they constituted the most important network of state enterprises in any Canadian provinces (Gouvernement du Québec, 1986b: 22).

Following the British model, governments around the world have initiated privatizations. However, contrary to the British example, most governments have merely streamlined their intervention in the economy, selling small state enterprises. The median size of stock market transaction exceeded $1,200 million (Canadian) in Great Britain but reached only $17 million in

---

3.   This section is based in part on Bernier (1994).

4.   For a longer explanation on the importance and development of Hydro-Quebec, see chapter 15 of Lachapelle et al. (1993).

Canada (Stanbury, 1994: 172). Provincial governments in Canada have sold mostly small state enterprises. Of the 61 privatizations for which the value of the transaction is known, 45 were under $100 million (Canadian), nine were between $100 and $300 million, four were between $300 and $500 million, and three were over $500 million. Of the 16 transactions over $100 million, four were by the Quebec government: the Albertan subsidiary of Soquip, assets of Soquem, Donohue Paper and four office towers (Stanbury, 1994: 211-214).[5]

According to the numbers published by the government (see Table 2), the average value of the 43 transactions in Quebec was $36.7 million, with a median value of $10.9 million. Twenty-one deals were under $10 million, 19 were between $10 and $100 million, and only three were over $100 million. After the first wave of privatization ending in 1988, the government decided to privatize the assets of only one SOE between 1989 and 1991. Privatization became popular once again between 1992 and 1994, when the average transaction value ($39.7 million) was similar to the 1986-88 average ($38.6 million). A comparison of Tables 1 and 2 illustrates that despite the privatizations, state enterprises in Quebec have generally continued to develop. The SGF continues to expand despite the sale of Donohue, its most profitable subsidiary. At the other end of the financial performance spectrum, SIDBEC was finally sold in 1994 after losing huge sums of money. In an almost zero-inflation economy, the total assets of the Caisse de dépôt and Hydro-Quebec have climbed tremendously. State enterprises in Quebec have been transformed, reduced in part but not closed down. The first wave has already been explained in terms of a rationalization cycle initiated in 1979 (Bernier, 1994). This paper attempts to explain that the need to adjust to the new North American free trade reality explains the second wave of privatization after 1992. Privatizations were achieved to avoid costly fights in front of the courts over unfair competition cases.

Even before the election of the Liberal Party in 1985, the importance of state enterprises in Quebec's economy was declining. Total investments by state enterprises (Hydro-Quebec included) declined steadily from around 4.5% of the GIP during the 1977-1979 period to 1.61% in 1985 and 1.71% in 1987 (Gouvernement du Québec, 1986A: 25). Excluding Hydro-Quebec, the investments of other state enterprises represent 0.24% of the GIP in 1985 and 0.23% in 1987. Until 1985, the Parti québécois government had initiated a few privatization attempts in a context of budgetary restraint. The end of Sidbec-Normines and other rationalization efforts reduced the drain on state finances, by getting rid of the lame ducks. A money-losing sawmill, Samoco, was privatized in 1980. The Société nationale de l'amiante (SNA) rationalized

---

5. In the latest data made available by the government, the value of the office towers sold has been reduced to $98.3 million.

its mining activites and sold subsidiaries. Shortly after his resignation as Finance Minister, the current Premier, Jacques Parizeau (1985), explained that mistakes had to be corrected and that state enterprises like Soquem had outlived their policy usefulness. He also suggested that the role of the investment vehicles, the Caisse de dépôt and the Société générale de financement (SGF), should be reconsidered. Before the Parti québécois stepped down in 1985, the SGF was reorganized, selling assets and becoming involved in joint-ventures to attract foreign investments to Quebec.

In addition to these few examples of privatization, the attitude of the government had changed. In his 1985 budget speech, the Parti québécois Finance Minister announced that the government was considering selling assets, moving into joint-ventures with the private sector, obtaining stock financing for some state enterprises and regrouping the operations of state enterprises undertaking similar activities. The Minister, Yves Duhaime, argued that it was essential to reconsider the role of the state sector, however crucial it had been in the past. The government also considered privatizing the Société des alcools du Québec, which was again up for sale in 1994.

In its political program of 1985, the Quebec Liberal Party suggested that some state enterprises should be privatized. The principle put forward was that the state should not compete with the private sector "without good reason." The program stated that, in a world where small enterprises create most jobs, the role of state enterprises as economic levers or industrial redeployment instruments was over. The program also suggested that a task force should be formed to decide which state enterprises should be privatized (Parti libéral, 1985: 96-99).

Once elected in 1985, the Liberal party moved one step ahead by appointing a Minister of Privatization, Pierre Fortier, whose mandate was to review all state enterprises and sell the commercial ones. The three objectives pursued were to stop financial losses, to improve Quebec's industrial structure by giving the private sector more room to manoeuver and to change the mandates of the remaining state enterprises that had fulfilled their initial mission. In his February 1986 policy statement, Fortier outlined six guidelines to achieve this (Gouvernement du Québec, 1986A):

1. Commercial production of goods and services in Quebec's economy belongs to the private sector, except in extraordinary circumstances justified by the public interest.

2. Privatization is not an end in itself. When it must take place, nationalization must be designed first to bolster Quebec's economic structure while assuring a presence in key economic sectors. Realization of a fair value for the assets transferred must also be considered.

3. Privatization must be done pragmatically, case by case, and may be carried out in many different ways, depending on the specific conditions of the corporation and its industrial sector.

4. Privatization is a public process which must comply with the equity and disclosure requirements applying to public companies.

5. The government will make certain that employees, communities and, where applicable, suppliers are fairly treated during implementation of any rationalization procedure which proves necessary.

6. Crown corporations that maintain their status will have to perform in accordance with rigorous production criteria and strict rules with a view to offering genuine competition on the market.

In his document, Fortier said that the state would no longer be an entrepreneur but would act as a "catalyst" for economic growth. Premier Robert Bourassa also established an Advisory Committee of businessmen that published a report in June 1986 (Gouvernement du Québec, 1986B). The Advisory Committee was to "advise the Minister responsible for Privatization on the advisability of transferring to the private sector in whole or in part, those Crown corporations whose activities are commercial or industrial in nature" (Gouvernement du Québec, 1986B). The Committee was also mandated to establish priorities among the corporations whose privatization was desirable and comment on procedures for the transition.

Starting its argument by stating how universal the privatization movement was, the report recommended that the ten "strategic" enterprises should be sold (see Table 1). These enterprises were "strategic" because they pursued economic development objectives and were in competition with private sector firms. According to the report, these enterprises set Quebec apart from other provinces in Canada and the American states. The report noted that many of them were in declining industries and that they had obtained mixed results. The authors of the report also stated that the enterprises, created between 1962 and 1975 to compensate for weaknesses in Quebec's economy, were no longer required because the new Francophone bourgeoisie was henceforth strong enough to manage Quebec's economic development. The report argued that the state enterprises had outlived their usefulness as policy tools to promote structural transformations; and Francophone management and control of major corporations in Quebec, as tools for carrying out specific projects. The report also considered that the procedure proposed by the Minister of Privatization was appropriate and that the impact of the transaction on the economic structure should prevail over financial profitability; in other words, that state enterprises should be sold to Quebec-based companies to respect the gains of the Quiet Revolution. Finally, the report suggested that the other state enterprises, the Caisse de dépôt, Hydro-Quebec, Loto-Québec, etc. should be reassessed to avoid becoming outmoded.

The government had already sold the Raffinerie de sucre du Québec in March 1986 to a competitor who closed it.[6] Québecair was also sold in January. The stake held by the Société québécoise d'initiatives agro-alimentaires (Soquia) in Provigo was sold for $48.4 million (and a capital gain of $37.5 million) in March. In July 1986, in order to put an end to its chronic deficits, the government rationalized the Société nationale de l'amiante (SNA) and sold it in 1993. In April of the same year, the profitable operations of Soquem were regrouped in Cambior and sold for $157.5 million, with Soquem retaining a 31% interest. A fish processing company, Madelipêche, was sold in 1987. In early 1987, the SGF sold its stake in the forest products company Donohue for $320 million. It was also announced that the SGF would no longer act as an industrial holding company, but would become a developer for industrial projects with private partners in key sectors of the Quebec economy. Later in 1987, Soquip, the oil and gas corporation, sold Soquip Alberta to Sceptre Resources for $227 million and became a minority owner of Sceptre (22%). In 1988, Seleine, Soquem's money-losing salt-mining operation, was sold for $35 million. But Domtar, the giant industrial conglomerate, has not been sold. Also, the Société des alcools du Québec has remained a state enterprise. A year after the privatization process was initiated, the government was already reconsidering the issue. What was supposed to be the sellout of the century has been downgraded to a more modest rationalization.

In its 1988 progress report, the government estimated that the 21 privatizations involving nine state enterprises completed in 1988 had a total value of $997.1 million. Of this amount, the government received $880.98 million and the new owners took over debts worth $116.12 million. The government also eliminated annual deficits of $66.6 million. Soquem and Soquip kept most of the money from the sales of their subsidiaries ($110 million). Other state enterprises kept $177.8 million for future projects. The government was able to put $102.9 million into the province's consolidated funds. Some $345.9 million were used to pay the debts of the state enterprises and $144.3 million to increase the SGF stake in Domtar to 28%.

Among the ten strategic enterprises to be privatized according to the 1986 government document, Madelipêche, the smallest of all, was sold early in the process (see Table 1). Sidbec and the SNA have been sold recently. The size of several others has been reduced. Soquem, the Société québécoise des transports (SQT) and Soquip are smaller than they used to be. The others have kept their development pace, as have the two most important state-owned enterprises, the Caisse de dépôt and Hydro-Quebec. The government announced in 1988 that the privatization operation had been a success and was complete

---

6.   The following numbers come from the progress reports published by the government in March 1987 and October 1988.

except for a few minor outstanding transactions. And as illustrated in Table 2, the only privatizations between 1988 and 1992 were the Rexfor subsidiaries.

In a dependent economic situation, or in the semi-periphery, the state intervenes because the private sector is unable to orient economic growth. In a situation of dependency, the state replaces a weak private sector. This was the case for Quebec in the 1960s, when the state enterprises were created. A weak state creates islands of autonomy by setting up state enterprises. In a state where the departments were enfeoffed to the private sector, state enterprises gave the state some room to manoeuvre (Bernier, 1989). State enterprises, when created in Quebec, were the instruments of policies that had yet to be drafted. Quebec's successive governments have chosen this form of intervention because of the lag between interventionist volition and weaknesses in available resources, particularly human resources. Acknowledging this discrepancy but wishing to act quickly, the state opted to delegate responsibility to autonomous organizations which were mandated to achieve major parts of the activities desired by the state. State enterprises were created to avoid having to establish coherent and comprehensive policies (Parenteau, 1980: 195). The privatizations completed an incremental and necessary rationalization process initiated in 1979. By privatizing Québecair, the SNA, etc., the government corrected its mistakes. It got out of industrial sectors where it had no place.

In general, state enterprises in Quebec have not constituted a severe drain on state finances. A few have: Sidbec, Raffinerie de sucre and Madelipêche, for example. Others never turned important profits because of their mandates. Partial privatization has left some of these enterprises in far better financial health than they had been before (see Gouvernement du Québec, 1988). Some state enterprises were not privatized for financial reasons. The ad hoc manner of the privatization drive also suggests that ideology was not the only reason. The privatization drive was a part of a larger pragmatic restructuring of the state enterprise sector in Quebec. But the realignment was not limited to Quebec, and the same could be said of other privatizations (see Laux and Molot, 1988; Molot, 1988).

It is worth noting that the rationale for privatization in Great Britain and Canada came along after some privatizations had been carried out. This was also the case in Quebec, where the nationalization of Hydro-Quebec and the creation of other state enterprises was not included in the 1960 Liberal program. In the United Kingdom, the government also developed privatization techniques through practice. Privatization was not included in the Conservative 1979 manifesto. Nonetheless, by 1986, 20% of all state industries had been privatized. In Canada, the rationale also came *post facto*. Eleven privatizations had been completed when a set of reasons was provided in May 1987 (Stanbury, 1988).

In his 1994 Budget Speech, André Bourbeau, the last Liberal Finance Minister, announced that a new wave of privatization would take place: Rexfor, SOQUIA, SOQUIP, the SEPAQ, the SIQ and the SGF were again for sale (Gouvernement du Québec, 1994: 9-10). Parts of the SAQ were also for sale. It should be noted that most of these state enterprises were involved in trade disputes following complaints by American companies. This Budget Speech followed the publication of *Les Finances publiques du Québec: vivre selon nos moyens,* which in 1993 had suggested that the government should reduce its activities because of the 1992 recession (Gouvernement du Québec, 1993).

The Quebec government did launch a second wave of privatization shortly before the general election they were likely to lose and effectively lost on September 12, 1994. They sold the Mont-Sainte-Anne ski resort, the main asset of SEPAQ, a week before the election. Although the estimated value was around $40 million, the sale price was just $11 million (Canadian).[7] Sidbec has also been sold to the Mexican branch of an Indonesian conglomerate. Full or partial privatization of the Société des Alcools du Quebec has been considered. The new government has announced that it will continue the privatizations (Lessard, 1995). These privatizations bring Quebec's economic policy instruments closer to the American tradition, as discussed in the fourth section. The new economic framework created by NAFTA forced the Quebec government to reconsider the possibility of privatizing state enterprises as it did. The second wave of privatizations was caused by external rather than domestic factors. The following comparison with Mexico, where a parallel privatization drive occurred during the NAFTA negotiations, could lead to a conclusion as to the effects of the trade deal.

STATE ENTERPRISES AND PRIVATIZATION IN MEXICO

In Mexico, confronted with the necessity of rebuilding after the revolution and the Great Depression, the state became increasingly involved in the economy. State enterprises are even mentioned in the Mexican constitution. In Mexico, "the public sector will be exclusively in charge of the strategic areas listed in article 28 paragraph 4 of the constitution, with the Federal Government as the owner and authority in charge of the entities created to that effect." (Article 25 of the constitution, from Aspe, 1993: 195.) The state can thus maintain an active role in the economy. As was the case in Canada, the state first created a central bank, an electricity production company, a national railway company and Petroléos Mexicano. In the 1970s, when the import substitution strategy

---

7.   Data from ASSELIN, Pierre, "Changement de garde au Mont-Sainte-Anne," *Le Soleil,* Quebec, September 9, 1994, page B-14.

had to be revamped or replaced, the government took the lead in the economy once again (Alpe, 1993: 180). Between 1970 and 1982, the number of state enterprises jumped from 272 to 1155.

The Mexican government decided to nationalize the domestic banking sector in 1982 in reaction to a debt crisis. As a result, the state became the owner of a wide range of commercial and industrial companies (Fraser, 1988: 166). By then, the state enterprise sector accounted for 18.5% of GDP, employed one million people and included all commercial banks. Of the 1155 firms under state control in 1982, 905 enterprises, plus another 87 still underway, have since been divested (Aspe, 1993: 177). A quarter of a million employees had been transferred to the private sector by the end of 1991.

As in Quebec, the government started with the privatization of its smallest enterprises (Aspe, 1993: 214). By 1988, the 765 firms authorized for privatization accounted only for 3% of state enterprise production (Schneider, 1990: 330). Privatization has enabled transfers to these enterprises to be reduced from 12% of GDP to 2% (Aspe, 1993: 218). As in Canada, the Mexican government divested to restore business confidence, and it streamlined its ownership rather than terminating its intervention in the economy (Schneider, 1990: 329-334; Molot, 1988). The sale process has twelve steps and has been rather pragmatic (Aspe, 1993: 201).

It could be argued that the Mexican government was learning how to privatize before tackling the larger enterprises. It could also be argued that, given the financial difficulties following the 1982 debt crisis, the Mexican government had other things to do before working seriously on major privatizations. Nevertheless, we consider that major privatizations would not have taken place without NAFTA (see Ramirez, 1995). Teléfonos de Mexico, the largest enterprise to be privatized, was sold late in 1990. The commercial banks were also sold in 1991. Until 1989, the revenues from privatization varied between 0.01% and 0.19 % of GDP. They jumped to 1.19% in 1990 and to 3.83% in 1991 (Aspe, 1993: 216-221). For the first six months of 1992, revenues from privatization equalled 1.98% of GDP. The privatization of infrastructures on the American model might follow (Silverstein, 1993: 38), as might increased privatization of the oil industry. As the signature of NAFTA approached, the privatization program apparently intensified.

One major public sector is expected to be maintained. In 1992, Mexico still owned 225 public enterprises (Barnes, 1992: 8). In Mexico, according to the National Program for the Modernization of State-Owned Companies, modernization will be carried out according to four basic criteria: the consolidation of executive organs within public companies; the promotion of greater management autonomy; increases in efficiency, effectiveness and productivity; and negotiation as a basis for viable relations both within and outside state-owned companies (Mexico, 1992: 32).

In June 1990, the Mexican and American presidents announced their intention to negotiate a free trade agreement between their countries. Canada joined the process in February 1991. Mexican trade liberalization began in the 1980s under international pressures but continued because of changing domestic factors (Pastor and Wise, 1994: 460-463). The implementation of NAFTA constitutes the final phase of these liberalization efforts. Privatization efforts in Mexico must be understood in the broader perspective of trade liberalization and economic reform (Barnes, 1992). As was the case in Quebec, privatization constituted an effort to modernize the economy. There was no dominant ideological transformation, but rather a necessary rationalization of government assets to improve its capacity to compete internationally. As discussed in the following section, privatization may also help avoid trade disputes.

In Quebec, the second wave of privatizations occurred after NAFTA was signed because the province needed to adapt to the new reality. In Mexico, the privatizations were achieved before NAFTA, to make it possible to sign the deal (see Ramirez, 1995). It will be interesting to see if, as new partners such as Chile enter the free trade zone, a similar process will occur. So far, the impact of NAFTA on privatization decisions might be more of an hypothesis than a proven fact. Further developments of the free trade zone will allow this to be verified.

THE UNITED STATES, NAFTA AND PRIVATIZATION EFFORTS

Comparisons of state interventions in the economy are often difficult. To some degree, all organizations are public (Bozeman, 1987). "No country, not even the United States, can distinguish unambiguously between its enterprises that are private and those that are not" (Vernon, 1988: 2). Research contracts granted to American companies by the government to develop new products in the computer or aerospatial sectors would be handled in many industrial countries by public companies. In Canada, most of these companies are or were owned by the state, as they have been in Great Britain or France.

The literature on state intervention in the United States does not generally mention the existence of major state enterprises as it is does in Quebec or Mexico. Infrastructure investments and sectoral targeting are discussed, but not direct investment by states, as Canadian provinces have been doing for decades (Dubnick and Holt, 1985; Fosler, 1988). At the same time, privatization of hospitals, race tracks and highways are underway in the United States but are still only at the preliminary stage in Quebec. Privatizations in Quebec, elsewhere in Canada and in Mexico are concentrated in sectors where the American federal or state governments have never been involved.

By comparison with the British or Canadian governments, the United States federal government has traditionally not involved itself directly in manufacturing or the supply of services. It has preferred regulation rather than ownership as an economic policy instrument. The 1988 Report of the Commission on Privatization suggested the privatization of public utilities, not the privatization of companies competing with the private sector, as was the case in Canada and Mexico (U.S. Government, 1988). Still, as MacAvoy and McIsaac write (1989: 77), the U.S. has at least 50 major federal enterprises, including the postal service. They employ over a million people, have revenues of $22 billion and in 1983 received at least $3.5 billion in subsidies. A decade ago they were producing 15% of the country's electric power, all intercity rail services and all freight rail services in the Northeast.

Like its Canadian neighbour, the American government has decided occasionally to buy private companies on the point of bankrupty in declining industries. In the railway industry, the government decided to create Amtrak (the National Railroad Passenger Corporation) in 1970 and Conrail (the Consolidated Rail Corporation) in 1973. The former still requires subsidies and the latter was sold in 1987 (Fraser, 1988: 156). The American government mostly created state public utilities: railways, airports, the postal service (Swann, 1988: 122-124). In most cases it was responding to market failures. The financial results achieved by the state enterprises have never been very good because of their statutory mandates. Efficency has never been a priority in the four cases MacAvoy and McIsaac (1989: 128) studied in more detail: the U.S. Postal Service, Amtrak, TVA and Conrail. They conclude that only privatization could solve the problem. The freight rail company, Conrail, was sold in 1987 (Henig, 1990: 649). Although a few exemptions exist, the U.S. economy is dominated by private companies. These companies have been confronted over the years by increased competition from foreign companies from countries with business-state relations far removed from the American tradition. American interests pressured American politicians for protection against what was often perceived as unfair competition. Local economic difficulties caused by trade conflicts were heard in Washington. Political mechanisms have been used efficiently by American interests.

Privatization drives in Canada and Mexico may come more from the need to deal with American interests than because of the intrinsic economic efficiency of privatization, although privatization might improve economic competitiveness. One of the difficulties of privatization is the absence of competition after the sale (Vickers and Yarrow, 1988). Because competition rather than privatization is the engine of efficiency, the free trade agreement has solved part of this problem. The American government could privatize its few public enterprises, but they are mostly in economic sectors where efficiency gains from competition are not likely to be important. The American postal service and Amtrak were created because the private sector could not generate profits from these activities. In Mexico as well as in Quebec, NAFTA has greatly increased the competitive pressure on private and public enterprises.

Economic intervention by the governments of Mexico and Quebec has come less from an ideological basis than from the necessity of serving the public interest, which is, however, not always very clearly defined. After 1980, the need for more economic efficiency made it difficult for governments to maintain money-losing state enterprises. NAFTA has increased this competitive pressure. Privatization of some of these state enterprises is part of a larger process of improving competitiveness. Some state enterprises have nevertheless been able to achieve results that could be compared with those achieved by the private sector. State enterprises in competition with the private sector do achieve efficiency (see Bernier and Fortin, 1994). For Quebec as for Mexico, adjusting to NAFTA means reducing state intervention in the economy. Historically, state enterprises have been more territorially bound than private companies, a factor that limited their capacity to compete. In both countries, rationalization/privatization has improved state intervention in the economy.

State enterprises were not privatized with a view to efficiency. The success of privatization in Mexico is due to an improved general performance of the economy and not to privatization as such (Barnes, 1992: 1). Both lame ducks and the most profitable enterprises were sold in Canada and Mexico. Some of the most profitable state enterprises were sold because they were easier to sell, and some of the worst performers were sold because governments could no longer afford to fund them. Privatization leaves a residual state enterprise sector that is smaller but perhaps not more efficient. The remaining state enterprises might be more capable of being a threat to American business, as they were perceived in 1979 by Lamont. In the long run, Lamont and Vernon are both right: post-privatization state enterprises could constitute a threat to American business, depending on their capacity to be efficient and competitive. And they are undoubtedly already perceived as such. Behind the environmentalist lobby's aggressive campaign against Hydro-Quebec, a number of powerful groups have vested interests: Ontario-Hydro or the coal and gas industries could sell the electricity supplied by Hydro-Quebec. State enterprises are also useful partners in joint-ventures. In Quebec, for example, the Société générale de financement has been involved in joint-ventures with foreign companies in areas such as aluminium, magnesium and paper. State enterprises will continue to exist on a larger scale in Mexico and Quebec than they ever existed in the United States. Partnerships with them could be seen as opportunities within the current NAFTA framework and also in the perspective of the arrival of new partners such as Chile in the coming years.

We do believe, however, that privatizations in Quebec and Mexico have occurred less for economic efficiency than to avoid trade disputes. One of the causes of current trade disputes is the possibility that state enterprises could be seen as channels for subsidies that create unfair competition. Whether they are or not is almost irrelevant. What matters is that the argument could be used to limit the capacity of Mexican or Canadian-based companies to export to the U.S. market. Trade disputes could also limit investment in Canada and Mexico by other foreign companies seeking access to the U.S. market. The dispute around the Honda cars assembled in Canada is a good example of such use of NAFTA by American interests. The dispute led to the conclusion that, to have access to the American market, Japanese companies should invest in the United States, not in Mexico or in Canada. To remain in line with NAFTA, state enterprises will have to operate more as private enterprises. The necessity of maintaining access to the U.S. market has led to privatizations.

Once the ideological arguments in favor of state ownership and/or privatization are taken into account, much has still to be done to understand when and how state enterprises can be efficient. Some studies have demonstrated that, *ceteris paribus*, state enterprises could be as efficient as private enterprises (Bernier and Fortin, 1994: 158-159). However, the *ceteris paribus* was often difficult to build. For Quebec, Mexico and the United States, NAFTA should make it easier in the coming years to compare the results of different ways of using the remaining state enterprises.

Many of the opponents of Quebec's independence have argued that Quebec would have to sign a free trade treaty that would be less favourable. Those in favor of sovereignty argue that NAFTA already includes a clause for the addition of new partners. As regards state enterprises, a jurisprudence is being developed. Trade disputes rather than constitutional discussions are imposing changes on the state enterprise sector. Some privatizations have already taken place as a result.

Trade disputes arising out of NAFTA have made some state enterprises obsolete. Further research will have to be done to verify the hypothesis developed in this chapter. Clearly, other factors cannot be excluded. The 1992 recession also forced the Quebec government to reconsider privatization. Nevertheless, the increased interest in privatization in Quebec and Mexico seems to have a common cause.

REFERENCES

ASPE, Pedro (1993), *Economic Transformation: the Mexican Way*, Cambridge: MIT Press.

BARNES, Guillermo (1992), "Lessons from Bank Privatization in Mexico," *Working Papers*, No 1027, World Bank, November.

BERNIER, Luc (1988), "The Foreign Economic Policy of a Subnational State: The Case of Quebec," in Duchacek, Ivo D., et al., *Perforated Sovereignties and International Relations*, New York: Greenwood: 125-139.

BERNIER, Luc (1989), *Soldiers of Fortune: State-Owned Enterprises as Instruments of Public Policy,* Ph D Dissertation, Northwestern University, Evanston, Illinois.

BERNIER, Luc (1994), "Privatization in Quebec," in Bernier, Robert, and James Iain Gow, *Un État réduit? A Down Sized State?*, Sainte-Foy: Presses de l'Université du Québec: 221-246.

BERNIER, Luc, and Jean-Pierre FORTIN (1994), "L'effet de l'entrepreneurship public sur la performance financière des sociétés d'État au Québec," in Charih, Mohamed, and Michel Paquin, *Les organisations publiques à la recherche de l'efficacité*, Sainte-Foy, ENAP: 155-179.

BOZEMAN, Barry (1987), *All Organizations Are Public*, San Francisco: Jossey-Bass.

DUBNICK, Mel, and Lynne HOLT (1985), "Industrial Policy and the States," *Publius*, 15: 113-129.

FOSLER, R. Scott, ed. (1988), *The New Economic Role of American States: Strategies in a Competitive World Economy*, Oxford: Oxford University Press.

FRASER, Robert (1988), *Privatization: the UK Experience and International Trends*, Harlow, Essex: Longman Group UK.

GOUVERNEMENT DU QUÉBEC (1986A), ministère des Finances, Ministre délégué à la Privatisation, *Privatisation de sociétés d'État: Orientations et perspectives*, Février. (Rapport Fortier)

GOUVERNEMENT DU QUÉBEC (1986B), ministère des Finances, *De la Révolution tranquille... à l'an deux mille*, Rapport du Comité sur la privatisation (Quebec: Gouvernement du Québec, 1986).

GOUVERNEMENT DU QUÉBEC (1988), ministère des Finances, Cabinet du ministre délégué aux Finances et à la Privatisation, *Rapport d'étape 1986-1988*, October.

GOUVERNEMENT DU QUÉBEC (1993), Ministère des Finances, *Les finances publiques: vivre selon nos moyens*, January 19.

GOUVERNEMENT DU QUÉBEC (1994), Ministère des Finances, *Budget 1994-1995, Discours*, May 12.

HENIG, Jeffrey R. (1990), "Privatization in the United States: Theory and Practice," *Political Science Quarterly*, 104: 649-670.

LACHAPELLE, Guy, BERNIER, Gérald, SALÉE, Daniel, and Luc BERNIER (1993), *The Quebec Democracy*, Toronto: McGraw-Hill Ryerson.

LAMONT, Douglas F. (1979), *Foreign State Enterprises: A Threat to American Business*, New York: Basic Books.

LAUX, Jeanne Kirk, and Maureen Appel MOLOT (1988), *State Capitalism: Public Enterprise in Canada*, Ithaca: Cornell University Press.

LESSARD, Denis (1995), "Québec veut accélérer les privatisations," *La Presse,* March 18, page A-21.

MACAVOY, Paul W., and MCISAAC (1989), "The Performance and Management of United States Federal Government Corporations," in MacAvoy, Paul W., et al., eds., *Privatization and State-Owned Enterprises*, Boston: Kluwer: 77-135.

McROBERTS, Kenneth (1993), *Quebec: Social Change and Political Crisis*, Third edition with a postscript, Toronto: McClelland & Stewart.

MEXICO, Presidencia de la República (1992), *Mexico: the Path Towards Modernity*, Mexico: Dirreccion General de Comunicación Social.

MOLOT, Maureen Appel (1988), "The Provinces and Privatization: Are the Provinces Really Getting Out of Business?," in Tupper, Allan, and G. Bruce Doern, eds., *Privatization, Public Policy and Public Corporations in Canada*, Halifax: The Institute for Research on Public Policy: 399-425.

North American Free Trade Agreement, Minister of Supply and Services Canada, 1992.

OCDE (1992), *Études économiques: Mexique*, Paris.

PARENTEAU, Roland (1980), "Les sociétés d'État: autonomie ou intégration," Montreal: École des HEC, document témoin de la rencontre du 8 mai.

PARIZEAU, Jacques (1985), "La privatisation des sociétés d'État au Quebec," *Gestion*, Vol 10, No 4: 43-46.

PARTI LIBÉRAL DU QUEBEC (1985), Commission politique, *Maîtriser l'avenir: Programme politique*.

PASTOR, Manuel, and Carol WISE (1994), "The Origins and Sustainability of Mexico's Free Trade Policy," *International Organization*, 48: 459-89.

PRICHARD, J. Robert S., ed. (1983), *Crown Corporations in Canada*, Toronto: Butterworths.

RAMIREZ, Miguel D. (1995), "The Political Economy of Privatization in Mexico, 1983-92," *Organization*, vol 2: 87-116.

SCHNEIDER, Ben Ross (1990), "The Politics of Privatization in Brazil and Mexico: Variations on a Statist Theme," in Sulieman, Ezra N., and John Waterbury, eds., *The Political Economy of Public Sector Reform and Privatization*, Boulder: Westview Press: 319-345.

SILVERSTEIN, Jeff (1993), "Wave of the Future," *Business Mexico*, April: 38-39.

STANBURY, William T. (1994), "Privatization by Federal and Provincial Governments in Canada: An Empirical Study," in Bernier, Robert, and James Iain Gow, *Un État réduit? A Down Sized State?*, Sainte-Foy: Presses de l'Université du Quebec: 165-219.

SWANN, Dennis (1988), *The Retreat of the State*, New York: Harvester.

U.S. GOVERNMENT (1988), *Privatization: Toward a More Effective Government*, Report of the President's Commission on Privatization, March.

VERNON, Raymond, ed. (1988), *The Promise of Privatization: A Challenge for American Foreign Policy*, New York: Council on Foreign Relations.

VICKERS, John, and George YARROW (1988), *Privatization: An Economic Analysis*, Cambridge, Mass.: The MIT Press.

TABLE 1
Total Assets of State-owned Enterprises in Quebec before and after the Privatization Drive
(in millions of current dollars)
Strategic SOEs Considered for Privatization in 1986

	1985	**1988**	**1992-93**[b]
SGF	1,160	1,140	1,224
SIDBEC	529	555	516
SOQUEM	272	124	108
SOQUIA	58	87	127
REXFOR	158	213	65
SOQUIP	437	166	213
Madelipêche	20	—	—
SNA	256	93	35
SQT (and Québecair)	144	10	3
SEPAQ	[a]	41	89
Other SOEs			
RADIO-QUÉBEC	48	48	50
SDI	147	436	1,546
SDBJ	1	19	21
Hydro-Quebec	27,129	31,659	44,864
Caisse de dépôt	22,502	29,918	40,598

a)   not operating yet

b)   1992-93 is the last year available in the public accounts.

Source: Gouvernement du Québec, 1988B, Annual Reports of Radio-Québec (1984-1985, 1987-1988), SDI (1984-1985, 1987-1988) and États financiers des entreprises du Gouvernement du Québec, 1992-1993.

TABLE 2
Privatizations in Quebec
Total Value per State-owned Enterprise
(in millions of Canadian dollars)
and Number of Transactions (1986-1994)

	1986-1988		1989-1991		1992-1994		1986-1994	
	$	N	$	N	$	N	$	N
SGF	348.7			3	90.0	1	438.7	4
SIDBEC					65.0	1	65.0	1
SOQUEM	223.4	3			53.7	1	277.1	4
SOQUIA	110.5	7			2.6	1	113.1	8
REXFOR	49.4	4	55.8	4	98.3	3	203.5	11
SOQUIP	196.5	1					196.5	1
Madelipêche[a]	16.1	1					16.1	1
SNA	25.4	7			36.9	2	62.3	9
SQT	73.8	1					73.8	1
SEPAQ					12.3	1	12.3	1
Others[b]					117.9	2	117.9	2
Total	1043.8	27	55.8	4	476.7	12	1576.3	43

a) Madelipêche is excluded in this table from SOQUIA in order to maintain the presentation of the 1986 reports used in Table 1.

b) Société immobilière du Québec (Place Desjardins, $98.3M.) and SOGIC (Disques Americ, $19.6M.).

Source: Gouvernement du Québec, Ministère des Finances, Direction des Sociétés d'État, Opérations de privatisation réalisées, September 7, 1994.

9

Trade Unionism and the State of Industrial Relations in Quebec

Serge Denis
University of Ottawa
Rock Denis
Université du Québec à Montréal

This chapter assesses the state of trade unionism and industrial relations in Quebec. The authors show that the recent evolution of the labour movement in that province is part-and-parcel of the transformations currently underway in Canada and the United States. However, they also draw attention to some particular features of the current developments, linking them to the specific historical and cultural heritage of Quebec. Following a description of the organizations and the numerical strength of the trade union movement, the chapter reviews the movement's ideological origins and political orientations, which reflect the concomitant influence of U.S., British and French traditions. Quebec labour organizations today are situated in a new economic and social environment that is producing a recomposition of the entire apparatus of industrial relations inherited from the post-war period. From confrontation to dialogue to partnership, the strategic evolution of the trade union movement is analyzed in light of its new practices and its internal tensions. A reorientation of the trade union movement, of the conception of its role and its forms of action, is underway. The outcome is difficult to determine, particularly in the new context of the Canada-United States-Mexico free trade agreement. In conclusion, the authors note that, notwithstanding exceptionally high membership figures, the capacity of Quebec's unions to achieve significant advances on behalf of their members has been severely tested in recent years, and the unions confront the current national and international conjuncture from a position that is highly unfavourable to them.

At first sight, the labour movement in Quebec is a complex subject. In their major features, the unions reflect the practices of continental Europe, the Anglo-Saxon countries and the United States. Yet Quebec trade unionism is a product of the particular culture of Francophone Quebec and the latter's unique history, traditions and institutions, which give it a specific national configuration within Canada and North America.

Industrial relations in Canada are largely under provincial jurisdiction, and for at least a half-century the evolution of the Quebec *Labour Code* has reflected not only its Canadian and American setting but the political and social relations within the province. This provincial dimension is of greater significance in Quebec than in other provinces: many economic, social and cultural projects, and the very life of its organizations, are defined by Quebec's specific institutional and cultural context. Whatever their respective constitutional options, successive provincial governments have claimed to speak on behalf of a distinct people. When community organizations decide to work together on a province-wide basis, they organize themselves as a "*national* coalition." Membership in political parties is determined on completely different bases in federal and provincial elections. The labour movement in Quebec operates within this environment, and has in fact helped to shape it. And when, for example, it is confronted with the issue of where and how to commit its own forces, the primary focus is provincial. The entire movement – including the local affiliates of the international unions of the AFL-CIO, such as the United Steelworkers of America – operates in French.

The internal life of the labour movement in Quebec, as it is in Europe, is, generally speaking, more centralized than that of the AFL-CIO and the independent unions in the United States. This is in part a reflection of certain social structures: for example, the hospitals in Quebec are almost entirely under provincial jurisdiction and dependent on provincial funding, and negotiations in this sector are centralized for each category of employees. This promotes union activities that affect all institutions in the health care sector. But Quebec unions also tend to engage in coordinated action more frequently than unions in the United States, since the top staff and leading bodies of the major union "centrals" enjoy greater authority with the local leaderships. As in many European countries, there is more than one union central in Quebec, and many independent – that is, unaffiliated – unions (more on that later). On more than one occasion over the past dozen years or so, the major collective bargaining contracts throughout the public and parapublic sectors, covering government departments and agencies and publicly-funded institutions, have been the targets of government decrees. Labour relations in some private sector industries such as construction are covered in whole or in part by other decrees, which in some instances go so far as to determine marketing and sales conditions (as, quite recently, in the hairdressing industry, for example).

Ventures in tripartite joint action by unions, employers and governments reflect the influence of the continental European models, and the level and form of social conquests (such as a free public health and hospital insurance plan) are comparable to those in the major Western countries with the exception of the United States. Like the Anglo-Saxon and more specifically the U.S. models, however, and in contrast to what is generally found in a country such as France, union life in Quebec has traditionally been defined by the decentralized structure of collective bargaining and the administration of contract provisions. Strikes and lock-outs are prohibited by law in Quebec while a contract is in force.

Another peculiarity of Quebec as a distinct national society, albeit one that it shares in common with the United States, is that its labour movement, unlike that of most developed countries, is non-partisan in its political action. It has never generated an independent labour party, although historically there have been tentative moves in this direction. This differentiates Quebec from both the Anglo-Saxon model of Great Britain and its former dominions, as reflected in English Canada in the NDP, and the great historical models of continental Europe.

It is of course the combination of these diverse characteristics that determines the originality of Quebec trade unionism. In view of the topics addressed by this book, our chapter, which is introductory in nature, will be devoted to the unions as institutions and to labour-management relations.[1]

One final introductory note. Canada and Quebec, like the United States, have been settled by immigrants. But in Quebec, immigration from Europe did not have the same significance for trade unionism and working-class history as it did in the United States. For many decades, the main contingents of immigrants were incorporated into the English-speaking minority (although more than 82% of the Quebec population has French as its mother tongue) and the middle and upper classes. During the 1960s a federal commission of inquiry found that French-speaking Quebecers ranked twelfth in average income in the province, just before immigrants of Italian origin and the aboriginal peoples (Royal Commission on Bilingualism and Biculturalism, 1965). In the last twenty years a larger share of Quebec's immigration has originated from non-European countries, many of which are seriously underdeveloped. The Quebec unions have adopted special measures to reach these new citizens.

Before situating Quebec trade unionism in its economic and social setting, it is necessary to present a brief outline of its numerical strength, its major organizations, and the principal features of its ideological and political evolution in recent years.

---

1.   In Quebec the bodies equivalent to U.S. union "federations" or "congresses" (as in American *Federation* of Labor and *Congress* of Industrial Organizations) are referred to as "centrals" or central labour bodies (*centrales syndicales*), and the counterparts of the individual U.S. "unions" are the "federations" (*fédérations syndicales*).

NUMERICALLY, AN IMPRESSIVE FORCE

About 1.1 million employees were covered by collective agreements in Quebec in 1993 (Racine, 1994: 29) – a spectacular 46.8% of the province's employed labour force.[2] This rate of union representation reflects the ratio between the number of employees covered by a collective agreement and the employment level in a given period. Thus it is always higher than the rate of union membership, which corresponds to the number of dues-paying members officially reported by the unions. Yet Quebec does post one of the highest rates of union membership in North America and, more generally, among the industrialized countries as a whole. Union membership has oscillated around 42% of the work force for a decade or so, well above the Canadian average of 37.6% and the 15.8% reported in the United States in 1992. The explanation of the relatively high rates of union membership and union representation lies in part in the extremely high level of union membership among the workers in the public and parapublic sectors in Quebec. Some 73.9% of the employees in these sectors are covered by agreements, compared with 34.7% in the private sector (see Tables 2 and 3).

These high rates of union membership in Quebec are indeed noteworthy. They are the result of a history, much of it recent, that has seen hundreds of thousands of hospital and educational employees win the right of association, the right to collective bargaining and the right to strike. In the early 1960s a Quebec premier responded to the initial manifestations of the new union upsurge with a formula directly inspired by the country's British legacy: "The Queen does not negotiate with her subjects." But the union organizing wave rolled over this opposition.

The tide of union organizing in Quebec in this period may also have drawn on the nationalist awakening of an entire generation that was discovering its language, its culture and its national distinctiveness and mobilizing in a challenge to the constitutional underpinnings of the Canadian state. Conversely, the mobilizing drive of an entire society was itself fuelled by the strengthening of organized labour, and the union movement served as a consciousness-raising school for wide segments of the working population that had until then remained unorganized. It would be interesting to measure to what degree the current level of union membership in Quebec reflects this context. But that cannot explain everything, since when all is said and done the rates of union membership in the rest of Canada are likewise relatively high. There, too, the gains of the public sector played a significant role. And from 1961 on, with the creation of the New Democratic Party, the unions were able to rely on an organized political expression of their interests.

---

2.   The statistical data in this section are derived from France Racine (Racine, 1994: 27-32).

Quebec has three union centrals with more than 100,000 members: the Fédération des travailleurs et travailleuses du Québec (FTQ, or Quebec Federation of Labour), the Confédération des syndicats nationaux (CSN, or Confederation of National Trade Unions), and the Centrale de l'enseignement du Québec (CEQ, or Quebec Teachers' Union). The FTQ was created in 1957, in the wake of the mergers between the AFL and the CIO in the United States and their respective counterparts in Canada. It includes the craft and industrial unions that, in Quebec, were the local affiliates of the major U.S. unions as well as a number of Canadian unions operating in Quebec, the importance of which increased during the 1960s, such as the Canadian Union of Public Employees (CUPE). The FTQ is now the leading union federation in the province, with 345,000 members. They account for 35.9% of all Quebec union members, or more than a third of the organized work force. Through its affiliation with the Canadian Labour Congress, the FTQ is an organic component of the Canadian labour movement, the only central labour body in Quebec to maintain such a direct link with a Canadian counterpart. The FTQ's membership is concentrated primarily in the private sector, where it represents close to 55% of all union members.

The CSN, with 232,772 members in 1993, represents about a quarter (24.3%) of Quebec union members. Formed in 1921 at the instigation of the Catholic Church, it sought to organize Quebec workers on the basis of their religious allegiance and thereby resist the inroads of North American trade unionism. Until the late 1950s it was called the Confédération des travailleurs catholiques du Canada (the Confederation of Catholic Workers of Canada). As a result of some major strikes and battles during that decade directed against the retrograde regime of Premier Maurice Duplessis, and the breakthrough in organizing the public sector that it spearheaded in the 1960s, the CSN was transformed into an authentic union central, breaking with its clerical and corporatist origins. The CSN is preponderant in the enormous parapublic sector: the health, social services and post-secondary educational institutions together account for more than half of its membership. In the private sector, it represents only 18.6% of union members (see Table 1).

The vast majority of the approximately 100,000 members of the CEQ are elementary and secondary school teachers. With a virtual monopoly on union representation in this sector, the CEQ is dominant in the educational system, although the majority of college and university professors are not affiliated to it. Teachers' unionism, as such, has a relatively recent history as well. In 1974 the CEQ officially designated itself as a union organization, capping a decade of large mobilizations that had effectively established the teachers as a component of the Quebec labour movement. It should be noted that in Quebec the process of organizing the teachers into unions was strewn with some exceptional obstacles. The Catholic Church had long dominated the entire French-language educational system, and collective action by the teachers put

TABLE 1

Distribution of Collective Agreements and Employees Covered by Trade Union Affiliation and Sector[a], 1993 (Racine, 1994: 28)

Sector	CEQ N	CEQ %[d]	CSD N	CSD %[d]	CSN N	CSN %[d]	FTQ N	FTQ %[d]	Independents[b] N	Independents[b] %[d]	Other[c] N	Other[c] %[d]	Total N	Total %[e]
Public														
Coll. agreements	—	—	—	—	—	—	—	—	12	100.0	—	—	12	0.2
Employees	—	—	—	—	—	—	—	—	62,789	100.0	—	—	62,789	6.5
Parapublic														
Coll. agreements	26	22.6	4	3.5	14	12.2	21	18.3	50	43.5	—	—	115	1.4
Employees	88,843	26.6	3,823	1.1	131,833	39.4	40,778	12.2	69,363	20.7	—	—	334,640	34.9
Peripublic[g]														
Coll. agreements	8	4.5	4	2.2	49	27.4	60	35.5	57	31.8	1	0.6	179	2.2
Employees	995	1.5	207	0.3	12,068	18.7	34,930	54.0	16,356	25.3	85	0.1	64,641	6.7
Private														
Coll. agreements	97	1.4	507	7.2	1,350	19.3	3,179	45.4	1,596	22.8	268	3.8	6,997	86.9
Employees	2,270	0.5	29,187	6.5	83,448	18.6	243,931	54.8	76,721	17.1	13,085	2.9	448,642	46.7
Municipal														
Coll. agreements	—	—	28	3.8	102	13.7	322	43.2	292	39.2	1	0.1	745	9.3
Employees	—	—	1,345	2.7	5,423	11.0	25,044	51.0	17,318	35.3	5	—	49,135	5.1
Total	N	%[f]	N	%[f]	N	%[f]	N	%[f]	N	%[f]	N	%[f]	N	%[f]
Coll. agreements	131	1.6	543	6.8	1,515	18.8	3,582	44.5	2,007	24.9	270	3.4	8,048	100.0
Employees	92,108	9.6	34,562	3.6	232,772	24.3	344,683	35.9	242,547	25.3	13,175	1.4	959,847	100.0

a) These data do not include the federal sector and employees subject to the Construction Decree.

b) The term "independents" should be considered in the sense of non-affiliation to any of the following organizations: CEQ, CSD, CSN, FTQ.

c) The "Other" category includes: The American Federation of Labor-Congress of Industrial Organizations (AFL-CIO), the Canadian Labour Congress (CLC), the Confederation of Canadian Unions (CCU), the Canadian Federation of Labour (CFL) and the Union des producteurs agricoles (UPA – the farmers' union).

d) This percentage expresses the ratio between the number of collective agreements or employees by union affiliation and the total number of collective agreements or employees per sector.

e) This percentage expresses the ratio between the number of collective agreements or employees in a sector and the total number of collective agreements in force or employees covered by a collective agreement.

f) This percentage expresses the ratio between the number of collective agreements or employees by union affiliation and the total number of collective agreements in force or employees covered by a collective agreement.

g) "Peripublic sector" in Quebec refers to publicly-owned firms: for example, hydro-electricity, liquor stores, auto-insurance.

them on a collision course with a system and an authority that were especially effective. Hiring and career advancement were for a long time determined by religious affiliation, not professional skill. Thus non-Catholic teachers were not members of the same organizations as the Catholics and, in keeping with the same ideological mindset, urban teachers were organized separately from rural teachers, and men from women. The very form of organization of the Catholic teachers reflected the official structure of the Church dioceses. If we add to these factors the extensive overlap of religious cleavages with linguistic divisions, we get a fair idea of the problems confronting those who sought to build organized, united collective action among Quebec teachers.

Over the last 15 years Quebec has also experienced a new phenomenon: the development of independent unions unaffiliated to any of the major union centrals. This movement has assumed such scope that a quarter of the organized labour force (25.3%) are now members of independent unions. This development has probably been encouraged in part by the absence of a single union central for Quebec workers, the rivalry between the different centrals diminishing the overall attractiveness of each individually.

IDEOLOGICAL TRADITIONS AND POLITICAL DEVELOPMENTS

As we indicated in our introductory comments, the orientations, structures and practices of the Quebec labour movement are analogous to the situation in a number of countries, albeit linked to Quebec's specific cultural development.

For example, the dominant characteristic of the social and political orientation of Quebec trade unionism, since the very dawn of its existence, has no doubt been its non-partisan nature. The concept of non-partisanship, which was developed in the United States as a means of defining a particular relationship between the unions and politics, does not connote a refusal by the labour movement to engage in political action. Rather, it connotes an orientation with three major dimensions: the labour movement must remain organically unaligned on the political level; it must bargain its support for the dominant electoral parties and candidates in return for potential favours and concessions; and it must not undertake to create its own third party, which would represent its own interests and the interests of the toiling classes as a whole. This approach is in stark contrast, of course, with the traditions of the British labour movement, which at the turn of the century initiated the formation of the Labour Party. It stands for political action, but in the form of pressuring and lobbying rather than initiative or organized membership. Albeit with derivations that are not uniquely North American, Quebec unions continue to practice an adaptation of non-partisanship that tends to define them politically as a pressure group.

Two major developments since the Second World War have informed this tradition, giving it a particular complexion. Toward the end of the 1950s, the Quebec labour movement was invited to join in creating a third party, as conceived by the new Canadian Labour Congress, the CLC, itself created in 1956. The FTQ was the Quebec relay for this project, but it is significant that the CSN was approached at one time, notwithstanding its firmly held traditions of "neutrality." However, the effort to found this new party in Quebec ended in failure, primarily because of differences between the Quebecers and the English-Canadian leaders of the CLC and the party they had formed, the New Democratic Party, over the Quebec national question and its constitutional recognition.

In fact, for a whole generation, beginning with the early 1960s, political action in Quebec became inextricably combined with a nationalist commitment, and the unions were no exception. As the nationalist movement progressed, so did their intervention and political presence. Thus, at the high point of the period of intensive union mobilizations and ideological radicalism of the 1970s, many union members, encouraged by similar developments internationally, lent their efforts to the construction and election of a new party... the nationalist and sovereigntist Parti québécois. In this context, it is noteworthy that in the minds of many union members, the union manifestoes of the early 1970s, with their sympathy for democratic socialism, paralleled a commitment to the Parti québécois, a new formation that, while not advancing a socialist program, advocated a set of social and democratic reforms reminiscent of social-democratic parties and proclaimed its sympathies for the workers.

The salient characteristic of the political evolution of Quebec unions over the last twenty years has undeniably been their non-partisan alliance with the Parti québécois. This alliance was strong between 1970 and 1982, and has been less pronounced since then. The PQ served two terms in office, from 1976 to 1985. The first was marked by a series of progressive reforms, particularly in labour legislation, language legislation, and recognition of the rights of the French-speaking population, automobile insurance, etc. The second term, however, witnessed a sharp confrontation with the labour movement, which resulted in a temporary breach in the unions' support of the PQ. Having turned its back on its social undertakings, the PQ likewise renounced its sovereigntist program for a period, and was torn by an internal crisis that resulted in the resignation of many members, a split in the cabinet, and, in 1985, an electoral defeat that was now unavoidable.

Throughout the 1990s the unions have followed what might be referred to as a policy of critical support for the PQ, the most recent application of their non-partisanship. But to all intents and purposes it is the party's constitutional program, once again officially sovereigntist, rather than its economic and social program, that differentiates it and wins it the support of a majority of unions.

This is an important point, since it confirms that the primary axis of the unions' political commitment is the national question. Since the demise of the federal-provincial constitutional accord of 1990, the three major Quebec labour centrals have come out in favour of the creation of an independent Quebec state. The implications of this position have been insufficiently analyzed, since it signifies in particular that the labour movement in one of the two major Canadian provinces officially advocates the break-up of the Canadian state. It is another matter, obviously, whether this stance can be translated into action, and if so, how. In keeping with this commitment, the Quebec unions have, on the federal level, supported the sovereigntist party that since 1993 has formed the Official Opposition in the House of Commons in Ottawa, the Bloc québécois.

THE SOCIAL AND ECONOMIC SETTING

Quebec unions today confront new problems and new challenges, not unrelated of course to the multiple transformations that have been experienced over the last fifteen years by the labour movements in the developed countries. The social, economic and political conditions of their day-to-day activity and their role within society have been altered in a way that tends to dilute the strength of their traditional forms of intervention. In membership levels, and as a percentage of the work force, they have held their own; but there is no doubt that the capacity of the unions to promote the interests of their members has been weakened.

During the 1960s and 1970s, since the period referred to as the "Quiet Revolution," the Quebec unions were in the forefront of the extensive process of political democratization, social development and redistributive justice that helped to define contemporary Quebec. Through their major activities and mobilizations, the unions' intervention combined with government reforms to produce the social and political fabric of today's Quebec. Comparative analyses of the labour movement in western countries generally present the parameters of union existence between the 1950s and the 1980s, albeit under various names, as the products of a "post-war settlement." The major social forces negotiated and accepted a reality that would be defined, in the words of Jenson and Mahon, by "mass production," "mass consumption," "collective bargaining," "Keynesian demand management" and the "welfare state" (Jenson and Mahon, 1993: 5). These were general features that obviously coloured and specifically structured the various particular local and national characteristics.[3] In Quebec, significant aspects of this settlement were not implemented until

---

3. An example that is still current: in the United States, working people's access to health care has not been guaranteed by comprehensive legislation but is promoted by collective agreement provisions.

more than twenty years after the end of the war. For our purposes, suffice it to note that the full recognition of union rights and the enactment of a *Labour Code* acceptable to both employers and employees, the promulgation of the major health insurance and hospital reforms, and of language rights in the industrial relations context,[4] etc., were orientations adopted between 1964 and 1977 in Quebec. Until the "Quiet Revolution," the legal standards for collective bargaining and social policies were essentially a legacy of the 1930s. In the early 1960s, the accumulated pressure of the growth of union membership, industrial development and democratic demands resulted in gains that paralleled and even exceeded in some respects what had been previously achieved in more advanced regions of Canada. For example, the new *Labour Code*, enacted in the mid-1960s, recognized the right of association, the right to bargain and the right to strike for all public and parapublic sector employees in the province, without exception. It even influenced the federal government which, confronted with similar demands from its own employment groups, conceded the right to strike to Canada's postal workers, for example. Public health and hospitalization insurance not only altered the social relationship of forces in health care, but significantly increased the economic security of manual and office workers.[5] In the late 1970s, the Quebec government adopted an "anti-scab" law, prohibiting employers from hiring people to do the work normally performed by employees engaged in a legal strike. After challenging this legislation, the employers ultimately agreed to live with it.[6]

During the 1960s and 1970s the Quebec labour movement played a leading role socially. Given the province's economic structure and employment pattern (there are few large industrial sectors), the dynamism of the public and parapublic sectors was decisive. These were the only sectors in which the labour relations framework favoured the united action of tens if not hundreds of thousands of unionized workers.

The unionization of public sector workers enabled the labour movement to register sustained growth between 1965 and 1975, and this gave a particular complexion to the tripartite and "social contract" initiatives adopted by the Parti québécois government when it convened major "economic summits" in

---

4.   That is, the predominance of French, a measure necessary for the achievement of what is referred to as the democratic and social citizenship of Quebec employees.

5.   By separating access to health care and hospitals from the employer-employee nexus, relative degrees of wealth or poverty, paid employment or unemployment, etc.

6.   "After nine years of proceedings, the Supreme Court of Canada held that the Conseil du patronat du Québec had a sufficient interest, as an association, to launch a substantive challenge to the constitutional validity of the anti-scab provisions of the Code (December 6, 1991). Notwithstanding this victory, the CPQ indicated that it would not pursue its case..., in deference to the spirit of collaboration then prevailing between the unions and the employers." (Brunet, 1992: 21-22.)

the late 1970s. Such initiatives were of course common in many advanced liberal countries at that time. In the initial phase of the crisis in the post-war settlement as it developed following the mid-1970s recession, the union leaders found they enjoyed "enhanced political influence." Seeking to reduce "labour costs" and promote the international competitiveness of their national industries, governments initially sought formulas that would enlist the aid of the labour movement in their national economic efforts (Pontusson, 1992: 30), offering in exchange to maintain the goal of full employment. In other words, they attempted to confront their difficulties through joint action and consultation, based on the realities and dynamics of the social relations established by the post-war consensus (Pontusson, 1992: 31). The tripartite economic summits in Quebec were consistent with these international processes but, in the particular context of the province's industrial relations, they were also viewed as an official acknowledgement of the new place and role of the unions in society, a recognition that encompassed far more than their mere right to exist.

This phase was followed by the turn of the 1980s, the subsequent upheaval in economic restructuring, and the decline of traditionally important economic sectors. The Quebec labour movement was now a massive, politically influential force with social and institutional accomplishments fully comparable to those of the labour movements in other developed countries. But, like them, and like working people everywhere, it was subject to harsh economic, social and political pressures, the nature and scope of which were new. These pressures would challenge the unions' practices and lead them into areas hitherto relatively unexplored.[7]

In our opinion, the foremost pressure now bearing down on the Quebec unions is the employment situation. Pierre Fortin, an economist, has demonstrated the long-term structural nature of unemployment rates in Quebec, which have been increasing since the 1960s irrespective of conjunctural fluctuations. In 1989 the unemployment rate was 9.3% (Fortin, 1990: 195-216). From then on, the structural problems were compounded by the severe downturn in the early years of the new decade and the ongoing transformations in the actual process of production: globalization, changing job structures, a new organization of the labour process, etc. In 1990 the unemployment rate rose to 10.1%, and by 1992-93 was oscillating around 13% (Zouali, 1992: 6). This of course exerted downward pressure on incomes: in 1992, the "effective increase in base wage rates" in the "major wage settlements" in Quebec was 1.2%, compared with a pan-Canadian average increase of 2.1% (2.4% in Ontario) (Statistics Canada, 1994: 70-71). What is more, poverty rates actually increased

---

7.   In a context in which governments view deficit reduction as a foremost priority and are redefining their overall role in a direction that challenges social programs and the type of action through which the unions have so far sought to influence politically the evolution of economic life.

during the 1980s in the 15-24 and 25-44 age groups, i.e., among the genera-tions that constitute the major labour force cohorts. The inverse relationship between labour force participation and poverty levels is well known (Zouali, 1991: 6-8, 71-80). With the recession, the situation worsened substantially: in August 1992 Quebec had some 423,500 welfare recipients (an "astronomical figure," according to the Minister of Income Security), and more than 400,000 unemployed, a total of more than 825,000 adults aged 15 and over, com-pared with about 2,900,000 persons who held a job.[8] Between 1990 and 1992, moreover, the total number of jobs in Quebec declined by 5% (Comité conjoint UQAM-CEQ, 1993: 8). These conditions had an impact, of course, on the economic demands of the trade union movement.

There are other pressures, too. Governments are reviewing and cutting back on social and economic programs, increasing the insecurity of wage earners. For example, the federal government, through legislation enacted in early 1993, reduced unemployment insurance benefits and withdrew benefits altogether from persons who are fired for "misconduct" or voluntarily quit their jobs (subject to a few exceptions) (Cantin, 1993: 15-26). In Quebec, some medical procedures and tests are no longer covered by the public insurance plan. Job security gradually became the primary concern in the early 1980s and again in the 1990-93 recession. Hence the pressure on the unions to make bargaining concessions, focused initially on attempts to get them to accept wage freezes or even decreases. There have been many substantial con-cessions, even among employees of public institutions, health services and governments.[9]

Not that there was no resistance to demands for concessions. In each province throughout Canada, there were significant instances of unions refus-ing to go along, sometimes successfully. But since the early 1980s the down-ward pressure has been present, and not easily evaded, it would seem. In Quebec, with its particular employment structure and the peculiar role of the public and parapublic sector, the tendency took effect socially and ideologically in 1982-83, when the major collective agreements in this sector (hospitals, schools, etc.) were being renegotiated. Since the late 1960s the public and parapublic sector negotiations had been conducted by the unions through inter-union "common fronts," and the breakthroughs and conquests of these govern-ment and public employees served as reference points and standards for the demands of other groups of employees. During the winter of 1982-83, through

---

8. See *La Presse*, Montreal, September 5, 1992, pp. A1 and A2; *Le Devoir*, Montreal, June 8, 1992, p. B10.

9. For example, Montreal bus and subway drivers (see Brunet, 1991: 11). In the private sec-tor, initial reductions in wages and/or benefits were sometimes followed by wage freezes with, in some instances, the possibility of recovery in future depending on the evolution of "net profits" (Brunet, 1992: 13).

extremely harsh legislation and notwithstanding an illegal strike in all the public schools and colleges, the Quebec government took back wages *previously* awarded to government employees, imposed a freeze on compensation and prohibited the unions by law from engaging in any protest action.[10]

This was a bitter defeat. It weakened the trade union movement and ended a whole period of social evolution and transformation. In retrospect, its impact on the Quebec unions appears to have been analogous with the impact on U.S. unions of President Reagan's attack on the air controllers in the same period. Since then, there have been no further "common fronts" in Quebec (Lipsig-Mummé, 1991: 95).

The government justified its position by referring to the state of the public finances. Deeper budget cuts were subsequently implemented in all public services, and wage gains were extremely tenuous, if not non-existent. From 1984-85 to 1993, successive governments in Quebec City sought to redefine the legal framework of collective bargaining in the public and parapublic sector, substantially limiting the union rights acquired during the 1960s; for example, strikes are now legal in health and social services institutions only if 55% to 90% of the employees, depending on the situation, remain on duty. Attempts are also being made to decentralize public and parapublic sector bargaining, and, as we write, there is a new generalized freeze on wages and an attempt to reduce the number of middle-level managers by 20% and the number of employees by 12% across the board (Leclerc and Quimper, 1994: 177-194; Harvey, 1994a).

Union rights have not come under comparable attack in the private sector. But, as the specialized publications of the government indicate, and as we wrote earlier, "industrial restructuring," "technological change," factory closures and layoffs have by themselves undermined the unions' capacity for struggle.

Politically, the signing of the Canada-U.S. Free Trade Agreement (FTA) and the Canada-U.S.-Mexico North American Free Trade Agreement (NAFTA) have also helped to transform the environment and conditions of trade union action. Its "horizon" is already being partially remodelled by this opening to "continental economic integration" (Jenson and Mahon, 1993: 13). It is interesting to note that a similar issue arose in the debates over the ultimate effect the FTA would have on Quebec's industrial relations. Would it weaken the unions' position or would it ultimately have a neutral effect? But no one argued that it would tend to improve the unions' status. And given the comparatively low level of Mexican incomes, it is generally conceded that the NAFTA will introduce an additional obstacle to wage gains, at least in some sectors.

---

10. Serge Denis has analyzed this episode in greater detail (Denis, 1984: 378-398).

Like the unions in English Canada and the United States, the Quebec unions were publicly opposed to the terms of the FTA and the NAFTA. In their opposition to the NAFTA, they emphasized that their position did not denote a "protectionist" stance; on the contrary, they wrote, they favoured in principle "increased trade with Mexico, as with the rest of the American continent," provided that the "social dimension" was reflected "in the economic integration process" (Coalition québécoise sur les négociations trilatérales, 1992: 3). Specifically, they criticized the NAFTA for threatening jobs in the "clothing, automobile, telecommunications and transportation" sectors, without providing any "adjustment mechanisms" and "compensatory financing" that would enable those regions and social groups most negatively affected to "recycle." This was in a context that is the opposite of what is occurring in the European Community: the "liberalization of trade" is not accompanied by any declaration of social rights; there is no clause guaranteeing the "rights of labour," protection of social programs, "individual and collective human rights," etc. (Coalition québécoise sur les négociations trilatérales, 1992: 3, 6-7). More fundamentally, perhaps, the Quebec unions argued that the NAFTA would deprive the various governments of the possibility of developing and implementing their own economic strategies: the NAFTA is in fact a continuation of the policies of "deregulation and disengagement of the state" that we have been experiencing since the 1980s, through an approach that would give further priority to the needs of the big American companies (Coalition québécoise sur les négociations trilatérales, 1992: 3, 12, 17-18). We might note, as well, that the NAFTA parallel agreements on the environment and labour failed to satisfy the major Quebec labour centrals (Coalition québécoise sur les négociations trilatérales, 1993).

For the unions, then, these agreements served to accelerate the "internationalization of capital" and production, undermining the "regulatory capacities of national governments," decreasing the significance of "tripartite corporatism" and, more immediately, tending to dislocate the major traditional patterns of collective bargaining.[11] Yet collective bargaining and nation-wide agreements were central to the unions' ability to exert influence on developments. And in Quebec the union centrals had also lost the leverage they once derived from their electoral influence, with the crisis in the relationship between the unions and the PQ in 1982-83, as we noted earlier.

Paradoxically, however, there has been no significant decline in the membership of the union centrals or the rate of union representation. As the following table illustrates (Table 2), the latter may even have increased between 1988 and 1992. It would appear that employment has remained relatively stable "in the sectors with a high rate of union membership (manufacturing, construction, public services)," despite the fact that since 1982 most of the new jobs

---

11.   The formulations are by Jonas Pontusson (Pontusson, 1992: 37).

have been created "in the private tertiary sector."[12] It should also be noted that under the generalized regime in Quebec union dues are deducted at source; a worker's contribution in a company where a union is certified is determined by his or her job status and not membership as such in the union, which remains optional. It would no doubt be interesting to gauge the impact of this system on the persistence of high rates of union membership and representation, in comparison to other countries in which unions cannot rely on a similar check-off system. However, it would appear that in 1993 the jobs crisis finally took its toll. The fall was dramatic.

TABLE 2
Overall Rate of Union Representation in Quebec, 1988-1993
(Racine, 1994: 31)

1988	45.3 %
1989	45.4 %
1990	46.9 %
1991	48.5 %
1992	49.7 %
1993	46.8 %

The situation is quite similar in both private and public sectors, notwithstanding some variations in the pattern as a result of specific government policies (for example, the increasing emphasis on hiring part-time workers in public institutions).

What the difficult social context means for unions and employees is most visible in quantitative terms in the figures on the number of disputes, strikes and "lost person-days" during the 1990s, all of which have been declining since 1989. The small rise witnessed in 1993 is entirely related to two specific disputes, the outcome of which had little to do with the industrial relations set-up between employers and unions. "Were it not for these disputes, a significant decline of over 20% would have been registered in the number of workers involved that year, in comparison to 1992" (Dompierre, 1994: 93).[13] That has been the dominant trend since the beginning of the decade: from 1991 to 1993 (inclusive) about 95% of all collective agreements entered into in Quebec

---

12. According to Jacques Rouillard, quoted by M. Leclerc and M. Quimper (Leclerc and Quimper, 1994: 95).

13. The two disputes in question were in the construction industry (a massive, largely spontaneous movement by workers in opposition to new statutory provisions governing residential construction) and a wave of work stoppages in childcare centres aimed at winning an increase in subsidies from the Quebec government, although the childcare workers' contracts are not with the government.

were negotiated without the occurrence of any work stoppage.[14] A similar and not unrelated situation existed throughout Canada: "the time lost through significant work stoppages in 1993 (work stoppages affecting 500 or more workers) represented (...) 0.02% of the total estimated labour time (...), the lowest level registered in the statistical series for work stoppages in close to fifty years" (Bureau of Labour Information, 1994a: 93).

TABLE 3
Evolution of Employment Level, Number of Employees Covered by a Collective Agreement and Rate of Union Representation in Quebec in the Public and Private Sectors, 1988-1993
(Racine, 1994: 31)

	Private sector			Public sector		
	Employment	Unionized employees	Rate (%)	Employment	Unionized employees	Rate (%)
1988	2,030,547	646,336	31.8	662,441	531,247	80.2
1989	2,032,868	659,186	32.4	669,052	536,419	80.2
1990	2,024,259	685,684	33.9	671,854	524,768	78.1
1991	1,917,163	673,971	35.2	687,755	530,234	77.1
1992	1,817,147	671,595	36.9	723,130	533,549	73.8
1993	1,826,312	634,757	34.7	723,846	534,692	73.9

The public sector corresponds to the education, health and social services and government sub-sectors. Since we do not have data on employment in the private component of the education and health and social services sectors, the rates presented for these two activities include private and public sector activities. Government includes the provincial, municipal and federal civil services. The total number of jobs and unionized employees listed in the public sector is derived from the sum of the jobs and unionized employees in the education, health and social services and government sub-sectors. The private sector is composed of all other sectors of activity.

An environment that, in the medium and long term, can promise only a deterioration in employment and living standards will of course tend to destabilize existing social relations, if not give rise to overt discontent. So far, as we have noted, it is the unions' fighting capacity that has been primarily affected. The need to save jobs is now paramount, leading some unions to agree to experiments that in earlier times would have been considered highly debatable.

For example, in Quebec as elsewhere in North America, collective agreements have begun to include two- and multi-tiered wage scales designed to

---

14.   See *Le marché du travail*, Ministry of Labour, Quebec, Les Publications du Québec, miscellaneous issues since 1989.

lower labour costs without affecting the wage structure of existing employees.[15] These first appeared in 1983; by 1986 they were found in 6.1% of the collective agreements signed that year, two thirds of these provisions being permanent. In virtually every instance they originated in employer demands, and they were accepted reluctantly as a means of promoting the profitability of the company (Pes and Blanchet, 1988: 88). Between 1985 and 1990 clauses of this nature were written into 6.3% of all contracts, especially those covering jobs in relatively low-paid sectors and the retail trades. However, it would appear that the phenomenon peaked in 1989, and the practice was found to be "discriminatory" by the Quebec Human Rights Commission (Turcot, 1992: 83).

TABLE 4
Overall Data on Labour Disputes, Quebec, 1984-1993
(Dompierre, 1994: 7)

	Number of disputes touched off during year	Number of disputes during year	Workers affected	Average number of workers affected	Lost person-days Number	Estimated % of labour time[a]	Average actual duration[b]	Average duration in working days[b]
1984	295	330	41,427	126	1,111,590	0.18	46.8	33.0
1985	244	283	44,491	157	1,143,768	0.18	53.3	37.4
1986	250	280	268,143	958	2,250,949	0.35	49.9	35.1
1987	249	291	95,574	328	1,465,490	0.22	54.0	38.6
1988	190	228	46,539	204	1,431,484	0.19	58.8	41.8
1989	219	244	297,672	1,220	1,609,763	0.21	53.5	38.1
1990	163	190	128,442	676	1,117,054	0.15	65.0	46.6
1991	138	169	43,096	255	641,787	0.09	47.9	34.3
1992	138	158	16,164	102	419,647	0.06	55.5	39.6
1993	145	170	47,872	282	529,136	0.07	60.2	43.1
Average	203	234	102,942	439	1,172,067	0.16	53.9	38.3

a. The annual average is computed from monthly data published in the *Labour Force Survey*, Statistics Canada, cat. 71-220. Only non-agricultural workers are considered.

b. The durations are computed from the number of disputes during the year.

Perhaps of greater significance in Quebec was the signing in the early 1990s of collective agreements containing so-called "social contract" clauses in mid-sized and large companies (625 employees of Abitibi-Price in Alma, 1,300 employees of Goodyear Canada Inc. in Valleyfield, 470 employees at

---

15. Essentially, this involves establishing lower salary scales for newly hired employees.

Aciers inoxydables Atlas in Tracy, etc.). These "social contracts" differ from the identically-named formulas that flourished in the latter half of the 1970s. Although strongly encouraged by the various services of the Quebec government, the current "social contracts" are binding solely on the employer and union(s) within a single firm. Typically, they include an undertaking not to resort to a strike or lock-out during a period exceeding the duration of traditional collective agreements (often six years), joint management "in implementing technological changes (and) job reclassifications while ensuring mobility of the workforce"; a guarantee of "minimum employment levels," the creation of employer-union committees to avoid "antagonistic relations," an "expansion in the principle of participative management at all levels of the organization" and an emphasis on "training, research and development" (Bureau of Labour Information, 1993: 91). It is too early to assess whether the "social contract" tendency as such will become fashionable. It is already obvious, however, that it has been the vehicle for the introduction in Quebec of a whole series of new concepts that are now being used throughout the western world to redefine, at least partially, the meaning of trade union action. We will discuss this in the following section. However, we should note at this point that the very idea of joint employer-employee action received its initial credentials in Quebec with the Parti québécois government's convening of "economic summits" in the late 1970s; that is, it was associated with nationalist discourse from the very beginning. The same consciousness, with its advocacy of a common effort to develop the province economically, now underlies many of the new experiments in labour relations.

Finally, we should note the emergence of a trend toward the implementation of what is referred to in the United States as "plant unionism," the negotiation within a firm of customized local agreements. Thus, in the mid-1980s, at the General Motors plant in Boisbriand (near Montreal), the autoworkers' union agreed to "renew" the industrial relations atmosphere and collaborate in redefining the way in which the work was organized, ostensibly to improve the quality and productivity of the labour force and keep the plant from closing. In the words of Professor Paul R. Bélanger, "the national pattern was broken and (...) it was decided to invent a new local agreement" (Bélanger, 1993-94: 34). Jobs were reclassified to expand mobility, and the job categories were reduced from 54 to 4. The teamwork concept was implemented, "eliminating first-line foremen" and providing for "voluntary rotation of tasks," creating "quality circles" and "parity committees" to supervise the introduction of "technological changes, training and staff transfers." While retaining a formal contract – at the request of the employees – the union and the employer agreed to a "statement of principles in which the parties acknowledge their respective and mutual interests and undertake to promote them jointly." Productivity rose spectacularly and the plant remained open (Bélanger, 1993-94: 35). This was an example of "plant unionism," in that the accepted conceptual framework for job preservation was the competition that General Motors has instituted between its various North American plants.[16] It is not hard to recognize the similarity between the methods adopted in Boisbriand and those characteristic of the "social contract" formulas outlined above. The trend toward regional and local customization of contract terms, and even competition for jobs between plants and companies, is also appearing within public institutions (in the social services sector, for example).

Thus the conditions in which the unions operate have been transformed, weakening their position in the traditional relationship between employers and unions. One academic specialist in industrial relations has even questioned whether the principle of free collective bargaining, the fulcrum of the existing labour relations regime, still exists in Quebec.[17] If the unions are to continue to defend the interests of their members and their role within the broader society, they must therefore revise their strategies.

THE NEW FORMS OF TRADE UNION ACTION

Pressures from many sources (the jobs crisis, the desire to lower labour costs, changes in the role of government, etc.) have brought the union centrals face to face with some substantial problems of orientation. In public and government services, it is the fiscal crisis of the state and the increased use of repression in labour disputes that, paradoxically, have prompted experiments in partnership and the reorganization of work;[18] in the private sector, concerns about the financial health of companies have had similar effects. On the other hand, since the early 1980s the internal life of the union centrals has revealed a genuine malaise. The questioning of prior areas of agreement, the manifestations of discontent with the proposed orientations, and the inability to influence the direction of social and economic developments in any sustained way fuel a decline in the membership's confidence and participation in the organizations. Some programmatic rethinking was necessary, and this has been undertaken in recent years.

---

16. It should be noted, however, that in the collective agreements between GM and the Canadian Auto Workers applying to all of the company's plants in Quebec and Ontario, effective September 1990 to September 1993, and from October 1993 to September 1996, there is one unified set of wage and benefit clauses. (See the summary of these agreements in Bureau of Labour Information, 1990, 1994b.)

17. Gérard Hébert, in an interview with the newspaper *Le Devoir*, was referring primarily to the many decisions by the Quebec and federal governments establishing the working conditions in the public and parapublic sectors by decree rather than negotiations (Amiot, 1994: E12). But the recent developments adverted to earlier also indicate the relevance of his remarks to the private sector, at least partially.

18. See the analyses by François Berger and by Bernard Doddridge, the national bargaining coordinator at the CEQ (Berger, 1991; Doddridge, 1993-94).

The three major union centrals in Quebec, which tend to set the pace for action by the labour movement as a whole, have begun to reassess the international context, to analyze the major contemporary economic and social trends, and to rethink their own activity. Through special symposiums and/or in their conventions, they have sought to get a handle on current developments and arm themselves with an orientation and strategies that will enable them to go beyond improvised reactions and define a new sphere of demands. Since 1992, for example, they have analyzed the means by which the production process is being reorganized and what this entails for the status of trade unionism within the corporate structure. It is important to note that the orientations adopted so far by all three centrals are very similar.

For our purposes let us recall, as many writers have done before us, that the current transformations in the organization of work are the result of both "technological changes" and "the changes that the individual firm (is undergoing) as a form of social organization of production." On the one hand, within the last ten years or so there has been "a quantitative [and] especially qualitative leap" in the use of "automation and computerization technologies"; their function is no longer simply one of "substituting for human labour" but of assisting in the design, manufacturing and diversification of production, which necessarily alters the roles and tasks of individuals. On the other hand, the reappraisal of rigid and repetitive production methods in the 1970s has produced "new philosophies of human resource management" which give greater emphasis to autonomy and "accountability" in the production process. The combined effect of these transformations, we are told, presupposes the disappearance and merging of existing positions, a flexible work mode, the "capacity to devote oneself no longer to the performance of a particular task but to the management of a work process," and a framework that will now accommodate a "less hierarchical distribution" of power; etc.[19]

The documents of the Quebec union centrals rely explicitly on the most recent works on economics and the politics and sociology of labour: the major European, and particularly French sources, in the case of the CSN, and primarily North American sources in the case of the FTQ. An overview of these documents shows that in many respects they complement each other or reiterate closely related themes: the exhaustion of the "Fordist" model of accumulation, the crisis of Taylorism, the globalization of the economy, etc.[20] The internationalization of production and its adaptation to the customization of tastes and needs weigh particularly heavily on the economy of Canada and Quebec, the CSN writes, because it is singularly dependent on exports and

---

19.   We are drawing directly here on Céline Saint-Pierre (Saint-Pierre, 1990: 68-69, 73).

20.   CSN, *Prendre les devants dans l'organisation du travail*, Montreal, 1992; FTQ, *Face aux changements: de nouvelles solidarités*, Montreal, 1993; CEQ, "L'organisation du travail," *Options*, Winter 1993-94, no. 9.

foreign trade. Yet the search for quality, the FTQ notes, is a consequence of the "globalization of the economy," which demands a reorganization of work and is linked, with the latter, to a desire to "reduce costs" (CSN, 1992: 5-10; FTQ, 1993: 20-24). Moreover, by "eliminating restrictions on the mobility of capital" and engaging in large-scale privatization, governments are no longer able "to play a decisive role in the orientation of development" and "investment decisions," thus facilitating "collusion by the multinationals on a world scale" (CSN, 1992: 10).

It is by acknowledging this general context as they have defined it that the Quebec union centrals are attempting to refurbish their policy objectives. The analysis has so far been focused on the reorganization of work, which the unions would like to be able to influence, and through which the major issues confronting the labour force and the individual firm are being addressed. The reorganization of work is viewed as the mechanism that will help to increase productivity and quality and thus the profitability of private firms and the efficiency of public services. In this framework, the objective is to preserve and create jobs. If there is any one place in which the ideological departure from the proclamations of the union manifestoes of the early 1970s is most evident, it is precisely in the establishment of a link between the profitability of each individual firm and the defence/promotion of the interests represented by the trade union movement. The unions, according to one central, should "propose ways to organize the work process that will be both interesting to the individuals and productive for the firm" (CSN, 1992: 69). And when, within a more comprehensive perspective of improving the jobs situation, a supplementary strategy of shortening the workweek is proposed, it is specified that the methods adopted should be "adapted to the particular conditions of each sector and each firm or institution" (CSN, 1994: 25).

These statements have led some Quebec economists to conclude that "the unions now agree to function within the rules of the market economy" (for example, Diane Bellemare in Boyer, 1994: E13), rules that include, of course, competition between firms and, more specifically, competition internationally. In the public and government services, the unions' action is similarly adapted to a difficult environment of spending cutbacks, the backdrop for work reorganization projects. Traditionally, in Quebec as elsewhere, the purpose of the trade union movement was "to take wages and conditions out of competition by setting standards" (*Canadian Dimension*, 1994: 3), and trying to attain such standards. Today, the attempt is more to fit within the logic of private enterprise and declining government budgets.

Convinced that these changes are irreversible, the Quebec union centrals are trying to prevent them from being implemented at the expense of union members – for example, to forestall the production of a "dual labour market" and a "dual society," characterized by systematic insecurity of employment and income for a large section of the population. They agree that they cannot "remain passive" or "limit themselves to defensive demands." As the title of the major orientation paper presented to the CSN's 1992 convention put it, they have decided to "make the first move" (*Prendre les devants*) by themselves proposing "some technological innovations and methods of organizing production" (CSN, 1992: 51-52). In this vein, they demand, for instance, the "right (of a firm's employees) to economic information" concerning "products, customers, competitors, suppliers,... market and employment trends, subcontractors, etc.," in order to "anticipate technological changes before (new) equipment and software are purchased." The idea is to be able to "foresee the necessary changes in the production process," "to find new forms of collaboration" in the management of the firms and institutions, "to enrich the content of the work,... (and) increase the autonomy, responsibilities and satisfaction" of the employees (CSN, 1992: 59-60).

All of these things, the FTQ president explains, dictate the "elimination of the (traditional) discrepancy between the principle of joint action and the interests of the workers" (Godbout in Harvey, 1994b: E5). If the unions' suggestions are to be relevant, firms must operate with greater openness. Thus, the 1,235-member Local 143 of the Canadian Communications Workers (FTQ) is now participating in the management of the Goodyear plant in Valleyfield: the "books are open," the federation explains, and the local is "represented at an annual meeting at headquarters in the United States" (FTQ, 1993: 88). Within this framework, the intention is to develop "forms of multi-skilling and flexibility (of duties) that are reskilling, instead of being simply an addition of dissimilar tasks or a roundabout way of increasing the workload" (CSN, 1992: 60). Underlying these demands, of course, particularly in the CSN and the FTQ, has been the desire since the 1980s for a greater emphasis on labour force training needs, to protect employment and promote adaptation to technological change. In the public and private sectors as a whole, the percentage of collective agreements under Quebec jurisdiction containing training provisions increased from 49.6% in 1980 to 72.3% in 1992 – and more specifically, "from 43% to 65% in the goods producing industries" in the private sector (Morissette, 1993: 7, 9).

That is why, at this stage, the reorganization of production can be seen as the focal point of the attempts by the Quebec union centrals to have some influence on employment and the evolution of the economy and to democratize social relations. There is even talk of "making collective agreements more flexible" by replacing the standard clauses in today's contracts with common declarations of principle or employer-union letters of agreement, to allow for "ongoing negotiations" and a permanent adaptation of labour relations (FTQ, 1993: 45). Be that as it may, however, it must be said that the attachment to the principle of the collective agreement is nevertheless very real, particularly with the union rank and file. When the CEQ convention in June 1994 discussed the advisability of teachers participating in the work reorganization process initiated by the government, the vigorous opposition (albeit ultimately defeated) rested on the fear that the province-wide contract would be broken down on an institution-by-institution basis, i.e., that the unified working conditions in the collective agreement would disappear. And in the private sector, even where there is a consensus on the need for long-term management-labour cooperation, the employees have always insisted that such formulas have no place in the definition of the contract. However, current developments are putting a question mark around the traditional role and place of the collective agreement.

Driving in the same direction, moreover, are some recent government initiatives. Toward the end of 1991 the Quebec government adopted a "Quebec Charter of Total Quality" aimed at encouraging managers and employees in private companies to develop ways and means of improving the quality of production. In 1993 some 5,500 firms had officially adopted a program of this nature; in perhaps 40% of the cases the unions, where present, were involved (FTQ, 1993: 22-23). At around the same time the government also announced a policy aimed at reorganizing the work process in the public and parapublic sectors, allegedly designed to involve "the employees," the "partners" and the "clients." But the unions say the search for "total quality" in this sector appears to be an attempt to do the same thing by cutting costs (and positions) (FTQ, 1993: 31-37). A number of government departments are promoting and initiating experiments in making technology and working conditions more "flexible" in private firms,[21] while at the same time the government has developed a "three-year strategic plan (1992-95)... that reinforces its commitment to redefine the traditional conception of labour relations... by developing greater expertise in the organization of production... (and striving to) establish a culture of joint action and cooperation" (Cantin, 1993: 18).

Government policies have therefore taken a very specific tack, which also serves to define the overall context of the unions' intervention. This context has pressured the unions into refocusing their discourse on the individual firm within the parameters of the market economy and its present evolution. There is still a desire for more general actions that might modify the course of developments in the labour market.[22] When they came out against the terms of the NAFTA, for example, the Quebec union centrals called for the inclusion of a side agreement that would require the three signatory countries to comply with strict standards governing labour relations and working conditions. This requirement might open the way to the type of demands that are now being raised in

---

21. See, for example, the speech by Jean des Trois Maisons, then Assistant Deputy Minister for Labour Relations in the Department of Employment (reproduced in des Trois Maisons, 1994).

22. This is a level at which the entire North American labour movement needs to intervene, according to J. Jenson and R. Mahon (Jenson and Mahon, 1993: 12).

Europe, for the adoption by governments of an international charter which would prohibit the pursuit of competitiveness at the expense of living conditions (jobs, skills) and incomes (wages), albeit allowing it on the basis of technological and managerial advances.[23]

But for the time being the FTA and NAFTA agreements, particularly the latter, represent, in the view of the Quebec union centrals, devices to exert downward pressure on social policies and conditions subject to collective bargaining; and although industry-wide inter-union links between the three countries are being discussed, these proposals have yet to get off the drawing board. In the framework of their participation in the Coalition québécoise sur les négociations trilatérales, the union centrals will be holding a symposium in 1995 to assess the first eighteen months of the NAFTA's existence and more specifically to fine-tune their position on the economic integration of the Americas. There is no doubt, however, that the individual firm's performance now constitutes the frame of reference *par excellence* for the development of the demands and programs of the Quebec unions, which makes the unions' economic orientation commensurate with a social and political program. With the struggle for jobs as its cornerstone, the priority in the unions' social program goes to the firm's performance, to productivity and quality, and thus to work-sharing and the reorganization of the work process.

A CLOUDED HORIZON

This new orientation of the unions has been accompanied by a retreat from their earlier political commitments as such. In this, the Quebec unions are not alone, as a similar phenomenon has been observed in many countries. The crisis has severely tested the labour movement. The period of upsurge and genuine advances of the 1960s and 1970s in Quebec has given way to a period of retreat, defeats in place of victories, and defensive struggles to preserve past gains that fail to stem the repeated blows of unemployment, factory closures and job losses. But it is precisely in such a context, this above all others, that the labour movement needs to extend its action to the political level. The failure in this regard has obscured the horizon. And what is now presented as an attempt to regain the initiative by modernizing its action, adapting it to the new context of the world economy, is to a large degree dictated by a situation in which Quebec trade unionism cannot anticipate any significant social or political breakthroughs.

Politically, the labour movement advocates a break with the existing constitutional order, while economically it attempts to adapt to the new economic order. The linkage between politics and economics, once provided by the special

---

23. See the analytical considerations suggested by Claude Julien (Julien, 1993: 1, 8-9).

relationship with the Parti québécois, is now absent. The major concerns of the movement appear to be focused on the economic sphere, while its political commitments are confined to statements of principle that provide no leverage for positive action.

Non-partisanship as a form of union representation in the political arena has been sorely tried. Paradoxically, the unions seem to cling to it with even greater fervour now that no major political formation, whether the Liberal party or the PQ, actually arouses their partisan allegiance. The PQ attracts the support of a majority of unions only by its position on the national question. But union non-partisanship can only exist in practice if the workers' organizations are in a position to bargain concessions for their members in exchange for the support they give to this or that party or candidate. It is precisely this capacity that has been eroded since the 1980s, with neither of the political formations agreeing to bargain for the unions' support in return for significant concessions. Thus, deprived of a political outlet, the unions have turned to the economic sphere as the area of predilection for action, as if it were possible to free up some space for social gains or advances without going the political route.

In fact, trade unionism has been weakened both economically and politically. In many countries this is particularly evident in the radical decline in union membership. In Quebec, it is less obvious, because from the standpoint of membership figures, the situation has until now remained relatively stable. But the numbers now seem misleading. The labour movement in Quebec is going through the same challenge to its role and its legitimacy as its counterparts in the other advanced capitalist countries.

REFERENCES

AMIOT, Marie-Andrée (1994), "L'action syndicale: point de vue de deux observateurs," *Le Devoir*, April 30 – May 1, p. E12.

BÉLANGER, R. Paul (1993-1994), "Après le taylorisme," *Options*, Montreal, CEQ, No. 9, Winter, pp. 23-36 (see pages 33-35 for the Boisbriand example).

BERGER, François (1991), "L'acceptation syndicale d'un gel de salaires inaugure-t-elle un *partenariat?*," *La Presse*, April 24, p. B6.

BOYER, Hélène (1994), "Les intérêts syndicaux convergent de plus en plus vers ceux du patronat," *Le Devoir*, April 30 – May 1, p. E13.

BRUNET, Anne-Marie (1991), "Les événements marquants," *Les relations du travail en 1991*, Quebec, Les publications du Québec, pp. 11-17.

BRUNET, Anne-Marie (1992), "Les événements marquants," *Les relations du travail en 1992*, Ministère du Travail, Quebec, Les publications du Québec, pp. 13-24.

BUREAU OF LABOUR INFORMATION (1990), *Revue de la négociation collective*, Labour Canada, November.

BUREAU OF LABOUR INFORMATION (1993), *Revue de la négociation collective*, Labour Canada, May, p. 91.

BUREAU OF LABOUR INFORMATION (1994a), *Revue de la négociation collective*, Labour Canada, March, p. 93.

BUREAU OF LABOUR INFORMATION (1994b), *Revue de la négociation collective*, Labour Canada, January.

Canadian Dimension (1994), "Editorial: Competing Visions Divide Labour," Winnipeg, January-February, p. 3.

CANTIN, Eugène (1993), "Les événements marquants," *Les relations du travail en 1993*, Ministère du Travail, Quebec, Les publications du Québec, pp. 15-26.

CEQ (1993-1994), "L'organisation du travail," *Options*, No. 9, Winter.

COALITION QUÉBÉCOISE SUR LES NÉGOCIATIONS TRILATÉRALES (1992), *L'Accord de libre-échange nord-américain: les gagnants et les perdants*, Montreal, December.

COALITION QUÉBÉCOISE SUR LES NÉGOCIATIONS TRILATÉRALES (1993), "Accord imparfait Les accords parallèles ne corrigent pas les impacts négatifs de l'ALENA," *Le Devoir*, September 13, p. A7.

COMITÉ CONJOINT UQAM-CEQ (1993), *Conjoncture et tendances économiques en 1993*, Montreal, UQAM: Services aux collectivités; a paper reproduced in part in *Correspondances*, Vol. 1, No. 3, June, p. 8.

CSN (1992), *Prendre les devants dans l'organisation du travail*, Montreal.

CSN (1994), *La réduction du temps de travail: éléments de réflexion*, Montreal, March.

DENIS, Serge (1984), "Développement, tensions et lignes de clivage du mouvement ouvrier au Canada," in BERNIER, G. and G. BOISMENU (ed.), *Crise économique, transformations politiques et changements idéologiques*, Montreal, ACFAS, pp. 373-398.

DES TROIS MAISONS, Jean (1994), speech reproduced in *Le marché du travail*, Vol. 15, No. 4, April, pp. 6-10, 83-84.

DODBRIDGE, Bernard (1993-1994), "Une nouvelle façon de faire en négociation," *Options*, Montreal, CEQ, No. 9, Winter, pp. 119-125.

DOMPIERRE, André (1994), "Grèves et lock-out au Quebec en 1993," *Le marché du travail*, Vol. 15, No. 5, May, pp. 6-10, 89-93.

FORTIN, Pierre (1990), "Y a t-il une voie québécoise vers le plein emploi?," in DUMONT, Fernand (ed.), *La société québécoise après 30 ans de changement*, Quebec, IQRC, pp. 195-216.

FTQ (1993), *Face aux changements: de nouvelles solidarités*, Montreal.

HARVEY, Claire (1994a), "Les compressions budgétaires se solderont par l'érosion du système de la santé," *Le Devoir*, April 30-May 1, p. E9.

HARVEY, Claire (1994b), "Chômage et déficit sont la toile de fond de l'action syndicale – Le néolibéralisme force les grandes centrales à revoir leurs priorités," *Le Devoir*, April 30-May 1, p. E5.

JENSON, Jane, and Rianne MAHON (1993), "North American Labour: Divergent Theories," in Jenson, Jane and Rianne Mahon (ed.), *The Challenge of Restructuring*, Philadelphia, Temple University Press, pp. 3-15.

JULIEN, Claude (1993), "Ces *élites* qui règnent sur des masses de chômeurs," *Le Monde diplomatique*, Paris, No. 469, pp. 1, 8-9.

LECLERC, M. and M. QUIMPER (1994), *Les relations du travail au Québec*, Quebec, Presses de l'Université du Québec.

LIPSIG-MUMMÉ, Carla (1991), "Future Conditional: Wars of Position in the Quebec Labour Movement," *Studies in Political Economy*, 36, Autumn, pp. 73-107.

MORISSETTE, Réal (1993), "Évolution de l'intérêt pour la formation dans les conventions collectives québécoises de 1980 à 1992," *Le marché du travail*, Vol. 14, No. 7, July, pp. 6-10, 63-72.

PES, Johanne and Anne-Marie BLANCHET (1988), "La rémunération à double ou à multiples paliers dans les conventions collectives en vigueur au Québec," *Le marché du travail*, Vol. 9, No. 3, March, pp. 78-89.

PONTUSSON, Jonas (1992), "Organizational and Political-Economic Perspectives on Union Politics," in Golden, Miriam and Jonas Pontusson (ed.), *Bargaining for Change*, Ithaca, Cornell University Press, pp. 1-41.

RACINE, Francine (1994), "La syndicalisation au Québec en 1993," *Les relations du travail en 1993*, Ministère du Travail, Quebec, Les Publications du Québec, pp. 27-32.

ROYAL COMMISSION ON BILINGUALISM AND BICULTURALISM (1965), Preliminary Report, Book III, in Denis, Roch, *Luttes de classes et question nationale au Québec*, Montreal, Paris, 1979, PSI, EDI, pp. 96-98.

SAINT-PIERRE, Céline (1990), "Transformations du monde du travail," in DUMONT, Fernand (ed.), *La société québécoise après 30 ans de changement*, Quebec, IQRC, pp. 67-79.

STATISTICS CANADA (1994), "Indicateurs-clés de l'emploi et du revenu," *Perspectives*, Catalogue 75-001F, Spring, pp. 70-71. [Published in English, Catalogue 75-001E, as "Key Labour and Income Facts," pp. 57 *et seq.*]

TURCOT, Yves (1992), "La rémunération à double palier dans les conventions collectives au Québec: évolution de la situation entre 1985 et 1990," *Le marché du travail*, Vol. 13, No. 11, November, pp. 9-10, 78-87.

ZOUALI, Siham (1991), "La pauvreté au Québec: une réalité à suivre," *Le marché du travail*, Vol. 12, No. 12, December, pp. 6-8.

ZOUALI, Siham (1992), "Incidences de la conjoncture sur la pauvreté et les revenus au Québec et au Canada," *Le marché du travail*, Vol. 13, No. 12, December, p. 6.

10

Uneasy Allies:
Quebecers, Canadians, Americans, Mexicans and NAFTA[1]

André Turcotte
University of Toronto

When NAFTA was announced on August 12, 1992, most observers agreed that the removal of trade barriers between the three countries offered advantages and disadvantages for all the parties involved. However, there was a lack of consensus among both analysts and citizens over the costs and benefits of the trade deal. In fact, the only common trend in this debate was sharp division over the perceived beneficiaries of the trade deal and its socioeconomic repercussions. It will be the aim of this study to explore further this lack of public support for NAFTA, and the sadly ironic commentary its enactment represents for democracy. In the end, only Mexicans majoritarily supported NAFTA, placing both American and Canadian elected representatives in the ironic position of ratifying and enacting a legislation contrary to the views of their constituents. It will be shown that trade-centred strategies have become the preferred option for government in the nineties despite public perceptions. It will thus be argued that trade liberalization is politically driven rather than an example of popular will endorsing the benefits of freer trade among nations. Without condemning or supporting the concept of free trade, the results of this analysis will at least identify the gap existing between the policy actions of the political elites in representative democracies and the views of citizens. The consequences of the existence of such a gap will also be considered.

1. The author would like to thank Mr. Jon Hugues, without whose help this paper would not have been possible. Mr. Hugues helped in the gathering of the information and provided critical insight which proved invaluable to the author.

" What is new in the so-called capitalist countries – and this is a vital point – is that the controlling contentment and resulting belief is now that of the many, not just of the few... The result is government that is accommodated not to reality or common need but to the beliefs of the contented. "

John Kenneth Galbraith

When NAFTA was announced on August 12, 1992, most observers agreed that the removal of trade barriers between the three countries offered advantages and disadvantages for all parties involved. Throughout the debate preceding the ratification, critics pointed to the small current trade between Canada and Mexico, Mexico's low labour costs, Mexican competition with Canadian goods in U.S. markets, and the alleged failure of the existing Canada–U.S. Free Trade Agreement as reasons for Canada to spurn the agreement. Concerns over the ratification of the trade deal were sufficiently salient that during the 1993 federal election campaign, Chrétien's Liberals expressed serious reservations about the agreement, and pledged to seek and obtain further concessions from the Mexican and American governments before ratifying it.

In contrast, proponents of the deal stressed the benefits in terms of economic growth, job creation and increased competitiveness as the main advantages of the Accord. Specifically, both the Canadian and Mexican governments had for objectives to achieve secure access to U.S. markets by improving their influence on application of U.S. trade laws. Moreover, supporters of the agreement stressed the inevitability of North American integration within the context of globalization.

Lack of consensus over the costs and benefits of continental integration was also found among citizens. In fact, the only common trend in this debate was the sharp division over the perceived beneficiaries of the trade deal and its socio-economic repercussions. In the end, only Mexicans majoritarily supported NAFTA, placing both American and Canadian elected representatives in the ironic position of ratifying and enacting a legislation contrary to the views of their constituents.

It will be the aim of this study to explore further this lack of public support for NAFTA, and the sadly ironic commentary its enactment represents for representative democracy. It will be shown that it is despite public perceptions of the issue that a strategy of continental integration has become the preferred option for government in the nineties. During the NAFTA debate, these policy initiatives were presented to the electorate as a way to deliver economic renewal and a higher standard of living. This promise was greeted by a dose of scepticism. It will thus be argued that continental trade liberalization is politically driven rather than an example of popular will endorsing the benefits of freer trade among nations. Without condemning nor supporting the concept of continental integration, the results of this analysis will at least identify the gap existing between the policy actions of the political elites in representative democracies, and the views of citizens. The consequences of the existence of such a gap will also be considered.

This study will present the results of public opinion surveys conducted in Quebec, Canada, the United States and Mexico. The analysis will concentrate on public perceptions of NAFTA, and will examine both national and regional attitudinal differences towards this deal. But first, to assist in the understanding of the data analysis, a brief profile stance of the four main regions under consideration will be presented.

QUEBEC

Quebec cannot ignore its position in North America. This position is multifaceted since it not only involves its cultural heritage, but must also take into consideration the economic and commercial relations with its continental partners – the rest of Canada, the United States and, to a lesser extent, Mexico. In short, Quebec's continental strategy, and its stance on continental integration, has been defined as being situated within a reconfiguration of power in the province that takes into account the new imperatives imposed by the global economy, and the structural constraints placed on its economy (see Rocher 1993: 450-468). Moreover, Quebec's strategy toward continental integration cannot be explained away as simply the conversion of political and/or business elites to the dogma of neo-liberal trade proponents, as it is partly the case in Canada, the United States, and to some extent in Mexico. It must be addressed within the context of the different phases in the development of Quebec's economic nationalism.

The Quebec economy is generally described as very open. The rest of Canada constitutes a larger market for most of Quebec's main products than does the domestic provincial market. However, in recent years, international exports of goods have consistently made a significant contribution to the provincial GDP, varying between 16% and 23% from year to year (see Langlois et al. 1992: 38).

Specifically, the United States are increasingly becoming Quebec's preferred trading partner. The percentage of Quebec's internationally exported products shipped to the United States fluctuated between 58.5% and 64.9% in the 1970s, and reached about 75% by the mid-1980s. For its part, Mexico remains a very minor actor in Quebec's trading picture, accounting for less than 1% of Quebec's total exports (Statistics Canada 1993). Nevertheless, Quebec has become more dependent on the U.S. market along with its other external markets – including the rest of Canada – than on its own domestic market for sales of its products (see Dutrisac 1989). Consequently, the structure of exports is strongly influenced by the continental market, and the dependence of Quebec upon both the Canadian and American markets cannot be underestimated. To some extent, Quebec's economy is particularly vulnerable to economic slowdowns that may arise in the United States, and to fluctuations in the demand for raw materials.

Faced with such economic realities, it is logical to conclude that the support for continental integration in Quebec rests on an acceptance of the liberal arguments that have driven public policy-making in the United States, and to a lesser extent in the rest of Canada. However, this constitutes only part of the argument.

First, the continentalist option was not a response to heightened concern about the issue. Throughout the period of the negotiations, more specifically between the spring of 1992 and the fall of 1993, no more than 3% of Quebecers perceived continental integration (North American Free Trade) as the most important issue facing the country (Perspectives Canada, Spring 1992 – Fall 1993). Thus, the impetus for negotiating continental integration did not stem from the public, but resided with the two classes that had more to gain from trade liberalization.

The support of a large portion of Quebec's business and political classes for continental integration is a reflection of their views on the new maturity of the francophone segments within those classes, and the need for structural changes that would allow those groups to achieve their objectives. In accordance with the democratic changes implemented in the province in the past thirty years, there is a sense that efficient public policy-making can best be achieved through more popular control and decreased governmental fine-tuning. As François Rocher (1993) has previously argued, it is within this context that the Quebec elites supported the free trade agreement negotiated by Ronald Reagan and Brian Mulroney in 1988. It is also the main reason for supporting the Chrétien-Clinton-Salinas trade deal, although the political circumstances surrounding the two agreements were quite different, as we will see below.

It is important to note that the business class does not unanimously support the continentalist option. During the NAFTA debate, business opposition to the trade deal was sectoral. According to the Quebec Minister of Industry and Commerce, of eighteen sectors examined, continental integration would benefit five industries – nonmetallic, minerals, sporting goods, tiles and linoleum, and wood products. In contrast, this option would negatively affect twelve sectors – printing and publishing, jewellery, instruments, plastic and rubber, electrical products, computers, metals, base metals transformation, footwear, machinery, furniture, and clothing, while it would not effect the agricultural sector and toys and games manufacturing (Blouin 1986: 102-103). The weaker businesses were obviously not enthusiastic about the idea of facing new competition, and demanded (and obtained) the adoption of government measures for the smooth transition toward continental integration. To this end, and as a way to minimize the negative effects of continental free trade, business representatives negotiated government aid for businesses in weaker competitive sectors and assistance in meeting changes in technology (Guay 1989: 154-155).

If aid to business was put forward as a condition for the opening of the Quebec market, continental integration was nevertheless business' answer to the structural problems of Quebec's economy. This option would give the necessary impetus to the removal of impediments to competitiveness, and would create new markets for Quebec's exports.

For the Quebec government, North American free trade was seen as a way to ensure that francophone capital would play a larger role in the continental economy by weakening federal powers to intervene in the economy. The Quebec government has always pursued a policy that promoted Quebec's place in the continental economy. In so doing, it has aimed at improving the socio-economic status of francophones through an interventionist state that also seeks to decrease the negative effects of the endemic structural weaknesses of the province's economy. The Quebec government wanted to distance itself from Canada's economic sphere, whose constraints are seen as having a negative influence on its economic development. The poor opinion of federal economic development policies, which are seen by many as favouring Ontario at the expense of Quebec, effectively reinforced support for NAFTA. The Quebec government saw continental integration as a way to develop economic relations with the rest of Canada, on a similar basis as the ties between Quebec and the United States, or between Quebec and Mexico.

Thus, both the business and political elites sought to maximize their utility, with little regards, as we will see, to the views of their constituents. The latter failed to see the benefits of continental integration, even if couched in terms of national development and affirmation.

CANADA

A major reticence voiced in Canada against joining NAFTA was the feeling that the Canada-U.S. Free Trade Agreement, at least from the perspectives of the general public, had been the major cause of the large number of job losses suffered between 1988 and 1993. This is especially the case for those that have occurred in the manufacturing sector since 1989 (Waverman 1993: 33).

In the new global economy, the Canadian situation is a particularly tenuous one. This is partly because Canada is adjacent to the most powerful nation of the world and is about one-tenth its size, measured by GDP. Canada depends upon the U.S. market for about 75% of its exports. The United States, moreover, own over 40% of Canada's manufacturing output – with another 25% owned by other foreign-owned firms – and engulfs Canadian culture via its television programs, movies, videos and magazines. Consequently, the political and business communities both see Canada's long-run interest as being intimately linked with the U.S. economy and with U.S. interests generally (see Wilkinson 1993: 35-36).

During the free trade debate, the rhetoric of business and government was widely disseminated. It was premised on the idea that Canada must privatize, deregulate, enter trade liberalization agreements, institute international as well as government-industry advisory committees based on the U.S. models and spend millions on trade missions. As a result, the largely private decisions of the market would produce economic growth, employment and prosperity for Canada.

More fundamentally, Canadian business people and politicians seemed to have generally accepted the idea of Adam Smith's "invisible hand" maximizing societal welfare as businesses pursue their own interests. However, this radically simplified assumption about human behaviour fell short of describing the reality under the Canada-U.S. Free Trade Agreement.

It was assumed that with trade liberalization, "national treatment" for capital would encourage Canada's new generation of ebullient entrepreneurs to conquer the enhanced market made secure by the Canada-U.S. Free Trade Agreement. Foreign investment would stream into Canada. Workers who lost their jobs in declining sectors would further the process of economic adjustment by finding jobs in more dynamic and technologically-sophisticated industries. As for noneconomic issues, prospects were equally promising since provinces would continue to develop their system of social services, while the federal government would play a more independent role on the world stage (see Crispo 1988; Lipsey 1988). However, in contrast to Quebec, Canadian nationalists perceived continental integration as a threat rather than a status-enhancing endeavour, and pondered the consequences of further U.S. cultural penetration.

The free trade scenario – as presented by the business sector – bears little resemblance to the drastic economic and political changes experienced in Canada over the last few years. In light of the state of the Canadian economy in the early 1990s – in terms of unemployment, poverty, homelessness, food banks, real incomes that have not increased in a decade – it is fair to say that the effects of the Canada–U.S. Free Trade Agreement left much to be desired. A major reason lies in the nature of the free trade agreements themselves. Free trade became the centrepiece of a political strategy designed to restructure Canada's economy and society for the "tough, new world of global competition" (Clarke 1993: 119; Campbell 1993). However, a central Canadian objective in signing the trade deal was to secure access to the U.S. market. Securing access to export markets requires the elimination of both tariff and nontariff obstacles to trade, and this has failed to materialize.

The Free Trade Agreement provided for a gradual ten-year phaseout of bilateral tariffs, to be coordinated through a dispute settlement mechanism. The reality of nontariff barriers is quite different. Before the trade deal, Canadian exporters to the United States faced ongoing harassment by border restrictions, bureaucratic red tape, technical and safety standards, and other restrictions (see Lazar 1981). The economic cost for Canada did not end with existing protective measures (Grinspun 1993: 106). The Free Trade Agreement disappointed Canadians in terms of the limited liberalization obtained in the area of nontariff barriers. Certainly, "secure access to the U.S. market" was not obtained in this critical area. Furthermore, little was achieved in terms of access to U.S. government procurement – another key objective of the Canadian negotiators (see Macdonald 1987).

Failure to achieve these key objectives did not stop the Canadian government from embarking upon negotiations to include a move from a bilateral trade agreement to a broader strategy of continental integration. The North American Free Trade Agreement came into effect despite the quickly-silenced objections voiced by the Chrétien government and despite the widespread public opposition to further trade liberalization in Canada's five geographical regions. However, as noted above, the nature of the debate over continental integration was much different from the debate over free trade with the United States.

First, the Canadian electorate never relented from its opposition to the Canada-U.S. Free Trade Agreement. During the negotiations, opposition to free trade in Canada hovered around 60%. Furthermore, a majority of Canadians in the five regions of the country were opposed to the Canada-U.S. Free Trade Agreement. (Perspectives Canada, Spring 1992-Fall 1993). But while Canadians were still reeling from the perceived negative effects of free trade with Americans, politicians had learned the lessons of 1988. Thus, the main difference between the 1988 free trade debate and the recent debate over continental integration lies in the fact that in the latter instance, Canadian politicians purposely avoided trying to make political gains out of the issue.

Unlike 1988, when Brian Mulroney successfully tied his government's survival to free trade, no efforts were made in 1993 to debate the issue of continental integration. The Liberals low-bridged the issue. Thus, for political and strategic reasons, no attempts were made to convince the electorate of the benefits of continental integration at a time when it was enjoying its highest saliency.

UNITED STATES

Although Canada and Mexico border upon the United States, many Americans are less aware of events occurring in those countries than in more distant places such as the Middle East. The Canadians and Mexicans, on the other hand, are well aware of their common neighbour. That anomaly may, perhaps, be explained by the fact that the United States has tended to dominate the other two North American countries and take them for granted. However, the decline of U.S. hegemony in the international political economy has led to a reconsideration of U.S. unilateralism and of the importance of both Canada and Mexico to achieve global trade liberalization.

Despite this heightened interest, the unequal stature of the three countries cannot be ignored. The U.S. population is roughly three times the population of Mexico. Mexico's population is three times Canada's. The U.S. economy is ten times the size of Canada's, and more than twenty times the size of the Mexican economy. Canada and the United States are each other's largest trading partners. Mexico is the third largest trading partner for the United States, but the United States is Mexico's largest. (McGaughey 1992: 45). A remnant of British colonial rule, Canada has a relatively small and static population residing in a large, well-irrigated territory that extends northward beyond the Arctic Circle. In contrast, Mexico, with its Spanish colonial heritage, has a large and fast-growing population in a relatively small, semi-tropical and mostly arid territory. Yet the two countries both border upon the United States, and that gives them something in common.

Canada and Mexico were invaded by U.S. troops in the 19th century. In the 20th century, they have been penetrated by U.S. economic, political and cultural influences. Both countries have developed an uneasy relationship with the American giant which translates into periodic re-evaluations of their role in North America. Until recently, the United States had little use for this type of self-evaluation.

The most contentious aspect of NAFTA for the United States is not what is in the agreement itself, but the very fact of having free trade with a developing country whose wages are so much lower – about 14% of the U.S. level for production workers in manufacturing (Weintraub 1993: 12). Ironically, most of the arguments raised in the United States were those raised in Canada prior to the ratification of the Canada-U.S. Free Trade Agreement.

Competitive concerns lay at the heart of the debate in the United States on approval of the agreement. At issue was not whether the United States should trade with Mexico and Canada or whether investment should be allowed to move freely within North America. As previously noted, Canada and Mexico are already among the most important trading partners of the United States and investment is already quite mobile. The question was how such increased trade and investment should take place.

Continental integration as presented in NAFTA will potentially harm long-term U.S. economic competitiveness and put in jeopardy the jobs of hundreds of thousands of U.S. workers. The central objection to the NAFTA was that it provided an incentive for U.S. producers to respond to market competition with a low-wage strategy, which would lower incomes and productivity over the long run, rather than the more difficult path of producing quality products more efficiently. With NAFTA in place, business will now be able to relocate to Mexico, pay dollar-an-hour wages, hire a young, eager work force, and have few pollution or environmental standards to worry about. Businesses remaining in the United States will have a difficult time competing on these terms. NAFTA will also put downward pressure on the wages of millions more U.S. citizens in sectors not directly affected by the agreement (Faux et al. 1993: 236).

Faced with such realities, two trade strategies were possible. One is modelled on the European path to integration, which was slow and gradual, sensitive to disparities of income and social institutions between countries, and committed to achieving integration without penalizing workers. The other is the neoconservative continental integration model implicit in the agreement signed by Chrétien, Clinton and Salinas, which aimed at rapidly removing all remaining barriers to the flow of capital, goods and services across borders within the North American continent, regardless of both short- and long-term consequences.

Despite the real cost of continental integration, alternatives were never seriously discussed. For instance, one way in which several of the European governments have attempted to guide their economies onto a high-wage, high-value-added growth path has been to shut off the low-wage option – by setting a relatively high minimum wage, regulating plant closings, and legislating levels of welfare, pension, and unemployment compensation benefits. This has forced companies to seek productivity improvements via investments in modern equipment and new technology and more interactive labour management (Faux et al. 1993: 245). NAFTA takes the United States in exactly the opposite direction – opening the door for U.S. corporations to seek the low-wage solution, obviating the need for investment in the labour force by either Mexico or the United States. While this may add to corporate profits in the short run, in the long run it will undermine the productivity and thus the competitiveness of the entire continent.

It is therefore incongruous that the NAFTA was ratified without a thorough discussion of the alternatives. The American people were presented with only one approach to continental integration. This is even more incongruous when one consider the level of U.S. opposition to the NAFTA, as will be demonstrated in this analysis.

MEXICO

At the start of the negotiation process, Mexico wanted an agreement to accelerate economic recovery, as the prolonged restructuring of the economy was seen to be taking considerable time to deliver tangible progress to the majority of Mexicans. Accordingly, the debate in Mexico over NAFTA was dominated by the fulfilment of people's expectations about well-paid jobs and an improved macroeconomic climate, reflected, above all, in low inflation. Fulfilling these expectations depended on high investment, which in turn called for substantial foreign capital inflows.

The main point of contention centred around the fact that increasing foreign capital would require the elimination of the remaining investment restrictions, which would threaten the monopolistic and oligopolistic positions of large Mexico industrial groups. Demands for protection from increased foreign domination would be loud, and it was argued that the government should resist them (De la O 1993: 84-85).

According to this line of argument, the Mexican government would be well-advised to resist these pressures, as it is generally accepted that Mexicans are poised to be the main beneficiaries of continental integration. In fact, much of the debate around the NAFTA was framed in terms that suggested that Canadian and U.S. losses will be Mexico's gains. However, nothing is that simple in Mexican politics.

First, although Mexico might benefit most from continental integration, many Mexicans will actually be adversely affected by NAFTA. Knowing precisely which Mexicans – that is, which sectors of the economy and which social classes – will gain or lose ground is difficult to predict. This climate of uncertainty leads to instability within a population that cannot afford to lose its few economic advantages. It is also difficult to establish who will benefit because of the closed authoritarian nature of the Mexican system.

The Mexican government gave NAFTA negotiations the equivalent status of a national security affair, keeping information almost a state secret, preventing any meaningful public debate, maintaining close vigilance over its opponents, and transmitting only general messages to the electorate (Zinser 1993: 207). This veil of secrecy stands as conundrum when one considers that proponents of continental integration think that the opening of the Mexican economy will not only solve economic woes, but will also create an environment conducive to political liberalization and freedom of expression.

Continental integration is also viewed as the impetus that will lead to adequate social and economic pressures, as well as incentives to clean up and strengthen the corrupt and unreliable Mexican legal system, and it may force Mexico to adopt, and actually enforce, international environmental standards to protect its own habitat and to preserve its natural resources (Zinser 1993: 205).

Opposition to NAFTA has less to do with the potential negative repercussions of elements of the deal than with a deep resentment and scepticism towards the ruling elite (the PRI in particular) held by a significant number of Mexicans. These people believe that anything that arouses the enthusiasm of the ruling party (PRI) and most of the economic elite will, by definition, turn out to be very rough on popular and middle-class Mexicans.

The views of the people in this group are not based on the specific details of NAFTA, or on a rejection of the continentalist option, but on their broader perceptions of past reality. Their experience suggests to them that they are no more likely to reap the benefits of continental integration than of any of the development programs instituted in the past. In general, these people do not know what, specifically, is going to happen to them under NAFTA, but they assume that it is not going to be good (Hellman 1993: 200).

The role of a social charter in improving working conditions, social benefits and environmental protection also generated opposition to NAFTA in Mexico. Some opinions support NAFTA on the condition that a parallel charter be attached. Others support trinational efforts to develop such a charter, but insist that no social charter can fix the flaws of this trade initiative (Comunes, 1992:128).

Despite the alleged secrecy and absence of an open debate, many Mexicans endorsed NAFTA. Much of this support for the trade initiative is based only on vague, ill-informed hopes of "better things to come," that nothing could be worse than the economic situation presently facing them. There is a sense that the free trade agreement has been negotiated over the heads of the Mexican citizenry, but ironically, the following analysis will show that, in contrast to Quebec, Canada and the United States, the Mexican government actually implemented a policy that reflected the views of the people it purports to represent.

WHO BENEFITS?

As shown by the preceding discussion, each region under study had a particular understanding of the costs and benefits associated with the continentalist option. This ambivalence is further reflected in the structure of public opinion in each region in the years leading up to the ratification of the North American Free Trade Agreement.

Two studies were conducted by the Gallup affiliates in Canada, the United States and Mexico concerning the perceived prospects of free trade for the citizens of the three countries. The same battery of questions was posed to representative samples in the three countries at two different points in time. The questions asked were as follows:

> As you may know, Canada and the United States now share a free trade agreement which ensures that trade between the two countries largely is not subject to tariffs or import quotas. It has been suggested that a wider free trade zone could be established, consisting of Canada, the United States, and Mexico. In general,

do you think a North American free trade zone consisting of these three countries would be mostly good for (respondent's country), or mostly bad for (respondent's country)?

Which of the three countries – Canada, the United States or Mexico – do you think would probably benefit most from a North American free trade zone?

Which, if any, of these three countries – Canada, the United, or Mexico – do you think would be more likely to be hurt than helped by the establishment of a North American free trade zone?

Interviews were conducted at two different points in time. In the first instance, a total of 1,039 personal interviews were conducted in Canada (including 253 in Quebec), and 1,009 personal interviews were conducted in Mexico, between March 6 and 9, 1991, as well as 1,005 telephone interviews conducted in the United States between March 14 and 17, 1991.

In the second instance, a total of 1,026 telephone interviews were conducted in Canada (including 253 in Quebec), between September 10 and 14, 1992, as well as 1,000 telephone interviews in the United States conducted between September 17 and 20, 1992. A further 1,005 personal interviews were conducted in Mexico, between September 11 and 15, 1992.

In 1991, 53% of Canadians maintained that establishing a Canada–U.S.–Mexico free trade zone would run counter to their country's best interests. Slightly more than one out of every four Canadians (28%) claimed that such a trade arrangement would be mostly good for Canada, while 6% maintained that creating a continent-wide free trade deal would neither be good nor bad for Canada.

An examination of this data set according to the home region of the respondent indicates that only in the province of Quebec did more people see North American free trade as a primarily positive, as opposed to negative, endeavour for Canada.

In specific terms, while 45% of Quebecers believed that such a trade arrangement would be mostly good for the country, 31% held the opposite view. In contrast, 50% of Atlantic Canadians, 52% of Prairie residents, 56% of British Columbians, and 66% of Ontarians perceived North American free trade as being mostly bad for Canada.

The results in the other countries were very different from those gleaned from the Canadian survey. More than seven out of every ten Americans (72%) believed a North American free trade deal would benefit the United States, while 66% of Mexicans thought that such an arrangement would be mostly good for Mexico. Accordingly, at this stage of the debate, the structure of opinion in the province of Quebec was closer to the United States and Mexico than to the rest of Canada.

This pattern was to be reversed a year later, when we witnessed a continent-wide erosion of confidence over the perceived benefits of the continentalist trade option, especially in the province of Quebec.

In 1992, 60% of Canadians believed that a Canada–United States–Mexico free trade zone would be detrimental to their country. This figure constituted a seven-percentage-point increase over a one-year period. Twenty-seven percent believed that such a trade arrangement would be beneficial to Canada, down marginally from 28% in 1991.

Unlike 1991, when Quebecers were more receptive to the continentalist option than Canadians in other regions of the country, in 1992 the free trade arrangement was negatively perceived across the country.

While 68% of British Columbians perceived the North American Free Trade Agreement as being mostly bad for Canada, 66% of residents in Atlantic Canada, 61% of Ontarians, and 59% of Prairie residents shared the same view.

In Quebec, where most respondents had viewed the arrangement in positive terms in 1991, the situation changed drastically in the 17-month period. In 1992, 53% of Quebecers believed that NAFTA would be mostly bad for Canada, up from 31% in 1991. Slightly less than one out of every four Quebec residents (24%) believed that it would be mostly good, down from 45% in 1991.

TABLE 1
Perceived Impact of NAFTA

	Good for Own Country	Bad for Own Country	Neutral
Quebec			
1992	24%	53%	23%
1991	45%	31%	24%
Canada			
1992	27%	60%	13%
1991	28%	53%	19%
USA			
1992	55%	24%	21%
1991	72%	15%	13%
Mexico			
1992	60%	17%	23%
1991	66%	20%	14%

We can only speculate, at this point, about the reasons behind Quebecers' change of heart with regards to NAFTA. The data set used in this study do not go beyond analyzing general attitudes towards NAFTA. However, part of the explanation may lie in the fact that unemployment reached record highs in the province of Quebec in the latter part of 1992. Specifically, the unemployment rate reached 13% in August 1993, the highest level since September 1984, and rose even further to 14.3% in November 1993. It was the first time unemployment had reached such a level since June 1983 (Statistics Canada, Cansim, D768478). Consequently, Quebecers were likely to be more sensitive to the potential repercussions of NAFTA on unemployment at a time when job loss was directly affecting them and their families.

In attitudinal terms, it would appear that these fears led Quebecers to reconsider the specific deal that was negotiated. Quebecers were having second thoughts about parts of the agreement and held the view that NAFTA should be renegotiated. In the fall of 1992, Insight Canada Research asked Canadians and Quebecers opposed to NAFTA if they would prefer to see the deal scrapped or renegotiated. In total, 51% of Canadians, but 64% of Quebecers, wanted to see the deal renegotiated rather than scrapped. (Perspectives Canada, Fall 1992). Hence, Quebecers were not rejecting continental integration as a policy option, but were rejected parts of the agreement negotiated by Mulroney, Bush, and Salinas. Nevertheless, their concerns fell on deaf ears.

As it was the case in 1991, Gallup affiliates in the United States and Mexico posed the same battery of questions to representative samples in those two countries. In both the U.S. and Mexico, initial optimism was replaced by caution. In the United States, 55% believed that NAFTA would be beneficial to their country, down from 72% in 1991. Similarly, six out of every ten Mexicans (60%) believed that the arrangement would be mostly good for Mexico, down from 66% in 1991.

At the heart of this scepticism lay a deeply-held view that others would likely reap the benefits of trade liberalization, while the costs would not be shared equally. Thus, despite the fact that the governments of the four regions enthusiastically pursued the continentalist option, the respective publics held clear reservations about the issue. That is, the population of Quebec, Canada, the United States and Mexico regarded the principal beneficiaries of North American free trade to be a country other than their own. This popular view was prevalent by 1991, and subsequent arguments presented in favour of NAFTA had little effects on it.

Specifically, 54% of Canadians, 53% of Quebecers and 52% of Mexicans believed the U.S. would be the country to benefit most from free trade. In contrast only 5% of Canadians, 8% of Quebecers and 23% of Mexicans maintained that their respective countries would be the chief beneficiary of trade liberalization, as suggested by the elites.

For their part, 53% of Americans believed Mexico would profit most from North American free trade. It would appear that the American people were receptive to the argument put forward by the opponents of NAFTA that competitive concerns were at the heart of the debate in the United States and that freer trade as presented in the NAFTA could potentially harm long-term U.S. economic competitiveness and threaten the jobs of hundreds of thousands of U.S. workers.

TABLE 2
Country to Benefit Most from NAFTA

	Canada	USA	Mexico	All	None	DK/NA
Quebec						
1992	6%	55%	29%	2%	–	8%
1991	8%	53%	21%	4%	1%	14%
Canada						
1992	4%	53%	36%	2%	–	5%
1991	5%	54%	29%	3%	1%	8%
USA						
1992	11%	19%	55%	3%	–	12%
1991	15%	20%	52%	3%	–	10%
Mexico						
1992	2%	57%	21%	13%	2%	5%
1991	2%	52%	23%	15%	–	8%

Canadians, Quebecers and Mexicans also believed that not only would the United States be most likely to reap the benefits of trade liberalization, but their own country would probably end up being the country most hurt by it. Furthermore, as it was the case with the perceived beneficiaries of NAFTA, Canadians and Mexicans had made up their minds by 1991, and proponents of the trade agreement were unsuccessful in their subsequent attempts to sway public opinion. For their part, Quebecers reacted negatively to the arguments favouring NAFTA, and grew more adamant in their beliefs that Canada would be more likely to be hurt than helped by further trade liberalization, and this for the aforementioned reasons.

In 1991, 63% of Canadians and 42% of Quebecers believed that Canada would be more likely to be hurt than helped by NAFTA. At the same time, slightly more than one out of every two Mexicans (53%) thought Mexico would be more likely to be hurt by the establishment of a North American free trade zone. One year later, 64% of Canadians, but 59% of Quebecers, believed Canada would be negatively affected by NAFTA, while 47% of Mexicans shared the same view as regards Mexico.

Americans were more likely to see NAFTA as a cost-free agreement. In 1991, 42% of Americans believed none of the participating countries would be more hurt than helped by the establishment of a North American free trade zone, while a further 26% believed the U.S. would be the most hurt. In 1992, slightly less than one out of every three citizens (32%) thought that none of the three countries would be hurt by NAFTA, while 32% believed the U.S. would be more likely to be hurt than helped by the continentalist option.

TABLE 3
Country to Be Hurt Most by NAFTA

	Canada	**USA**	**Mexico**	**All**	**None**	**DK/NA**
Quebec						
1992	59%	13%	15%	2%	1%	11%
1991	42%	6%	20%	–	9%	23%
Canada						
1992	64%	7%	14%	1%	4%	9%
1991	63%	4%	16%	–	7%	10%
USA						
1992	5%	32%	9%	1%	32%	21%
1991	6%	26%	11%	–	42%	15%
Mexico						
1992	7%	4%	47%	2%	32%	9%
1991	1%	2%	53%	–	28%	16%

ATTITUDES TOWARDS NAFTA

Such perceptions and attitudes towards NAFTA were not conducive to a subsequent popular endorsement of continental integration. A comparison of public opinion data in the fall of 1993 indicates that NAFTA was rejected by a majority of citizens in Canada's five geographical regions, as well as in all regions in the United States. However, a slim majority of Mexicans supported the North American Free Trade Agreement.

This comparison is based on three different datasets. In Canada, the results are based on 1,100 telephone interviews (285 in Quebec) conducted between October 27 and November 1, 1993. In the United States, the results are based on 1,000 telephone interviews conducted between November 2 and 4, 1993, while the Mexican results are based on 3,500 personal interviews conducted on November 19 and 20, 1993. Respondents in each country were asked if they supported or opposed the North American Free Trade Agreement between Canada, the United States and Mexico.[2]

---

2.   The author would like to thank Michael Marzolini, Chairman of Insight Canada Research, for the use of Perspectives Canada's data. The author would also like to thank the Gallup Organization for the U.S. data and the Roper Centre for the Mexican data.

In Quebec, slightly less than three out of every five residents (57%) opposed NAFTA, while 32% were in favour and 11% were opposed. Opposition to NAFTA was lower in the province of Quebec than in the rest of the country. At the national level, 69% of Canadians opposed NAFTA. Specifically, while 64% of residents in Atlantic Canada were opposed to NAFTA, this figure increased to 67% in the Prairies, 75% in British Columbia and 77% in Ontario.

TABLE 4
Attitudes towards NAFTA (Fall 1993)

	Support	**Oppose**	**DK/NA**
Quebec	32%	57%	11%
Canada	23%	69%	8%
Atlantic	27%	64%	9%
Ontario	18%	77%	5%
Prairies	23%	67%	10%
BC	18%	75%	7%
USA	38%	46%	16%
East	33%	44%	23%
MidWest	40%	45%	15%
South	37%	47%	16%
West	41%	47%	12%
Mexico	52%	20%	28%

Opposition to NAFTA was weaker in the United States, where significant segments of the population remained ambivalent towards the trade agreement. In total, 46% of Americans were opposed to NAFTA, while 38% were in favour and 16% were unsure. On a regional basis across the U.S., opposition to the trade agreement stood at 47% in both the south and the west, 45% in the midwest, and 44% in the east. In contrast, support for NAFTA was higher in the west (41%) and the midwest (40%) than in the south (37%) and the east (33%).

As noted previously, the continentalist option was greeted with a dose of scepticism in Mexico, and this is reflected in the structure of the public opinion environment in that country. It was generally argued that Mexicans had most to gain from trade liberalization, and support for NAFTA was based on vague hopes of "better things to come." However, partly because of the shroud of secrecy surrounding the trade negotiations, historical reasons, and general suspicion of politicians, a significant number of Mexicans distrusted NAFTA despite the alleged benefits. Consequently, while 51% of Mexicans supported the North American Free Trade Agreement, more than one out of every four residents (28%) remained unsure. In contrast, opposition to NAFTA stood at 20% – the lowest in the four regions analyzed in this study.

CONCLUDING REMARKS

Democracy must enable its citizens to influence, if not determine, government policy. Over the last 30 years, Quebec governments have made efforts to democratize the political process, passing various acts to increase citizens' participation (Lachapelle et al. 1993: vii). It has even been argued that few other democracies have done as much to reform voting procedures, party financing, party structure, and electoral behaviour (ibid.). However, reforms of the political process must go beyond a restructuring of the processes of politics to restore a climate for responsible government where public opinion is no longer seen as a hindrance to policy-making.

The above analysis explored the lack of public support for NAFTA and the sadly ironic commentary its enactment represented for democracy. It was the aim of this study to look at public attitudes towards NAFTA to identify the existing gap between the policy actions of the political elites in representative democracies and the views of the citizens.

It was demonstrated that continental integration – as embodied in the North American Free Trade Agreement – became the preferred trade policy alternative for governments in North America despite public opinion. In this sense, the Quebec government, like the Canadian and the American governments, chose to ignore the popular will in their support for NAFTA. Paradoxically, the Mexican government, although not recognized for its democratic tendencies, was able to claim that the enactment of NAFTA represented the wishes of a majority of the Mexican population. However, the veil of secrecy and the lack of open debate in Mexico over the merits of NAFTA are not reflective of a government poised to embrace democracy.

The dynamics of the debate over continental integration shed light upon the apparent breakdown in the public's capacity to influence policy-making. In Quebec, Canada, and more strikingly in Mexico, efforts were made to avoid presenting the issue for general discussion. In the case of Canada and Quebec, the Liberal Party carefully avoided making NAFTA a central element of its electoral strategy. The party remembered the pitfalls of the 1988 free trade debate and circumvented the issue. This was also the preferred strategy of the Democrats and Republicans in the United Sates until Ross Perot forced the issue onto centre stage.

It is disquieting to see political actors who believe that they now have the right to exclude purposely their constituents from public policy decisions. While elitist and interest group literature discusses at length the forces that lead to this kind of policy formulation, it is more important to reflect on the attitudes held by politicians and their advisers which allow them to justify their actions.

As John Kenneth Galbraith recently pointed out, there is evidence that politicians operate in a culture of contentment (see Galbraith 1992). Leaders seek to accommodate the contented. They operate under the cloak of democracy, but it is not the democracy of all citizens, but the democracy of those who support them. According to Galbraith, this, and not the much celebrated circumstance of charismatic political leaders and leadership, is what shapes modern politics. Dominating and omnipresent on television, in the polls and in the press, political leaders are passive or accommodating as regards political reality (ibid.:144). He further argued that older democracies are more likely to suffer from this erosion of representativeness (ibid.: 155).

The consequences of the culture of contentment are important. The mutual understanding between citizens and government necessary for effective democracy becomes distorted. Elected officials do not respond to the electorate, and act in such a way as to ensure that citizens are cut out of the politics pertaining to the most important public policy decisions. In the case of NAFTA, the governments involved responded to a set of narrow interests, rather than to the concerns of their respective constituencies. Restoring a climate for responsible government will require a paradigmatic change in the way politicians now perceive the views of ordinary citizens. Instead of distancing people from government decisions, efforts should be made to bring citizens back into the process and, above all, to accept the consequences of the democratization of the political process. Failure to do so will lead to a further decline in public respect for government institutions and a further sense of alienation from the political process. The public will increasingly become convinced that the political system is irrelevant to their lives and will become even more alienated from the political process. Politicians will have difficulty implementing policy changes that require public support (such as social security reform or health care reform), leading to a political incapacity to make important decisions.

Unfortunately, despite the consequences of the present situation, the current climate of quiet accommodation and silent leadership is not conducive to the implementation of such changes.

REFERENCES

BÉLANGER, Yves, "Economic Development: From Family Enterprise to Big Business," in Gagnon, Alain (Ed.), *Quebec: State and Society*, 2nd edition, Scarborough: Nelson Canada, 1993.

BLOUIN, Jean, *Le libre-échange vraiment libre?*, Quebec: Institut québécois de recherche sur la culture, 1986.

CAMPBELL, Bruce, "Restructuring the Economy: Canada into the Free Trade Era," in Grinspun, Ricardo, and Maxwell A. Cameron (Eds.), *The Political Economy of North American Free Trade*, Montreal: McGill-Queen's University Press, 1993.

CHOMSKY, Noam, *Deterring Democracy*, New York: Hill and Wang, 1992.

CLARKE, Tony, "Fighting Free Trade, Canadian Style," in Sinclair, Jim (Ed.), *Crossing the Line*, Oshawa: The Alger Press, 1992.

COMUNES, Fronteras, "Fighting Free Trade, Mexican Style," in Sinclair, Jim, (Ed.), *Crossing the Line*, Oshawa: The Alger Press, 1992.

CRISPO, John (Ed.), *Free Trade: The Real Story*, Toronto: Gage, 1988.

DE LA O, Rogelio Ramirez, "A Mexican Vision of North American Economic Integration," in Globerman, Steve (Ed.), *Continental Accord: North American Economic Integration*, Vancouver: The Fraser Institute, 1991.

DE LA O, Rogelio Ramirez, "The North American Free Trade Agreement from a Mexican Perspective," in Globerman, Steve, and Michael Walker (Eds.), *Assessing NAFTA: A Trinational Analysis*, Vancouver: The Fraser Institute, 1993.

DUTRISAC, Robert, "Le Québec sous influence," *Le Devoir économique*, 5, no. 6, 1989.

FAUX, Jeff, and Thea LEE, "Implications of NAFTA for the United States: Investment, Jobs, and Productivity" in Grinspun, Ricardo, and Maxwell A. Cameron (Eds.), *The Political Economy of North American Free Trade*, Montreal: McGill-Queen's University Press, 1993.

FLORES, Maria Davila, "The Social Impact: A Mexican Commentary," in McKinney, Joseph A., and M. Rebecca Sharpless (Eds.), *Implications of a North American Free Trade Region: Multidisciplinary Perspectives*, Ottawa: Carleton University Press, 1992.

FRY, Earl H., "The North American Free Trade Agreement: U.S. and Canadian Perspectives," in McKinney, Joseph A., and M. Rebecca Sharpless (Eds.), *Implications of a North American Free Trade Region: Multidisciplinary Perspectives*, Ottawa: Carleton University Press, 1992.

GAGNON, Alain (Ed.), *Quebec: State and Society*, 2nd edition, Scarborough: Nelson Canada, 1993.

GALBRAITH, John Kenneth, *The Culture of Contentment*, Boston: Houghton Mifflin Company, 1992.

GAMBLE, John King, Zachary T. IRWIN, Charles M. REDENIUS and James W. WEBER, *Introduction to Political Science*, 2nd edition, Englewood Cliffs: Prentice-Hall, 1992.

GUAY, Jean-H., "Le patronat," in Monière, Denis, *L'année politique au Québec, 1988-1989*, Montreal: Québec/Amérique, 1989.

GLOBERMAN, Steve (Ed.), *Continental Accord: North American Economic Integration*, Vancouver: The Fraser Institute, 1991.

GLOBERMAN, Steve, and Michael WALKER (Eds.), *Assessing NAFTA: A Trinational Analysis*, Vancouver: The Fraser Institute, 1993.

GREIDER, William, *Who Will Tell the People: The Betrayal of American Democracy*, New York: Simon & Schuster, 1992.

GRINSPUN, Ricardo, and Maxwell A. CAMERON (Eds.), *The Political Economy of North American Free Trade*, Montreal: McGill-Queen's University Press, 1993.

HELLMAN, Judith Adler, "Mexican Perceptions of Free Trade: Support and Opposition to NAFTA," in Grinspun, Ricardo and Maxwell A. Cameron (Eds.), *The Political Economy of North American Free Trade*, Montreal: McGill-Queen's University Press, 1993.

LACHAPELLE, Guy, Gérald BERNIER, Daniel SALÉE and Luc BERNIER, *The Quebec Democracy: Structures, Processes & Policies*, Toronto: McGraw-Hill Ryerson Limited, 1993.

LANGLOIS, Simon, et al., *Recent Social Trends in Quebec, 1960-1990*, Montreal: McGill-Queen's University Press, 1992.

LAZAR, Frank, *The New Protectionism: Non-Tariff Barriers and Their Effects on Canada*, Toronto: Lorimer, 1981.

LIPSEY, Richard, "The Case for Trilaterism," in Globerman, Steve (Ed.), *Continental Accord: North American Economic Integration*, Vancouver: The Fraser Institute, 1991.

MACDONALD, D., *Canada, Royal Commission on the Economic Union and Development Prospects for Canada*, Report, Vol. 1, Ottawa: Supply and Services Canada, 1985.

MCGAUGHEY, William, *A US-Mexico-Canada Free Trade Agreement: Do We Just Say No?*, Minneapolis: Thistle Rose Publications, 1992.

MCKINNEY, Joseph A., and M. Rebecca SHARPLESS (Eds.), *Implications of a North American Free Trade Region: Multidisciplinary Perspectives*, Ottawa: Carleton University Press, 1992.

MIRAMONTES, Eduardo Zepeda, "The Economic Impact: A Mexican Commentary," in McKinney, Joseph A., and M. Rebecca Sharpless, (Eds.), *Implications of a North American Free Trade Region*: Multidisciplinary Perspectives, Ottawa: Carleton University Press, 1992.

MONIÈRE, Denis, *L'année politique au Québec, 1988-1989*, Montreal: Québec/ Amérique, 1989.

NEY, Edward, "The Evolution of Trilateral Relations," in Randall, Stephen (Ed.), *North America Without Borders: Integrating Canada, the United States, and Mexico*, Calgary: University of Calgary Press, 1992.

NOËL, Alain, "Politics in a High Unemployment Society," in Gagnon, Alain (Ed.), *Quebec: State and Society*, 2nd edition, Scarborough: Nelson Canada, 1993.

RANDALL, Stephen (Ed.), *North America Without Borders: Integrating Canada, the United States, and Mexico*, Calgary: University of Calgary Press, 1992.

REYNOLDS, Clark W., "A United States Vision of North American Economic Integration," in Globerman, Steve (Ed.), *Continental Accord: North American Economic Integration*, Vancouver: The Fraser Institute, 1991.

ROCHER, François, "Continental Strategy: Quebec in North America," in Gagnon, Alain (Ed.), *Quebec: State and Society*, 2nd edition, Scarborough: Nelson Canada, 1993.

RITCHIE, Mark, "Fighting Free Trade, U.S. Style," in Sinclair, Jim (Ed.), *Crossing the Line*, Oshawa: The Alger Press, 1992.

SILVERMAN, Sheldon A., "Reflections on the Cultural Impact of A North American Free Trade Agreement," in Randall, Stephen (Ed.), *North America Without Borders: Integrating Canada, the United States, and Mexico*, Calgary: University of Calgary Press, 1992.

SINCLAIR, Jim, (Ed.), *Crossing the Line*, Oshawa: The Alger Press, 1992.

STATISTICS CANADA, cat. no. 65-003, 1993.

THE ECONOMIST, "Mexico's Second-Class Citizens Say Enough Is Enough," January 8th, 1994.

TRAYNOR, Ken, "The Origins of Free Trade Mania," in Sinclair, Jim (Ed.), *Crossing the Line*, Oshawa: The Alger Press, 1992.

VAILLANCOURT, François, "The Economic Status of the French Language and Francophones in Quebec," in Gagnon, Alain, (Ed.), *Quebec: State and Society*, 2nd edition, Scarborough: Nelson Canada, 1993.

WATSON, William G., *North American Free Trade Area*, Kingston: Queen's University Press, 1991.

WAVERMAN, Leonard, "A Canadian Vision of North American Economic Integration," in Globerman, Steve (Ed.), *Continental Accord: North American Economic Integration*, Vancouver: The Fraser Institute, 1991.

WAVERMAN, Leonard, "The NAFTA Agreement: A Canadian Perspective," in Globerman, Steve, and Michael Walker (Eds.), *Assessing NAFTA: A Trinational Analysis*, Vancouver: The Fraser Institute, 1993.

WEINTRAUB, Sidney, "The North American Free Trade Agreement as Negotiated: A U.S. Perspective," in Globerman, Steve, and Michael Walker (Eds.), *Assessing NAFTA: A Trinational Analysis*, Vancouver: The Fraser Institute, 1993.

WILKINSON, Bruce W., "Trade Liberalization, the Market Ideology, and Morality: Are We a Sustainable System?," in Grinspun, Ricardo, and Maxwell A. Cameron (Eds.), *The Political Economy of North American Free Trade*, Montreal: McGill-Queen's University Press, 1993.

ZINSER, Adolfo Aguilar, "Authoritarianism and North American Free Trade: The Debate in Mexico," in Grinspun, Ricardo, and Maxwell A. Cameron (Eds.), *The Political Economy of North American Free Trade*, Montreal: McGill-Queen's University Press, 1993.

11

Editorials and the Free Trade Agenda:
Comparison of *La Presse* and the *Toronto Star*

Andrea M.L. Perrella
Université de Montréal

Quebec's support for free trade and Ontario's opposition to it appear to be linked to the editorial stands of the two provinces' main mass newspapers, La Presse and the Toronto Star. *However, quantitative links are weak, in that changes in the amount of editorial coverage do not correspond well to changes in opinion or changes in salience. Moreover, free trade was less salient in Quebec than in Ontario, although this was not reflected by differences in the amount of editorial coverage. A qualitative analysis, however, reveals striking differences, in that the* Toronto Star *related free trade to job losses and other highly salient concerns, while* La Presse *emphasized less salient and more abstract reasons to support both FTA and NAFTA. This may explain why free trade remained more salient in Ontario than in Quebec. Free trade was not highly salient in either province, but it was slightly more so in Ontario.*

EDITORIAL ATTEMPTS TO MOBILIZE THE PUBLIC AGENDA

Free trade climbed up the policy agenda from the fringes to centre stage during the mid-1980s, pushing the public into giving it serious thought. From the start, the free trade negotiations between Canada and the United States, followed by a sequel involving Mexico in the early 1990s, split opinion in central Canada along the Quebec–Ontario border throughout much of the Progressive Conservative reign. Ontarians put up greater opposition to both the Canada–U.S. Free Trade Agreement (FTA) and the North American Free Trade Agreement

(NAFTA), while Quebecers were more supportive of both. Opinion seems to have aligned according to the principal mass newspapers of both provinces, with *La Presse* endorsing free trade and the *Toronto Star* vehemently opposing it. This apparently neat link between the newspapers' editorial positions and public opinion within their respective provinces deserves an insightful examination to determine just how much influence the editorials had in mobilizing the public.

Overall, it appears that the editorials had a hard time influencing the public on free trade, given the issue's persistent low salience. However, while polls show that Quebecers lost interest in free trade shortly after the 1988 federal election, Ontarians seemed to maintain a modest level of interest. Why did free trade interest Ontarians more and for a longer period than Quebecers? The multivariate nature of public opinion makes a simple answer difficult, but this study provides some insight by examining two variables.

Since editorials seek to persuade the public, they are likely candidates for an agenda-setting study. Editorials on free trade printed by both newspapers throughout the PC reign from 1984 to 1993 were examined, content analyzed and word counted to determine their influence on the public agenda as measured by Gallup polls which tracked the public's top concerns and their opinions on free trade. However, there appears to be nothing more than a weak *quantitative* link between the amount of editorial coverage and public opinion on free trade, and even this weak link appeared only during part of the 10-year study period. Given that the *quantity* of editorial coverage printed on free trade had little measurable effect on the public agenda, perhaps editorial content, or a *qualitative* study, would prove more revealing. In fact, it was found that *La Presse's* editorials presented free trade – a low-salience issue – in light of abstract concepts, thus failing to link the issue to something with which the public could easily relate. In contrast, the *Toronto Star's* editorials connected free trade with other and more salient issues, including unemployment, an issue that has been at the top of public concern for years. Hence, *La Presse* failed to entice the public while the *Toronto Star* succeeded in making free trade more relevant, and thus more salient.

Given the public's consistent and persistent concern with unemployment, the unemployment rate should enter as another variable. Here, the results are even more revealing. It appears that Quebec's support for free trade is inversely related to the unemployment rate, with few exceptions. Quebecers' support for free trade grew in proportion to reductions in the unemployment rate. Editorials seemed to have *no* influence along this pattern. Ontario, on the other hand, seemed more ambivalent. Polls measuring Ontario's opposition to free trade show a slight zig-zag pattern. Reductions in Ontario's unemployment may have reduced opposition to free trade, but the *Toronto Star's* anti-free-trade editorials seems to have acted as a counter force.

As this study will show, editorials do not always affect opinion, though their potential must never be overlooked. Robinson (1974) notes that although few people read editorials, many could accurately indicate their favourite newspaper's editorial positions. Hurd and Singletary write that, like most other forms of mass communication, editorials have "some effect under some conditions some of the time" (1984: 332). One such condition is an election, when the media increases its coverage of various issues and hence mobilizes the public's views, or the public agenda. In such cases, editorials have been known to sway public opinion and cause some voters to deflect their vote from a certain candidate in favour of an opposing candidate (McCombs 1967, Coombs 1981).

General elections certainly are hot agenda-setting periods because they engender participation by a large segment of the population, whose peaked interest in various issues draws them to the press for information, thus setting the stage for the press to mould opinion (McCombs and Shaw 1977). Whether or not elections are the main stimulant behind an issue's peak salience, several conditions generally lead to its rise and decline in the public agenda. Research has identified different conditions which move an issue up the public agenda from obscurity to salience. Amid a sea of issues, each competing for attention at the public and policy-making level, few are taken seriously enough to develop into appropriate legislation.

Cobb, Ross and Ross (1976) outline three agenda-building models: 1) the *outside* model, consisting of non-governmental organizations, such as lobby and interest groups, which promote an issue to gain prominence within the public agenda in order to compel policy officials to admit the issue within the formal (policy) agenda; 2) the *mobilization* model which includes policy initiated by government which promotes the issue for public acceptance (from public to formal agenda); and 3) the *inside* model, similar to mobilization in that government officials initiate an issue or policy, but in this case it is prevented from spilling over into the public agenda.

Free trade seems to fit the mobilization model, since the issue originated with the government. The Liberal-appointed Royal Commission on the Economic Union and Development Prospects for Canada, known as the Macdonald Commission, recommended in 1985 that Canada embark on free trade with the United States. Prime Minister Mulroney took up this policy proposal and steered Canada towards negotiations in 1986, with the media reporting on the activities and events surrounding the negotiations. The public grew more concerned and elevated free trade in the public agenda, as was shown by various public opinion polls. Concern about free trade peaked in 1988, the year of a federal election which focused on the FTA. After the election, free trade nosedived in Quebec's public agenda, and over time dropped into obscurity. However, Ontario's interest in free trade seems to have persisted right up to the early 1990s, during the rise of NAFTA, but weakened too much for press coverage of the issue to make much of a difference in the 1993 federal election.

Editorials yield their greatest effects when the iron of public opinion is hot, which was not the case here. Jian-Hua Zhu (1992) notes that people can generally list and rank no more than five concerns. Gallup polls show respondents consistently ranking free trade as not very important, often placing it towards the end of a top-10 list. Hence, free trade was not a hot iron ready to be struck by newspaper editors. Its temperature approached "warm" at best, and this was only during a brief period in the 1988 election year. After the election, the issue's salience withered, leaving editorials fairly impotent in their mission to persuade.

The red-hot issues over the 10-year period were bread and butter questions such as unemployment and inflation, two issues which clearly affect everyone's standard of living. Unemployment appears to have been a pivotal issue within the question of free trade, which was sold as a means to generate jobs. Editorials mentioned jobs in their treatment of free trade, but the *Toronto Star* was far more vigilant in linking free trade with job losses than *La Presse* was in promoting free trade as a job-generating policy. This difference of approach appears to have made a difference in public opinion. The *Toronto Star* was slightly more effective in generating interest for free trade in Ontario and persuading the public to reject it than *La Presse* was in trying to generate support.

This is consistent with a study by Aileen Yagade and David M. Dozier, which shows that the more abstract an issue, the lower the media's effect, because "individuals find it difficult to attach salience to something they don't comprehend" (1990: 5). However, they also include another variable, issue obtrusiveness: the more obtrusive an issue, i.e., the more personal experience people have with regard to a certain issue, the less influence the media has over its salience, because people do not need to rely on the media for information on issues with which they personally have experience. Free trade was not tested to determine its abstractness or obtrusiveness, but since it is not a concrete thing but an inter-state contractual commercial agreement, it can be considered to be abstract. Survey results showing free trade's low salience suggest that it might qualify as an abstract concept which fails to arouse excitement. Free trade is not an easy concept to grasp, unlike other and more salient issues, such an unemployment, inflation and the environment, all three of which have a direct link to something concrete, namely money and health. In order to comprehend abstract concepts such as countervailing duties, protectionism, subsidies and other issues that surrounded the free trade negotiations, they would have to be presented in terms of concrete factors such as wages, jobs, prices, or something people can generally relate to quite well. Only then can the media wield some measure of influence over the public's agenda. The *Toronto Star*'s emphasis of salient issues seems to have kept Ontario more interested in free trade than was the case in Quebec, where the issue was presented in a more abstract form by *La Presse*.

METHODOLOGY

As mentioned earlier, editorials on free trade printed by both newspapers between 1984 and 1993 were searched and analyzed. This 10-year period was selected principally because it heralded the rise of the free trade profile from an idea stretching back to Confederation more than a century ago towards the top of the policy agenda. Free trade was not an overly important issue before 1984, despite the then-Liberal government's attempts at a "limited" or "sectoral" free trade arrangement with the United States. After the Liberals lost power in the 1984 Tory sweep, free trade was granted more legitimacy in the newly elected neo-Conservative executive. The beginning of the free trade negotiations in May 1986 compelled the public finally to take notice of this policy proposal and its potentially far-reaching consequences. As a result, free trade rose up the public agenda from 1984 and peaked around the late 1980s, before falling back to obscurity and reaching its low point towards the final days of PC rule in the early 1990s. Sometime during this 10-year period, free trade may have been salient enough for editorials to have had some mobilizing effect.

This mobilizing effect was measured by comparing public opinion polls on free trade to a careful examination and coding of the contents of all relevant editorials published during the PC years. Most editorials indicated at least one reason to either support or oppose free trade. Each reason was coded and noted in appropriate categories. It is not the number of mentions that were coded, but the number of reasons. If, for instance, an editorial mentioned "job growth" three times and "improved trade" once, each reason – job growth and trade – was coded separately as *one* – not three and one – for that specific editorial. Two of the main reasons mentioned were jobs and trade relations. Often, an editorial would be vague. It might, for instance, mention how free trade would be good for the economy without discussing anything specific such as job growth. This was coded in the "Overall gain" category for *La Presse* and "Overall loss" category for the *Toronto Star*. Also, the number of editorials written by specific editors were noted for *La Presse* only, since the *Toronto Star*'s edtorials are not signed. The coded number of reasons in the editorials were added and presented in Tables 3 to 5, showing the issues that were emphasized by each paper.

All the editorials on free trade published by both newspapers within the 10-year period were not included for analysis. Many mentioned one of the two free trade deals as part of another theme, such as GATT, and thus were excluded. Also excluded were columns about free trade. *La Presse*, like many other newspapers, prints editorials either along the top or down the left-hand side of the editorial page, leaving the rest of the page for letters or columns. Many of the columns were written by editors who used them to endorse free trade. Columns are generally perceived as presenting the personal views of the writer and could be considered less authoritative than editorials, which present views generally believed to be representative of the newspaper.

In order to measure the editorials' effect on readers, the following assumptions were considered in formulating a set of hypotheses. It seems intuitively obvious that the more editorial space a newspaper devotes to a certain issue, the more that issue is noticed by readers, and hence, the greater the probability that it will be read. A similar approach has been used in many content analyses (McCombs and Shaw 1972), where front-page lead stories have been attributed more agenda-setting weight than a four-inch story tucked away as a space filler at the bottom of a page towards the end of the paper. Such an approach is not fully adaptable to the study of editorials because the editorial page is generally a fixed section that every reader can easily identify and locate. In such a case, what may determine an editorial's agenda-setting weight – at least in part – is size. Most editorial pages carry two to four editorials, varying in size from three paragraphs to more than 1,000 words. Smaller editorials are generally placed below larger ones, similar to the layout for news articles. In this context, editorials compete for attention through size, measured by a word count. The greater the number of words, the more prominent the issue. This assumption led to the following hypotheses:

1. Support for free trade and its salience in Quebec varies according to the amount of editorial coverage endorsing free trade in *La Presse*;

2. Opposition to free trade and its salience in Ontario varies according to the amount of anti-free trade editorial coverage in the *Toronto Star*.

Editorial coverage is simply a word count, calculated to the nearest 10. Once assessed, it was compared to Gallup poll results on free trade to determine whether public opinion followed editorials published within the four previous months (the lag between media publication and its effect on the public agenda has been measured at between three and five months (McCombs 1977)).[1] Data were graphed to locate patterns between changes in editorial coverage and shifts in public opinions.

Gallup conducted several different polls to track views on free trade. In order to avoid inconsistencies, the polls used here were those that asked respondents whether they felt free trade would make Canada *better* or *worse*

---

1.   Results showed no improvement with other time-lag periods, including one- to three-month lags, as well as five- to six-month lags.

off. Gallup asked this question on several occasions from the 1950s right up to 1990. The influence of editorials over opinion on the FTA can be tracked using these poll results, especially during the crucial one-year period between October 1987, when negotiators reached an agreement, to the fall of 1988, when a general federal election returned the PC to power in a majority government that passed the FTA in January 1989. During this period, the free trade issue peaked in the public agenda.

Another type of poll simply asked respondents if they were for or against free trade. Though the question is more blunt and would appear to extract a more accurate response, the average number of respondents who were either undecided or had no opinion (non-committed) hovered around 25 per cent and often reached more than 30 per cent, raising doubts as to whether such polls reveal much about editorial influence. The better/worse-off polls had a slightly lower average of non-committed respondents. Also, Gallup only began the favour/oppose polls in November 1988, a year after free trade's rise in salience, and hence too late for our purposes. However, these polls were used to gauge editorial influence over the issue of NAFTA, since it moved up the policy agenda in 1991, when Canada, the United States and Mexico began NAFTA negotiations.

In any case, the proportion of non-committed respondents was high enough to undermine confidence in all the polls. Also, shifts in opinions on free trade as expressed by the polls' raw data do not fit neatly with shifts in editorial coverage, perhaps indicating that the high non-committed respondent rate is responsible. It may be that the large non-committed block in all these polls reflects free trade's low salience, which would explain why correlations between poll results and editorial coverage is not very strong. However, if we factor out the non-committed respondents (i.e. redistribute them proportionally), the results appear more promising and show a firmer link between opinion shifts and changes in editorial coverage.

Another problem with the reliability of Gallup's poll concerns sample size. Since the polls used a national sample of more than 1,000 respondents, regional breakdowns elevate the margin of error to around 6 per cent 19 times out of 20 due to the significantly smaller sample size (around 270 in Quebec for some polls[2]).

Despite these problems, both papers were found to influence public opinion to some extent, though it appears that the *Toronto Star* was more effective in mobilizing opinion in Ontario than *La Presse* was in Quebec. Here we must ask whether or not there were differences in content between the two

---

2. This information was provided by Jon Hughes, research analyst with Gallup Canada in Toronto, Ont., during a telephone conversation in August 1994.

newspapers' editorials and, if so, whether or not those differences would account for the fact that Ontario seems to have been far more strongly opposed to free trade than Quebec was in favour of it.

EDITORIAL PRONOUNCEMENTS AND FREE TRADE'S SALIENCE ON THE PUBLIC AGENDA

Given the public's persistently low concern with free trade, it is no surprise that a weak link appears between editorial coverage and shifts in public opinion. This does not undermine previous research on the influence of editorials on the public agenda. Links exist here too, but free trade's low salience presents a unique challenge. The goal here is to find a link between changes in editorial coverage and the salience of free trade, an issue about which most people seemed to have cared very little.

Increases in media attention to free trade seem to have had a weak influence on the public, as can be seen by Table 1 and Figures 1a and 1b, which compare the number of news articles listed in the *Canadian News Index* and its French counterpart, *L'Index de l'Actualité*, with results of Gallup polls that asked respondents to indicate the top problem of the day.

FIGURE 1A
French Press Coverage and Free Trade's Salience in Quebec

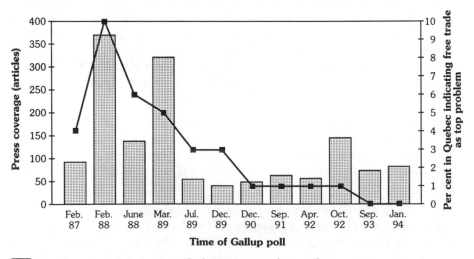

French press free-trade coverage in Quebec over previous four months
Per cent in Quebec indicating free trade as top problem

FIGURE 1B
English Press Coverage and Free Trade's Salience in Ontario

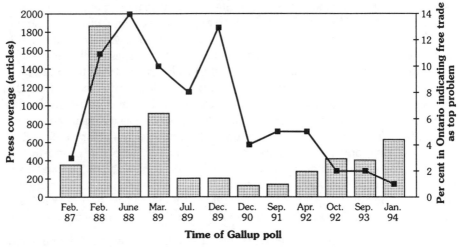

English press free-trade coverage in Canada over previous four months
Per cent in Ontario indicating free trade as top problem

TABLE 1
Media Attention and Salience

Time of poll	Quebec		Canada	
	Coverage	Salience	Coverage	Salience
Feb-87	93	4	354	3
Feb-88	370	10	1,876	11
Jun-88	138	6	776	14
Mar-89	321	5	921	10
Jul-89	54	3	206	8
Dec-89	41	3	206	13
Dec-90	49	1	128	4
Sep-91	63	1	140	5
Apr-92	58	1	279	5
Oct-92	146	1	420	2
Sep-93	74	0	411	2
Jan-94	83	0	643	1

Source: Gallup polls on "top problem" from 1987 (when "U.S. Trade Relations" was first included as a category) to 1994, *Canadian News Index*, *L'Index de l'Actualité*.

Note: Coverage reflects the number of articles printed during the four months prior to the poll. Salience represents the Gallup poll respondents who indicated "U.S. Trade Relations" as the nation's top problem.

Although news indexes generally list selected articles from various papers, they provide a good proxy measure of changes in media coverage of various issues. As expected, the indexes indicate that newspapers peaked their free-trade coverage in 1988 and 1989, before and after a general election in which the FTA was an issue. Changes in coverage seem to follow changes in salience, with increases in media attention matching increases in salience. However, this applies only to Quebec, and only from February 1987 to June 1988, after which time increases in coverage did not seem to be reflected by increases in free trade's salience, as can be seen from the March 1989 sample. For Ontario, media coverage has an even looser connection to saliency. The *Canadian News Index* cited 354 articles during the four months prior to the February 1987 poll, and 1876 articles the following year, with the proportion of Ontario respondents indicating free trade as the top problem jumping from 3 to 11 per cent. However, in June 1988, concern increased to 14 per cent, while citations dropped to 776. From then on, increases and decreases in media coverage do not always correspond with similar changes in saliency.

Overall, after 1988, coverage dropped significantly, as did salience. However, coverage rose once again in 1992 to 1994, a period during which NAFTA emerged, although it received far less coverage than the FTA. The reduced attention perhaps accounted for NAFTA's lower salience. However, while polls show free trade's continued drop in salience from September 1991 to January 1994, media coverage increased, although it never equalled the amount of coverage devoted to the FTA, suggesting that a *critical mass* of media attention may be needed to push an issue up the public agenda. There will be no attempt here to identify this critical mass.

Editorial coverage may have contributed to salience. Table 2 and Figures 2a and 2b compare salience with editorial coverage. The results differ very little. Increases in editorial coverage do not relate well to increases in salience, except perhaps for Quebec during the period between February 1987 and June 1988. The same applies to Ontario, with changes in editorial coverage producing virtually no effect on salience.

Free trade's drop in salience in Ontario after 1992, despite increases in both media attention and editorial coverage, may reflect the end of the issue cycle according to Downs' model (1972), with other issues capturing more interest. Polls in the fall of 1992 show "National Unity" as a relatively high concern in Canada, far ahead of "U.S. Trade Relations." This poll, conducted in October, shows 13 per cent of Quebecers and 9 per cent of Ontarians indicating "National Unity" as the top problem, while only 2 and 1 per cent respectively indicated "U.S. Trade Relations." The top problem was "Economy/ Inflation," which was checked off by 34 per cent of Ontarians and 32 per cent of Quebecers. The number two spot went to "Unemployment," checked off by 22 per cent of respondents in both provinces, although many other polls show unemployment as the top problem.

FIGURE 2A

FIGURE 2A
La Presse's Editorial Coverage
and Free Trade's Salience in Quebec

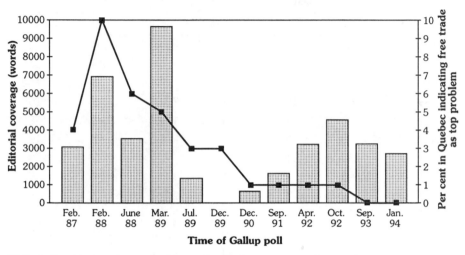

La Presse's editorial coverage of free-trade in Quebec over previous four months
Per cent in Quebec indicating free trade as top problem

FIGURE 2B
Toronto Star's Editorial Coverage
and Free Trade's Salience in Ontario

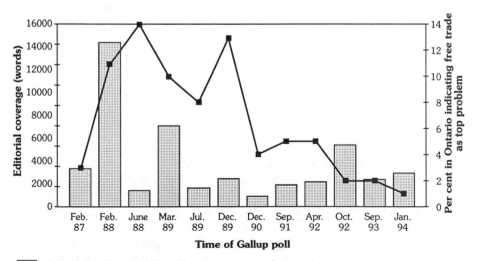

Toronto Star's editorial coverage (words) over previous four months
Per cent in Ontario indicating free trade as top problem

TABLE 2
Editorial Coverage and Salience

Time of poll	Quebec			Ontario		
	Coverage	Qty	Salience	Coverage	Qty	Salience
Feb-87	3,060	6	4	3,340	8	3
Feb-88	6,910	14	10	14,380	37	11
Jun-88	3,520	9	6	1,440	6	14
Mar-89	9,360	17	5	7,100	6	10
Jul-89	1,330	2	3	1,660	5	8
Dec-89	0	0	3	2,450	7	13
Dec-90	630	1	1	870	2	4
Sep-91	1,590	3	1	1,890	4	5
Apr-92	3,200	5	1	2,110	7	5
Oct-92	4,550	9	1	5,400	12	2
Sep-93	3,210	6	0	2,410	7	2
Jan-94	2,700	5	0	2,970	9	1

Source: Gallup polls on "top problem" from 1987 (when "U.S. Trade Relations" was first included as a category) to 1994, *Canadian News Index*, *L'Index de L'actualité*

Note: Coverage reflects the amount of editorial coverage in words printed and Qty is the number of editorials printed during the four months prior to the poll. Salience represents the Gallup poll respondents who indicated "U.S. Trade Relations" as the nation's top problem.

The rise of the national unity issue surrounded the nation-wide referendum on the Charlottetown constitutional agreement. Here we have to acknowledge Zhu's (1992) "zero-sum" phenomenon of the public agenda. Although decreases in media attention have been known to reduce an issue's salience, Zhu notes that issues also drop down the public agenda because they are displaced by the rise of other issues. The public can only accommodate a few concerns at a time, and in this case, NAFTA may have been pushed aside by the rise of other issues such as national unity, making it harder for editorials about NAFTA to penetrate the public agenda.

Perhaps editorials – and the press in general – do not necessarily influence the public agenda by emphasizing an issue through the quantity of words printed, as noted by Kosicki (1993) in his review of agenda-setting research. Also, issues have been known to capture the public's concern and maintain their saliency long after the press coverage falls away (Salwen 1988). In this case, given a weak – if any – quantitative link between editorial coverage and opinion of free trade, perhaps the content of the editorials would provide an explanation as to why Ontario's interest in free trade lasted longer than Quebec's. In fact, qualitative analysis shows striking differences between the two papers. *La Presse's* reliance on promoting free trade as a means to improve exports and circumvent American protectionist moods may have had less of an impact than the *Toronto Star's* emphasis of more concrete issues such as job losses. As mentioned earlier free trade may not be something ordinary people can easily visualize. Issues such as unemployment, inflation, and even the environment have become salient more easily. Jobs, prices and ecological issues have a direct link with survivability and living standards. Tariffs, countervailing duties, exports and subsidies are more abstract concepts that are difficult for the average person to imagine. In order for the public to become serious about free trade, it would have to be linked to something concrete. The *Toronto Star's* persistence in linking free trade to unemployment seems to have helped maintain the issue's salience in Ontario, while *La Presse's* pattern of linking free trade to other abstract and vague concepts, such as improved exports and "economic development," seems to have failed in maintaining the concern of Quebecers, whose support for free trade died too soon for opinion to mobilize around NAFTA.

TABLE 3

Reasons Mentioned by *La Presse* in Favour of FTA

Number of editorials mentioning the following reasons by publication year

Reasons	'84	'85	'86	'87	'88	'89	'90	'91	'92	'93
Job growth	2	2	1	4	4				1	
Pay increases		2			1	1				
More products	1			3	1					
Lower prices				2						
Better trade	3	5	7	12	11	1	1	1	5	
Overall gain	1	6	6	12	9	2	1		1	1
Other		1	3	2	7	1		1		
Author										
Roy		1	2	2						
Wagnière	3	11	18	29	22	5	1	4	10	
Dubuc					11	2	1		3	
Other		1	4	2	8					
Summary										
Number of editorials	3	13	24	33	41	7	1	5	13	1
Coverage (in words × 10)	159	649	1,221	1,590	2,019	375	200	265	677	290

Source: *La Presse* editorials on free trade printed during 1984-1993 period.

TABLE 4
Reasons Mentioned by the *Toronto Star* against the FTA
Number of editorials mentioning the following reasons by publication year

Reasons	'84	'85	'86	'87	'88	'89	'90	'91	'92	'93
Job losses	11	4	6	11	10	6	4	2	6	11
Wage losses				5	3	1			1	
Price rises			1		2		1			
Worse jobs	2	1		1						
Auto Pact		1	2	6		1				
Worse trade	6	2	1	9	10	3	4	3	12	5
Overall loss				2	1	1				
Demise of Medicare		2	1		1	1				
UIC cutbacks										
Demise of other social progs.	1	3	2	1	8	3		1		
Demise of reg. policies	24	13	5	21	20		1	1		
US corporate takeovers			3	11	6	1	1		1	
Demise of culture		6	7	11	2	1	1	2		
Undermining of sovereignty	7	7	4	6	12	3	2	1		2
Other			1	3	2	2	1			
Summary										
Number of editorials:	13	22	27	66	46	18	10	10	17	9
Coverage (in words × 10)	624	1,038	970	2,510	1,608	613	431	364	628	324

Source: *Toronto Star* editorials on free trade printed during 1984-1993 period.

TABLE 5

**Number of Editorials of Both Newspapers Containing
Specified Reasons to Support or Oppose NAFTA**

Reasons	*La Presse* editorials (number) per year				*Toronto Star* editorials (number) per year			
	'90	'91	'92	'93	'90	'91	'92	'93
Job gains/losses			1	1	1	1	4	1
Wage gains/losses				2			1	
Better/worse trade	2	3	3	1	1		5	6
Loss of Auto Pact						1	1	
Overall gain/loss	1	2	1	3				
Demise of culture						2	1	
Undermining sovereignty								3
Other		1	5	3	1			1
Author								
Roy								
Wagnière	3	4	9	11				
Dubuc	1	1	2	3				
Other		1						
Summary								
Number of editorials	4	5	11	14	4	4	14	17
Coverage (in words × 10)	176	275	607	758	163	151	629	664

Source: *La Presse* and *Toronto Star* editorials on free trade printed during 1990-1993 period.

Over the 10-year period, *La Presse* printed only 14 editorials that mentioned job growth as a likely benefit of the FTA, and two editorials linking job growth to NAFTA (see Tables 3 to 5). The *Toronto Star* linked job losses to the FTA in 71 editorials, and job losses to NAFTA in seven. Such a wide discrepancy cannot be overlooked and may provide a plausible explanation as to why Ontarians felt more concerned about free trade than residents of Quebec. The following excerpts show the *Toronto Star*'s approach at linking free trade with job losses:

"... U.S. companies would be able to sell freely in Canada and that could well knock out a lot of smaller Canadian companies and cause massive lay-offs" (*Toronto Star*, February 13, 1984).

"From the perspective of U.S. multinationals, the importance of free trade rests primarily on the word *free* – they would be free to shut down branch plants and supply the Canadian market from U.S. plants, and free to threaten Canadian workers with plant closures to get wage concessions" (*Toronto Star*, September 14, 1987).

"It was a year full of layoffs, with announcements week after week of plant closings" (*Toronto Star*, January 1, 1990).

"... [NAFTA] would mean wiping out another economic border, and freeing companies now located in Canada to supply the entire North American market from low-cost plants in Mexico, not just Tennessee" (*Toronto Star*, November 28, 1990).

"... Mexico will take all the low-skilled jobs it can get" (*Toronto Star*, October 8, 1992).

The Auto Pact also received a lot of coverage, with 10 editorials linking the FTA with the demise of the popular managed-trade agreement, while only two editorials mentioned NAFTA's threat to the Pact. The Pact was shown as a job-creating arrangement which free trade would sacrifice, taking jobs away from Ontario. It was often mentioned in the light of on-going negotiations that the *Star* feared would include a bargaining-away of the Pact and, hence, the bargaining-away of jobs. Also, the *Toronto Star* refuted many claims of free trade's proponents, who often referred to the Auto Pact as an example of free trade's lucrative payoff. The *Toronto Star* explained that the Pact is not free trade, but a "market-sharing agreement" involving quotas as to how many cars the American auto makers are required to assemble in Canada (*Toronto Star*, 18 June 1986). This angle was emphasized further in another editorial titled "The Auto Pact Myth" (*Toronto Star*, 10 December 1987), which added that the only reason other parts of Canada did not benefit under the Pact as much as Southern Ontario was because the American manufacturers located their Canadian plants close to "its markets," and that under free trade manufacturers would be free to relocate their plants outside Canada.

The *Toronto Star* did not mince words in explaining how free trade would eliminate jobs or, at the very best, would create fewer and poorer quality jobs – "McJobs" (*Toronto Star*, 3 July 1987). The Star cited several studies that reached dire conclusions, such as one by the Computer Services Association which estimated that its industry would see "500,000 computer-related and administrative jobs" move to the United States if the Canadian government provided no protection under a freer trade arrangement (*Toronto Star*, 24 February 1984). This estimate was repeated in several other editorials throughout that year, and even found its way into editorials printed as late as 1985.

The *Star* cited various other sources to substantiate arguments about how free trade would lead to more unemployment. In a July 1987 editorial, Queen's University economists Richard Harris and David Cox were mentioned as having forecast job losses in 13 out of 22 manufacturing sectors under free trade.

An August 1989 editorial cited a *Businessweek* article about free trade being a "one-way street" in which businesses would relocate to the United States. Even Benoit Bouchard, a PC cabinet minister, was quoted in several editorials after he said in Parliament that free trade could cost Canada 500,000 jobs. Such clear links between job losses and free trade, substantiated by sources including university professors, a renowned business magazine and a well known federal cabinet minister, turned free trade from an abstract esoteric international commercial treaty to something concrete and understandable: unemployment.

La Presse relied on fewer studies to substantiate its belief in free trade's potential for job growth. In fact, its editorial treatment of free trade often echoed a remark made by Donald Macdonald, the head of the Royal Commission that recommended free trade, who said in 1985 that Canadians should take a "leap of faith" towards a closer economic alliance with the United States. *La Presse*'s approach was similar in its expression of *faith* over the economy's ability to generate jobs under free trade, as demonstrated by the following excerpts:

> "L'importance du libre-échange réside dans sa capacité d'augmenter le commerce et de créer un plus grand nombre d'emplois." ("Free trade's importance lies in its ability to increase trade and create more jobs," *La Presse*, October 11, 1984.)

> "Le libre-échange signifie que les industries dynamiques devront créer de nouveaux emplois plus rapidement que des emplois sont perdus dans les entreprises peu productives." (Free trade means that dynamic industries will have to create more jobs more quickly than the less dynamic industries lose them," *La Presse*, November 22, 1984.)

> "... il faut maintenant montrer que la libéralisation des échanges est la seule façon de sauver des emplois et d'en créer de nouveaux." ("We must now show that liberalizing trade is the only way save jobs and to create new ones," *La Presse*, November 27, 1985.)

> "Si on veut moins de chômage, plus d'argent dans nos poches et de meilleurs programmes publics, il faut ouvrir les portes des marchés étrangers." ("If we want less unemployment, more money in our pockets and better public programs, we must open our doors to foreign markets," *La Presse*, November 19, 1988.)

La Presse also printed several editorials containing more substantive links between free trade and job growth, along the following lines: more trade means more economic activity, hence more jobs. With regard to NAFTA, Mexico's economic development would generate a demand for products manufactured in Canada and the United States, as shown by the following excerpt:

> "En effet, il n'y a pas de meilleure façon d'assurer une croissance de l'emploi et des salaires aux États-Unis et au Canada qu'en favorisant le développement économique du Mexique." (There is no better way of assuring job and salary growth in the United States and Canada than by encouraging Mexico's economic development," *La Presse*, July 23, 1993.)

Although much of *La Presse*'s praise of free trade appears to have been based on an assumption that it would generate more trade and more job-developing economic activity, some editorials made more substantive claims by citing "economists" in an attempt to lend scientific credence to its editorial endorsements. Very rarely did *La Presse* identify particular economists, although, in one case, the Canadian Economic Council's estimate that Ontario would obtain 95,000 new jobs in the first decade of a free trade was cited in a November 1988 editorial. *La Presse* often tried to portray Ontario as a potential winner under free trade in an apparent attempt to quell anti-free trade fears emanating from that province. However, after the ratification of the FTA, job losses from the recession in the early 1990s in both Ontario and Quebec eroded support for free trade, making NAFTA an even tougher sell. *La Presse*, recognizing the increased and wide-spread opposition to free trade, tried to give NAFTA a positive spin.

> "Les études économiques montrent qu'il y a eu une croissance plus forte et plus d'emplois créés que s'il n'y avait pas eu de libre-échange." ("Economic studies show that growth has been stronger and more jobs have been created than if free trade had not existed," *La Presse*, August 13, 1992.)

The few references to job growth were dwarfed by *La Presse*'s emphasis of FTA and NAFTA potential to improve trade, since they are, after all, trade treaties. *La Presse* printed 36 editorials that mentioned improved trade. Free trade was seen as a solution to protectionism and a means to circumvent American harassment and countervailing duties. A 1984 editorial tried to rally Canadians into seizing the opportunity to negotiate a good free trade agreement with the United States by emphasizing the elimination of tariffs, which the editor – Frederic Wagnière, who wrote most of *La Presse*'s free trade editorials – called a "tracasserie pour le consommateur," or a nuisance for the consumer, whose purchasing power, he added, would remain limited without free trade (*La Presse*, March 31, 1984). Trade, countervailing duties and other abstract concepts within free trade as an international commercial treaty were often not linked to concrete issues like job growth.

La Presse was more generic in its advocacy for free trade, relying on words such as "prosperity," "stability," "efficiency," "economic development," "economically dynamic," "economic liberalization" and others to validate the "virtues of free trade." These all-encompassing, perhaps vague, expressions were often not linked to concrete concepts such as jobs and prices. As a result, these rather *soft* expressions were not strong enough to make free trade something worth considering. The following excerpts provide some good examples:

> "Le libre-échange est sans doute un des buts qu'il faut poursuivre pour assurer notre prospérité." ("Free trade is without a doubt one of the goals that must be pursued to assure our prosperity," *La Presse*, May 17, 1985.)

"... [le libre échange pourrait] rendre l'économie canadienne plus efficace et plus dynamique." ("Free Trade would make the Canadian economy more efficient and more dynamic," *La Presse*, March 13, 1987.)

"Même à court terme, le libre-échange pourrait assurer une croissance plus stable de l'économie que la protection des marchés et des industries," ("Even in the short term, free trade could lead to more stable economic growth than protectionism," *La Presse*, August 17, 1985.)

In contrast to *La Presse*'s vague terms, the *Toronto Star* was very specific in linking free trade to adverse consequences, not just unemployment. Five editorials mentioned the potential for free trade to force the elimination of Medicare as a result of the American perception that social programs gave Canadians an unfair competitive edge. Another 19 editorials mentioned free trade's threat to other social programs, such as day care, unemployment insurance and pensions, all forms of government intervention disliked by many advocates of free trade.

In a similar vein, 85 *Toronto Star* editorials mentioned the possibility that free trade would erode the Canadian government's right to legislate regulatory policy, such as regional development, which Americans might perceive as subsidies and therefore illegal under free trade. The *Star* tied regulatory policies closely to national sovereignty, another issue that was given considerable coverage, in 44 editorials on the FTA and another three editorials on NAFTA. Culture was another related issue connected to Canadian sovereignty. The *Toronto Star* was concerned that Canada's heavily subsidized cinema, recording, television and publication industries would not survive if forced into competition with the United States' mammoth cultural industries.

In sum, the *Toronto Star*'s emphasis and *explanation* of more concrete issues such as unemployment and how jobs would be lost under free trade seems to have penetrated further than *La Presse*'s reliance on more abstract notions of the benefits of free trade. As a result, free trade was more salient in Ontario than in Quebec, giving the *Toronto Star* more leverage in influencing opinion.

However, even in Ontario, free trade could never be considered an overly salient issue. With a peak of 14 per cent of respondents who mentioned free trade as the nation's top problem, the media's impact in sensitizing opinion remained rather weak. However, this may simply reflect a methodological flaw. People may have been concerned about free trade, but they may not have indicated it as a top problem. Nonetheless, other polls which asked respondents to name issues about which they were very concerned still reflected a more significant drop in salience in Quebec after the 1988 election than in Ontario. A July 1989 Gallup poll covering 14 issues shows that very few Quebecers and Ontarians were concerned about free trade. They ranked it 10th in Quebec, where less than 30 per cent of respondents said it was an issue about which they were very concerned, and 7th in Ontario, where 44 per cent of respondents said they were very concerned about the issue. Taxes and the environment occupied the top two spots, although the list is curious in its omission of unemployment and inflation, two highly salient issues throughout the 1980s. In any case, the poll clearly demonstrates that free trade ranked quite low when compared to other issues, although it remained more salient in Ontario than in Quebec.

Quebec's interest in free trade peaked between the winter of 1987 and the fall of 1988, while Ontario's "high-salient period" lasted from the fall of 1987 to the fall of 1990. Any authoritative analysis of how editorials affected opinion about NAFTA is therefore very elusive. Editorials have the most effect during relative high-salience periods. The two provinces' high-salience periods reflect a link between public opinion on free trade and editorial coverage (see Tables 6 and 7, and Figures 3a to 4b).

During the four-month lag period before February 1987, *La Presse* printed 3,060 words of editorials endorsing free trade. Coverage increased to 5,200 words during the lag period before September of that year, and increased again to 6,910 words during the lag period before January 1988. During this time, support for free trade in Quebec rose from 43 per cent to 65 per cent. Until October 1988, Quebecers' support for free trade seems to have followed editorial coverage, as can be seen from Figure 3a.

Outside this "high-salience period," editorial coverage seems to have had far less or no effect on opinion about free trade, which appeared to be erratic and unstable. However, the large dip in opinion in Quebec in 1986, with a September poll showing only 36 per cent of respondents feeling that Canada would be better off with free trade, may be explained by the increased media coverage of the FTA, with much of the news not being very good. Newspapers printed several articles about the potentially adverse effects of the FTA on industry, including textiles, an important sector in Quebec. Perhaps this made many Quebecers feel insecure about free trade, but confidence seems to have been restored soon after, with sharp increases in *La Presse*'s editorial coverage. However, editorials appear to have had their sharpest effect when free trade was relatively high in salience during 1987 and 1988.

However, the picture changes somewhat when controls are added for unemployment. Quebec's support for free trade seems to fluctuate with improvements in economic conditions; rises in the unemployment rate bring about reductions in the support for free trade (see Table 8 and Figures 5a to 6b). During the high salience period, opposition to free trade peaked at 40 per cent in September 1987, when the unemployment rate was at 10.1 per cent. Interestingly, during the same period, opposition reached an all-time low of 22 per cent in January 1988, when unemployment also was lower, at 8.9 per cent.

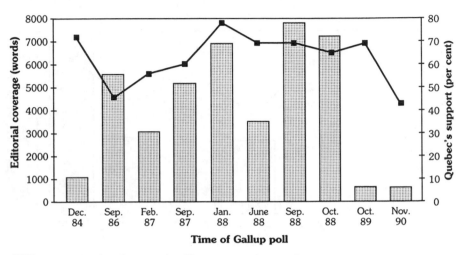

FIGURE 3A
La Presse's Editorial Coverage and Quebec's Support for FTA

La Presse's editorial coverage (words) over previous four months
Per cent in Quebec supportive of FTA, with non-committed factored out

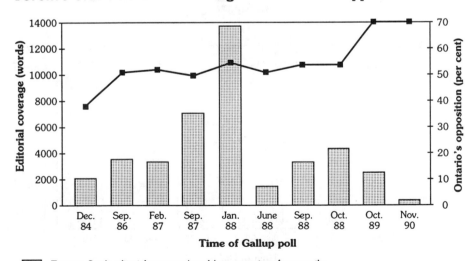

FIGURE 3B
Toronto Star's Editorial Coverage and Ontario's Opposition to FTA

Toronto Star's editorial coverage (words) over previous four months
Per cent in Ontario opposed to free trade, with non-committed factored out

FIGURE 4A
La Presse's Editorial Coverage and Quebec's Support for NAFTA

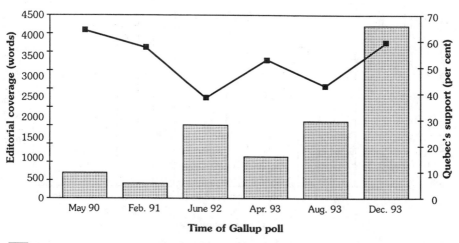

La Presse's editorial coverage (words) over previous four months
Per cent in Quebec supportive of NAFTA, with non-committed factored out

FIGURE 4B
Toronto Star's Editorial Coverage and Ontario's Opposition to NAFTA

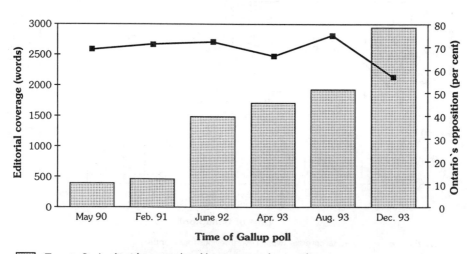

Toronto Star's editorial coverage (words) over previous four months
Per cent in Ontario opposed to NAFTA, with non-committed factored out

TABLE 6
Editorial Coverage and Support for Free Trade

Time of poll	Quebec				Ontario			
	Coverage	Fav.	Opp.	None	Coverage	Fav.	Opp.	None
FTA								
Dec-84	1,070	59	23	18	2,100	52	32	16
Sep-86	5,580	36	42	22	3,570	39	41	19
Feb-87	3,060	43	34	23	3,340	40	44	17
Sep-87	5,200	44	29	27	7,060	40	40	20
Jan-88	6,910	65	18	17	13,760	37	46	17
Jun-88	3,520	56	25	19	1,440	41	42	17
Sep-88	7,810	57	26	16	3,330	39	46	15
Oct-88	7,230	51	27	22	4,350	34	40	26
Oct-89	650	55	25	20	2,580	24	57	19
Nov-90	630	30	39	31	410	24	56	21
NAFTA								
May-90	630	53	29	18	380	27	59	14
Feb-91	370	45	33	22	460	26	64	10
Jun-92	1,810	32	50	18	1,480	25	64	12
Apr-93	1,040	46	41	13	1,710	32	63	5
Aug-93	1,890	33	44	23	1,930	23	69	8
Dec-93	4,230	49	33	17	2,940	36	47	17

Source: Gallup polls tracking public opinion about free trade from 1984 to 1993, *La Presse* and *Toronto Star* editorials on free trade printed from 1984 to 1993.

Note: Coverage is editorial coverage. Fav. represents respondents in favour of NAFTA or who feel that Canada would be better off with the FTA. Opp. represents those who oppose NAFTA or feel Canada would be worse off with the FTA.

TABLE 7
**Editorial Coverage and Support for Free Trade
with Non-Committed Respondents Factored Out**

Time of poll	Quebec			Ontario		
	Coverage	Fav.	Opp.	Coverage	Fav.	Opp.
FTA						
Dec-84	1,070	72	28	2,100	62	38
Sep-86	5,580	46	54	3,570	49	51
Feb-87	3,060	56	44	3,340	48	52
Sep-87	5,200	60	40	7,060	50	50
Jan-88	6,910	78	22	13,760	45	55
Jun-88	3,520	69	31	1,440	49	51
Sep-88	7,810	69	31	3,330	46	54
Oct-88	7,230	65	35	4,350	46	54
Oct-89	650	69	31	2,580	30	70
Nov-90	630	43	56	410	30	70
NAFTA						
May-90	630	64	35	380	31	69
Feb-91	370	58	42	460	29	71
Jun-92	1,810	39	61	1,480	29	72
Apr-93	1,040	53	47	1,710	34	66
Aug-93	1,890	43	57	1,930	21	75
Dec-93	4,230	60	40	2,940	43	57

Source: Gallup polls tracking public opinion about free trade from 1984 to 1993, *La Presse* and *Toronto Star* editorials on free trade printed from 1984 to 1993.

Note: Coverage is editorial coverage. Fav. represents respondents in favour of NAFTA or who feel that Canada would be better off with the FTA. Opp. represents those who opposed NAFTA or feel Canada would be worse off with the FTA.

The picture in Ontario is even more revealing. Opposition mounted from 44 to 56 per cent (50 to 70 per cent with non-committed respondents factored out), although public opinion seems to have zig-zagged regardless of editorial coverage. Ontario seems to have behaved ambivalently with respect to free trade, with opposition high, but bouncing up and down. Improved economic conditions with lower unemployment may have encouraged some Ontarians to feel less hostile towards taking a chance with free trade, but the *Toronto Star*'s editorial coverage pushed hard against such a risk, reminding the public about inevitable job losses. As unemployment grew, opposition skyrocketed towards the 70 per cent mark. Here, the joint effects of the worsening economic conditions and negative press coverage may have caused an increase in the opposition to free trade.

FIGURE 5A
Quebec's Unemployment Rate and Support for FTA

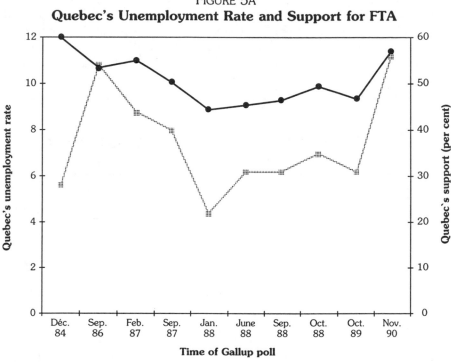

Time of Gallup poll

—●— Quebec's unemployment rate
—■— Per cent in Quebec opposed to FTA, with undecided factored out

Opinions of NAFTA also seemed to follow shifts in unemployment, an over-riding relationship that remained clear from the beginning of the issue cycle. However, even when economic conditions are taken into consideration, the *Toronto Star* seems to have been more successful in fighting against free trade than *La Presse* was in generating support for it. The lowest unemployment rate during the six poll dates was 9.5 per cent for Quebec and 5.7 per cent for Ontario, both in May 1990. At this time, 69 per cent of Ontarians opposed free trade while support in Quebec reached 64 per cent. The difference was small, considering the relatively worse economic situation in Quebec. But when both provinces are compared at similar unemployment levels, opposition in Ontario is still higher than support in Quebec. Quebec's unemployment rate was 9.5 per cent in May 1990, and a similar rate was recorded in Ontario in February 1991 (9.7 per cent). The preceding four-months' editorial coverage in *La Presse* amounted to about 630 words, while the *Toronto Star* printed about 460 words. Unemployment rates were relatively similar, although Quebec's was slightly lower, and *La Presse* had slightly more editorial coverage than the *Toronto Star*; nevertheless, support for free trade in Quebec was 53 per cent (64 with non-committed factored out) while opposition in Ontario was 64 per cent (71 with non-committed factored out). The tilt towards Ontario lends some validity to the claim that the *Toronto Star* was more effective in mobilizing opposition to NAFTA in spite of *La Presse's* relatively higher editorial coverage. It should be borne in mind that free trade was no longer an important issue in Quebec in 1990, while in Ontario it still raised popular concern, a condition that gave the *Toronto Star* far more influence than *La Presse*, which had a harder time penetrating public opinion.

FIGURE 5B
Ontario's Unemployment Rate and Opposition to FTA

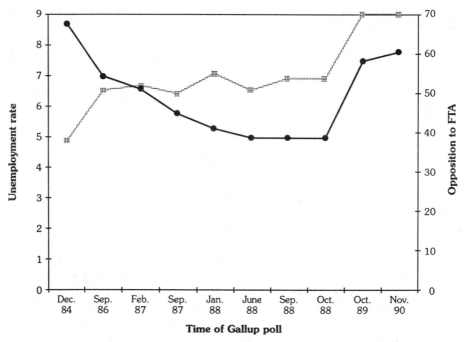

- Ontario unemployment rate
- Per cent in Ontario opposed to FTA

Another point of comparison occurred between Quebec in January 1988 and Ontario in November 1989, when both provinces had a roughly similar level of unemployment. Support for free trade in Quebec was much higher than opposition in Ontario, 65 to 56 per cent respectively (or 78 to 70 per cent with the non-committed portion factored out). The gap is similar to the previous example, but here we are faced with a slightly different situation, in that *La Presse's* editorial coverage peaked during 1988, with close to 7,000 words in the four-month period prior to the January poll, while the *Toronto Star* printed only about 400 words during the four-month period prior to the

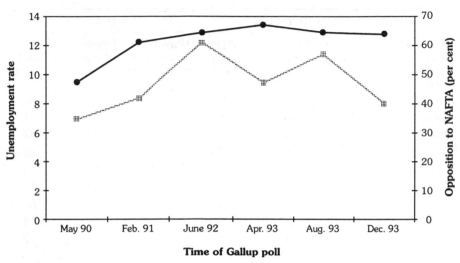

FIGURE 6A
Quebec's Unemployment Rate and Opposition to NAFTA

Time of Gallup poll

—●— Quebec's unemployment rate
—■— Per cent in Quebec opposed to NAFTA, with non-commited factored out

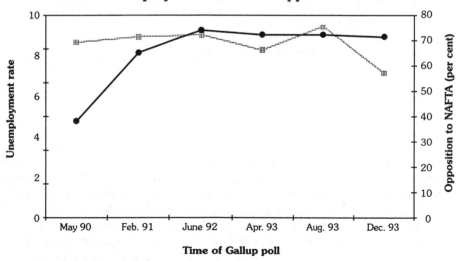

FIGURE 6B
Ontario's Unemployment Rate and Opposition to NAFTA

Time of Gallup poll

—●— Ontario's unemployment rate
—■— Per cent in Ontario opposed to NAFTA, with non-commited factored out

TABLE 8
Unemployment and Opinion on FTA and NAFTA

Time of poll	Quebec			Ontario		
	Unemploy-ment rate	Oppose (raw)	Oppose (adj.)	Unemploy-ment rate	Oppose (raw)	Oppose (adj.)
FTA						
Dec-84	12	12	28	8.7	32	38
Sep-86	10.7	42	54	7	41	51
Feb-87	11	34	44	6.6	44	52
Sep-87	10.1	29	40	5.8	40	50
Jan-88	8.9	18	22	5.3	46	55
Jun-88	9.1	25	31	5	42	51
Sep-88	9.3	26	31	5	46	54
Oct-88	9.9	27	35	5	40	54
Oct-89	9.4	25	31	7.5	57	70
Nov-90	11.4	39	56	7.8	56	70
NAFTA						
May-90	9.5	29	35	5.7	59	69
Feb-91	12.2	33	42	9.7	64	71
Jun-92	12.9	50	61	11	64	72
Apr-93	13.4	41	47	10.8	63	66
Aug-93	12.9	44	57	10.8	69	75
Dec-93	12.8	33	40	10.7	47	57

Source: Statistics Canada (catalogue: 71-201); Gallup polls on opinion about free trade from 1984-1993.

Note: Oppose represents Gallup poll respondents who were opposed to NAFTA or felt that Canada would be worse off with the FTA. The raw data are based on results without factoring out the non-committed, while the adjusted data (adj.) factor out the non-committed portion of Gallup's results.

November poll. Although quantitative links between editorial coverage and opinion are weak, such a huge discrepancy should have resulted in a wide spread of opinion, whereas in fact the spread remains the same as in the previous situation. This suggests that, although *La Presse* appears to have had a huge influence, it may have persuaded opinion through sheer quantity of coverage, whereas the *Toronto Star*'s far less extensive coverage was not followed by opposition in Ontario. Indeed, the amount of editorial coverage as a variable appears rather weak, while editorial content seems to have a much greater effect, and the unemployment rate perhaps even more.

Two comparisons are, however, insufficient for the results to be overly authoritative. Stretching a contrived argument too far will not help validate them. Nevertheless, considering unemployment as a constant factor in determining support for free trade in both Ontario and Quebec, editorial coverage seems more significant in setting the public agenda in Ontario. The link between the *Toronto Star*'s editorials and Ontario's opposition to free trade appears firmer than that between *La Presse*'s editorials and Quebec's support of free trade. Quebec's support of free trade seems entirely dependent on economic conditions, with the January 1988 observation providing the only exception and accounted for by *La Presse*'s peaked coverage during a high salience period. Outside this one exception, *La Presse*'s editorial coverage does not seem to have had any influence.

CONCLUSION

The Canada-U.S. Free Trade negotiations were imposed on the public agenda by the Mulroney government and attracted considerable media attention. The issue climbed a few notches up the public agenda, although it remained well below other issues such as unemployment. Free trade's relatively low saliency made it difficult for the editorials to penetrate public opinion. However, Ontarians remained more concerned about free trade than Quebecers, thus allowing the *Toronto Star* more room to persuade.

A qualitative analysis of editorial coverage appears to shed some light on why Quebecers lost interest sooner. *La Presse* emphasized abstract reasons such as improved exports for favouring free trade, while the *Toronto Star* editorials linked free trade, an issue consistently low in salience, with higher salience issues such as unemployment. As a result, it seems that the *Toronto Star* was more successful in mobilizing opposition to free trade than *La Presse* was in trying to generate enthusiasm.

Although the results of this study are not overly conclusive, given the few Gallup polls from which the effects of editorial coverage could be gauged, and given the small regional sample sizes, the persistent pattern of free trade's higher salience in Ontario than in Quebec cannot be overlooked. The clear difference in the two newspapers' approaches to editorial coverage of both the FTA and NAFTA removes some of the doubt that the *Toronto Star*'s campaign against free trade was more successful than *La Presse*'s attempt to inspire faith in the trade treaties. Here, we have to accept quantitative analyses as a relevant and critical factor in accounting for changes in public views.

REFERENCES

COBB, Roger, Jennie-Keith ROSS and Marc Howard ROSS. 1976. "Agenda Building as a Comparative Political Process." *The American Political Science Review* 70 (March): 126-138.

COOMBS, Steven Lane. 1981. "Editorial Endorsements and Electoral Outcomes." In *More Than News*, (Ed.) Michael Bruce MacKuen, 146-226. Beverly Hills, CA: Sage Publications, Inc.

DOWNS, Anthony. 1972. "Up and Down with Ecology — The 'Issue Attention Cycle'." *The Public Interest* 28 (Summer): 38-50.

GOVERNMENT OF CANADA. 1994. *Historical Labour Force Statistics, 1993*. Ottawa: Minister of Industry, Science and Technology.

GOVERNMENT OF CANADA. 1985. *Royal Commission on the Economic Union and Development Prospects for Canada*. Ottawa: Minister of Supply and Services Canada.

HURD, Robert E., and Michael W. SINGLETARY. 1984. "Newspaper Endorsement Influence on the 1980 Presidential Election Vote." *Journalism Quarterly* 61 (Summer): 332-338.

KOSICKI, Gerald M. 1993. "Problems and Opportunities in Agenda-Setting Research." *Journal of Communication* 43 (Spring): 100-127.

MCCOMBS, Maxwell. 1967. "Editorial Endorsements: A Study of Influence." *Journalism Quarterly* 44 (Autumn): 545-548.

MCCOMBS, Maxwell. 1977. "Agenda Setting Function of Mass Media." *Public Relations Review* 3 (Winter): 89-95.

MCCOMBS, Maxwell E. 1972. "The Agenda-Setting Function of Mass Media." *Public Opinion Quarterly* 36 (Summer): 176-187.

MCCOMBS, Maxwell E., and Donald L. SHAW. 1977. "Agenda-Setting and the Political Process." Chap. in *The Emergence of American Political Issues: The Agenda-Setting Function of the Press*. St. Paul: West Publishing Co.

ROBINSON, John P. 1974. "The Press as King-Maker: What Surveys from Last Five Campaigns Show." *Journalism Quarterly* 51 (Winter): 587-594, 606.

SALWEN, Michael B. 1988. "Effects of Accumulation of Coverage on Issue Salience in Agenda Setting." *Journalism Quarterly* 65 (Spring): 100-106, 130.

YAGADE, Aileen, and David M. DOZIER. 1990. "The Media Agenda-Setting Effect of Concrete versus Abstract Issues." *Journalism Quarterly* 67 (Spring): 3-10.

ZHU, Jian-Hua. 1992. "Issue Competition and Attention Distraction: A Zero-Sum Theory of Agenda-Setting." *Journalism Quarterly* 69 (Winter): 825-836.

Sectorial Analysis:
Making Public Policy in North America

12

Environmental Policy in Quebec*

Fredric C. Menz
Clarkson University

This paper suggests that environmental policy-making in Quebec will be influenced increasingly by external considerations. This will occur not only because of greater awareness of global and transfrontier environmental issues, but also because of North American economic integration. The North American Free Trade Agreement (NAFTA) will not have a significant environmental impact either in Quebec or elsewhere, although it will lead to harmonization of environmental regulations among NAFTA member nations. Quebec should consider the use of economic incentives instead of direct regulations in environmental policy. Other countries are making greater use of incentive-based environemental regulations, and it would be in Quebec's interests to do so. The possible use of tradeable emissions allowances to control cross-border sulfur dioxide pollution is also discussed.

INTRODUCTION

The process of negotiating and approving the North American Free Trade Agreement (NAFTA) resulted in greater awareness across the entire continent of environmental issues in individual member countries. It also refocused attention on transfrontier environmental concerns such as air and water pollution in the Mexican–U.S. border region and pollution in the Great Lakes and St. Lawrence River watersheds. In addition, there now is greater recognition that environmental issues can spill across borders so that countries must cooperate

* I would like to thank William Vitek for helpful comments.

in order to manage shared pollution problems effectively. Cooperative efforts to combat environmental problems can result in mutual gains, just as there can be mutual gains from cooperative efforts to reduce international or interregional trade barriers.

The concern about environmental spillovers among states, provinces and countries means that no political jurisdiction, including Quebec, enjoys complete environmental independence. In the future, environmental policy-making in Quebec will be influenced more by external factors than it has been in the past. This will occur not only because of increased awareness of global and transfrontier environmental problems but also as a direct consequence of a more integrated North American economy. External pressures will also result from international agreements which obligate signatory countries to develop new regulations to deal with global environmental problems.

Perhaps the best example in North America of how external pressures can shape environmental policies occurred in conjunction with the recent NAFTA deliberations. Because of widespread concern about pollution in the Mexican-U.S. border region, Mexico was forced to strengthen its environmental enforcement measures in order to gain Canadian and U.S. approval of the agreement. An example involving Canada and the United States is the problem of acid rain. The two countries had been disagreeing since 1979 about sulfur dioxide pollution, with Canada taking the position that much of Canada's acid rain originated in the United States. Even before the United States enacted a program to control acid rain, Canada's federal government and the seven eastern provinces agreed to adopt stringent controls on sulfur dioxide emissions. Though Canada may have taken this action to signal to the United States that it was willing to act unilaterally, it was also required as a defensive measure to control acid rain damages in Canada. Another example involves Hydro-Quebec's proposed Great Whale hydroelectric project in James Bay. The environmental assessment of the Great Whale project by provincial and federal officials has undoubtedly been influenced by concerns expressed outside Canada about the impact of the project on the environment and on native communities.

The first section of this paper provides a discussion of environmental considerations in NAFTA itself (including the supplemental environmental agreement) and the anticipated environmental impact of freer North American trade. The next section suggests why actions in Quebec that affect the environment are likely to be increasingly influenced by considerations outside Quebec. Subsequent sections consider several issues in the design of environmental policy, including the rationale for the use of market-based policies, the effective management of transfrontier pollution, and the need for Quebec to emphasize a regional perspective in designing its environmental policies. It is concluded that Quebec's environmental policies should be reconsidered in light of the renewed interest in transfrontier environmental problems and the implementation of NAFTA.

NAFTA AND THE ENVIRONMENT

The environmental impact of freer North American trade has been the subject of several recent studies.[1] It can be expected that the direct effect of NAFTA on the environment will be limited for a number of reasons. First, NAFTA is not expected to have significant economic impacts in either Canada or the United States because Canadian and U.S. tariffs on Mexican goods were quite low before the agreement was implemented. Thus, the incremental environmental damage from trade-related economic growth is likely to be very small. Second, the expected rise in Mexican income levels as a result of NAFTA should increase pressure for stricter pollution controls in Mexico and eventually lead to improved environmental conditions. Third, NAFTA should not affect firms' relocation decisions because expenditures for compliance with pollution regulations are not a significant component of costs for most manufacturing sectors and international trade is due more to differentials in other costs (such as labor, natural resources, and capital) than to differences in pollution abatement costs.

If pollution problems worsen anywhere as a result of freer North American trade, they will most likely involve transfrontier pollution in the Mexican-U.S. border region. Environmental problems in Mexico and in the border region were an important issue in the negotiations and debate over NAFTA. Mexico's pollution problems near the U.S. border are a result of the explosion of economic growth in this region during the 1980s, coupled with lax enforcement of environmental regulations. Even prior to the NAFTA negotiations, concerns were expressed that the border region's pollution problems were not being adequately addressed by the Mexican and U.S. governments and that conditions would further deteriorate with freer North American trade.[2]

Environmental advocacy groups, particularly in the United States, were critical of NAFTA not only because of existing pollution problems in Mexico, but also because of a perceived conflict between freer international trade and a healthy environment. It was argued that freer trade would lead to more pollution not only because of trade-related economic growth but also as a consequence of the relocation of pollution-intensive industries from countries with strict pollution regulations to others where environmental standards are less stringent. The agreement also was criticized by some who thought it did not deal directly enough with environmental protection issues. After protracted debate in the United States, NAFTA was ratified by the U.S. Congress in late 1993, but only after supplemental agreements were developed to deal with concerns related to the environment, labor, and import surges.

---

1. See, for example, Anderson (1993), Grossman and Krueger (1993), and Pastor (1992).

2. For discussion of environmental problems in the border region, see National Wildlife Federation (1990), Ortman (1991), U.S. General Accounting Office (1992), U.S. House of Representatives, Committee on Ways and Means (1993), and U.S. Senate, Committee on Finance, Subcommittee on International Trade (1992).

While there is no chapter devoted exclusively to the environment or to environmental concerns in NAFTA, environmental issues are addressed in several chapters in the document. Furthermore, much of the language in the agreement relating to the environment is either new to trade agreements or clarifies ambiguous provisions in the GATT rules that govern international trade. While NAFTA does not meet all environmental concerns, it stands as a landmark accord for handling environmental issues in an international trade agreement (Hufbauer and Schott, 1993: 91).

The focus in NAFTA is to ensure that existing environmental standards are maintained and enforced rather than to force the adoption of enhanced standards or regulations. The text of NAFTA affirms a country's right to determine its own environmental regulations and enforcement measures, but requires that member countries work together on joint environmental concerns. The agreement states that it is inappropriate for member nations to relax their environmental standards or enforcement to attract foreign investment and it allows them to adopt appropriate measures to ensure that foreign investment is "undertaken in a manner sensitive to environmental concerns" (*The NAFTA*, 1992, Chapter 11, article 1114). Member countries are allowed to impose environmental requirements on inward foreign investment but only if those requirements also apply to investment undertaken by domestic firms.

The supplemental environmental accord that was adopted with NAFTA established a new North American institution – the North American Commission on Environmental Cooperation (CEC). The functions of the CEC include: (1) monitoring environmental conditions in North America; (2) promoting compliance with environmental laws and regulations in the three countries; and (3) administering new procedures for settling environmental disputes among the three countries (*The NAFTA, Supplemental Agreements*, 1993). The side accord recognizes the interrelationship of the countries' environments and stresses the importance of cooperation among the countries to protect the North American environment. It also calls for establishing a public advisory committee with an equal number of members from all three nations to provide advice to the commission on environmental issues in the NAFTA region.

While the environmental side accord explicitly states that the parties have no right to undertake environmental enforcement activities in the territory of another party, anyone (including non-governmental organizations, the public, and the parties themselves) in a member country can bring a complaint alleging that another country has persistently failed to effectively enforce an environmental law. If the affected parties cannot resolve the dispute, the CEC will attempt to resolve the matter, appointing arbitration panels if necessary.[3] The offending country can be fined up to $20 million per violation and, in the case

---

3.   Actions about a complaint can be undertaken only after a two-thirds vote of the members, thus preventing one country from initiating action by the panel on its own.

of Mexico and the United States, face trade sanctions if the fine is not paid or the problem not corrected. The CEC also has a mandate to design work plans to limit specific pollutants and assess projects that might cause transboundary environmental problems. The environmental side agreement should serve as a stimulus for the member countries to work jointly to address environmental problems, especially transboundary pollution in border regions.

Under the terms of the agreement creating the CEC, Mexico and the United States immediately became members of the trilateral body, but Canada will not become a member until a number of provinces with a total of 55 percent of Canada's population formally agree to bring their environmental regulations under the commission's purview.[4] The commission is headquartered in Montreal with a staff of 25 and an annual budget of about $15 million, funded equally from the three countries. Until Canada's membership on the CEC gains the necessary approvals, the commission's ability to pursue complaints by Canadians about violations of Mexican or U.S. environmental regulations will be limited to alleged violations of laws that would fall under federal jurisdiction in Canada. Since most Canadian industries are regulated by provincial environmental regulations, this severely curtails the ability of Canadians to make use of the commission. For example, Canadians would not be able to bring to the commission a complaint that a Canadian firm had relocated to Mexico or the United States because of lax environmental standards or enforcement.

EXTERNAL INFLUENCES ON QUEBEC

As North America becomes more integrated, Quebec's economic policies and economic development efforts are likely to be increasingly subject to external pressures because of perceived transborder (in some cases global) impacts of activities undertaken in Quebec. If the CEC adheres to its mandate, there will be pressure on Quebec to harmonize its environmental regulations with those of other North American countries. In addition, because transborder environmental problems like acid rain and pollution of the St. Lawrence River cannot be solved effectively through independent actions by individual countries, there will be more interest in cooperative agreements to manage regional pollution problems. Quebec may also find it advantageous to utilize new environmental regulatory tools such as emissions trading, effluent charges, or other market-based instruments (as other countries are doing) rather than using the traditional approach of forcing firms to invest in technological improvements to comply with more stringent emission standards.

---

4.   No provinces had agreed with Ottawa to have themselves covered by the CEC as of late 1994. Quebec's Minister of International Affairs introduced a bill in February 1995 providing for the approval of numerous international trade agreements including NAFTA and the Environmental Cooperation Agreement.

The impact of North American economic integration on various sectors of Quebec, including the economy, is addressed in several other chapters of this book and will not be repeated here. One important issue that arose in the NAFTA debate is whether Canadian and U.S. firms would have an incentive to relocate to Mexico because of differences in Mexican environmental regulations or enforcement. As stated above, it is unlikely that firms currently located in Quebec would relocate to Mexico for environmental reasons because pollution abatement costs are generally a small share of total production costs and there is little evidence that differences in environmental compliance costs are an important factor in firms' relocation decisions.[5] For the same reason, it is unlikely (and also expressly prohibited by NAFTA itself) that Quebec would be put in the position of having to lower its environmental standards in order to maintain its current competitive advantage in certain key economic sectors.

Even without NAFTA, Quebec's environmental policies would have been subject to greater influence by external factors for a number of reasons. For one thing, there is greater recognition that environmental problems such as stratospheric ozone depletion and climate change can only be managed through multinational agreements that require countries to take appropriate pollution abatement actions. This has resulted in numerous international environmental agreements like the Montreal Protocol, signed in 1987, in which 24 nations agreed to limit the production and consumption of ozone-depleting substances. Quebec industries are being forced to curtail emissions of ozone-depleting substances in order to comply with the Montreal Protocol. Emissions of carbon dioxide and other greenhouse gases will also need to be stabilized at their 1990 levels by the year 2000 to comply with the Framework Convention on Climate Change signed by 167 countries, including Canada, at the United Nations Conference on Environment and Development at Rio de Janeiro in June 1992. The convention was transformed into an international treaty in March 1993.

There is also greater recognition that pollution problems are often regional in scope and do not respect jurisdictional boundaries, whether the boundaries are between nations, provinces, or states. Acid rain, for example, which is caused by the long-range atmospheric transport of emissions of sulfur dioxide, does not respect political boundaries either within or between countries.[6] It was only in 1990 that the U.S. Clean Air Act was amended in recognition of the regional scale of the acidic deposition problem. While acid-gas emissions had been controlled in the United States prior to 1990, the primary concern was on controlling damages at sites located close to sources rather than acidic deposition at distant receptor sites. The regional scale of acid rain

---

5.   For evidence on this issue, see Harrison (1993), Leonard (1988), Walter (1982), and World Bank (1992).

6.   For discussion of the Canada-U.S. acid rain issue, see Menz (1992).

was also recognized in Canada with the federal-provincial agreement in 1985 to reduce sulfur dioxide emissions to one-half of their allowable 1980 level by 1994. Quebec was the first province to take action following this agreement by adopting modifications to existing regulations on air quality and pollution from pulp and paper plants. The regulations set tighter controls on the use of fossil fuels for combustion systems and established maximum allowable amounts of annual emissions for each of four major corporate sources of sulfur dioxide. The other affected provinces (from Manitoba eastward) introduced similar regulations or otherwise agreed to comply with the 1985 federal-provincial agreement (House of Commons Special Committee on Acid Rain, 1988).

Existing binational agreements between Canada and the United States will continue to influence Quebec's environmental policies in the future. Canada and the United States signed an Air Quality Agreement in 1991 following more than ten years of bilateral discussion and debate on the issue of transboundary acidic deposition. This agreement obligates the two countries to meet their emissions targets for sulfur dioxide and nitrogen oxides and to coordinate efforts in atmospheric modeling and in monitoring the effects of transboundary air pollution. It also requires the countries to undertake assessments of proposed or continuing actions that might cause significant transboundary air pollution. The accord established a bilateral air quality committee to assist in the implementation of the agreement and to review progress made in achieving the accord's environmental objectives (U.S. Environmental Protection Agency, 1992).

Quebec also has cooperative agreements with several states, and some of these agreements address environmental concerns. One such agreement was the Quebec-New York Agreement on Acid Precipitation, which was the first agreement on this issue between a state and a province. The agreement called for coordinated efforts to address the acid rain problem, including joint studies, exchange of scientific information and data, and coordinated efforts to undertake, on a national basis, corrective actions to reduce acid precipitation (Quebec, 1986). This agreement was followed by a more general agreement on environmental cooperation between Quebec and New York which called for exchange of information, consultations regarding environmental issues of joint concern, and establishment of a joint committee to oversee and report progress regarding cooperative efforts. Quebec is also involved with the states of Vermont and New York in joint endeavors to control pollution in Lake Champlain.

ENVIRONMENTAL POLICY DESIGN

Given the implementation of NAFTA and the rising interest in transfrontier pollution, Quebec should reconsider the design of its environmental policies. NAFTA's impact provides all the more reason for Quebec to take a wider outlook in setting pollution control policies and in its other actions with signifi-cant environmental impacts in Quebec and elsewhere. Quebec's existing envi-ronmental regulations may have been entirely appropriate before, but there is a need for Quebec to develop coherent, long-range environmental policies that allow strict environmental standards to be met without sacrificing other politi-cal and economic objectives. Most importantly, Quebec should consider the use of economic incentives to control pollution rather than relying on tradi-tional methods that require sources to adopt a certain type of pollution control technology or some other specified abatement approach.

Economists view pollution as a consequence of the failure to charge appropriate prices for the use of scarce environmental resources such as clean air and water. Pollution tends to occur whenever rights governing the use of these resources are not clearly specified or their use is not otherwise regulated by non-market forces. If profit-maximizing firms or utility-maximizing individu-als are not charged appropriate prices for the use of scarce resources, they will engage in socially excessive levels of polluting activities. The standard approach in environmental economics characterizes pollution as an external cost resulting from "waste discharges" associated with the use of certain types of resources for which rights to use have not been clearly specified.

If the economic process will not automatically achieve a socially efficient allocation of resources, then the question arises as to what sort of corrective action might be taken to address the problem. Economic analysis suggests two possible approaches: (1) private negotiations and legal action among the affected parties, or (2) intervention to alter the structure of prices to reflect external costs or to change the structure of property rights in order to encourage scarce environmental resources to be used more efficiently.

The possibility of resolving environmental problems through private actions among the affected parties was first suggested by Coase (1960). The "Coase Theorem" states that as long as negotiation costs are negligible and the number of affected parties is small, bargaining will automatically achieve the socially efficient outcome so long as the rights to the use of the resource are clearly specified. If the victim has rights to an unpolluted environment, then the polluter would have to compensate the victim for damages. Alternatively, if the polluter has the right to use the resource, then the victim should pay the polluter to curtail its polluting activities. Regardless of who holds the property rights, the socially efficient level of polluting activities (and the efficient level of environmental degradation) will tend to be achieved through bargaining. In real world situations, the number of parties involved in typical examples of pollu-tion is large, making it costly to negotiate and enforce private solutions and suggesting that government intervention may be a more efficient way to cor-rect the problem. In fact, environmental policy actions by governments can be regarded as remedies for situations with high private bargaining costs.

Government intervention to control pollution can take a number of different forms, including regulations which directly force the polluter to reduce emissions (so-called "direct" regulations), moral suasion to encourage polluters to act responsibly, and economic incentives that provide financial rewards to polluters for reducing their emissions. In the past, virtually all countries' environmental policies (including strongly market-oriented ones like the United States) entailed the use of direct regulations that require dischargers to employ a particular type of abatement technology or production process to comply with pollution control standards (OECD, 1994: 37). In the United States, regulations often require new sources to adopt the "best available control technology" or to use a particular technology in a given industry to control pollution. Canadian provinces also regulate pollution sources directly, but their regulations are less rigid than in the United States. Canadian regulatory schemes do not involve the same rigidities because it is the usual practice of provincial authorities to negotiate acceptable methods of pollution abatement on a case-by-case basis (particularly with large sources) rather than forcing all sources to control emissions in a particular way.[7]

In Quebec, the framework environmental protection legislation is the Environmental Quality Act, originally approved in 1972 and amended on several occasions since then. The act sets limits on air and water emissions, and sets standards for water quality, sewage treatment and hazardous wastes. The law also incorporates criteria for project evaluation which require that major development projects undergo an evaluation to assess possible environmental impacts.[8] The Environmental Quality Act gives the Minister of the Environment authority to order the installation of "any class or type of apparatus which he indicates to abate or eliminate the emission, deposit, issuance or discharge of a contaminant" (Quebec, 1991: 10). The government also has adopted specific regulations to address other environmental problems. For example, regulations

---

7. An important difference between Canadian and U.S. environmental policy making involves the roles of different levels of government. In the United States, authority for developing environmental policy rests primarily with the federal government. The U.S. Environmental Protection Agency (EPA) has the authority to set emission standards for all new sources of common air pollutants and Congress itself established the emission standards that cars (and later trucks) would have to meet. The states have the authority to control emissions from existing sources within their boundaries, but their plans must be approved by the EPA. In Canada, authority for developing environmental regulations rests almost exclusively with provincial authorities. The authority of the federal government is limited to dealing with interprovincial and international transboundary pollution concerns.

8. The procedures are similar to the environmental impact statement process required in the United States under the National Environmental Policy Act. An important difference is that Quebec's Minister of the Environment makes a recommendation to the provincial government, which then authorizes or rejects the project. In the United States, approval authority rests with a single government agency (whatever government agency has jurisdiction over the project) rather than the entire cabinet.

were adopted in 1984 to reduce sulfur dioxide emissions by one-half of their 1980 levels by 1995, and strict regulations requiring pulp and paper mills to cut pollutants discharged into the air and water were passed in 1985 and again in 1991. Such regulations usually require a certain percentage cutback in emissions within a specified time frame, but the methods for achieving the standards are developed through consultations between the industrial sources and the ministry. Government grants or subsidies are also often provided to companies which must modernize their plants to comply with the regulations. This form of direct environmental regulation is similar to methods followed by other Canadian provinces.

A disadvantage of direct regulations is that they provide little or no incentive for sources to control their emissions at minimum cost, so the costs of achieving environmental targets are likely to be higher than they otherwise might be. Economic analysis suggests that so-called *economic instruments* might achieve the same pollution abatement objectives as direct regulations, but more efficiently. This could be achieved by charging polluters a "price" equal to the marginal external cost of the polluting activity to induce the agent to act in a socially efficient manner. By forcing the polluter to bear the full social costs of its activity, the level of the polluting activity (and the associated amount of pollution) would be reduced to the amount that is economically efficient from the social perspective. Such a price incentive can take the form of a tax or charge levied on discharges – an effluent charge – or through the use of marketable emissions permits.

Economic incentives for pollution control are being increasingly used by environmental authorities looking for more cost-effective methods to meet their pollution control objectives.[9] By changing incentives, market-based policies can achieve the same level of pollution abatement as direct regulations, but at a lower cost. Another important advantage of economic instruments is that polluters are given a continuing incentive to develop new methods for controlling pollution because there is a market value on reducing emissions.

Effluent charges are a per-unit charge paid by a source for each unit of its emissions. The charge is set at the level necessary to achieve the target reduction in emissions (the environmental standard). Under an effluent charge system, sources have the option of either reducing their emissions to avoid the charge or continue emitting and pay the charge. Faced with the effluent charge, polluters have an incentive to find the most cost-effective pollution abatement techniques, and sources that find it less costly to reduce their emissions will do so to avoid paying the charge. Effluent charges internalize the costs of pollution without requiring regulators to specify how the sources should reduce their emissions, thus reducing the administrative burden on environmental authorities.

---

9.   For discussion of different types and applications of market-based environmental policies, see OECD (1989). See also Canada (1992).

Marketable emission allowances offer the same promise of efficiency as effluent charges, but have the advantage of insuring that the total emissions of a pollutant can be limited to whatever target amount is allowed by environmental regulations. Under an emission allowance system, enough allowances or permits are issued by the environmental authority to meet the desired level of total emissions of a particular pollutant. Emissions from an individual source are limited to the amount corresponding to the allowances it holds and any further emissions would be subject to a steep monetary fine. It is not important whether the allowances are initially distributed by auction or simply given to sources based on historical emission patterns, so long as they are transferable among sources after the initial distribution. By allowing the permits to be traded, sources have the option of either purchasing an emissions permit or emitting less in order to comply with the emission standard. As long as polluters have different abatement costs, allowances will tend to be sold by polluters with low abatement costs to polluters with high abatement costs. The trading of emission allowances among sources insures that the total cost of meeting the environmental standard will be minimized because it enables marginal pollution abatement costs to be equalized among sources.

The 1990 amendments to the U.S. Clean Air Act featured a transferable emission allowance program for the control of acidic deposition. The legislation was designed to achieve an approximate 50 percent reduction in sulfur dioxide emissions from their 1980 levels over a ten-year period, with a national limit of 8.95 million tons by the year 2010 on emissions from utility sources. The acid rain control program was aimed primarily at reducing emissions from existing sources since emissions from new sources were already limited by other regulations. Enough sulfur dioxide emission allowances will be issued by the U.S. EPA each year beginning in 1995 to meet the targets established by the legislation. Instead of requiring all polluters to reduce their sulfur dioxide emissions to the maximum allowable amount, sources are free to use the allowances to meet sulfur dioxide emission standards. Most of the allowances are to be issued annually by the EPA based on historical emission patterns, but a small percentage (less than 3 percent) are to be sold in an auction to provide polluters an additional source of allowances and a price signal to the emission allowance markets. Once the allowances are issued, they are freely transferable among sources, private citizens, brokers, municipalities, environmental advocacy groups, or other interested parties located anywhere within the continental United States.

Another interesting feature of the U.S. acid rain control program is that it also allows sources to sell "excess" emissions reductions (i.e., those beyond the emissions standard) to other sources who find it cheaper to purchase allowances than to implement the necessary pollution controls. This provides an incentive for sources with relatively low pollution abatement costs to reduce their emissions beyond the emissions standard and further lowers the costs of meeting the overall emissions target.

There is no formal emissions trading program in Canada, but Ontario's acid rain program allows Ontario Hydro to shift or "trade" emissions among its electricity generating stations (Ontario Ministry of the Environment and Ministry of the Energy, 1989). It is known that the marginal costs of controlling sulfur dioxide vary greatly among the major sources in Ontario, so allowing them to trade emission rights has the potential for considerable savings in pollution control costs (Dewees, 1990). The possibility of allowing sulfur dioxide emissions trading to take place between sources located in different provinces in Canada or between Canadian and U.S. sources has also been raised (Canada, 1992; Menz, 1993). Allowing emissions trading among sources located in different provinces or with U.S. sources would expand the market for permits, thereby introducing cost savings and making the permit market more competitive.

There is limited experience with the use of environmental charges in Canada. The province of British Columbia bases its fee for an air pollution permit on the amount of emissions (OECD, 1994: 57). Fees are reduced if applicants can demonstrate that actual emissions are below permitted emissions. When actual emissions exceed permitted emissions, a new permit must be issued and fees revised accordingly. The provinces of Alberta, British Columbia, and Quebec also levy a charge for certain types of water pollutants, with rates varying by degree of toxicity of pollutants (OECD, 1994: 68).

TRANSFRONTIER POLLUTION

Quebec's extensive border with several American states suggests a need for Quebec to consider environmental issues from a regional perspective rather than the perspective of an isolated government jurisdiction. Problems such as air or water pollution in the St. Lawrence valley obviously go beyond Quebec's borders. Effective management of activities with effects in other political jurisdictions requires cooperative efforts among the affected parties.

Environmental externalities involving different political jurisdictions (states, provinces, or countries) can take a number of different forms. First, they can involve physical flows of pollutants across political boundaries, either within a given country (between states or provinces) or across international boundaries. Examples in North America include pollution in the Great Lakes watershed, acid rain between Canada and the United States (or even within each of the two countries), and air and water pollution in the Mexican-U.S. border area. Environmental linkages can also result because citizens in one country are simply concerned about environmental resources in another jurisdiction. For example, pollution in the U.S. portion of the St. Lawrence River may be of concern to citizens of Quebec because of its direct or indirect effect on their economic welfare.[10] Third, environmental problems can link different political jurisdictions as a consequence of trade-related economic activity.

With transfrontier pollution, neither the polluters nor the jurisdictions where their emissions occur face the proper incentives to institute efficient pollution abatement measures. Since independent efforts at pollution control are likely to be inefficient, the affected parties must negotiate environmental standards and pollution abatement responsibilities in order to achieve what might be termed *international efficiency*. To accomplish this, rights to the use of shared resources must be defined, understood and enforced. Transfrontier pollution problems could conceivably be settled through private negotiations or in courts if everyone (polluters and victims) had access to courts, if the sources and effects of pollution could be readily identified and if rights to the use of resources were defined. However, since large numbers of emitters and victims are often involved, it is too costly for private litigation to achieve a solution. An example is Canadian-U.S. acidic deposition, where there are numerous victims and emitters on both sides of the border and it is impossible for them to identify each other. In such cases, governments must act on behalf of their citizens to resolve the problem.

Effective management of transborder pollution involves the same basic economic principles as managing pollution within a single jurisdiction's borders. However, because international rights and responsibilities for the use of shared resources are not well defined, implementing control measures can be far more complex than managing pollution within a single country.[11] If a polluting country has absolute sovereignty over the use of its resources, this implies that victims must bear the costs of reducing pollution. On the other hand, holding countries responsible for any extra-territorial pollution their activities cause implies that polluters must bear the costs of pollution control (the principle of "external responsibility").[12] If rights can be established, transborder pollution can be remedied by having either the polluter compensate the victim for damages or the victim bribe the polluter to reduce emissions (the Coase Theorem). Either of these solutions will achieve the efficient level of pollution by internalizing the external costs of the activity. However, to achieve this result it

---

10. For an excellent discussion of pollution in the St. Lawrence River, see Canada (1991).

11. Even within a nation, wide disparities can prevent remedial action if rights are unclear. In the debate over acid rain in the United States during the 1980s, the northeastern states took the position that emissions in the midwest had to be reduced to control acidic deposition in the northeast. Midwestern states argued that it was unfair for them to bear the burden of reducing acid rain damages elsewhere. Similar debates occurred in Canada. The Atlantic provinces argued that their emissions were inconsequential compared to those from major industrial provinces and that external sources were major contributors to their acid rain problem (House of Commons Special Committee on Acid Rain, 1988: 13).

12. For discussion of the issue of state responsibility for transboundary pollution, see D'Arge and Kneese (1980).

is necessary to establish the property rights to the environmental resource, measure the external costs (environmental damages) to determine the appropriate amount of compensation, and monitor the payments or transfers.

Dealing with transborder pollution issues is difficult because there are disagreements among countries over fundamental principles concerning the rights and responsibilities to shared environmental resources. With disagreements about fundamental principles of responsibility, effective joint solutions in difficult transboundary pollution problems may not be possible (Scott, 1986). There is precedent, however, for adopting the "polluter pays principle" which states that responsibility for the costs of pollution control, if not any remaining damages, rests with the source of pollution. The United Nations Stockholm Declaration on the Human Environment in 1972 supported the principle that a nation has the responsibility to ensure that activities within its borders do not cause damage in areas beyond their jurisdiction. The polluter pays principle was also adopted by the Organization for Economic Cooperation and Development (in 1974) because of concern that not requiring polluters to bear the cost of pollution control measures might result in distortions of international trade and investment patterns (OECD, 1994: 41).

If bargaining costs among parties affected by transfrontier pollution are large enough to warrant government regulatory actions, any of several policies can be employed to achieve whatever environmental targets are set, including direct controls on emissions, effluent charges and transferable emissions permits. Prior to the implementation of policies, however, it will be necessary to agree on rights and responsibilities governing the use of extraterritorial resources.

The experience of Canada and the United States in numerous disputes suggests an inability to agree on which principle of responsibility should apply to transborder pollution problems. In some instances, the two countries have accepted the principle of external responsibility, while in others the principle of territorial sovereignty has been adopted. In the Boundary Waters Treaty of 1909, the two countries agreed that neither country should use boundary waters so as to injure the other country. This principle was confirmed in the *Trail Smelter Case* in which an international tribunal held a Canadian smelter responsible for sulfur dioxide emissions coming into the state of Washington. On the other hand, in disputes involving marine fisheries and acid rain, the positions of the two countries have reflected the principle of absolute territorial sovereignty.

In the Canada-U.S. Air Quality Accord (1991), the two countries reaffirmed that nations have the responsibility to ensure that their activities do not cause damage in areas beyond their jurisdiction and established a bilateral air quality committee to monitor transboundary air pollution. However, the committee was not given authority to specify joint environmental targets or policies for meeting those objectives. While the North American environmental commission created with NAFTA also has been given numerous responsibilities, it too lacks the authority to develop its own policies to control transboundary pollution.

Quebec must take action jointly with other governments for several reasons. First, actions taken by one country alone may be insufficient to solve a shared pollution problem, making it difficult for a single country to warrant taking any action at all. While this may be especially true for global environmental problems, it can also occur when pollution involves only two different political jurisdictions. Second, one country's actions to reduce pollution can be undermined if polluters facing high pollution control costs can move to another location with less stringent environmental controls. Third, sharing pollution control responsibilities among a larger number of sources can reduce the costs of pollution control and still environmental quality standards to be met. Finally, and perhaps most important, nations that act independently are less willing to invest in pollution abatement because they ignore the benefits from their emissions abatement activities on other nations.

Beyond simple cooperative efforts, Quebec should consider the use of economic instruments such as effluent charges or transferable emissions rights for the control of transboundary pollution. If emission allowances were used, they would need to be freely transferable within the environmental problem area, including across international borders. For example, consider the problem of water pollution in Lake Champlain or along the St. Lawrence River. An emissions cap on discharges to a certain geographic portion of the water body could be set based on the need to meet a pre-determined water quality standard. Discharge permits would be distributed annually to sources and the allowances would be freely transferable within the prescribed region, including across international borders. Each year, the amount of emissions allowances issued by the authority could be reduced to meet more stringent pollution control objectives. Transfers of pollution control responsibility among sources located in Quebec and elsewhere could be monitored to insure that environmental standards in each jurisdiction were maintained. Emissions trading would minimize the costs of meeting the environmental quality standard within this designated region. The scope of trading could be determined either through a cooperative agreement or by a supranational authority, but should be based on comparisons of the additional cost savings from enhanced emissions trading with the need to meet environmental targets in receptor areas.[13]

A joint agency should have the authority to establish environmental targets as well as to administer policies such as tax mechanisms or marketable emissions permits. The agency must collect information about emissions,

---

13. The larger the trading area, the greater the number of possible sources for trades and the greater the potential savings from an emissions trading program. For discussion, see Tietenberg (1990).

pollution deposition, and damages. Unless the overseeing body has the authority to tax the polluting country or define the structure of rights and liabilities, there will be reluctance on the part of sovereign nations to take the necessary actions to control transboundary pollution.

CONCLUSIONS

Quebec's actions in the future will be influenced to a much greater extent by external considerations rather than being governed by domestic factors alone. This will occur because there is greater interest in issues involving transfrontier pollution and also as a result of the increased interdependency among economies, particularly in North America. In an interdependent world, each country's rights to the use of their natural resources must be reconciled with the interests of others within the shared ecosystem. This suggests that there will be greater sharing of pollution control responsibilities among all countries, including Quebec. Faced with this challenge, Quebec should redesign its environmental policies to allow more strict environmental standards to be met without sacrificing other important political and economic objectives.

Despite the potential gains in social welfare from coordinated pollution control efforts, it is difficult to achieve such agreements among nations. The task is complex because of differences in underlying legal and regulatory structures and lack of consensus on how much environmental protection is appropriate. Nonetheless, Quebec and several states have in the past acted cooperatively to address pollution of shared resources. While these efforts have brought the affected governments together, they have yet to involve the actual "trading" of pollution control responsibilities across an international border. An emissions trading program or other market-based method could also be used in controlling transboundary air pollution or in allocating other scarce resources in the border region. Implementing such policies could very well be in Quebec's best interests.

REFERENCES

ANDERSON, Terry L. (ed.). 1993. *NAFTA and the Environment*. Vancouver: Fraser Institute.

CANADA. 1991. *The State of Canada's Environment*. Ottawa: Minister of Supply and Services Canada.

CANADA. 1992. *Economic Instruments for Environmental Protection*. Discussion Paper. Ottawa: Minister of Supply and Services Canada.

COASE, Ronald H. 1960. "The Problem of Social Cost." *The Journal of Law and Economics* 3: 1-44.

D'ARGE, Ralph C., and Allen V. KNEESE. 1980. "State Liability for Environmental Degradation: An Economic Perspective." *Natural Resources Journal* 20: 427-50.

DEWEES, Donald E. 1990. "The Regulation of Sulphur Dioxide in Ontario," in G. Bruce Doern, Ed., *Getting It Green: Case Studies in Environmental Regulation*, pp. 129-54. Toronto: C.D. Howe Institute.

GROSSMAN, Gene M., and Alan B. KRUEGER. 1993. "Environmental Impacts of a North American Free Trade Agreement," in Peter M. Garber, Ed., *The Mexico-U.S. Free Trade Agreement*, pp. 13-56. Cambridge, MA: The MIT Press.

HARRISON, Glenn W. 1993. "Environmentally Sensitive Industries and an Emerging Mexico." *The North American Journal of Economics and Finance* 4(1): 109-26.

HOUSE OF COMMONS SPECIAL COMMITTEE ON ACID RAIN. 1988. *Report of the Special Committee on Acid Rain*. Ottawa: House of Commons.

HUFBAUER, Gary CLYDE, and Jeffrey J. SCHOTT. 1993. *NAFTA: An Assessment*. Revised Edition. Washington, D.C.: Institute for International Economics.

LEONARD, H. Jeffrey. 1988. *Pollution and the Struggle for World Product*. Cambridge: Cambridge University Press.

MENZ, Fredric C. 1992. "Transboundary Acid Rain: A Canadian-U.S. Problem Requiring a Joint Solution," in Jonathan Lemco, Ed., *Tensions at the Border: Energy and Environmental Concerns in Canada and the United States*, pp. 45-60. New York: Praeger.

MENZ, Fredric C. 1993. "Minimizing Acidic Deposition Control Costs through Transboundary Emissions Trading." *American Review of Canadian Studies* 23: 247-66.

The NAFTA. 1992. *North American Free Trade Agreement between the Government of the United States, the Government of Canada, and the Government of the United Mexican States*. Washington, D.C.: United States Government Printing Office.

The NAFTA Supplemental Agreements. 1993. *North American Agreement on Environmental Cooperation*. Washington, D.C.: United States Government Printing Office.

NATIONAL WILDLIFE FEDERATION. 1990. "Environmental Concerns Related to a United States-Mexico-Canada Free Trade Agreement." Mimeo. Washington, D.C.: National Wildlife Federation.

ONTARIO MINISTRY OF THE ENVIRONMENT AND MINISTRY OF ENERGY. 1989. "A Review of Ontario Hydro's Acid Gas Report." Mimeo. Downsview: Ontario Ministry of the Environment

OECD. 1989. *Economic Instruments for Environmental Protection*. Paris: Organization for Economic Cooperation and Development.

OECD. 1994. *Managing the Environment: The Role of Economic Instruments*. Paris: Organization for Economic Cooperation and Development.

ORTMAN, David E. 1991. "On a Comprehensive North American Trade Agreement." Testimony on Behalf of Friends of the Earth, National Wildlife Federation, and the Texas Center for Policy Studies before the Subcommittee on Trade, Committee on Ways and Means, U.S. House of Representatives.

PASTOR, Robert A. 1992. "NAFTA as Center of Integration Process." In Nora Lustig, Barry P. Bosworth and Robert Z. Lawrence, Eds., *North American Free Trade: Assessing the Impact*. Washington, D.C.: Brookings Institution.

QUEBEC. 1986. *Annual Report 1985, Quebec–New York Agreement on Acid Precipitation*. Quebec: Minister of the Environment.

QUEBEC. 1991. *Environmental Quality Act*. R.S.Q., chapter Q-2. Quebec: Éditeur officiel.

SCOTT, Anthony. 1986. "The Canadian-American Problem of Acid Rain." *Natural Resources Journal* 26: 337-58.

TIETENBERG, Thomas H. 1990. "Economic Instruments for Environmental Policies." *Oxford Review of Economic Policy* 6(1): 17-33.

U.S. ENVIRONMENTAL PROTECTION AGENCY. 1992. United States/Canada Air Quality Agreement. Progress Report. EPA/400/1-92/002. Washington, D.C.

U.S. GENERAL ACCOUNTING OFFICE. 1992. *U.S.-Mexico Trade: Assessment of Mexico's Environmental Controls for New Companies*. Washington, D.C.

U.S. HOUSE OF REPRESENTATIVES, COMMITTEE ON WAYS AND MEANS. 1993. *NAFTA and Supplemental Labor/Environmental Pacts*. Washington, D.C. 103rd Congress, 1st session, March 11.

U.S. SENATE, COMMITTEE ON FINANCE, SUBCOMMITTEE ON INTERNATIONAL TRADE. 1992. 102nd Congress, 2nd session, September 16, 1992.

WALTER, Ingo. 1982. "Environmentally-Induced Industrial Relocation to Developing Countries." In S.J. Rubin and T.R. Graham, Eds., *Environment and Trade*. New Jersey: Allanheld, Osmun, and Co.

WORLD Bank. 1992. *World Development Report, 1992*. New York: Oxford University Press.

13

Agricultural Policy

Benoît Mario Papillon
Université du Québec à Trois-Rivières

Quebec is a net importer of food and farm products. However, with over $1 billion of exports, foreign markets are important to Quebec's farm producers and food processors. The second section briefly surveys export records. In Quebec, Canada and elsewhere, government involvement in agriculture is pervasive. The third section of the paper gathers some economic facts about agricultural markets which have been conducive to government involvement. However justified it may be, any trade negotiation is a challenge to this involvement, or more precisely to its diversity among negotiating partners. Competition from foreign businesses will be acceptable to domestic businesses if this competition is fair. This demands that the amount of government support should not differ significantly between countries. The fourth section discusses this issue and surveys government support to agriculture in Quebec and elsewhere in North America. There is a need to reconcile agricultural policy with the objective of gaining access to foreign markets. The last section proposes a guiding principle for this reconciliation.

INTRODUCTION

Operating under severe climatic constraints, Quebec's farm production has always been complemented by a wide variety of imported products in order to meet local food requirements. Traffic over borders has **not**, however, been one-way. With specialization in some production, producers in Quebec have also acted as suppliers to other countries' markets. Quebec trade records in food and farm products are surveyed in the first section of the chapter. On the overall importance of imports and exports, recent years are consistent with earlier periods.

As in most other states around the world, the agricultural sector in Quebec has been constrained, as well as supported in its evolution, by public policies. Although governments in power at different times and places have had different political orientations, there is a set of economic conditions specific to agriculture that has been conducive to very similar policy initiatives among them. In order to recognize the various sources of pressures on the policy process, the specificity of agricultural markets needs to be well-understood. The second section of the chapter surveys conditions on these markets.

In some areas of policy, the "live hand of the past" is particularly strong in setting the current agenda. Trade policy regarding farm production is one of those areas. The third section of the chapter describes government support to farm production in Quebec. The quantitative assessment of government support has become an issue in trade negociations; references are made to assessments from several sources.

The NAFTA, as well as its precursor the FTA, facilitates broader integration of national markets in North America. Agriculture was given special treatment in the agreement with a separate chapter, chapter 7. However, this was not really because a lot of progress had been made in this sector.

The objective is rather to introduce a number of exemptions and special rules for agriculture which have priority over the general provisions of Chapter 3. Special agreements regarding market access for a number of agricultural commodities contained in the FTA are further extended to recognize Mexican interests. The inability of the agricultural sector to live with the more general provisions on market access has much to do with the level of government support received by a number of agricultural commodities.

Laws, regulations and related programs left in statutes following past crises and compromises are not wholly consistent with the pursuit of present opportunities on a broad front. The last section of the chapter discusses the need for a new agenda with respect to agricultural policies and its composition.

QUEBEC TRADE RECORDS IN FOOD AND FARM PRODUCTS

Over recent years, the value of Quebec's exports in farm and food products has fluctuated above the $ 1.1 billion mark. In comparison, imports increased from $1.7 billion to $1.9 billion between 1989 and 1992; this makes Quebec a net importer in this category of products. As shown in Table B-1, the value of exports in recent years represents approximately 15% of the estimated value of domestic production.

As indicated in Table B-2, approximately half the total value of exports is composed of livestock products. Within the livestock product category, a closer look at the data indicates that meat is the single largest item, accounting for more than half of the category total. Aside from a residual category ("Others") in which beverages form the largest sub-category, the shares of other categories are of the order of 10% or less.

TABLE B-1

**Trade Flows between Quebec and Other Countries
in Farm and Food Products
1989-1992**

Year	Exports ($000)	Imports ($000)	Exports as % of dom. prod. in same cat.[1]
1989	1,131,458	1,679,218	15.71
1990	1,293,756	1,757,737	16.32
1991	1,200,947	1,808,470	15.55
1992	1,254,705	1,863,331	16.47

1: Domestic production in the same categories of products is estimated by the sum of market receipts at the farmgate plus the value added in food processing.

Source: Computations from Quebec Department of Agriculture, Fisheries and Food, 1993: 5, 7.

TABLE B-2

**Farm and Food Product Exports by Category of Products
1989-1992**

Product Category	1989		1992		1989-1992 - % -
	$000	% - share	$000	% - share	
Grain & Oilseeds	83,343	7.4	95,578	7.6	14.7
Livestock	639,317	56.5	628,923	50.1	(1.6)
Fish	122,060	10.8	130,725	10.4	7.1
Fruits and Veget.	61,870	5.5	71,251	5.7	15.2
Others	224,870	19.8	328,228	26.2	45.9
Total	1,131,458	100.0	1,254,705	100.0	10.9

Source: Quebec Department of Agriculture, Fisheries and Food, 1993: 11

In 1989, the share of exports to the United States was 56.6%. As shown by Table B-3, this share had risen to 66.6% in 1992. A closer look at the years between indicates that this increase was continuous, suggesting more to come. The share of all other regions decreased, including Mexico, whose share in 1992 was down to less than one percent.

TABLE B-3
Percentage Distribution of Farm and Food Product Exports
by Destination
1989-1992

Destinations	1989	1992
United States	56.4	65.9
Mexico	2.3	0.7
European Community	11.1	9.9
Japan	10.7	8.1
Others	19.5	15.4
Total	100.0	100.0

Source: Quebec Department of Agriculture, Fisheries and Food, 1993: 13

Table B-4 reports dollar amounts of exports and percentage increases between 1989 and 1992. The growing share of the U.S. as an export destination is accounted for by a 23.4% increase in exports to U.S. between 1989 and 1992. All other destinations listed in Table B-4 report decreasing dollar amounts of farm and food product exports.

TABLE B-4
Farm and Food Product Exports by Destination
1989-1992 ($000)

Destinations	1989	1992	1989-1992 – % –
United States	640,617	835,784	30.5
Mexico	24,752	8,859	(64.2)
European Community	126,399	125,096	(1.0)
Japan	121,863	102,965	(15.5)
Others	221,828	195,450	(11.9)
Total	1,131,458	1,254,705	11.7

Source: Quebec Department of Agriculture, Fisheries and Food, 1993: 13

Tables B-5 and B-6 give information in dollar amounts and in percentage shares about the main categories of exports to the U.S. and Mexico. In the case of the U.S., a very large decrease is recorded for the category "Meats" between 1989 and 1992. This reduction is more than compensated by a very large increase in the residual category "Other." In the case of Mexico, most of Quebec's exports were in the product category "Powder Milk" in 1989; powder milk was still the largest category in 1992, but the dollar amount is four times smaller than in 1989.

TABLE B-5
Main Exports in Farm Products and Food to U.S. and Mexico
1989-1992

Product Category	1989	1992	1989-1992 – % –
U.S.			
Meats	318,305	178,104	(44.0)
Fish Products	65,612	79,717	21.5
Beverages	85,647	111,167	29.8
Other	171,053	466,796	17.9
Total **(U.S.)**	640,617	835,784	30.5
Mexico			
Powder Milk	17,731	3,961	(77.7)
Meats	5,913	1,624	(72.5)
Other	1,108	3,274	19.5
Total **(Mexico)**	24,752	8,859	(6.2)

Source: Computations from Quebec Department of Agriculture, Fisheries and Food, 1993: 13

TABLE B-6
Main Exports in Farm Products and Food to U.S. and Mexico
Percentage Share
1989-1992

Product Category	1989	1992
U.S.		
Meats	49.69	21.31
Fish Products	10.24	9.54
Beverages	13.37	13.30
Other	26.70	55.85
Total **(U.S.)**	100.00	100.00
Mexico		
Powder Milk	71.63	44.71
Meats	23.89	18.33
Other	4.48	36.96
Total **(Mexico)**	100.00	100.00

Source: Computations from Quebec Department of Agriculture, Fisheries and Food, 1993: 13

TABLE B-7
Market Receipts for Various Commodities
1992

	$000	% – total
Milk	1,098,988	34.8
Livestock	888,709	28.1
Poultry	321,955	10.2
Eggs	95,907	3.0
Other	29,693	0.9
Sub-Total – Livestock and Livestock Products	2,435,252	77.0
Corn	149,013	4.7
Wheat	10,324	0.3
Barley	22,591	0.7
Oat	8,960	0.3
Potatoes	59,308	1.9
Vegetables	170,437	5.4
Apples	31,113	1.0
Other Fruits	25,639	0.8
Flower	100,805	3.2
Maple Products	59,736	1.9
Other	87,951	2.8
Sub-Total – Crops	725,877	23.0
Total	3,161,129	100.0

Source: Department of Agriculture, Quebec, 1994: 76

AGRICULTURAL MARKETS IN ECONOMIC PERSPECTIVE

Labour Productivity and Structural Changes

No other sector of activities has experienced structural changes of the same order of magnitude as agriculture. Over the period since World War II alone, the share of agriculture in total employment in Quebec declined from nearly one-third to less than 5%. This represents a reduction of more than 25 percentage points. In comparaison, the equally discussed reduction in the share of manufacturing employment is a small blip of a few percentage points and the equally discussed increase in services (trade and finance excluded) has been around 10 percentage points.

The good news in these changes is the very significant labour productivity gains which caused them. There is a very close correlation between the income per capita of a country and the share of its population engaged in agriculture (Suits, 1982: 1). The bad news is the downwards pressure on farm income that these reductions in the relative as well as the absolute farm labour force require-ments have generated, and the predictable cry for government help.

The pattern of structural changes in the U.S. has been very similar to Quebec's, and the share of the U.S. population engaged in farming is now less than 4%. In the case of Mexico, the same forces are at work but the transfor-mation of the national economy is still at a middle point; more than a quarter of the population is engaged in agriculture (Canadian International Trade Tribunal / Research Branch, 1993: 97).

History is not the only factor which makes the agricultural sector some-what unique. Beyond productivity gains, also achieved in some sectors other than agriculture, a special combination of economic factors still present today has contributed to make this history what it is, with its long series of crises.

Organization of the Industry and Exit Barriers

In terms of industrial organization, the agricultural sector represents an extreme. Although the typical farm has grown continuously in size, farming is still a small business industry. For example, in 1992 Quebec dairy production was carried on by more than thirteen thousand farms, the vast majority of them being family-type enterprises with one or two people working full time.

The agricultural sector is frequently used in academic textbooks on applied economics as an illustration of the perfect competition model (Weiss, 1980: 21-89). It implies that no individual producer is large enough to make produc-tion decisions which would have a noticeable impact on market prices. In other words, all producers are price-takers. This abstracts from government regula-tions which allow producers of some categories of products to act together to restrict output and force market prices upwards.

With labour productivity growing faster than demand for farm products, manpower requirements in agriculture – as mentioned above – have been decreasing continuously. Although not in the same order of magnitude as for agriculture, the reallocation of manpower resources between various industrial sectors is a common event in a dynamic economy.

However, what makes the reallocation of manpower unique in the case of agriculture is not only its magnitude. Given the very atomistic structure of the industry with non-diversified ownership in the hands of people at work in agriculture, the reallocation of manpower resources away from agriculture could mean extensive losses in personal wealth among those leaving the sector.

Farmers who leave agriculture lose much more than a job. The location of farms in rural areas exacerbates these losses, since the reallocation of man-power will also mean a move to the city for those involved. In other words, there are significant exit barriers in the agricultural sector, in comparison to sectors where ownership of productive assets is widely distributed among the population and whose location is shared with other sectors.

Output Uncertainties and Demand Characteristics

Volume of output produced by a manufacturing enterprise will normally be fairly close to the originally-planned production level. Unless a new production method is introduced, uncertainty over the expected amount of output is lim-ited. This is not the case in crop farming and, to a lesser degree, in some types of livestock farming.

A same amount of seed can generate significantly different returns, depending on the weather and the presence or absence of insects or diseases. More advanced technology and greater knowledge can mitigate the impact of these factors but do not eliminate them, as long as farming is carried on in an uncontrolled atmosphere.[1] Beyond the discriminated impact of these factors on individual farms – the assessment of which is a source of hazard as is the case of any other insurance if government support is involved – market factors also come into play, and in specific ways when it comes to farming.

Farmers, like other businessmen, are not concerned by production levels alone but by what they mean in terms of sales revenue. If market prices at farmgate increased proportionately to unexpected reductions in actual levels of industry output, and decreased no more than proportionately to unexpected increases in levels of industry output, consumers and food processors would have more reasons to be concerned by farm production uncertainty than farmers themselves. But this is not the case.

The value of farm production is derived from what consumers are willing to pay for it, where they get it, when they get it and in what form they get it. The costs of transporting, distributing and processing, in a transformation from wheat to bread, for example, are substantial. Therefore, the raw product price at the farmgate is low in comparison to the consumer price.

More explicitly, transportation and distribution costs account for around 35% of the consumer price of food and beverages. Of the remaining 65%, around 47% is accounted for by processing expenses other than the purchase of the farm output, such as wages, energy, capital expenditures for the

---

1.   Again, this characterization of the farm output is more relevant to crop farming than to livestock farming.

processing plant, etc.[2] This means that for every consumer dollar spent on food, the share allocated to the purchase of the product at the farmgate is around 18%. It also means that the consumer price will not be very sensitive to price changes at the farmgate. For instance, based on the quoted average figures, an increase of 50% in the farmgate price would increase the consumer price by only 9%.

Furthermore, the consumption of items such as eggs, milk, butter and basic vegetables or fruits such as potatoes and apples is relatively insensitive to price. This is either because such items account for only a small proportion of the overall food budget, for instance potatoes, or because they are considered necessities, for instance milk. There are two major implications to all this.

First, a very good crop is not necessarily a blessing to farmers and can very well mean a reduction in sale revenues. Farmers have to accept price reductions that are larger than the percentage increase in realized output if they want to sell all their output. Second, unexpected increases in farm product imports do not need to be very large to reduce significantly the price of those products on the domestic market.

GOVERNMENT SUPPORT TO DOMESTIC PRODUCTION

A Trade Policy Issue

The relation between competition and economic activity is a complex one. As the old saying goes, "two heads are better than one," and competition is a way of using the creativity of many people to find new and better ways to satisfy human needs.

Businesses, in purchasing goods or services that they make more valuable, and consumers both enjoy choice. Both groups value the ability to buy from more than one source or to contract with new suppliers. But when it comes to selling, the issues are quite different. The nature and extent of competition are among the main determinants of business profitability and, by the same token, of the probability of survival.

The extent of competition as well as the extent of specialization is limited by the size of the market. The benefits for a given customer of buying from a given producer is net of all sorts of transaction costs, including very tangible costs such as transportation. When these costs are too high, the customer will be in the market for the producer's goods.

---

2. Computations from tables on the structure of the Canadian economy (Statistics Canada, 1994).

The last century has been one of continuous reductions in transportation and communications costs. It has become increasingly beneficial to trade with businesses located far away. An important feature of the global economy since World War II "was that, in almost every year, the increase in the volume of international trade exceeded the increase in the volume production. In other words, trade led economic growth." (Kenwood and Lougheed, 1983: 299). Businesses with markets beyond national borders have emerged in growing numbers, and more domestic businesses find themselves competing with businesses from abroad.

Businesses expect governments to address their concern for fair competition with laws and regulations to exclude some practices, for instance predatory pricing and false advertising. With international trade, businesses living under different tax regimes and having access to different forms of government support must compete for the same market. For businesses based in countries where government support is limited, the actual or apparently more generous support enjoyed by some foreign businesses is viewed as a source of unfair competition.

It can be claimed, for instance, that one-third of the production costs of a foreign business are covered by subsidies from its government, while the domestic firm needs to recover all its costs in the price for its output. Businesses viewing themselves as victims of such unfair competition will expect protection and defensive action from their governments. The most obvious action would be to erect a tariff wall.

The use of tariffs as a defensive action against unfair competition can open the door to various kinds of abuses. In order to protect tariff reductions and related trade liberalization achieved through various rounds of negotiation since 1947, countries participating in the GATT have adopted a code to regulate the recourse to tariffs as a means of retaliatory action.[3]

Under Article VI of the GATT, a country can levy a Countervailing Duty on a good whose production is subsidized in the country of origin. The duty should not exceed "the estimated bounty or subsidy determined to have been granted." In the case of agriculture, a sector that is subsidized in many countries, the issue becomes one of comparative levels of support. The meaning of the word subsidy, however, is not obvious.

From the standpoint of a domestic producer who has to compete with foreign producers, it makes very little difference whether the foreign producers are supported by their government through direct subsidies paid out of taxes or through a regulation which raises the price consumers have to pay on their own domestic market.

---

3. This code is very similar in application to the anti-dumping code, also included in the GATT. For instance, evidence of subsidy, like evidence of dumping, is not sufficient. It must also be proved that the domestic industry has suffered or been injured.

Forms and Measurement of Government Support

Very many policies may impact directly or indirectly on businesses in a particular sector, especially in agriculture. There is no simple answer to the question of what constitutes government support to a particular industry or group of producers and what does not.

The concept of producer subsidy equivalent (PSE) has been proposed to measure the degree of assistance to agricultural production. It has been used extensively by the OECD in recent years to monitor the evolution of agricultural policies in a number of countries. In agriculture, government intervention has taken many forms and has cumulated over the years. The PSE measure constitutes an attempt to interpret a very large set of information about government programs and regulations in terms of assistance to producers.

More specifically, the PSE measures "the value of the monetary transfers to farmers from consumers of agricultural products and from taxpayers resulting from agricultural policy" (OECD, 1992: 127). A PSE value represents the value of these transfers as a percentage of the value of production.[4]

The PSE measure can be broken down into five components, with some of these components including more than one factor.[5] The first component is the price gap between the domestic market and the world market multiplied by the domestic production. The second component is the amount of direct payments by governments to farmers, and the third component is composed of the other kinds of support from public funds, for instance subsidies to carriers for the transportation of the product. The fourth component is made up of the amount of levies on production and the fifth element, specific to livestock, measures the effect of government programs on market feed prices paid by livestock producers (taxes as well as market price support programs) affecting products used to manufacture animal feed. The PSE value is the sum of the first three elements minus the last two.

The origin of the PSE goes back to work by Tim Josling for the Food and Agriculture Organisation in the early 1970s.[6] It was adopted by the OECD in 1982 for the implementation of a Ministerial Trade Mandate requiring estimates of assistance to farm production (by commodity) in OECD countries. This same mandate also required a method for assessing the impact on domestic and world markets of a gradual reduction of government assistance,

---

4.   More specifically, a value of production adjusted to include the amount of direct transfers from government in farmers' cash receipts.

5.   This five-component breakdown of the PSE measure is used by the OECD to represent the method followed in the computation of the PSE values.

6.   Some theoretical basis for this concept can be found in the work of a number of authors, in particular Max Corden (Cahill and Legg, 1989-1990: 14).

recognizing the effect of inter-commodity linkages (Cahill and Legg, 1989-1990: 14). Since then, PSE estimates are published every year by the OECD under **AGRICULTURAL POLICIES, MARKETS AND TRADE Monitoring and Outlook – *the year* –**.

PSEs, along with other concepts like the "effective rate of protection" and the "trade distortion equivalent," fall within the category known as aggregate measures of support (AMSs). AMSs in general and PSEs in particular can play two roles in trade liberalization in agriculture. First, they provide a common denominator for a wide range of government policies (nontariff barriers like quotas, export subsidies, input subsidies, deficiency payments, etc.) and can be used as a basis for inter-country comparisons. This allows an aggregate approach and therefore simplifies negotiations on the matter of government support.

Second, they can be used as a monitoring device to determine whether countries taking part in a trade agreement actually reduce the amount of support to their agriculture according to commitments made.

As pointed out by specialists, there is no single best AMS; "the most appropriate measure can be selected only after careful consideration of the objectives of the analysis" (Meilke, 1991: 823).

For instance, to achieve fair competition among red meat animal producers from different Canadian provinces, a number of agreements were signed in the 1980s (National Red Meat Tripartite Stabilization Agreements). To be eligible for federal contributions, provinces had to maintain their support to local production under certain ceilings. Given the importance of feed, also a farm product, and transportation (subject to significant government programs related to farm production) in the total cost of red meat animal production, the standard PSE methodology was extended "by incorporating more policy interactions than is typically the case, in particular by allowing for some cross commodity policy effects" (Meilke, 1991: 824).

Records of Support

Government expenditures provide the most obvious form of government support. The answer to the question of which portion of a particular program applicable to many sectors represents support to agriculture is less obvious. In the case of a government program specific to agriculture but applicable to many commodities, the answer to the question of which portion goes to a given commodity will be even less obvious. Government expenditures, however, remain a well-documented form of support in public accounts, and one that is directly interpretable. It therefore provides a good starting point.

Tables D-1, D-2, and D-3 report on public expenditures on agriculture. The first table (D-1) provides a detailed breakdown of expenditures by the Quebec government, distinguishing up to fourteen categories of programs, as well as operating and capital expenditures by departments and tax expenditures. The single largest category of expenditures in the recent years has been

TABLE D-1

Provincial Support to Quebec Agriculture in the Form of Government Expenditures (1987-88, 1992-93 (forecast))

	1987-88		1992-93	
	$ 000	% of total	$ 000	% of total
A. Operating Expenditures (1)	138,902	25.89	175,813	26.28
B. Capital Expenditures (2)	3,494	0.65	3,684	0.55
C. Program Expenditures (3)				
C.1. Dir. Comm. Paym. (4)	141,485	26.37	217,131	32.45
C.2. Dir. Suppl. Paym. (5)	11,825	2.20	27,869	4.17
C.3. Crop Insurance (6)	12,846	2.39	16,647	2.49
C.4. Financial Assistance (7)	93,928	17.51	76,103	11.38
C.5. Storage & Freight (8)	0	0.00	0	0.00
C.6. Social & Labor (9)	2,280	0.42	1,747	0.26
C.7. Research (10)	4,645	0.87	6,706	1.00
C.8. Food Inspec. (11)	5,360	1.00	5,371	0.80
C.9. Food Aid (12)	0	0.00	0	0.00
C.10. Mkting & Trade (13)	16,143	3.01	15,755	2.35
C.11. Rural & Reg. Devt. (14)	19,267	3.59	11,245	1.68
C.12. Environment (15)	13,360	2.49	17,532	2.62
C.13. Education (16)	13,534	2.52	17,773	2.66
C.14. Extension (17)	8,950	1.67	9,003	1.35
D. Tax Expenditures (18)	56,532	10.54	72,034	10.77
Total Gross Expenditures	542,551	101.12	674,413	100.81
Recoveries (19)	(6,015)	(1.12)	(5,398)	(0.81)
Total Net Expenditures	536,536	100.00	669,015	100.00

Source: Agriculture Canada – Policy Branch, 1993: 37, 49.

TABLE D-1 (cont'd)
Provincial Support to Quebec Agriculture in the Form of Government Expenditures

(1) Includes all expenses associated with day-to-day operations of the Department including salaries and purchases of goods and services and the cost of administering various programs.

(2) Includes expenditures for acquisition and renovation of land and buildings and acquisition of capital items such as property, furnitures and large equipement.

(3) Includes money directly transferred to individuals and agencies through programs or indirectly transferred through funds (e.g. crop insurance fund) and through transfers to other levels of government.

(4) Grants and contributions made under ongoing price and commodity programs: for example: WGSA, ASA, etc.

(5) Grants and contributions made under ad-hoc programs and for factors of production, for example: input subsidy programs, artificial insemination costs, land rental assistance, special drought assistance, etc.

(6) Government premiums to the Crop Insurance Funds.

(7) This category includes interest sudsidies, loan defaults and other credit programs.

(8) This category includes grants and contributions made under transportation assistance programs and storage programs.

(9) Included in this category are grants and contributions to community organizations and for general skills training.

(10) Grants and contributions for research activities including research for improvement of product quality. This category does not include administrative costs (for example researchers' salaries) related to research. These costs are included in Category A (Operating expenditures).

(11) Grants and contributions for animal health, veterinary services, products testing, disease control, food quality. This category does not include admistrative costs (for example inspectors' salaries) related to inspection. These costs are included in Category A (Operating expenditures).

(12) Grants and contributions for food aid assistance and to international agriculture organizations.

(13) Grants for activities related to product promotion and development of new markets.

(14) Grants for activities related to rural and regional development. General irrigation projects, community pastures and general development projects would be included in this category.

(15) Grants and activities related to the conservation of farm-related resources and wildlife. Included in this category are expenditures for securing water supplies.

(16) Grants to agricultural educational institutions.

(17) Grants for activities related to the provision of information, training and services to farmers. This category does not include administrative costs (for example salaries to government employees) related to extension.

(18) Tax expenditures are restricted to provincial property and fuel tax rebates and exemptions and federal fuel tax rebates.

(19) The recoveries include revenues from the following items: transfers from one level of government to another, licences and permits, leases and rentals, sales, fees and royalties, previous year recoveries, land sales and other miscellaneous revenues. The repayments of loans or advances and return on investments are not included in the recoveries.

direct commodity payments (32.45% of total support in the form of Quebec government expenditures). These payments are direct cash transfers from government to producers and are usually considered as straight forms of subsidy. Next in line, after departmental operating expenditures, is the category of programs known as financial assistance, composed of interest subsidies and other forms of subsidized credit programs.

Table D-2 shows the total dollar amount of support to Quebec agriculture from provincial and federal governments in 1987-88 and 1992-93. Recoveries are entered as negative support.[7] Program expenditures still constitute the largest category of support. The last two columns of the table indicate the percentage share of each level of government in the total amount of support for the two-year average. In the case of program expenditures, two-thirds come from the Quebec government.

TABLE D-2
**Total[1] Support to Quebec Agriculture
in the Form of Government Expenditures
(1987-88, 1992-93 (forecast))**

	Total $000,000		% Share by Level of Government[2]	
			Provincial	**Federal**
	87-88	**92-93**	**87-93**	**87-93**
Operating & Capital	246.2	308.9	57.95	42.05
Program & Tax	659.9	735.2	63.95	36.05
Recoveries	20.6	22.9	26.35	73.65
Total	885.5	1,021.2	63.05	36.95

1. Provincial and federal combined.

2. Average over the two years of previous column.

Source: Agriculture Canada – Policy Branch, 1993: 31, 32

Table D-3 compares the amount of government support in the form of payments to producers, composed primarily of the direct commodity programs referred to above, with market receipts. It provides a partial assessment of the contribution of government support to farmers' incomes, and therefore to total production cost. Government payments to producers represent between 15% and 20% of the total cash receipts of farmers in Quebec and Canada. The table also shows that agriculture in Quebec is more specialized in livestock than agriculture in Canada as a whole.

7. Recoveries are made of items such as licences and leases paid by farmers to governments. See note at the bottom of Table D-2.

TABLE D-3
**Composition of Farmers' Cash Receipts
(1992 (forecast))**

	Quebec		Canada	
	$ million	**%**	**$ million**	**%**
Crop Receipts	716	18.9	8,161	35.1
Livestock Receipts	2,422	64.6	11,254	48.4
Total Market Receipts	3,138	83.5	19,415	83.5
Program Payments	622	16.5	3,831	16.5
Total Cash Receipts	3,760	100.0	23,246	100.0

Source: Agriculture Canada – Policy Branch, 1993: 2.

When all forms of government support are included, the Table D-3 percentages nearly double. As Table D-4 indicates, the resulting figure is of the order of 30% for Quebec and Canada. Table D-4 also gives a more detailed breakdown by category of products than Table D-2. The highest levels of support are recorded for Supply Management products: dairy, eggs and poultry. Here, support mainly takes the form of market price regulation with quotas on imports and domestic production to sustain prices.

TABLE D-4
**Total Support (including border protection) to Farm Commodities
Quebec, Canada 1991/92**
(in % of value of production[1])

	Quebec	Canada
Livestock/Red Meats	15.88	9.90
Grains & Oilseeds	32.56	42.97
Supply Management	46.81	45.90
Forages	8.88	10.22
Special Crops	20.48	30.07
Horticulture	22.17	20.67
All Commodities	31.39	31.99

1. Measured as a three-year average value of production plus direct financial transfers provided by governments, including tax expenditures.

Source: Estimates of financial transfers to producers from expenditure programs and regulation, Agriculture Canada, upon special request.

Sources tend to agree on the order of magnitude of government support to agriculture. The figures reported in Table D-4 were produced by Agriculture

Canada using a methodology very similar to PSE computations. Similar computations by the U.S. Departement of Agriculture produced very similar results. According to this latter source, total support to Canadian agriculture is of the order of 34% (Table D-5), compared with just 23% in the U.S. and Mexico.[8] Differences also exist in the distribution of government support between commodity groups.

TABLE D-5
Percentage Producer Subsidy Equivalent (PSE)
Canada, U.S., Mexico
1982-91 Average

	Canada	U.S.	Mexico
Livestock	35	20	7
Crops	33	27	49
Total	34	23	23

Source: Estimates of producer subsidy equivalents for Canada, Mexico and the United States, USDA, upon special request.

Livestock production receives slightly more support than crop production in Canada, while the reverse is true in the U.S. and even more so in Mexico. The breakdown of total government support by type, as shown in Table D-6, reveals other differences between the three countries. Market price intervention is the main form of support in all three cases. However, in Canada and the United States the next form of support in importance is direct income support, while in Mexico it is input assistance. The picture differs considerably among commodity groups.

TABLE D-6
Percentage Breakdown of total PSE
Canada, U.S., Mexico
1982-91 Average
Total

Forms of Support	Canada	U.S.	Mexico
Market Price Intervention	58 .	42	62
Direct Income Support	23	28	4
Input Assistance	1	12	34
Other[1]	18	18	0
Total	100	100	100

1. Other includes the following: marketing assistance, infrastructures, regional support, economy-wide policies.
Source: See Table D-5.

8. The results reported in Table D-5 were obtained by special request to the USDA. These same results are been presented in summary form in the review *Choices* (Nelson et al., 1994).

A comparison of Table D-7 for crops and Table D-8 for livestock shows that market price intervention is used more extensively for livestock than for crops in all three countries. This is consistent, for Canada and Quebec, with the observations reported in Table D-4 on the relative importance of supply management commodities (all livestock) in total support.

TABLE D-7
**Percentage Breakdown of total PSE
Canada, U.S., Mexico
1982-91 Average
Crops**

Forms of Support	Canada	U.S.	Mexico
Market Price Intervention	40	13	61
Direct Income Support	36	54	5
Input Assistance	2	14	34
Other[1]	22	19	0
Total	100	100	100

1. Other includes the following: marketing assistance, infrastructures, regional support, economy-wide policies.
Source: See Table D-5.

TABLE D-8
**Percentage Breakdown of total PSE
Canada, U.S., Mexico
1982-91 Average
Livestock**

Forms of Support	Canada	U.S.	Mexico
Market Price Intervention	74	72	71
Direct Income Support	11	-1	-1
Input Assistance	1	10	30
Other[1]	14	19	0
Total	100	100	100

1. Other includes the following: marketing assistance, infrastructures, regional support, economy-wide policies.
Source: See Table D-5.

The above qualifications on variations in the amount of support by commodity group are clarified in Table D-9, which shows commodity-specific PSE values ranked from the highest to the lowest. The two commodities in which Quebec agriculture is specialized – dairy and pork – are those for which Canada records its highest rank (the highest of all the country's commodities) and its lowest rank, respectively.

TABLE D-9
Comparison of PSEs by Commodity
1982-91 Average

Country	Commodity	PSE Percentage
Canada	Dairy	69
U.S.	Sugar	60
Mexico	Corn	58
U.S.	Dairy	49
Mexico	Soybeans	48
Mexico	Sorghum	46
U.S.	Rice	44
Canada	Barley	41
U.S.	Wheat	40
Canada	Rye	40
Mexico	Wheat	39
Mexico	Dry beans	38
Mexico	Sesame seed	36
Canada	Wheat	36
U.S.	Barley	36
Mexico	Poultry	32
U.S.	Sorghum	31
Canada	Oats	30
Canada	Rapeseed	28
U.S.	Corn	28
Mexico	Pork	28
Canada	Flaxseed	28
Canada	Sugar	27
Canada	Poultry	22
Canada	Corn	20
Mexico	Cotton	16
Canada	Soybeans	13
Canada	Beef	12
Canada	Pork	11
U.S.	Oats	10
U.S.	Poultry	9
U.S.	Beef and veal	8
U.S.	Soybeans	8
U.S.	Pork	6
Mexico	Dairy	(2)
Mexico	Beef	(5)
Mexico	Eggs	(9)

Source: See Table D-5.

There is no reason to suggest that the figures in Table D-5 and the following tables, which show higher amounts of support in Canada than in the U.S., overestimate support in Canada compared to the U.S. The 1990 figures, as estimated by the OECD, which correspond to the total Canada and U.S. P.S.E. of 34% and 23% reported in Table D-5, are respectively 49% and 27% (OECD, 1994: 126, 155). This shows that U.S. support is significantly lower than the average among OECD countries, while Canadian support is slightly higher.[9]

FREER TRADE AGENDA FOR AGRICULTURAL POLICIES

Extensive government support for domestic production of some commodities and access to foreign markets for those commodities cannot be reconciled as policy choices. FTA and NAFTA provide two more illustrations of this long-standing principle in international trade; commodities which rank first in Table D-9 because of their high level of government support tend also to be those for which exemptions from the more general rules are the most extensive. This is the case particularly for Canadian dairy products and American sugar.

Furthermore, agricultural commodities for which government support is more limited, for instance pork, may still be vulnerable to market access restrictions in the form of countervailing duties.[10] This is the case, for example, when the support they receive is greater than that received by their competitors in the export destination country. Bi-national panels can remove unjustified trade restrictions, but the effect of the original trade disruption remains.

These considerations suggest that the freer trade agenda for agricultural commodities must also include an agenda for domestic policy changes. The elimination of government support in the form of direct payments to producers should be a definite objective for the years ahead. It is not a question of replacing this type of support with more hidden forms. Given the monitoring system in place at the OECD and elsewhere, this would be a fruitless venture.

The issue is a more fundamental one. It is a matter of insuring that production decisions in the agricultural sector are based on needs as revealed by market signals. The current organization of the industry is not always consistent with this approach. An integrated approach to the valuation of farm output is required.

---

9. More precisely, the ratio of U.S. to OECD PSE is 0.63 for 1990 while the ratio of Canada to OECD PSE is 1.14 (OECD, 1994: 129, 155).

10. These duties are applicable when it can be shown that domestic producers suffer material injury from competition by foreign producers who are subsidized by their home governments.

The demand characteristics and output uncertainties that apply to many farm products, especially crops, were mentionned above. Given these factors, few small independent farmers will survive for long with sale revenues wholly based on spot market valuations of their product as it becomes available. The value of farm production originates with the consumer who buys processed products at the end of the value chain. Government support, rather than substituting for spot market valuations that fall too low, should facilitate closer integration of farm output with the value chain.

The use of futures markets provides an initial form of integration. By using these markets to value their products, farm producers rely on commodity specialists who routinely monitor the value of commodities in the value chain. Since the specialists end up bearing much of the risk, they have a strong incentive to do a good job. The strong competition on the futures markets ensures that users benefit from the process.

Futures markets have their limitations, however.[11] Another form of integration in the value chain is closer contracting with product processors. This provides benefits for farm producers in terms of risk sharing, and benefits for processors in terms of better coordination of product standards. Some initiatives in this direction have already been taken, and more should follow (Gagné and Lefèvre, 1993: 233-245; George Morris Center/Food Industry Research Group, 1993).

Government support and protection for farm producers are costly for consumers, in terms of higher prices, and for taxpayers, in terms of higher taxes. However, these costs constitute transfers. More fundamentally, they are costly for the economy and the farm producers themselves, in terms of dependency upon government intervention and lost economic opportunities.

Lost economic opportunities for farm producers take the form of lower quantities demanded by the product processors, who will frequently suffer from negative protection rates.[12] If these issues are dealt with other than by a bold change in the principles guiding government support, this is likely to lead to further restrictions on market access rather than improved market opportunities. A very good example of this are the food processors, especially those using dairy products, following implementation of the FTA.

With the elimination of tariffs on processed foods from the United States, Canadian processors, such as frozen pizza manufacturers who have to pay a higher price for processed farm products like cheese, find themselves at a disadvantage. This was recognized early in the process by an advisory council on

---

11. The many sources on futures markets include Chafin and Hoepner, 1989, and Leuthold, et al., 1989.

12. This will be the case when the benefits from the protection enjoyed by processors are lower than the costs they bear because of the protection given to their input suppliers.

trade agreement adjustment[13] and then by the Canadian Dairy Commission, which in 1991 announced a rebate program to assist "manufacturers that use dairy products as ingredients in finished food products" (OECD, 1994: 126). This kind of measure, which pushes back full integration of farm products in the value chain, can only be temporary.

What this amounts to is cross-subsidization between, on the one hand, a clientele for the product – fresh milk buyers – that is captive because of exemptions in trade agreements or because of high natural barriers to trade in the form of transportation costs, and, on the other hand, the sector exposed to foreign competition. It is closely monitored by trade partners and also by the OECD, which lists it among domestic support measures in its PSE estimates for Canada (OECD, 1994: 126).

As regards freer trade, longer-term prospects for farm production include domestic processing. Processing raises the ratio of unit value to transportation costs, which makes trade more beneficial. Furthermore, with processing the potential for product differentiation grows exponentially, and along with it grows the potential for intra-industry trade, which is much less conducive to frictions than trade in staple products. Greater integration of farm output in the value chain remains a basic condition for taking advantage of these longer-term prospects. Agricultural policies, inasmuch as trade is concerned, should be guided by this objective.

Among agriculture policies, the supply management system, specially as it applies to dairy, is the one most in need of a change. In the country-commodity classification of PSE values (Table D-9), dairy makes Quebec/Canada showing up with the highest level of support in North America. It is not a mere coincidence that dairy products rank among the worst in terms of export performance while pork, which is among the least supported (Table D-9, ranks among the best.

The importance of dairy makes it a central issue of Quebec agricultural policy; more than one-third of farm market receipts in Quebec are for milk production (Table E-1). More than half of this production, basically all uses other than fresh milk for table consumption,[14] is in a critical condition. Its survival under the current regime and, to a lesser degree, the survival of processing activities for poultry, depend upon exemptions embodied in free trade agreements. As time goes on and everybody else must live with the general provisions of trade agreements, these exemptions will become non-defensible.

Supply management regulations should be pro-actively revised. These revisions should insure that farm production is growingly self-supported and

---

13. For further details, see Advisory Council on Adjustment, 1989: 113-124.
14. Tables 2 and 3, Statistics Canada, August 1994, pp. 4, 9.

valued according to market conditions for the processed products further down the values chain, at volumes of sales which reflect production potential. Only those conditions will allow processing activities from milk as well as from poultry produced by Quebec farms to remain possible.

REFERENCES

ADVISORY COUNCIL ON ADJUSTMENT, "Agrifood," in *Adjusting to Win, Report of the Advisory Council on Adjustment*, Ottawa, 1989, pp.113-123.

AGRICULTURE CANADA, *Farm Income Financial Conditions and Government Expenditures Data Book*, Ottawa, August 1993.

CAHILL, C., and W. LEGG, "Estimation of Agricultural Assistance Using Producer and Consumer Subsidy Equivalents: Theory and Practice," *OECD Economic Studies*, No. 13, winter 1989-1990, pp. 13-43.

BALLENGER, N., "PSEs: What They Are and Their Role in Trade Negotiations," *Choices*, first quarter 1988, pp. 36, 37.

BODDEZ, T.M., and M.J. TREBILCOCK, *Unfinished Business: Reforming Trade Remedy Laws in North America*, C.D. Howe Institute, Policy Study 17, Toronto, 1993.

CANADIAN INTERNATIONAL TRADE TRIBUNAL / RESEARCH STAFF, *Competitiveness of the Canadian Cattle and Beef Industries in the North American and World Markets*, Ottawa, August 1993.

CHAFIN, D.G., and P.H. HOEPNER, *Commodity Marketing from a Producer's Perspective*, Interstate Publishers, Illinois, 1989.

JOSLING, T., and R. BARICELLO, "Agriculture in the NAFTA: A Preliminary Assessment," *C.D. Howe Institute Commentary*, The NAFTA Papers, No. 43, April 1993.

JOSLING, T., "NAFTA and Agriculture: A Review of the Economic Impacts," in *North American Free Trade: Assessing the Impact*, ed. by N.Lustig et al., Brookings, Washington, 1992, pp. 144-175.

LEUTHOLD, R.M. et al., *The Theory and Practice of Futures Markets*, Lexington, 1989.

LIPSEY, R.G., D.D. Purvis and P.O. Steiner, *Microéconomique*, Gaëtan Morin, Montreal, 1988.

OECD, *Agricultural Policies, Markets and Trade Monitoring and Outlook 1993*, Paris, 1994.

MEILKE, K.D., "Methods of Measuring Net Benefits for Agriculture," *Canadian Journal of Agricultural Economics*, 39, 1991, pp. 823-834.

NELSON, F.J., et al., "Agricultural Subsidies in Canada, Mexico, and United States, 1982-91," *Choices*, first quarter 1994.

QUEBEC DEPARTMENT OF AGRICULTURE, FISHERIES AND FOOD, *Profil sectoriel de l'industrie bioalimentaire au Québec, édition 1993*, Quebec, 1993.

STATISTICS CANADA, *The Diary Review,* cat. 23-005, Ottawa, August 1994.

SUITS, D.B., "Agriculture," in *The Structure of American Industry*, edited by W. Adams, 6th ed., Macmillan, pp. 1-35.

WEISS, L.W., ed., "Pure Competition in Agriculture," in *Case Studies in American Industry*, 3rd ed., John Wiley & Sons, New York, 1980, pp. 31-89.

14

Public Culture and Political Culture

Kevin V. Mulcahy
Louisiana State University

Quebec's ministry of culture and its cultural policy merit intellectual consideration for a variety of reasons that relate both to the administrative structures
involved and the political importance of culture in debates about the future of
Canada.

- Quebec's arts agency is the only cabinet-level department of cultural
  affairs within North America.

- Per capita expenditure in support of the arts in Quebec is higher than
  federal and other provincial expenditures despite a generally lower level
  of economic development.

- From its creation in 1961 until 1993, what is now termed the
  Ministère de la Culture et des Communications in Quebec has been
  administered along lines more similar to the French model of direct
  state management. The recent creation of the Conseil des Arts et des
  Lettres represents a shift to "arm's length" administration of the arts.

- Quebec's cultural policy has long been at the center of debates over
  the character of its political culture. Support for cultural activities has
  involved questions about their relation to the expression of a Quebecois
  cultural identity.

In sum, Quebec's ministry of culture represents an important case study
of public administration and arts policy-making. First, there has been a significant, and historically unique, shift in the mode of cultural administration with
the creation of an independent, or arm's length, advisory council on the arts.

Second, public support for the arts in Quebec has had a political significance because of the association of cultural values with debates about the future of nationalism. Any cultural policy will also involve issues of cultural politics within the Canadian federal system.

In the period 1990-93, Quebec went through a theoretically self-conscious, administratively innovative, and artistically sensitive revision of its cultural policy. This new *politique culturelle* will be elaborated here with reference to five elements of public policy-making. First, what constitutes the political theory that underlies Quebec's cultural policy; second, what is the role of the ministry of culture in the administration of public culture; third, what will be the "arm's-length" relationship between the ministry and the cultural milieu; fourth, what will be the extent of cultural development and diffusion. Finally, some observations will be offered about the relationship between Quebec's cultural politics and the political culture of a "distinct society."

PRINCIPLES OF THE CULTURAL POLICY

The new cultural policy was promulgated in 1992 by the *Act respecting the Ministère de la Culture*[1] and the *Act respecting the Conseil des Arts et des Lettres du Québec*.[2] Preceding this legislation was a two-year-long process of policy development involving independent analysis and review and a publicly-conducted inquiry that culminated in the ministry's official *politique culturelle*. The process began with proposals for a Quebec cultural policy by a council of private citizens who held prominent positions in the cultural community. The advisory group was chaired by Roland Arpin, who is general manager of the Musée de la Civilisation (a government supported institution devoted to Quebec's *patrimoine* or cultural heritage) and a former deputy minister of cultural affairs. The *Arpin Report* of June, 1991 provided a philosophical and theoretical framework as well as a detailed set of recommendations. These recommendations were further elaborated in a series of hearings before a Parliamentary Committee on Culture for eight weeks in the fall of 1991, with the participation of 181 organizations and 264 witnesses; and formalized by the staff of the cultural ministry in June, 1992 into the first comprehensive plan for the future of Quebec's commitment to public culture.

The *Arpin Report* was rooted in three basic assumptions about the proper place of cultural policy as a public policy. First, that culture is an essential public good and the cultural dimension is necessary for the life of a society. Second, that cultural activities need to be accessible to all citizens. Third, that the state has the obligation to support and promote the cultural dimension of

1. Bill 52, National Assembly, second session, thirty-fourth legislature, December 22, 1992.
2. Bill 53, National Assembly, second session, thirty-fourth legislature, December 22, 1992.

society.[3] Arpin has said that the report could be summarized as a proposal "to put culture at the heart of things, at the same level as the social and economic missions of the state."[4]

To further these goals, the Arpin Report recommended that a cultural policy for Quebec should proceed along three broad lines.

The first is to develop the cultural world by policies that encourage artistic creation, maintain the professional quality of cultural industries, protect intellectual property and assure the stability and *épanouissement* (blossoming) of cultural institutions.[5]

Secondly, in order to encourage access to the life of culture, there should be a heightened emphasis on arts education for adults and children and a concerted program of cultural development in the regions that favors both local heritage and contemporary artistic works.[6]

Finally, to increase the effectiveness of the government in the management of its cultural mission, the cultural ministry should concentrate on elaborating the overall policy, filling the role of initiator, assuring support for the arts, and functioning increasingly as a *ministère d'intervention*: coordinating its partners in other ministries, local governments, arts organizations, the artistic milieu and the private sector.[7]

Overall, the cultural ministry was to be marked by three broad directions: to effect an integrated effort with other governmental departments in related areas; to decentralize the powers of the ministry and to devolve its services to the regions; and for the Quebec government (through the ministry) to be solely responsible for public support of the arts.[8]

The fullest official expression of the political underpinnings of Quebec's cultural policy is found in the 1992 report of the ministry of cultural affairs,

---

3. *Une politique de la culture et des arts du Québec*. Proposition présentée à la ministre par le groupe-conseil sur la politique culturelle du Québec sous la présidence de M. Roland Arpin (Les Publications du Québec, 1991), p. 51. Hereafter referred to as the *Arpin Report*. Interview with M. Arpin, Managing Director, Musée de la Civilisation, August 18, 1993.

4. "...inscrire la culture au coeur du projet, à la même hauteur que les missions sociales et économique de l'État." Roland Arpin, "Enjeux de la politique de la culture du Québec," *Revue française d'administration publique*, 65 (janvier-mars, 1993), p. 45. Hereafter referred to as "Stakes of Cultural Policy." Interview with Gerald Grandmont, Research Director, Musée de la Civilisation, July 17, 1993.

5. *Arpin Report*, pp. 53-106.

6. *Ibid.*, pp. 107-176.

7. *Ibid.*, pp. 177-290.

8. *Ibid.*, p. 30.

Notre Culture, Notre Avenir. Our Culture, Our Future[9] specifies three general orientations of the cultural policy: affirmation of cultural identity as an issue concerning society as a whole; support for artists and the arts; promotion of access to and participation by individuals in Quebec's cultural life. These three foci are directed to the needs of three distinct clienteles: society, artists and individuals. Government policy directions and objectives have been designed to take into account each clientele's concerns within each focus.[10] (See Figure 1.)

FIGURE 1

**Cultural Objectives and Directions
by Sector in Quebec's Cultural Policy**

I.	**Sector**	– Society
	Objectives	– Affirmation of Cultural Identity
	Directions	– Promote French language
		Preserve Cultural heritage
		Strengthen inter-cultural dialogue
II.	**Sector**	– Artistic Community
	Objectives	– Support for Artists and the Arts
	Directions	– Encourage artistic creation
		Improve working conditions of artists
		Ensure the stability of arts organizations
		Develop cultural industries
III.	**Sector**	– Individual
	Objectives	– Increased Access to Culture
	Directions	– Strengthen arts education
		Facilitate Access
		Promote participation

The first focus of the cultural policy is the affirmation of Quebec's cultural identity. This is to be realized "through the promotion of the French language as a means of expressing culture and gaining access to it," the preservation of the cultural heritage and intercultural dialogue.[11]

Certainly, there is no question of the centrality of language as a component of cultural identity. What primarily defines Quebec culture is its French-speaking character; "Quebec is identified first and foremost with the French fact." "In particular, the French language characterizes Quebec's cultural uniqueness in North America. Its importance for the future of Quebec and

9. *La politique culturelle du Québec: notre culture, notre avenir. Quebec's Cultural Policy: Our Culture, Our Future* (Gouvernement du Québec, Ministère des Affaires culturelles, 1992). Hereafter referred to as *Notre Culture, Notre Avenir.*
10. *Ibid.*, p. 101.
11. *Ibid.*, p. 21.

Quebecers is decisive."[12] French is the official language of Quebec and its promotion is a reminder that the vast majority of Quebec's citizens share French culture. Accordingly, Quebec's cultural policy intends to foster the dissemination and consumption of French-language cultural products.

The presentation of Quebec heritage is the oldest field of cultural intervention in which the government has been engaged. The three state museums – the Musée du Quebec, the Musée d'art contemporain and the Musée de la Civilisation – as well as the Centre de conservation du Québec, the Bibliothèque nationale, the Archives nationales, and the Grand Théâtre de Québec are "national" institutions established "to preserve, restore and disseminate Quebec's heritage in the interests of society as a whole."[13] It is the particular mission of these state museums, along with the 342 other cultural institutions that constitute Quebec's museum network, to make this cultural heritage accessible to the citizenry. The need was also expressed to insure that the regions and municipalities would have access to their indigenous history and heritage.

"Quebec society is first and foremost French-speaking, but not exclusively so."[14] Through its cultural initiatives, the government will seek to foster dialogue among the various communities that make up Quebec's society – most noticeably English-speaking Quebecois and the indigeneous (Amerindian and Inuit) peoples. Furthermore, intercultural exchanges are designed to bolster the presence of Quebec's cultural products in the international art network and to foster a *culture mondiale* rather than a *culture provinciale*.

The second objective of the cultural policy is support for artists and the arts. The specific policy goals include recognizing the centrality of artistic creation and the financial and professional independence of artists, implementing a strategy for the development of cultural industries, ensuring the vitality of arts organizations and their economic stability. These goals are in themselves rather conventional aspects of a cultural policy. However, *Notre Culture, Notre Avenir* recommended a major overhaul in the administrative machinery that dispenses the public funding to autonomous arts organizations.[15] For example, public funding for arts organizations is to be placed on a three-year rather than an annual basis.[16] Given the extent to which any arts organization in Quebec is dependent on public support – between 30 and 45 percent – this would provide an important measure of financial stability. This is particularly true for the newer, more locally-oriented, budgetarily smaller organizations that have the greatest dependence on public subsidy.

---

12. *Ibid.*, pp. 16, 21.
13. *Ibid.*, p. 31.
14. *Ibid.*, p. 39.
15. *Ibid.*, p. 61.
16. *Ibid.*, p. 62.

Most important, Quebec's cultural policy proposes to further guarantee the autonomy of the artistic community through the creation of an arts council as an independent management agency responsible for elaborating and implementing specific programs of artistic creation in the visual arts, multidisciplinary and multimedia sectors, literature, performing arts, variety shows, crafts, architectural research.[17] (The new arts council will be discussed in detail in a subsequent section.)

The cultural policy's third objective is to facilitate greater individual access to, and participation in, the arts. Accomplishing this objective involves the cultural ministry in a variety of cooperative ventures with other governmental entities.

- Implementing, under the aegis of the ministry of education, a plan to revitalize arts education through support for school projects aimed at encouraging the cultural development of all students and, as part of a review of basic school regulations, a reexamination of the place of the arts in the curriculum.

- Entering into agreements with private radio and television networks, such as those with Radio-Quebec, to play a leading role in cultural education through a stable presence in arts programming.

- Setting up a touring office responsible for increasing the circulation of the works, exhibitions and live performances of the State cultural institutions in the different regions of Quebec.

- Elaborating, in collaboration with the regions, master plans that pinpoint each region's priorities with respect to the development of libraries, archives, performance halls, cinemas, museums, exhibition centers and heritage interpretation sites.

- Devising, in collaboration with the ministry of recreation, fish and game, measures to insure that groups involved in cultural leisure activities have access to professional expertise.[18]

Overall, the new cultural policy seeks to inaugurate a new philosophy of administration for the ministry of culture. The disappearance of direct management of programs in support of the arts and the heightened emphasis on decentralization and local cultural development is designed to transform the cultural ministry into a *ministère d'impulsion*, that is, one that provides the impetus for local efforts and partnership with the municipalities and other public agencies concerned with cultural life. The ministry's relations with the cultural community are to be governed by the long-demanded arm's-length principle and the substitution of a broad policymaking power for the narrow power of

---

17. *Ibid.*, pp. 47, 51.
18. *Ibid.*, pp. 80-81, 86, 89.

budgetary decisionmaking. Finally, with this new cultural policy, the state assumes responsibility for the insertion of the citizenry into the culture scene through increased availability of the arts, especially at the local level.[19]

THE MINISTRY OF CULTURE

The creation of the Ministère des Affaires culturelles (ministry of cultural affairs) in 1961 by the reformist government of Jean Lesage distinguished Quebec as the only government entity in North America to have a cabinet-level department dedicated to support for the arts. The Arts Council of Canada was founded in 1957, but is located in the Department of Communications, as are most of the provincial arts councils. The American National Endowment for the Arts, founded in 1965, is an independent executive agency of the federal governement, but its chairman does not have cabinet status and its policy-making powers are decidedly limited. Typically, state arts councils are administered like the National Endowment. From 1961-92 the administration of culture in Quebec was in a direct and centralized fashion as in France; the other governments have used "arm's length" administrative systems like the British Arts Council. The new Conseil des arts et lettres du Québec is an "arm's length" agency that will be discussed presently.

The Minister of Culture and Communications (to use the 1994 designation) is an elected member of the 125-member National Assembly and has often been a person of some political prominence in the cabinet. Premier Parizeau himself held the job for the first six months of the Parti québécois government elected in 1994. The first minister in the Lesage government, Georges-Émile Lapalme, was simultaneously attorney-general and a past leader of the Liberal Party; a more recent minister, Lise Bacon, was deputy premier in the Bourassa government. Camille Laurin, the minister of state for cultural development in the Lévesque government, was the author of Bill 101, the Charter of the French language in Quebec.

Starting with the Quiet Revolution (*la révolution tranquille*) in 1960, Quebec governments – Liberal, Union Nationale, Parti québécois – have sought to replace the long-dominant influence of the English-speaking minority with a self-confident and modernized cultural identity. This revolution has largely been won and the *épanouissement* of Quebec's artistic and intellectual life transformed a provincial culture into one with an international standing. As *The Economist* observed in 1987, "Although officially one of Canada's ten provinces, Quebec is, in cultural terms, a nation."[20]

---

19. See Arpin, "Stakes of Cultural Policy," pp. 46-48; see also "Politique culturelle du Québec: Un an déjà," *Municipalité*, November, 1993, pp. 31-32.

20. *Economist*, November 28, 1987, p. 95.

What clearly distinguishes Quebec's cultural policy from the rest of Canada is the magnitude of its support for the arts and arts organization. Table 1 shows provincial spending on culture in relation to total spending. With cultural spending amounting to 0.74% of total public expenditures, Quebec ranks first among the ten provinces with Ontario second. The ministry of culture's share of the government's budget has also grown steadily in the past decade from 0.5% in the early 1980s to its current level. This spending level compares favorably with the 1.00% of budget goal realized by Jack Lang when he was minister of culture in France during the Socialist governments of the 1980s.

TABLE 1
**Provincial Spending on Culture and the Cultural Budget
as a % of Total Budget***

Provinces	Cultural Budget ($ million)	Total Budget ($ million)	%
Quebec	259.5	34,993.6	.74
Ontario	283.5	42,057.2	.67
Alberta	99.3	14,492.7	.68
All Provinces & Territories	852.9	128,014.2	.67

* Expenditures on radio and television broadcasting are not included. All figures expressed here are in Canadian dollars. For the period discussed, $1.00 U.S. = $1.20 C.

Source: Ministère des Affaires culturelles, Direction de la Recherche et de la Statistique, 1991.

Quebec's support for the arts and culture is decidedly superior to that of the federal government of Canada. Table 2 shows support for culture in Quebec by level of government. Some 47% of cultural spending is done by the government of Quebec, 31% by the government of Canada, and 22% by the municipalities. Moreover, while the budget of the ministry of culture has increased markedly over the past two decades, the Canada Council has shown only modest increases. Where federal and Quebec government spending was about equal in 1970, the Canada Council's budget in 1990 of about $100 million was less than half the approximately $230 million budget of the ministry of culture. Table 3 shows the evolution of the budget of the ministry of cultural affairs from 1971-72 to 1991-92, along with the annual variation, and the cultural budget as a percentage of the total budget. If one adjusts for inflation and follows the budget in constant dollars, the spending increases are not nearly so dramatic. Nonetheless, the budget allocation for the ministry of cultural affairs still had a four fold increase over twenty years, compared to a total budget that was two and a half times greater.[21]

---

21.   *Arpin Report*, p. 242.

TABLE 2
Support for Culture in Quebec by Level of Government (1990)*

	$ Millions	%
Government of Quebec $232 M (29%) for the Ministère des Affaires culturelles	422	47
Government of Canada $145 M (16%) for Telefilm Canada/National Film Office	283	31
Municipalities $100 M (11%) for libraries	200	22
Total	905	100

* Funds for public broadcasting of Radio-Quebec and Radio-Canada are not included.

Source: *Une politique de la culture et des arts du Québec*. Proposition présentée à la ministre par le groupe-conseil sur la politique culturelle du Québec sous la présidence de M. Roland Arpin (Les Publications du Québec, 1991), p. 239-40.

TABLE 3
Evolution of the Budget of the Ministry of Cultural Affairs, 1971/1972 – 1991/1992

Year	Cultural Budget	Variation	% of Total Budget	Total Budget of Quebec
1971/1972	19,153,000	12.61	0.42	4,543,808,000
1972/1973	18,204,000	–4.95	0.39	4,656,910,000
1973/1974	21,540,000	18.33	0.40	5,402,707,000
1974/1975	30,706,000	42.55	0.42	7,289,266,000
1975/1976	38,958,000	26.87	0.43	9,027,710,000
1976/1977	45,586,000	17.01	0.43	10,596,504,000
1977/1978	60,405,000	32.51	0.51	11,774,931,000
1978/1979	67,318,000	11.45	0.49	13,877,871,000
1979/1980	70,567,000	4.83	0.46	15,360,837,000
1980/1981	99,977,000	41.68	0.56	17,760,134,000
1981/1982	108,705,000	8.73	0.52	20,712,872,000
1982/1983	120,379,000	10.74	0.51	23,547,306,000
1983/1984	127,222,000	5.68	0.51	25,105,579,000
1984/1985	142,788,000	12.24	0.55	26,113,061,000
1985/1986	177,904,000	24.59	0.64	27,686,339,000
1986/1987	173,335,000	–2.57	0.60	29,022,553,000
1987/1988	182,785,000	5.45	0.59	30,800,903,000
1988/1989	221,264,000	21.05	0.69	32,022,642,000
1989/1990	234,403,000	5.94	0.71	33,213,000,000
1990/1991	261,800,000	11.69	0.72	36,477,000,000
1991/1992	288,700,000	10.27	0.74	38,863,507,000

Source: Ministère des Affaires culturelles, Direction de la recherche et de la statistique, 1991.

The cultural ministry's budget has been allocated among four programmatic categories: (1) planning, evaluation, and internal management; (2) development of the cultural milieux; (3) national institutions; (4) state cultural organizations. Table 4 details the funds allocated for each category as a percentage of the total budget.

(1) The 14% of the ministry's budget that goes for planning, evaluation, and management includes the cost of administering the programs as well as the planning and evaluation component, which is a major emphasis of the new cultural policy. In particular, the director-general of planning assists the Minister in developing a general policy orientation and will evaluate its implementation.[22]

(2) Part of the responsibility for development of the cultural milieux has been transferred to the new Conseil des Arts et Lettres with $42,000,000 for grants to artists and arts organizations.

(3) The national institutions supported are the Archives nationales, the Centre de conservation du Québec and a regional network of conservatories of music and dramatic arts. One of the goals of the cultural policy is to transform all of these institutions into autonomous cultural organizations.

(4) The state cultural organizations are autonomous institutions that receive most of their general operationg expenses from the ministry. These include the Bibliothèque nationale, the state museums (the Musée d'art contemporain and the Musée du Québec), the Société de la Place des Arts de Montréal and the Grand Théâtre de Québec as well as the Société générale des industries culturelles (SOGIC) which has been reorganized under the cultural plan as the Société de développement des entreprises culturelles (SODEC) and will be discussed presently.

TABLE 4
The Cultural Budget By Programmatic Element, 1992-1993

Program 1:	Planning, Evaluation and Internal Management	$45,857,000 14.13%
Program 2:	Development of the Cultural Milieux	$133,597,400 41.18%
Program 3:	National Institutions	$23,235,300 7.16%
Program 4:	State Organizations and Societies	$121,774,000 37.53%

Source: Ministère de la Culture, *Rapport annuel, 1992-1993*, p. 13.

---

22.   Interview with Marie-Claire Lévesque, Director-General of Planning, Ministère de la Culture, August 18, 1993.

Figure 2 represents a summarized organization chart of the ministry of culture. Approximately 550 people work for the ministry proper (after the transfer of about 50 persons from the Direction générale des arts, des lettres et des industries culturelles to the new Arts Council); of these, about 50 are senior civil servants, 250 are in the professional category and 250 are office workers. There are an additional 200 civil servants in the conservatories of music and dramatic arts; 100 of these are teachers.[23] These figures do not include the personnel of the formally independent ministry of communications.

FIGURE 2
Summary Organization Chart of the Ministry of Culture

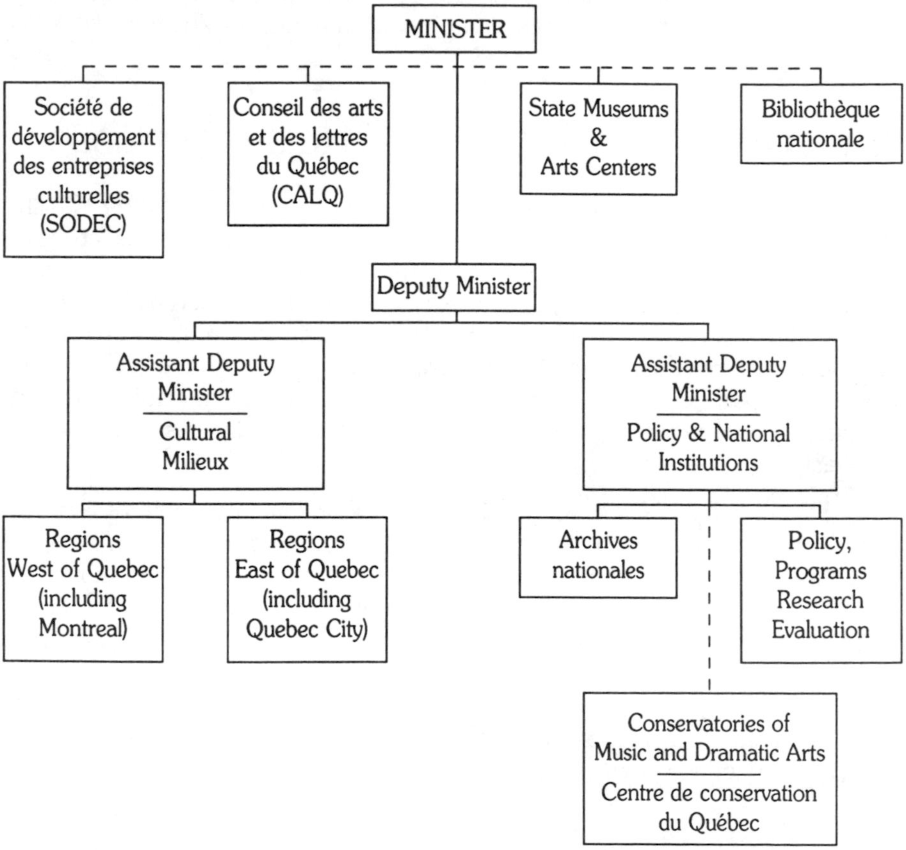

Source: Adapted from Ministère de la Culture, *Rapport annuel*, pp. 34-35, and *Livre d'ici*, 19 (April, 1994), p. 25.

23. Ministère de la Culture, *Rapport annuel*, *1992-93*, p. 11.

In sum, the overall goal of the reorganized ministry of culture is fourfold.[24]

(1) to remove the ministry from "hands on" administration of grant-making activities and the management of institutions;

(2) to devolve grantmaking responsibility to an independent entity (the Conseil) so as to create a "buffer" between the ministry and its clientele;

(3) to facilitate the diffusion of opportunities for cultural participation to the regions and to assist in the development of for-profit cultural enterprises;

(4) to permit the ministry to focus on cultural constituencies in the regions and, most important, on programmatic evaluation and policy planning.

THE CONSEIL DES ARTS ET LETTRES DU QUÉBEC

The "pièce de résistance" of the new cultural policy according to the Minister responsible for its creation, Liza Frulla, is the Conseil des arts et des lettres du Québec (CALQ).[25] The importance of CALQ cannot be overestimated as it represents not only the formation of a new entity for the administration of public cultural programs, but also a profound shift in the political philosophy guiding arts administration in Quebec. Essentially, the law that established the Conseil in 1992 reflected a more basic decision to replace a centralized form of cultural decision-making with what has been characterized as "arm's length administration."

The mandate of the council involves the always contentious issue of awarding grants to artistic creators and not-for-profit arts organizations. Essentially, the ministry of culture has devolved to the Arts Council responsibility for the annual process of discretionary grant-making. In 1993-94, this amounted to $42 million (or almost one-third of the ministry's budget before the addition of public broadcasting in 1994). However, the council is not just in the business of allocating grants. It also exists to interpret the ministry's overall policy orientation and guidelines as these affect the cultural milieu and to serve as the cultural community's spokesman to the ministry.[26]

---

24. Interviews with Louise Bourassa, Department of Intergovernmental Relations, Ministère de la Culture, July 24, 1993, and Gérald Grandmont, Director of the Research Department, Musée de la Civilisation, July 18, 1993. See also André Giroux, "Le train quitte le quai," *Livre d'ici*, 19 (April 1994), p. 22.

25. *Le Devoir*, May 12, 1993.

26. Interview with Guy Morin, President-Director-General of the Conseil des arts et des lettres du Québec, August 17, 1993.

The council, then, is an autonomous public agency that awards grants to individual and institutional applicants pursuant to the general orientation of the ministry's cultural policy. The head of the Arts Council is appointed by the minister of culture after consultation with the Premier of Quebec and the cabinet. With the title president-director general, Guy Morin, who was appointed in 1993, is both the chief executive officer and the chief administrative officer of CALQ; that is, he administers the grant-making process and chairs the twelve-member advisory council.

Accordingly, he wears "two hats": first, as the official accountable for managing the council's 60-member staff (for the most part, former functionaries of the ministry of culture) and for selecting and coordinating the members of the advisory panels from the various artistic disciplines (music, theater, dance, visual arts, literature); second, as the chair of the body appointed by the Minister to serve on a volunteer basis to represent the arts community and as the council spokesman to the ministry on the concerns of the cultural milieu. (Figure 3 diagrams the organization of cultural policy-making in Quebec.)

FIGURE 3
The Organization of Cultural Policy-making in Quebec

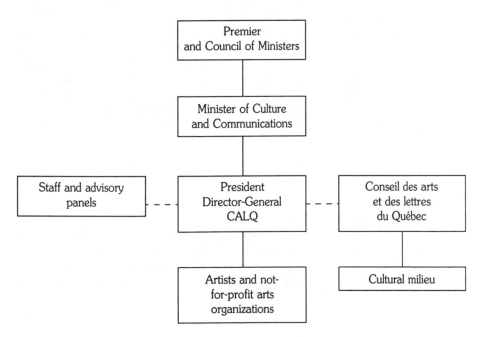

In the appointment of Guy Morin and the twelve members of the council, there appears to be wide agreement that the selection is broadly representative of the arts community of Quebec. Morin is past director-general of the Place des Arts de Montréal (comparable to the Kennedy Center) and a former president of the Société générale des industries culturelles (SOGIC). The appointments to the council are clearly designed to represent the diverse artistic disciplines and to achieve a balance between men and women and among the different regions of Quebec.[27] One newspaper headline spoke of this as a "dream council," in which "everyone works astonishingly well together because they know each other and share the same objectives."[28] The council, which meets monthly, is composed of half men and half women; a little more than half are from Montreal and the rest from Quebec City and the regions; of the artistic disciplines, 3 members are associated with music, 3 with theater, 1 with dance, 2 with literature, 3 with the visual arts; in addition to their artistic professions, most of the appointees are managing and/or artistic directors of arts organizations and three are academics.

The members of the council by artistic disciplines and institutional affiliations are as follows:[29]

> Monique Mercure, actress, Managing Director of the National Theater School; Ginette Laurin, choreographer, Managing and Artistic Director of the "O Vertigo" dance company; Marie Laberge, author, actress; Jovette Marchessault, writer, sculptor, President of the Conseil de la culture de l'Estrie; Élise Paré-Tousignant, teacher at the school of music at Université Laval, Artistic Director of the Domaine Forget de Charlevoix; William Saint-Hilaire, musician, Managing Director of the chamber orchestra "I Musici de Montréal"; Guy Rodgers, scriptwriter, Managing Director of the Fédération d'art dramatique du Québec; Melvin Charney, artist, architect, Full Professor of Architecture at the Université de Montréal; Jean-Claude Germain, writer, dramatist, historian; Luc Plamondon, songwriter and author of musicals, President of the Société professionnelle des auteurs-compositeurs du Québec; Giles Maheu, author, Artistic Director of "Troupe Carbone 14"; Godefroy Cardinal, Full Professor at the Université du Québec à Montréal, and an art gallery director.

For evaluating the nature of this new mode of arts administration in Quebec, it is important to note certain aspects of the policy-making arrangements.

First, the council is an autonomous agency, but not one that has complete independence. While having authority over the allocation of grants to individual artists and arts organizations with the advice of panels of jurors, the council functions under the policy umbrella of the ministry of culture.[30] Put another way, the ministry determines the orientation of cultural policy, while

---

27. *Le Soleil*, August 13, 1993.

28. *Le Soleil*, February 25, 1994.

29. *Bulletin du Conseil de la peinture du Québec*, 58 (December, 1993), p. 7.

30. *Le Soleil*, December 18, 1993.

the council makes specific applications in the grants that are awarded.[31] It has also been noted that the president-director general and the council's members are ministerial appointees with the former serving a three- to four-year term and the latter serving for three-year terms.

Second, the double role of Guy Morin as president and director-general has been the subject of some criticism on the grounds that such an arrangement undermines the Arts Council's "arm's- length" relation with the ministry of culture.[32] It should be noted that the law that created the council is explicit about having a president-director general; that is, someone who would serve simultaneously as chairman and managing director or chief executive officer and chief administrative officer.[33] This is also the case in the United States, where the chairman of the National Endowment for the Arts wears two hats as the agency's chief and the chair of the presidentially-appointed National Council on the Arts for its six-times-a-year meetings. On the other hand, state arts councils have executive directors distinct from council chairmen. Clearly, there is no one form of "arm's length" administration. Moreover, as will be discussed shortly, while Quebec's arm's length cultural policy-making has been constructed as a major departure from French-style centralized administration, it is different from both the National Endowment and the Canada Council. Basically, the Council is an arm's length agency, but closer to ministerial control than a pure model would suggest.[34]

Third, some members of the arts community have expressed dissatisfaction with CALQ's new grant-making process. As *Le Devoir* observed, "Very quickly, a section of the artistic milieu, instead of thanking Mme Frulla for the program, has begun to complain publicly that the organization will be too subservient to the minister."[35] For his part, Guy Morin has pledged to survey the opinion of all the arts disciplines about establishing a permanent decision-making process during a five-year period of laying the council's foundations. "The artists themselves will be deciding their priorities from now on."[36] Moreover, the fundamental change for the cultural community in the making of

31. Interview with Roland Arpin, Managing Director of the Musée de la Civilisation, August 18, 1993.

32. Serge Turgeon, President of the Union des artistes, "Le fait de nommer un président-directeur général et non un président me semble a priori relever d'une certaine volonté du gouvernement de diminuer la distance (arm's length) entre elle et le conseil." *Le Devoir*, July 11, 1993.

33. *An Act respecting the Conseil des arts et des lettres du Québec*, p. 4.

34. *Le Devoir*, May 12, 1993.

35. *Le Devoir*, May 14, 1993. "Mais rapidement, une section du milieu artistique, au lieu de remercier Mme Frulla pour son beau programme, s'est publiquement plainte de ce que l'organisme serait trop inféodé à la ministre."

36. *La Presse*, July 9, 1993. "Les artistes décideront désormais eux-mêmes de leurs priorités."

government decisions is that "the council permits artists and arts organizations to have a voice close to the government."[37]

A great deal of emphasis has been placed in the creation of CALQ on its provenance as an "arm's length" institution similar to the Arts Council of Great Britain (1945) and the Canada Council on the Arts (1958). Yet, what exactly is meant by "arm's length" administration? And, to what extent does the Quebec situation approximate such a model?

With arm's length arts councils, a *Patron State* determines the aggregate level of government support, although not which artists or arts organizations should be supported. The council is appointed by the government, but acts as a board of trustees in making grants while usually relying on the advice of arts professionals in making their decisions. The Arts Council of Great Britain was the first arm's length council and was organized in this fashion to distance the arts from government and bureaucracy. The Canada Council for the Encouragement of the Arts was created as an arm's length council on the advice of the 1951 Royal Commission on National Development in the Arts, Letters and Sciences which recommended the British model while rejecting directing funding of the arts through a ministry of culture. Other provinces, including Saskatchewan, Manitoba, Ontario and Newfoundland, have adopted the British model, as well as a number of Canadian cities including Vancouver, Toronto, Ottawa and Montreal. Other Commonwealth countries with arm's length councils include New Zealand and Australia.[38]

By contrast, the Architect State funds the arts through a ministry of culture. Granting decisions concerning artists and arts organizations are generally made by ministerial functionaries. The *Architect State* tends to support culture as part of more general public policy objectives and often with a great emphasis on community, rather than professional, development.[39]

The role of Architect originated with the monarchies of the seventeenth century that sought to celebrate the grandeur of their dynasties. The most notable example is Louis XIV, who, with his principal minister Colbert, supported theater, music and the visual arts, undertook major building projects in Paris and, of course, created a visual manifestation of *la gloire de France* and

---

37. *Le Soleil*, December 18, 1993. "Le CALQ doit permettre aux artistes et organismes d'avoir une voix auprès du gouvernement."

38. Harry Hillman-Chartrand and Claire McCaughey, "The Arm's Length Principle and the Arts: An International Perspective – Past, Present and Future," in Milton C. Cummings, Jr. and J. Mark Davidson Schuster, Editors, *Who's to Pay for the Arts: The International Search for Models of Support* (New York: American Council on the Arts, 1987), pp. 153-57. This discussion is heavily indebted to the theoretical analysis of Hillman-Chartrand and McCaughey.

39. *Ibid*, pp. 49-50.

le roi soleil at Versailles through architecture, decoration and landscape. The conjunction of art and state at Versailles was widely imitated throughout Europe by Frederick the Great of Prussia, Catherine the Great of Russia and a myriad of lesser princelings such as the rulers of Saxony and Bavaria. In France, to this day, the Presidents of the Republic have taken a great interest in the arts, as exemplified by the Centre Pompidou and the *grand projets* of François Mitterrand – The Musée d'Orsay, the renovated Louvre, the new Bibliothèque nationale. Mitterrand's very visible minister of culture, Jack Lang, initiated an ambitious program of public support for literary, media, visual and performing arts with a particular emphasis on cultural development in the regions and among underserved cultural constituencies such as the young and Arab immigrants.[40]

There are two other possible models for arts funding, but these are not relevant to this discussion. The *Facilitator State* is one that stands at the greatest distance in its artistic patronage by relying on tax deductions for contributions to the arts by individuals and corporations. This was the case in the United States before 1965 when the National Endowments for the Arts (NEA) was created.[41] It should be noted that tax deductible contributions for the arts (as part of the not-for-profit sector) are a source of artistic patronage that is not commonly available outside the United States and should be taken into account in any cross-national study of public support for the arts.[42] It should also be noted that the American federal government has long been a patron of the arts in providing line-item appropriations for the various museums in the Smithsonian complex, the National Gallery of Art, the National Archives, the Library of Congress.

The state as cultural Engineer stands to the extreme side of the architect model. The *Engineer State* owns all the means of artistic production, determines who is an artist, and coordinates the aesthetic content of cultural products in accordance with ideological principles. Funding decisions are made by "cultural commissars" and are intended to further political indoctrination; artistic production must adapt to any changes in the party line. The engineer model was used in totalitarian states like Nazi Germany and the Soviet Union. For example, Stalin decreed in the 1930s that the official cultural aesthetic was to provide art that was immediately apprehensible by the masses.

---

40. François Avenas, "La politique culturelle en France depuis 1981," paper presented at the Annual Meeting of the Conference on Social Theory, Politics and the Arts, October 21-23, 1994, Louisiana State University, Baton Rouge, Louisiana.

41. Kevin V. Mulcahy, "Government and the Arts in the United States," in Milton C. Cummings, Jr. and Richard S. Katz, *The Patron State: Government and the Arts in Europe, the United States and Japan* (Baltemore; Johns Hopkins University Press, 1987), pp. 311-32.

42. Margaret J. Wyszomirski and Pat Clubb, Editors, *The Cost of Culture: Patterns and Prospects of Private Arts Patronage* (New York: American Council for the Arts, 1989).

Henceforth, all art produced in the Soviet Union had to be "socialist realism"; that is realist in form and socialist in content. Artistic activity was organized into "creative union" to monitor new works and ensure conformity with the aesthetic principles of the Communist Party. Under this scheme, the social responsibility of the artist lies in "satisfying" the "owners," that is producing works that can be immediately accepted by the masses.[43]

These four models for supporting the arts are summarized in Figure 4.

FIGURE 4
Models for Supporting the Arts

Role	Model Country	Policy Objective	Funding	Artistic Standards
Patron	Great Britain	excellence	arm's length arts council	professional
Architect	France	public policy	ministry of culture	communitarian
Facilitator	USA (before 1965)	diversity	tax deductions	personal
Engineer	Nazi Germany Soviet Union	political indoctrination	ownership of the means of artistic production	ideological

Source: Adapted from Harry Hillman-Chartrand and Claire McCaughey, "The Arm's Length Principle and the Arts: An International Perspective – Past, Present, Future" in Milton C. Cummings, Jr. and J. Mark Davidson Schuster, Editors, *Who's to Pay for the Arts* (New York: American Council for the Arts, 1987), pp. 54-55.

Where does Quebec's cultural policy fit into this scheme? The answer is that Quebec represented a hybrid of the Patron State and the Architect State. Until 1992, Quebec's ministry of culture was clearly based on the French-style, patron-state model. Until the new cultural policy, the ministry directly awarded grants to artists and arts organizations. Inevitably, this led to accusations that the grant-making process was politicized.[44] The creation of the Conseil des arts et des lettres represents an effort to create a distance between arts administration and politics. However, this arm's length relationship does not apply to all the ministry of culture's functions, which still include responsibility for national institutions, regional development and relations with autonomous arts organizations. In particular, the minister of culture will provide the overall policy orientation to guide the council in specific grant determinations. This relationship between the ministry (deciding policy) and the council (making decisions)

43. Hillman-Chartrand and McCaughey, "The Arm's Length Principle," p. 53. See also Kevin V. Mulcahy, "The Case of Dmitri Shostakovich," *Journal of Arts Management and Law.*

44. See, for example, *The (Montreal) Gazette*, August 17, 1993.

has been frequently cited as the distinguishing characteristic of the Quebec model of arts administration.[45] In sum, the council exists to keep politicians and bureaucrats at arm's length as it implements the minister's policy directives. In doing this, the decision-making status of arts grants is upgraded and the council provides the minister with an institutionalized vehicle with which to have a dialogue with the cultural milieu.[46]

DEVELOPMENT AND DIFFUSIONS

The organizational complement to the Conseil des arts et des lettres du Québec is the Société de développement des entreprises culturelles (SODEC) which has replaced it predecessor, the Société générale des industries culturelles (SOGIC), established in 1978.[47] As with many administrative name-changes, the new SODEC reflects a change in policy emphasis. In particular, SODEC has been designed to emphasize the economic impact that the arts have on the economy, especially the film industry.

SODEC is, like its predecessor, an autonomous organization but one that is under the policy umbrella of the ministry of culture. The management and advisory council membership are appointed by the government for fixed terms and the administrative staff is nominated by the cultural industry. Essentially, its mission has been to assist for-profit cultural enterprises through loans at below-market interest rates.[48] SODEC is to work with businesses involved with film, books, communications records and videos, interpretive arts and applied arts. For these enterprises, SODEC is supposed to be the synthesizer and subsidizer in the for-profit arts world as CALQ is for artists and arts organizations in the not-for-profit world.[49]

The often stated purpose of SODEC's creation was (1) to bring the cultural enterprises under the "orientation" of the new cultural policy;[50] (2) to consolidate the various "interventions" of the Ministry in the development of cultural enterprises;[51] (3) to allow this new organization to be less bureaucratic

---

45. This model was frequently cited in interviews at the ministry of culture; for example with Marie-Claire Lévesque, Director-General of Planning; Pierre Lafleur, Assistant Deputy Minister; Louise Bourassa, adviser, Department of Intergovernmental Relations.

46. Interview with Pierre-Denis Cantin, Director-General, Direction générale des arts, des lettres et des industries culturelles, July 27, 1993.

47. *Le Soleil*, June 9, 1994.

48. *Le Soleil*, December 28, 1993.

49. "Création de la Société de développement des entreprises culturelles; Un visage attendu," Communiqué du Cabinet de la Ministre de la Culture et des Communications. April 28, 1994, p. 10.

50. *Ibid.*, p. 11.

51. *Le Devoir*, April 29, 1994.

and more risk-taking in its interventions.[52] In fact, many of the clientele of SODEC claim that its primary mandate is to promote the growth of Quebec's film industry at the expense of other applied arts. This is particularly the case since SODEC will be administered by two directors-general: one for cinema and the other with responsibility for all the other cultural industries. As Lise Bissonette editorialized in *Le Devoir*, "Too bad for the others, SODEC will be the creature of the film industry."[53] (It might be noted here parenthetically that culture is Quebec's sixth largest industry, with expenditures of $3.5 billion and employing 75,000 people directly and 125,000 indirectly.)[54]

As yet, the least developed aspect of Quebec's cultural policy is regional development, particularly the ministry's planned agreements with the municipalities for partnerships in the arts. As with the creation of an arm's- length arts council, collaborative relations between the ministry and the municipalities represents a major change from the traditional top-down administration. As with SODEC and CALQ, the ministry will set the global policy and serve as coordinator while the regions will formulate and manage specific programs.[55] In particular, regional cultural development represents an effort to realize the third axis of Quebec's cultural policy, which is to improve popular access to culture.[56]

For the most part, Quebec's support for the arts has traditionally gone to artistic creators and to national-level arts organizations rather than to the localities and folk arts. Put another way, the ministry's orientation has been "elitist" rather than "populist"; that is, the emphasis has been on artistic excellence and the marketability of cultural products, especially for export. For the future, however, according to Pierre Lafleur, assistant deputy minister in charge of the cultural milieux, "energizing the localities" will be a primary emphasis.[57] Guy Morin, the head of CALQ, describes the policy as "decentralization as well as excellence."[58] Both appear aware that grass-roots and avant-garde interests may not be so easy to serve equally.

---

52. *Le Devoir*, May 5, 1994.

53. *Le Devoir*, May 7, 1994. "Tant pis pour les autres, la Sodec sera la créature du milieu du cinéma."

54. Marie-Agnès Thellier, "Madame Culture voit rouge," *Actualité*, 19 (May 15, 1994): 52.

55. Michelle Courchesne, Deputy Minister, Ministère de la Culture, "Enjeux et défis de la décentralisation de l'action culturelle," in Mario Beaulac and François Colbert, Editors, *Décentralisation, régionalisation et action culturelle municipale* (Montreal: École des Hautes Études commerciales, 1993), p. 363.

56. Marie-Claire Lévesque, Director-General of Planning, Ministère de la Culture, "Le patronage des compétences entre les paliers de pouvoirs publics en matière culturelle du Québec" in *ibid*. p. 235.

57. Interview with Pierre Lafleur, July 28, 1993.

58. Interview with Guy Morin, August 17, 1993.

Municipalities in Quebec have certainly been involved in the promotion of cultural affairs, especially through libraries, concert halls, leisure activities and promoting the local heritage. In particular, "they support cultural events which contribute to giving them a specificity which distinguishes them from neighboring municipalities."[59] According to Marie-Claire Lévesque, Director-General of Planning,

> Our priority will be to make agreements with the cities that assume the role of regional center and which have equipped themselves with a cultural policy or objectives in regard to cultural development.[60]

In sum, the goals of Quebec's cultural policy toward its regions are:

- First, to diffuse artistic opportunities beyond the metropole (Montreal) and the capital (Quebec City) to the 1,500 municipalities that are often in remote areas;

- Second, to create developmental partnerships involving the ministry with any overall policy, CALQ with its support for artists and arts organizations and the municipalities with their local venues;

- Third, to promote local cultural participation and to preserve particular cultural heritages;

- Fourth, to protect the French language and culture.

The next goal that needs to be addressed by Quebec's cultural policy is the future of the arts and letters in the light of the North American Free Trade Agreement (NAFTA) of 1994. In particular, there will be a need to balance the requirements of internal cultural development with those of external cultural diffusion. For example, is the celebration of heritage and local cultural diversity at odds with a global culture that must compete in a hemispheric economy that is overwhelmingly non-francophone? More specifically, will the already overwhelming presence of American culture completely engulf what is left of the cultural uniqueness of its near neighbors? Or has this largely been accomplished anyway, meaning that NAFTA might simply accelerate a process of dominant cultural absorption that has been in effect at least since the 1930s?

Ironically, the traditionally dominant anglophone culture experienced more concern over the possible consequences of NAFTA than did francophone Quebec. Many liberals and intellectuals in English Canada were in vigorous opposition to the 1988 Free Trade Agreement with the United States. "Quebec, on the other hand, hailed the agreement as the greatest development in Canada in the 20th century."[61] There are a number of possible

---

59.   Lévesque in *Décentralisation, régionalisation et action culturelle municipale.*

60.   *Ibid.*

61.   Guy Lachapelle, Gérald Bernier, Daniel Salée, Luc Bernier, *The Quebec Democracy: Structure, Processes and Politics* (Toronto: McGraw-Hill Ryerson, 1993), p. 306.

explanations for Quebec's strong support for free trade, including a residual resentment against the rest of Canada after the failure of the Meech Lake and Charlottetown agreements and a consequent pro-Americanism. More positively, its has been argued that the free trade agreement meant that Quebecers had "come of age." "They felt confident that they had the competence, ability, and expertise to meet successfully the challenges of a highly competitive international environment." It may also be that Quebec's linguistic distinctiveness has given it some insulation from the full brunt of the overwhelming influence of American culture, especially its popular culture.

This is not to say that Quebec is not threatened by the pervasiveness of American "cultural imperialism." Concern has been expressed, especially by Quebecois intellectual elites, about the dependency of Quebec on massive U.S. cultural input.[62] Indeed, two-thirds of Quebecois feel francophone culture in Canada to be jeopardized "by other cultures" of which the U.S. is seen as the principal threat.[63] Again, this is particularly the case with popular culture. For example, American movies dominate the Quebec market, as is the case in the rest of Canada (as well as in France) with about 80% of attendance. This led *Le Soleil* to observe that "in the movie business, Quebec is perhaps the 51st American state."[64] Similarly, *Le Devoir* saw Montreal as "occupied territory" where the giant American film companies control the movie houses and, hence, guarantee the best distribution for their products."[65] Similarly, the Canadian magazine market is heavily penetrated by American publications, particularly in English Canada, which has led to measures to bar non-Canadian magazines with advertising directed at Canadians.[66]

Under the terms of the North American Free Trade Agreements, Canada has claimed the right to protect its publishing and audiovisual industries from open competition with the United States. On the other hand, the United States has asserted the right to object if this "cultural exemption" were used to discriminate against its interests. Again, the problem here is one that pits the two anglophone societies against each other. It was the introduction of a Canadian edition of *Sports Illustrated* – a so-called "split-run" with American editorial content and Canadian advertising – that raised the prospect of Canada imposing an 80 per cent tax on the revenues of such ads and the United States threatening retaliatory action.[67]

62. See Yvan Lamonde, "American Cultural Influence in Quebec: A One-Way Mirror," in *Problems and Opportunities in U.S.-Quebec Relations*, Ed. Alfred O. Hero, Jr. and Marcel Daneau (Boulder, CO: Westview Press, 1989), pp. 106-26.

63. Alfred Oliver Hero, Jr. and Louis Balthazar, *Contemporary Quebec and the United States, 1960-1985* (Boulder, CO: Westview Press, 1986), p. 198.

64. *Le Soleil*, March 23, 1994.

65. *Le Devoir*, August 28, 1993.

66. *The (Montreal) Gazette*, April 2, 1994.

67. *Le Soleil*, April 1, 1994.

The challenge for Quebec's cultural industries is not the need for greater protectionism but to develop greater competitiveness. Given Quebec's small size and francophone character, the best strategy may be to develop "cultural niches" where its arts and letters could predominate rather than attempt a frontal assault on American cultural hegemony. Also, the very distinctiveness of Quebec society provides a solid foundation for the cultural tourism that characterizes many areas of Europe. With its distinct society and distinctive culture, Quebec should be able to find a broader market for its artistic and intellectual products.

DISTINCT SOCIETY, DISTINCTIVE CULTURE

What should be clear from this discussion of Quebec's new cultural policy is that its guiding principles and administrative reorganization represent an innovative and ambitious public commitment. In particular, the shift from the direct management of the arts to the administrative distance of the council was itself an unprecedented bureaucratic development. Related to this devolution of grant-making authority was a plan for administrative decentralization that was also designed to further a more representative public culture. This is not to suggest, however, that Quebec's cultural policy is beyond criticism. For example, it is unclear how the council will translate the minister's policy orientation into specific grants and what will be the role of advisory panels in shaping the council's grant-making decisions. Furthermore, a radical decentralization of cultural affairs will necessitate new relationships among metropole, capital and the regions. Empowering the regions culturally may diminish the powers of others in the artistic community. Also, questions arise about the relative weights to be accorded to a "global culture" that seeks to compete in the international cultural mainstream and a "provincial culture" that celebrates the uniqueness of its local folk arts.

What is most peculiar about Quebec's cultural policy, and which may account for the seriousness with which it is engaged in the public arena, is the relationship between cultural identity and political identity. Cultural policy in Quebec is not just support for artists and the arts, but is also a matter of support for the heritage and for the development of the French language. To put a complex matter simply: the cultural inheritance to be enhanced is a francophone heritage as the contemporary cultural expressions to be supported are, for the most part, French-Canadian.[68] Quebec's cultural policy, then, is intertwined with constitutional and linguistic matters that have been at the heart of the debates about nationalism and federalism.

---

68. It should be remembered that Quebec's cultural policy recognizes the cultural contributions and concerns of anglophones and indigenous people. See *Notre Culture, Notre Avenir*, pp. 39-42.

The creation of the ministry of cultural affairs can be seen as a manifestation of the cultural nationalism of the 1960s that predated the political nationalism of later decades. It was established by the government of Liberal Premier Jean Lesage, "for the purpose of maintaining and fostering all those traits and characteristics of the people of Quebec as a distinct cultural group on the North American continent."[69] This cultural distinctiveness was its "Frenchness" and, in addition to goals of cultural development, the ministry also included an "Office de la langue française," under Jean-Marc Léger, a well known nationalist intellectual, that was designed to oversee the "correctness and enrichment of French in Quebec as well as the promotion of greater francisation of Quebec society."[70] In sum, the ministry was charged with the task of supporting the enhancement of French language and culture in Quebec.[71]

The ministry's commitment to the revalorisation of French culture was an official counterpart to the more general explosion of cultural ebullience during the Quiet Revolution that saw "a new maturity of French-Canadian artistic, dramatic, lyric, and literary production."[72] In this highly-charged, nationalistic environment, language emerged as a potent symbol of French-Canadian cultural affirmation, political emancipation, and group identity.[73] This was especially true for the Quebecois intelligenstia or so-called "language workers": teachers, administrators, journalists and policy analysts, whose occupational skills involve the manipulation of knowledge and information.[74] (Later, the *Parti québécois* of René Lévesque would come to power on a wave of nationalist sentiment with strong support in academic and artistic circles, the civil service and the media.[75]) For this technically skilled, francophone middle class, the survival and blossoming of Quebec society required the reconciliation of its French-Canadian cultural heritage with the realities of a modern, urbanized world. "Otherwise, the French language and culture would survive in Quebec, as it did in Louisiana, merely as folklore, while English dominated the dynamic elements of Quebec life and inexorably threatened the cultural survival of the French-speaking people."[76]

---

69.   Herbert F. Quinn, *The Union Nationale: A Study in Quebec Nationalism* (Toronto: University of Toronto Press, 1963), p. 181.

70.   Lachapelle et al., *Quebec Democracy*, p. 332.

71.   Levine, *Reconquest of Montreal*, p. 53.

72.   Louis Balthazar, *French-Canadian Civilization* (Washington, D.C.: The Association for Canadian Studies in the United States, 1989), p. 32.

73.   Lachapelle et al., *Quebec Democracy*, p. 331.

74.   Levine, *Reconquest of Montreal*, p. 45; see also Kenneth McRoberts, *Quebec: Social Change and Political Crisis* (Toronto: McClelland and Stewart, 1988), pp. 147-57.

75.   Balthazar, *French-Canadian Civilization*, p. 19.

76.   Levine, *Reconquest of Montreal*, p. 45.

It is crucial to note that the cultural nationalism of the decades beginning with the Quiet Revolution is of a fundamentally different character than the "will to survive" of the previous two centuries. There is arguably a remarkable continuity between the ethos of survival and that of blossoming. Both are rooted in the efforts of French-Canadians after the Conquest in 1759 to resist assimilation and "a determination to survive, a 'will to live' as a cultural group."[77] As a result of this determination to retain their cultural distinctiveness, French-Canadians have been engaged "in an intermittent, and at times bitter, struggle against assimilation by the dominant English group."[78] In describing the decades after Quebec was ceded at the Treaty of Paris in 1763, historian W.J. Eccles concluded as follows:

> The French-Canadians, concentrated in their seigneuries, bound together by their language, their old culture, and their religion – which now assumed far greater importance in their lives than it had since the early seventeenth century – successfully resisted the continual fumbling efforts of the Anglo-Canadians and British officials to assimilate them, to make them over into English-speaking Protestants, or at least to exorcize their divisive language. All that this accomplished was to strengthen what the conqueror had sought to eradicate.[79]

The underpinnings of the Quebecois social order were institutionalized religion, the Catholic school system and the provincial government; these were francophone institutions in a Canada that was Protestant, English, British Empire and, with the exception of bilingual New Brunswick, anglophone.[80] At root, the ethos of "survival" preached a defensive nationalism that encouraged social isolation and economic underdevelopment as the keys to French-Canadian cultural survival.[81]

The "blossoming" ideology, by contrast, was a modernizing nationalism that sought the economic empowerment of the francophone majority in Quebec. Although highly symbolic, the blossoming of French-Canadian culture and the concommitant rise of the language issue as a matter of cultural survival mobilized the ethnic pride of francophones and "formed the impetus for a tremendous effort toward economic self-reliance."[82] It is important to point out that the type of nationalism we are discussing here is of the defensive rather than the expansionist kind. "It is concerned with the maintenance of existing rights and

---

77. Quinn, *Union Nationale*, p. 3.

78. *Ibid.*, p. 4.

79. W.J. Eccles, *France in America* (New York: Harper and Row, 1972), p. 247.

80. See the discussion by Hubert Guindon of "The Church as the embodiment of the nation" in *Quebec Society: Tradition, Modernity and Nationhood* (Toronto: University of Toronto Press, 1988), pp. 104-10.

81. Levine, *Reconquest of Montreal*, p. 45.

82. Lachapelle et al., *Quebec Democracy*, p. 346.

interests... It may be looked upon as the national reaction of a minority ethnic group when confronted with a serious threat to its cultural survival."[83]

Ironically, Quebec nationalism can be seen as the "illegitimate child of Canadian nationalism." If, as Louis Balthazar has argued, the Canadian nation-state gave rise to the Quebec nation-state,[84] Quebec cultural nationalism is a response to the attempt to define a common Canadian culture. Marc Levine argues, in his book on the language-policy controversies in Montreal, that the ministry of cultural affairs was established by the Lesage government "as a French-speaking, provincial government counterpart to the federal government's Canada Council, which Francophone nationalist intellectuals viewed as an attempt to impose 'Canadian' culture on Quebec Francophones."[85]

As has been noted, the instinct for cultural survival is deeply rooted in Quebecois consciousness. It may be that this sense of cultural distinctness has been heightened in the post-World War II period by the perception that any "hegemonic" Canadian culture would be a threatening development. For the Royal Commission on National Development in the Arts, Letters and Sciences, chaired by Vincent Massey from 1949 to 1951, it was an article of faith that there was an identifiable "Canadian" culture that would serve as a unifying principle of national identity.[86] The administrative manifestations of this ethos were the Arts Council of Canada, the Canadian Broadcasting Corporation and the National Film Board. In fact, this belief system is a highly contentious issue, especially for French-Canadians who insist upon having a culture of their own, separate from the culture of other Canadians.[87] This was certainly the case for the traditionalist Premier of Quebec in the 1940s and 1950s, Maurice Duplessis, but also for the liberalizing government of Jean Lesage and the Quiet Revolution of the 1960s, and certainly for René Lévesque and the Parti Québécois governments from 1976 to 1985.

It may be that an unanticipated consequence of the Massey Commission's emphasis on a distinctive Canadian culture (even while reaffirming Canada's bilingualism) was to encourage artists and intellectuals in Quebec to become

---

83. Quinn, *Union Nationale*, p. 27.

84. Louis Balthazar, "The Faces of Quebec Nationalism," in Alain Gagnon, editor, *Quebec: State and Society* (Toronto: Nelson Canada, 1993), p. 17.

85. Levine, *Reconquest of Montreal*, p. 53.

86. See Paul Litt, *The Muses, the Masses and the Massey Commission* (Toronto: University of Toronto Press, 1992). Louis Balthazar observes that, "Ironically enough, Radio-Canada, a federal institution devised to bring Canadians closer to each other, was one of the institutions that contributed the most to the development of Quebec nationalism." The CBC's French programming on television and radio was essentially a Quebec network that brought French-speaking Québécois closer to one another, providing "a mirror of themselves forming a nation." See Balthazar, "Forces of Quebec Nationalism," p. 14.

87. Balthazar, *French-Canadian Civilization*, p. 1. Interview with Louis Balthazar, Department of Political Science, Université Laval, August 10, 1993.

maître chez nous, that is, to assert the distinctiveness and primacy of their francophone culture. Just as the efforts in the 1980s to forge a Canadian constitutional arrangement to replace the British North America Act of 1867 opened up questions of political identity, the Massey Commission's creation of Canadian cultural institutions may have exacerbated Quebec's concerns about its cultural survival in a Canadian polity.

Not surprisingly, the result has been a vigorous assertion of provincial rights – long a characteristic of Quebec politics – in certain fundamental areas such as education, immigration, language and culture. In 1945, Maurice Duplessis spoke of the right to autonomy – meaning laws "for us and by us."[88] In general, the Quebecers "have used the... provincial government as an instrument of cultural survival and, because the stakes are so high, provincial rights have been guarded with a rigor unknown in the United States."[89]

In 1966, the Union Nationale premier, Daniel Johnson, expressed Quebec's wish "to be master of its own decision-making in areas that concern the human growth of its citizens... their economic affirmation... their cultural development – not only the arts and letters, but also the French language..."[90] In 1991, the Bélanger-Campeau Report recommended constitutional changes that would provide "the exclusive attribution to Quebec of powers and responsibilities related to its social, economic and cultural development, as well as to language."[91] The *Arpin Report* recommended that, because of the distinct character of Quebec society, the Quebec state should have control over culture and that, whatever the constitutional status of Quebec, the federal government should leave the cultural field completely.[92] In her introductory message to *Notre Culture, Notre Avenir*, Minister Liza Frulla, noting the fundamental importance of culture in Quebec especially because "Quebec is the only majoritarily French-speaking society in North America," argued for the necessity of Quebec having mastery over cultural matters within its territory.[93]

---

88. "C'est le doit d'être maître chez soi... L'Autonomie, c'est le droit... de faire des lois pour nous et par nous..." Quoted in Quinn, *Union nationale*, p. 191.

89. Roger Gibbins, *Regionalism: Territorial Politics in Canada and the United States* (Toronto: Butterworth, 1982), p. 192.

90. Quoted in Balthazar, "Faces of Quebec Nationalism," p. 20.

91. *Report of the Commission on the Political and Constitutional Future of Quebec*, 1991, p. 48.

92. "... à cause du caractère distinct de la société québécoise, l'État, par l'intermédiaire de son ministère des Affaires culturelles, doit se poser en seul maître-d'oeuvre. Le gouvernement fédéral doit se retirer complètement du champ culturel, quel que soit le futur statut constitutionel du Québec." *Arpin Report*, pp. 31-32.

93. "Dans le contexte constitutionnel présent, comme ministre des Affaires culturelles, j'entends réaffirmer la nécessité pour le Québec d'obtenir la maîtrise d'oeuvre en matière culturelle sur son territoire." *Notre Culture, Notre Avenir*, pp. vii-viii. This viewpoint is not expressed in the cultural policy itself and the minister's introductory message is not included in the English edition.

Whatever the political and constitutional recognition of Quebec as a distinct society, it is already recognized as having a distinctive culture and it is the cultural distinctiveness of Quebec that distinguishes its approach to public support for the arts. For the members of the Massey Commission and its disciples, opposition to American mass culture was the basis of a Canadian cultural identity.[94] As Seymour Martin Lipset has put it, "Canadians are the world's oldest and most continuing un-Americans."[95] Indeed, many English-Canadian intellectuals mobilized to fight the Canada-U.S. Free Trade Pact because they saw it as a threat to their national culture and distinct Canadian values."[96] For Quebec, on the other hand, national identity is centered around the language as the expression of the cultural heritage of its francophone population.

A formulation of this sense of politics and culture might be: the language is the culture; the culture is the people; the people are the nation. If for no other reason than this, Quebec's ministry of culture is on the frontlines as a crucial combattant in the battle over national identity and cultural identity involving the federal government of Canada and the state of Quebec.

94. See John Meisel, "Government and the Arts in Canada," in Cummings and Schuster, Editors, *Who's to Pay for the Arts,* pp. 82-83; see also John Meisel and Jean Van Loon, "Cultivating the Bushgarden: Cultural Policy in Canada," in Cummings and Katz, Editors, *The Patron State,* pp. 276-310.

95. Seymour Martin Lipset, *"Continental Divide: The Values and Institutions of the United States and Canada* (New York and London: Routledge, 1990), p. 53.

96. *Ibid.,* p. 221.

15

Telecommunications and Information Technology

Hervé Déry*
Industry Canada

Telecommunications in the last 20 years have had a dramatic influence on personal, business and social life styles. Hence, adequate communications facilities are necessary to promote economic development. As economies continue to shift toward service-based economic structures, the relative importance of communications is undeniably increasing. In the telecommunications industry, change is perhaps the only constant. The development of the telecommunications industry has traditionally taken place within a heavily regulated environment characterized by intense public policy debate. This chapter presents an overview of the Canadian and Quebec Telecommunications and Information Technology industry as well as an analysis of its regulatory and public policy environment in the context of a continental economy. It analyses the North American Free Trade Agreement (NAFTA) in relation to this industry and outlines the industry's Research and Development capacity. Furthermore, it introduces key concepts (such as information highway) and key activities (such as spectrum management) related to this industry.

*   Thanks are due to Hélène Asselin, Richard Bourassa, Keith Chang, Denis Lachance, Jean-François LeMay, Alain Robillard, Len St-Aubin and Michael Tiger for information provided or comments on initial version of the paper. The views expressed in this chapter are those of the author alone and should not be attributed to Industry Canada or the individuals named above.

INTRODUCTION

In the last 20 years, telecommunications have had a dramatic influence on personal, business and social life styles. Telecommunications and information technologies are influencing the growth of national economies and their level of development. The increasing impact of technology is also creating new opportunities; so much so, that in the telecommunications industry, change is perhaps the only constant. The social and economic benefits of telecommunications investment are now widely understood, and it is recognized that adequate communications facilities are necessary to promote economic development. Telecommunications services are no longer considered a supportive industry but rather a forerunner of development. It is also recognized that adequate telecommunications foster important objectives such as national integration and decentralization of economic activities. As economies continue to shift toward service-based economic structures, the relative importance of communications increases. Necessarily, the benefits of improved telecommunications services are more evident in information-intensive sectors such as banking and finance, wholesale and retail trade, transportation, storage and distribution and accommodation and tourism. Furthermore, automated teller machines, point-of-sale systems, and credit and debit cards have already changed the way consumers bank, shop and make payments. Large businesses spend up to 5% of their total expenditure on telecommunications services, accounting for a significant portion of their overhead costs. Undeniably, telecommunications has become an important element of competitiveness in an increasingly global market.

The development of the telecommunications industry has traditionally taken place within a heavily regulated environment characterized by intense public policy debate. This chapter presents an overview of the Canadian and Quebec Telecommunications and Information Technology industry. It is divided into four sections. The first section deals with the terms and conditions of the 1987 Canada-US Free Trade Agreement (FTA) and the subsequent North American Free Trade Agreement (NAFTA) as they related to the telecommunications industry. The subsequent section presents the regulatory and public policy environment in which the industry operates. Include in this section are policy issues related to the creation of a Canadian information highway. The third section presents a statistical overview of the Canadian and Quebec Telecommunications and Information Technology industry. Included in this section is information on Northern Telecom, the largest Canadian manufacturer of telecommunications equipment. The fourth section presents an outline of the industry's Research and Development capacity, including information on Canadian regime of spectrum management.

INTERNATIONAL TRADE AND NAFTA

The 1987 Canada-US Free Trade Agreement (FTA) was the first bilateral agreement with a significant trade-in-services component. The FTA guaranteed a national treatment[1] for all future government measures that affected the provision of enhanced telecommunications or computer services. The FTA also confirmed that markets for such services would remain open and competitive. However, basic telecommunications networks and services were excluded from the overall Agreement.

The North American Free Trade Agreement (NAFTA) is similar to the FTA but goes a few steps beyond in some obligations. It has created the world's largest telecommunications equipment and computer market. All internal tariffs will be eliminated over ten years and, at the end of that period, a common regulatory approach for "access and use of" the public telecommunications transport network will have been adopted. However, the three governments have not taken the next step, i.e., opening basic telecommunications network and services, such as local or long distance voice telephony to foreign competition. When examining both Agreements, the key principle is that access to and use of the public network is to be on "reasonable and non-discriminatory terms and conditions." Furthermore, it is worth noting that NAFTA contains a list of government measures of what constitutes "good regulatory behaviour." It can therefore be argued[2] that NAFTA goes beyond the traditional application of the national treatment principle. In general, national treatment only means that government should treat foreign and domestic businesses equally, but it does not tell a government what it should do.

Under NAFTA, the government will still be able to protect confidentiality of messages and technical integrity. This is important in the context of the creation of the information highway. NAFTA limits the government's ability to impose conditions on access to and use of public networks to three general cases:

1. to safeguard the public service responsibility of the public network operators;

2. to protect the technical integrity of the public networks and services;

3. to safeguard the confidentiality of messages and the privacy of subscribers.

---

1. National treatment means treating foreign and national companies similarly, i.e., non-discriminatory become the guide for government regulations or policies.

2. This is the case for example of Michael Tiger, in his paper entitled "NAFTA's New Code Book for the World's Largest Market."

Furthermore, NAFTA preserves Canadian control of basic telecommunications services and improves business and investment opportunities for the industry in one of the world's fastest growing markets.[3] NAFTA does not open the door for foreign-owned telephone companies to provide facilities-based telecommunications services in Canada. Canada's 20% limit on foreign ownership remains in effect. As under the FTA, foreign companies such as AT&T may operate in Canada, but only as resellers of telephone services or as providers of enhanced services. Both FTA and NAFTA maintain a competitive environment for the provision of computer and enhanced telecommunications services[4] but NAFTA contains broader rules which guarantee that providers of enhanced services and companies can operate their own private networks and establishes a program to recognize compatible equipment standards.

Telecommunications and Information Technology What Is in the NAFTA

1. As under the Canada-U.S. Free Trade Agreement (FTA), protection of basic telecommunications, such as telephone services;

2. Elimination of Mexican trade barriers to the provision of enhanced services (e.g. advanced data processing services);

3. Guaranteed access to and use of telecommunications networks in the three countries;

4. Future compatibility of standards for telecommunications equipment in Canada, the U.S. and Mexico;

5. Immediate removal of Mexican tariffs on all telecommunications equipment, except central switching apparatus, telephone sets, printed circuit boards and televisions, which are phased out in five years.

6. Elimination of all Mexican and Canadian duties within ten years for information technology products;

7. Better access to a range of government procurement contracts and other business such as state monopolies in Mexico for high-technology equipment in the Mexican and U.S. market;

8. Clearer and more precise rules of origin, narrowing the scope for disputes;

9. Extension of duty drawback for two years beyond the FTA expiry in 1994. This will be replaced in 1996 by a permanent duty refund system that will reduce input costs for Canadian manufacturers who still pay duties on goods shipped into other NAFTA countries;

10. All parties agree to apply identical tariffs for computers, microelectronics and related equipment from non-NAFTA countries within ten years.

---

3. According to experts, Mexico's demand for imported telecommunications products is expected to grow by 42% by the year 2000 as Mexico modernizes and integrates its telecommunications with the rest of the North America. Overall, the Mexican market for imported technology products is expected to grow up to 20% per year over the next five years.

4. Enhanced telecommunications services means anything beyond basic telephone services. This would include automatic answering services, E-mail services and data processing services.

It is worth noting that Canadian firms had interests in Mexico even before NAFTA. For instance, Northern Telecom has had a plant in Mexico since 1991. Bell Canada Enterprises Inc. (BCE) has a significant interest in two cellular phone companies, and other Canadian firms are also becoming active in the Mexican market.

REGULATORY AND POLICY ENVIRONMENT

In Canada, virtually all facilities-based telecommunications carriers are regulated by the Canadian Radio-television and Telecommunications Commission (CRTC), an agency of the federal government[5] under the 1993 *Telecommunications Act.*[6] The major exception is Saskatchewan Telecommunications (SaskTel), which is exempted from federal regulation until 1998. Where the use of the radio frequency spectrum is involved, carriers are also subject to technical regulation under the federal *Radiocommunication Act.*[7] Regulated common carriers are obliged to provide access and tariffed services to all users on a non-discriminatory basis at just and reasonable rates. Resellers, who do not own or operate transmission facilities, are not subject to regulation.

The Minister of Industry, assisted by his/her Department, is responsible for policy formulation and any necessary legislation that may be required regarding spectrum, information technologies and telecommunications.

The 1993 *Telecommunications Act* signals a clear preference for competition as the driving force in the telecommunications industry. It provides the tools required to complete the transition to a competitive integrated national market. Telecommunications markets are becoming increasingly competitive.

---

5.   A 1989 Supreme Court Decision (AGT Case) confirmed federal jurisdiction over Alberta Government Telephones and, by extension, all members of Telecom Canada (now Stentor). On April 26, 1994, the Supreme Court confirmed federal jurisdiction over Téléphone Guèvremont, an independent telephone company in Quebec, and by extension over all independent telephone companies.

6.   In the United States, Telecommunications policy involves a complex combination of federal, state and local authorities. At the federal level, the Federal Communications Commission (FCC) regulates interstate and international communications and manages private spectrum usage. The Department of State conducts foreign relations and the National Telecommunications and Information Administration (NTIA) is the President's principal advisor on telecommunications policies. The NTIA ensures that its views and the views of the Department of State are presented to FCC and Congress, works with the US Trade Representative (USTR), manages all Federal Government use of the spectrum and conduct R&D. The responsibility for regulation also involves the FCC and 50 state regulatory bodies that regulate within each state. The FCC has a very broad policy-making role, but the level and nature of regulation varies considerably from state to state. Many carriers are subject to regulation by the FCC and states in which they operate.

7.   There was a major updating of the *Radiocommunications Act* in 1989 and passage of a new *Broadcasting Act* in 1991.

Slowly, regulation is giving way to market forces as the best means to ensure that users have access to high quality, innovative services at competitive prices. The role of regulation is evolving away from the control of rates, profits and level of service, towards the facilitation of competition through the establishment of non-discriminatory access to bottleneck facilities.

An essential part of the *Act* concerns the Canadian ownership and control of Canadian facilities-based carriers. The *Act* and its ownership regulations implement the 80% ownership[8] and control policy announced by the government in 1987 in its Telecommunications Policy Framework for Canada. Previously, there had been no generally applicable statutory restriction on foreign ownership and control of the Canadian telecommunications carriage industry.[9] Regulations issued under the *Radiocommunications Act* govern the issuing of radio licences.

In Canada and internationally, there has been a trend over the last decade towards greater reliance on market force in the provision of communications services. Competition stimulates investment and innovation and reduces the gap between the development and deployment of new technologies, products and services, thereby quickly expanding the range of products and services available to consumers. Competition can also serve to reduce prices.

Canada's progress has been considerable on the competition front: competition has been open in the sale of telecommunications terminal equipment and in the resale of telecommunications services; cellular and personal communications services were launched with licensing of competitive suppliers; and competition has been adopted in the public long-distance telephone service market. One should note that Canada–U.S. crossborder services are provided on a competitive basis pursuant to agreements between a number of carriers on both sides of the border. Since September 1994, all services, including local services, are open to competition by cable companies, wireless carriers, or any other service provider. Also, telephone companies will be allowed to deliver

---

8. Participation by foreign entities in Canadian facilities-based carriers is limited to 20%. However, companies which are at least two-thirds Canadian-owned are considered "Canadian" investors. Foreign-owned common carriers as of July 22, 1987 are eligible to hold a telecommunications licence to continue operating as Canadian carriers. These carriers are required to at least maintain the level of Canadian ownership and control that existed on July 22, 1987.

9. In the United States, the 1934 *Communications Act* prohibits the granting of any radio licence to a foreign government or its representative. The Act also limits direct foreign (or "alien") ownership in common carrier radio licensees to 20% and indirect ownership to 25%. However, the Federal Communications Commission (FCC) has the authority to allow more indirect ownership and has on occasion permitted alien control of a common carrier radio licence. There are no foreign investment restrictions on wired (fibre optics, coaxial cable) facilities. In Mexico, foreign ownership is allowed to a maximum of 49%.

broadcast programming, as carriers, on behalf of licensed broadcasters (video dial tone) and the door is open for them eventually to provide information-based content services.

Excerpt from the *Telecommunications Act*
Canadian Telecommunications Policy

7. It is hereby affirmed that telecommunications performs an essential role in the maintenance of Canada's identity and sovereignty and that the Canadian telecommunications policy has as its objectives

(a) to facilitate the orderly development throughout Canada of a telecommunications system that serves to safeguard, enrich and strengthen the social and economic fabric of Canada and its regions;

(b) to render reliable and affordable telecommunications services of high quality, accessible to Canadians in both urban and rural areas in all regions of Canada;

(c) to enhance the efficiency and competitiveness, at the national and international levels, of Canadian telecommunications;

(d) to promote the ownership and control of Canadian carriers by Canadians;

(e) to promote the use of Canadian transmission facilities for telecommunications within Canada and between Canada and points outside Canada;

(f) to foster increased reliance on market force for the provision of telecommunications service and to ensure that regulations, where required, are efficient and effective;

(g) to stimulate research and development in Canada in the field of telecommunications and to encourage innovation in the provision of telecommunications services;

(h) to respond to economic and social requirements of users of telecommunications services; and

(i) to contribute to the protection of the privacy of persons.

The only remaining monopolies are Telesat's monopoly provision of fixed domestic satellite services and Teleglobe's monopoly provision of overseas services. All local telecommunications services are now open to competition by cable companies, wireless carriers, or any other service provider.[10] Although the technological change which is leading to convergence and the information highway will further expand the horizon for competition, the market dominance enjoyed by the major telephone companies will continue to raise concerns about the potential for anti-competitive behaviour.

---

10. On September 16, 1994, the CRTC issued its decision on the Regulatory Framework (CRTC Telecom Decision 94-19), in which the Commission outlines how it will approach the regulation of telephone companies. This is a major decision which covers a number of important issues.

The CRTC is an administrative tribunal constituted under the *CRTC Act* (R.S.C. 1985, c. C-22) as amended by the *Broadcasting Act* (S.C. 1991 c. 11) and the *Telecommunications Act*. It is vested with the administrative and quasi-judicial authority to supervise and, where required, to regulate telecommunications common carriers that fall under federal jurisdiction. It regulates rates and other aspects of the services offered by telecommunications common carriers under federal jurisdiction. The Commission is an independent agency operating at "arms length" from government and reporting to Parliament through the Minister of Canadian Heritage.

Virtually all facilities-based telecommunications carriers are subject to the jurisdiction of the CRTC, including all telephone companies except SaskTel which, by federal-provincial agreement, will not be CRTC-regulated until October 1998. Other carriers within CRTC jurisdiction include Unitel, Sprint Canada and other interexchange carriers, cellular telephone service providers (e.g. Rogers Cantel), Telesat Canada, Teleglobe Canada and other wireless service providers.

In the area of telecommunications, the primary role of the regulator is to implement the policy in Section 7 of the *Telecommunications Act* and to ensure that rates are just and reasonable and that carriers provide non-discriminatory access to services.

With respect to competition, the Commission decision in the 1970s and 80s allowing resale and sharing and decision 92-12, which permitted Unitel to compete in the provision of public long distance telephone services, are very important milestones in the transition from a fragmented market dominated by powerful, regionally-based, monopoly telephone companies towards an integrated, increasingly competitive national market with a growing number of service providers. As set out in the 92-12 decision, the Commission believes that its decision will result not only in lower long distance rates, but in an environment characterized by increased responsiveness in which competitive suppliers offer improved customer service and by the development of an increased number of service features.

On September 16, 1994, the CRTC issued its decision on the Regulatory Framework (CRTC Telecom Decision 94-19). This is a major decision which covers a number of important issues and outlines how the Commission will approach the regulation of the telephone companies. It is a multi-element decision which establishes the regulatory framework for the telecommunications industry for the next 5 to 10 years. This decision completes decision 92-12. However, on December 13, 1994, the Industry Minister announced that an important element of the decision – the rate rebalancing proposal which authorizes an increase in local monthly telephone rates of $2 in 1995, 1996 and 1997 – has been put on hold by the federal government pending a further study of costs. The Commission has been asked to complete its work by

October 31, 1995. Local rates have been virtually unchanged over the past decade. Also, every dollar generated from the local rate increases would have been used to lower long distance rates, targeting those services used by residential and small business subscribers. On the other hand, contribution payments of competitors would have been lowered on January 1, 1995 in proportion to changes in local rates. The request to the CRTC from the government is a response to appeals from consumer groups concerned about the proposed rate increases, and appeals from members of the industry regarding the impact on competition of the rate rebalancing proposals contained in CRTC decision 94-19. Although the federal government has agreed to a fuller review of rate rebalancing, the federal cabinet did not exercise its power to reject or change the CRTC's decision. "The government is not opposed to some rebalancing, as long as the need for specific rate adjustments is clearly identified for each company and as long as the principle of affordable telephone service is not compromised," said the Industry Minister.[11] The federal government remains committed to the regulatory reform process undertaken by the CRTC and anticipates rapid implementation of other aspects of the regulatory reforms contained in decision 94-19. The Commission has delivered its statutory requirement to rely more on market forces and has adopted a regulatory framework based on incentive regulation that will eventually lead to forbearance and deregulation.

- Regulation to focus on monopolies, areas where there is market dominance, and in cases where there are bottleneck facilities.

- The Commission will adopt price caps in 1998, whereby prices can be adjusted within predetermined limits usually related to the rate of inflation. In the interim the CRTC has instituted specific measures, including rate rebalancing, to prepare for the adoption of price caps.

- As of January 1995 the CRTC will, for regulatory purposes, separate the telephone companies into two components, Utility (local and access) and Competitive (Split Rate Base Approach). Any increases in rates for Utility services will be justified only on the basis of the utility segment. Telephone companies will have considerable freedom in pricing competitive services, as long as they cover all causal costs, but shareholders will have to absorb any drops in revenue.

- The Commission will use its power to forbear from regulation, starting immediately with terminal equipment, but has explicitly cautioned the telephone companies that they cannot expect forbearance in the absence of equitable treatment of competitors, i.e., they must stop playing games with equal access.

---

11.   Source: Industry Canada, December 13, 1994, News release.

With respect to price regulation, in the case of telecommunications regulated prices have increased much more slowly that the general rate of inflation since 1980.

As regulation is diminished, the *Competition Act* may increasingly be relied upon to address the key issues of access and entry. The Commission (CRTC Telecom Decision 94-19) acknowledged that the Director of Investigation and Research (Bureau of Competition Policy) has jurisdiction once forbearance is in place.

Enforcement of the *Competition Act* in Canada

The Director of Investigation and Research of the Bureau of Competition Policy has statutory responsibility for the administration and enforcement of the *Competition Act* with the objective to maintain and encourage competition in the Canadian economy. The *Act* comprises six components:

1. **Merger Review** administers the provisions of the *Act* relating to mergers. This component is responsible for the examination of proposed merger transactions in Canada and subsequent application by the Director to the Competition Tribunal where appropriate. In 1993-94, 236 examinations had been completed and, in two cases, applications before the Competition Tribunal were required.

2. **Criminal Matters** administers and enforces the criminal provisions of the *Act* relating to anticompetitive behaviour, excluding misleading advertising and deceptive marketing practices but including such offences as conspiracy and bid-rigging. In 1993-94, 90 examinations were completed and 10 formal inquiries completed. In seven cases there were referrals to the Attorney General.

3. **Civil Matters** administers and enforces the civil provisions of the *Act* relating to anticompetitive behaviour (such as abuse of dominant position, exclusive dealing, tied selling and refusal to deal), excluding mergers. The reviewable practices provision of the *Act* require adjudication by the Competition Tribunal. In 1993-94, 45 examinations were commenced and 25 completed. Eight formal inquiries commenced (five completed) and two applications to the Tribunal were made.

4. **Marketing Practices** administers and enforces the provision of the *Act* relating to misleading advertising and deceptive marketing practices. These provisions are criminal in nature and apply to all industry sectors in Canada. In 1993-94, some 1,150 investigations were initiated and 70 formal inquiries completed. Fifty cases were referred to the Attorney General.

5. **Economic and International Affairs** provides economic analysis of enforcement cases and policies, competition analysis of federal legislation, regulation of economic policies and representation of Canadian interests relating to competition and related issues in international fora.

6. **Compliance and Operations** provides compliance and enforcement strategy initiatives, legal research on enforcement cases, public consultations, information programs including information bulletins, guidelines and speeches, program management, information management, and resource management.

Source: Expenditure Plan of Industry Canada, Part III of the 1994-95 Estimates.

The *Competition Act* is a law of general application, which pertains equally to all industries, except where specific exemptions exist either within the *Act* or in other legislation. Its approach differs substantially from industry-specific regulation. Under the *Act*, the Director of Investigation and Research, who heads the Bureau of Competition Policy (the Bureau) is responsible for the *Act*'s administration and enforcement. This includes: conducting inquiries (in response to complaints or on the Director's initiative); appearing before regulatory boards; and, where warranted, bringing matters before the courts or the Competition Tribunal. The Bureau of Competition Policy – an arm's length organization under the responsibility of Industry Canada since June 1993 – is a strong advocate of competition, especially in the context of an industry as dynamic as the telecommunications services industry. It has been a frequent intervenor in CRTC public hearings, and has welcomed decisions introducing greater competition. The role of the *Competition Act* and the Bureau's enforcement activity is to prohibit activities that impede competition or entry into an industry. The *Telecommunications Act* requires the CRTC to forbear from regulation where it finds that a service or class of service is, or will be, subject to sufficient competition to protect the interest of users. The *Act* also authorizes the CRTC to exempt classes of Canadian carriers from its application, where doing so is consistent with Canadian telecommunications policy objectives.

Although the telecommunications services industry has never been exempt from the *Competition Act*, it has benefited from what is known as the "regulated conduct defence." This defence is based on the courts' long-standing recognition that industry behaviour approved by a regulatory authority must be deemed to be in the public interest. This has limited the Bureau's ability to apply the *Competition Act* to regulated industries.

It is important to note, however, that the *Telecommunications Act* gives the CRTC tremendous flexibility in the use of its powers. For example, it can exempt classes of carriers from the *Act* subject to conditions; similarly, it can forbear from regulating services in whole or in part, and with or without conditions. Exemption and forbearance will not necessarily constitute "deregulation." Accordingly, the Bureau's ability to apply the *Competition Act* will depend on the extent of exemption or forbearance and, therefore, on the validity of a "regulated conduct defence" in a given circumstance.

It is also important to point out that under the *Telecommunications Act*, resellers, and others who provide telecommunications services but are not "Canadian carriers" within the definition of the *Act* are not subject to regulation. Their activities are clearly subject to the full application of the provisions of the *Competition Act*.

International Services

Canada has adopted a unique and highly specialized approach to the management of intercontinental communications. Teleglobe Canada Inc. was established in 1949 as a crown corporation (then known as Canadian Overseas Telecommunications Corporation). It came under formal CRTC regulation when it was privatized in 1987 after a competitive bidding process. Teleglobe Canada's headquarters is located in Montreal (Quebec).

Teleglobe Canada Inc. is the sole provider of facilities for the provision of overseas telecommunications services. It offers extensive expertise in the development and management of intercontinental telecommunications; in the installation, maintenance and repair of submarine cables; and in the set-up and financing of international facilities in countries other than Canada. When Teleglobe was privatized, this was to provide a stable period of adjustment from a crown corporation to a privately owned company.

At the time of privatization, the federal government announced restrictions on Teleglobe's ownership structure. It restricted Canadian telephone companies, which then accounted for 90% of Teleglobe's traffic, from owning more than one-third of the voting shares in Teleglobe, in order to prevent them from extending their dominant domestic position to the overseas market. Furthermore, the general telecommunications policy is to prohibit non-Canadians from owning or controlling more than 20% of Teleglobe's voting shares. Teleglobe's monopoly was renewed for five years in 1992, because of rapid economic and technological changes in international telecommunications and because telecommunications were considered an instrument of economic development. Teleglobe's monopoly comes up for review in 1995. It charges the third lowest price for intercontinental calls among countries of the Organization for Economic Cooperation and Development (OECD). On average, prices decreased by 40% between 1987 and 1992 and will benchmark those charged by U.S. carriers by the year 1995. However, Teleglobe Canada does not offer domestic long distance services (it does not generally even provide Canada–U.S. services).

As an intercontinental carrier, Teleglobe is the sole authorized operator of international telecommunications facilities linking Canada with more than 240 countries through an extensive network of submarine cables, membership in the INTERSAT and the International Maritime Satellite Organization (INMARSAT) satellite systems and nearly 200 bilateral agreement overseas correspondents. Teleglobe also represents Canada's interest in the Commonwealth Telecommunications Organization, INTERSAT, and in INMARSAT.

In Canada, International Simple Resale is permitted to use private circuits under some conditions (registration with Teleglobe and CRTC, payment of monthly contribution charges, reciprocity). There is no additional specific condition for foreign-owned firms and resellers are not limited in the types of services they are allowed to offer.

Teleglobe has recently signed a ten-year agreement with Stentor (the alliance of phone companies, including Bell) which specifies the arrangements governing the interconnection of their respective networks for the supply and development of international services. Under this agreement, Stentor will subscribe to the Globeaccess service and commit to routing all its outgoing overseas traffic over Teleglobe's network. Domestic carriers have exclusive responsibility for the routing of traffic within Canada and between Canada and the United States. Both parties have committed to aligning their rates with those of competing carriers, primarily from the U.S. The agreement is non-discriminatory: the same terms and conditions are offered to resellers and other carriers. The agreement was approved by the CRTC on September 27, 1993 (Telecom Decision CRTC93-15).[12]

The CRTC also regulates other aspects of Teleglobe's business. For instance, Teleglobe enjoys a maximum 12.75%-14.75% return on equity, higher than Bell's to allow for greater business risks, including foreign exchange. Teleglobe wants an incentive system to encourage cost reduction, traffic growth and profitability.

Teleglobe Canada Inc. has formed a 21-member international consortium to lay a transatlantic fibre-optics cable. The cable to connect North America with West and East Europe, dubbed Cantat-3, is the first major undersea communications cable to be spearheaded by Teleglobe. The total cost of the project to build the 7,537-kilometre cable is estimated at $385 million (Can.). The Cantat-3 cable is estimated to have 300% more capacity than all existing cable under the Atlantic Ocean.

Information Highway

So far, in Canada, firms in the telecommunications, broadcasting, cable and information industries have operated in separate markets, without all the benefits of either competition or collaboration. The term "information highway" is used to designate an advanced information and communications infrastructure that will become a network of networks, linking Canadian homes, businesses, government and institutions to a wide range of information-based services from entertainment, education, cultural products, and social services to data banks, computers, electronic commerce, banking and business services. Its enabling effects will be felt in all industry sectors. As traffic on the information highway

---

12.   CRTC accepted the 10-year term of the Agreement but if Teleglobe's mandate is terminated by the Government, the approval of the Agreement will remain in force only until one year after the effective date of the Government's decision.

moves into the fast lane, as new technology and new services appear, public policy will be increasingly challenged to catch up. In its January 1994 Speech from the Throne and its subsequent February Budget, the government of Canada announced its intention to implement a Canadian strategy for an information highway. It has set out three policy objectives and four operating principles which will provide the fundamental direction for Canada's strategy to build the highest quality, lowest cost information network in the world. The policy objectives are:

1. To create jobs through innovation and investment in Canada.

2. To reinforce Canadian sovereignty and cultural identity.

3. To ensure universal access at reasonable cost.

The four operating principles are:

1. an interconnected and interoperable network of networks;

2. collaborative public and private sector development;

3. competition in facilities, products and services;

4. privacy protection and network security.

The government has created an Information Highway Advisory Council to provide it with advice and guidance on the development of the information highway. The Council will consider all-important policy issues such as the proper balance between competition and regulation, the Canadian ownership issue, the standards issue, and the copyright, intellectual property and protection of personal privacy and security of information issues.

Industry Canada indicated that the government would adopt a pro-competition approach to the development of the information highway. In a public speech,[13] the Director of Investigation of Research under the *Competition Act* stated that a pro-competition approach to the information highway must include six elements:

1. Legislative and regulatory impediments to competition – such as line of business restrictions imposed upon telephone companies, broadcasters and others – would have to be reduced or eliminated.

2. Where any firms – telephone, cable or whatever – control network facilities which are essential for competition entry, an obligation needs to be created for these firms to provide open access to such facilities on a non-discriminatory basis.

---

13. Addy, George N., *The Competition Act and the Canadian Telecommunications Industry*, speech by the Director of Investigation and Research under the Competition Act to the Institute for International Research Telecommunications Conference, Toronto, March 1994 (and Montreal, March 1994), 15 pages.

3. Policies permitting telephone and cable companies to expand their range of services must also include requirements for them to provide network capacity to unaffiliated program and service providers on a nondiscriminatory basis.

4. Collaboration and cooperation among industry participants should not involve anti-competitive market sharing, or otherwise go beyond what is necessary to facilitate interconnection and open access.

5. Competition is most likely to occur between cable and telephone companies. Therefore, mergers and acquisitions involving these firms, particularly in the same geographic market areas, will have to be subject to very close scrutiny. It should be noted that in the United States, the Clinton Administration is proposing to prohibit telephone companies from acquiring cable systems in their local exchange areas.

6. The current policy of pricing local service/access below cost and relying upon contributions from long distance service will have to be reconsidered.

Le Groupe Vidéotron, a Quebec-based company with total revenues of almost $600 million (Can.) is the second-largest cable TV company in Canada. It is actively involved in providing cable and television services in England and has been a pioneer in the introduction of interactive television services known as Videoway. It has recently formed a consortium – UBI (Universal Bidirectional Interactive) – which will pilot a range of IH services (primarily electronic) in the region of Saguenay–Lac-St-Jean (in Quebec).

THE INDUSTRY

The Canadian telecommunications services industry includes nine regionally based major and 49 smaller telephone companies. All of the major companies – members of Stentor alliance – provide long-distance service. In addition, Unitel Communications provides a wide range of services including long-distance telephone service in competition with Stentor. Satellite-based services are provided by Telesat Canada, while overseas services are provided by Teleglobe Canada. Other telecommunications service providers include two national cellular telephone carriers, CellNet and Rogers Cantel Inc. (reaching 80% of Canadians and serving over one million subscribers), approximately 200 radio common carriers and more than 200 resellers. In 1990-1991, operating revenues for the Canadian telecommunications services industry totalled $14 billion (Can.).

Bell Canada Enterprise (BCE) is the largest telecommunications company in Canada. In 1993, it generated revenues of $19,827 million (Can.). BCE's principal subsidiary, Bell Canada (50,982 employees and revenues of $7,957 million Can. in 1993), serves Ontario and Quebec, with more than seven million business and 9.5 million network access lines (some 58% of the Canadian total).[14]

Canada has one of the best wireline telecommunications network infrastructures in the world. It can count on an increasingly digital[15] (more than 90%) coast-to-coast optic network. Almost 99% of households have telephone service and 92% of households are passed by cable, with a 79% subscription rate for households passed.

There are also several telecommunications equipment manufacturers (revenues over $6B (Can.) in 1992), Northern Telecom – also a BCE subsidiary – being the largest company.

Yet, in terms of revenues generated, Canadian long-distance service providers ($8 billion Can.) are small compared to American interexchange carriers ($64 billion Can.).

It would be relevant to compare Canadian and U.S. rates, but such a comparison is difficult because rate structures and services differ among regions and service providers. Nevertheless, in general, substantial gaps remain in newer, private-line, high-capacity services (lower rates in the U.S.) and basic local telephone service (higher rates in the U.S.). However, competition, strategic alliances and changing regulation have substantially reduced long-distance rates, making them more competitive with those in the U.S. Since 1987, rates have decreased between 26% (for 800 Service) and 51% (Long Distance MTS), depending on the service. In Canada, big businesses have been the prime targets, users and beneficiaries of these innovative and competitive services. Residential long-distance rates are now being targeted with discount packages. All in all, competition is continuing the downward pressure on long-distance rates, though it has not yet fully developed since the CRTC authorized competitive long-distance service in 1992. In the U.S., after more than ten years of competition, AT&T (which is still regulated by the Federal Communications Commission (FCC)) controls 60% of the long-distance market.[16]

---

14. BCE has a 58.5% interest in Telesat Canada, whose satellites transmit TV and radio signals and business telecommunications across Canada in United States and a 22.5% investment in Teleglobe Inc., whose subsidiary Teleglobe Canada Inc. is Canada's sole carrier for overseas telecommunications, via satellite and submarine cable. BCE also has at 52.1% interest in Northern Telecom Limited and a 30% interest in Bell-Northern Research Ltd. (Source: BCE 1993 Annual Report.)

15. Conversion of network to digital technology improves network performance, increases the carrier's ability to manage installations, multiplies the service offered and lowers costs.

16. According to some economists, [**Dr. J.M. Bauer**, Associate Director and Professor of Telecommunications, Institute of Public Utilities, Michigan State University, in his presentation on "The Role and Rationale of Public Utility Regulation," NARUC Annual Regulatory

A natural outcome of competition will be that the prices charged for services will move towards the cost of providing them. As rates for long-distance and business services decline, there will be upward pressure on local rates. The government and the regulator will face public pressure on this issue. In rural and remote areas, the cost of providing service may not attract competitive service providers, and therefore different rules may need to be applied in these areas. The issue of how to deal with the revenues shortfall attributable to local telephone services is one of the issues being considered by the CRTC in the context of major public hearings on the regulatory framework for telephone companies involved in both monopolies and competitive services.

In Canada most of the telecommunications carriers are privately owned and controlled. Exceptions include two of the major telephone companies which are provincially owned (SaskTel and Manitoba Telephone System) as well as several municipally owned local independent telephone companies.

Resellers can lease telecommunications facilities from the telecommunications carriers. Canadians can also lease or buy terminal equipment from numerous telecommunications suppliers, the largest being Northern Telecom, or directly through retailers of their choice.

Rogers is Canada's largest cable television distributor with 14 cable television systems in and aroud metropolitan areas of Southern Ontario, Alberta and British Columbia. Following the $3.1-billion transaction with Maclean Hunter and the Shaw transaction, Rogers shares over one-third of the total number of cable subscribers in Canada. In Quebec, Vidéotron controls approximately two-thirds of the cable market.

With the convergence of telephone, cable, broadcast, wireless and computer technologies, it is becoming increasingly important to consider the telecommunications sector not only alone but as a subset of the larger class of the industry of Information Technologies Goods and Services. For the purpose of this section, IT includes telecommunications services and products, computer hardware, software products, and computer services and equipment. Current global revenues are $1.9 trillion, with Canada's share at 3%. According to SRI International, the world's IT industry is projected to grow at an annual rate of 9.2%, and is forecast to exceed $3.2 trillion by the year 2000. By then, the industry will account for nearly $1 of every $6 of global Gross Domestic Product (GDP). The creation, movement and application of information and

Studies Program, MSU, August 1993; **Dr. John E. Kwoka**, evidence submitted to the CRTC for public hearings leading to Decision 92-12 which authorized competitive long-distance service, and **W. G. Shepherd**, "Converting Dominance to Competition: New Regulatory and Management Strategies in a Changing Market Environment," MSU Public Utility Paper, 1987, for competition to be fully effective in a previously monopoly market, no firm should possess more than a 40% market share.

knowledge are redefining the world economy and politics at all levels. All major nations either have, or are developing, national information strategies and infrastructures.

In Canada, the IT industry is a major source of employment, innovation, trade and wealth creation, contributing almost 5% to Canada's GDP in 1990-1991. Over the past six years, Canada's IT industry has experienced an average growth of approximately 7% annually. The industry consists of some 11,744 establishments which employ over 250,000 people. The supply industry is largely characterized by smaller firms that are innovative, have excellent growth potential and have established strong niche positions in which they provide competitive solutions.[17]

In 1990-1991, the Telecommunications Goods and Services Sector accounted for 3.02% of the total GDP and for two-thirds of the information technology industry.

Information Technology which can be subdivided into several smaller sectors, is now considered one of the primary sectors in Quebec's economy. As shown in Tables 1 and 2, revenues and jobs generated by the various firms evolving in this large sector are notable. In the province of Quebec, the Telecommunications Goods and Services Sector generated $4,869.4 million, almost a quarter of Canada's total $20,277.3 million, while the Computer Goods and Services Sector generated $2,493.9 million and $10,509.2 million Canada-wide. In 1990-1991, the Telecommunications Goods and Services Sector employed 37,784 salaried employees in Quebec, 63,858 in Ontario and 55,883 in the rest of Canada. Interestingly, 69.3% of the jobs were linked to the Telephone Services Sector. Furthermore, in 1990-1991, the number of firms operating in the Telecommunications Goods and Services Sector was estimated at 348. More specifically, Quebec accounts for almost 28% of these firms and employs 24% of the total 157,525 employees. As shown in Table 4, in 1990-1991 the Telecommunications Goods and Services Sector accounted for 3.02% of the GDP (3.16% in Quebec).[18]

Manufacturing capability in the Quebec Information Technology sector can be classified into three groups: (1) telecommunications equipment (77 firms, 12,465 employees and revenues of $1,833.4 million (Can.), (2) fabrication of computer equipment (103 companies, 8,199 employees, revenues of $1,068 millions (Can.), and (3) other manufacturing capability with firms who have other primary interests, such as aerospace or audio-visual production.

---

17.   Source: Industry Canada: Canada's International Trade Business Plan 1994-1995, and the Canadian Information Highway.

18.   Industry Canada, *Statistiques économiques sur la production des industries canadiennes des communications 1990-1991*, Direction des industries de communications et de services, Quebec Regional Office, March 1994.

For a third straight year, the Telecommunications Equipment and Material group was ranked number one in exported Quebec products by the Ministère des Affaires internationales du Québec and the Quebec Bureau of Statistics (table 5). In 1993, Quebec's international exports went mostly to the United States (79.4%), a number which has been increasing for the last three years (exports to the U.S. totalled 73.4% in 1991 and climbed to 76.3% in 1992). Northern Telecom accounted for about one-quarter of these exports, supported by a large number of small and medium-sized enterprises (20 to 200 employees).

TABLE 1
Information Technology
Revenues 1990-1991 (in millions of Can. $)

	Quebec	%	Ontario	Others	Canada
Telecommunications Goods and Services Sector					
Telecommunications Equipment	1,833.4	29.9	3,477.2	824.0	6,134.6
Telecommunications Services	135.1	23.0	242.5	209.7	587.3
Telephone Services	2,900.9	21.4	5,095.6	5,559.0	13,555.4
Sub-total	4,869.4	23.9	8,815.3	6,592.7	20,277.3
Computer Goods and Services Sector					
Computer Equipment	1,067.9	22.6	3,220.7	434.9	4,723.5
Software	185.3	20.9	495.1	208.2	888.6
Computer Services	1,240.7	25.3	2,686.8	969.6	4,897.1
Sub-total	2,493.9	23.7	6,402.6	1,612.7	10,509.2
TOTAL	**7,363.3**	**23.9**	**15,217.9**	**8,205.4**	**30,786.5**

Source: Industry Canada, Direction des industries de communications et de services, Quebec regional office.
Data are from Statistics Canada.

TABLE 2
Information Technology
Jobs 1990-1991 (number of salaried employees)

	Quebec	%	Ontario	Others	Canada
Telecommunications Goods and Services Sector					
Telecommunications Equipment	12,465	28.3	26,000	5,600	44,065
Telecommunications Services	978	23.0	1,754	1,517	4,249
Telephone Services	24,341	22.3	36,104	48,766	109,211
Sub-total	37,784	24.0	63,858	55,883	157,525
Computer Goods and Services Sector					
Computer Equipment	8,199	27.5	18,047	3,540	29,786
Software[1]	—	—	—	—	—
Computer Services	19,371	30.7	30,492	13,255	63,118
Sub-total	27,570	29.7	48,539	16,795	92,904
TOTAL	**65,354**	**26.1**	**112,397**	**72,678**	**250,429**

Source: Industry Canada, Direction des industries de communications et de services, Quebec regional office. Data are from Statistics Canada.

1. In 1990, Quebec counted between 400 to 500 enterprises manufacturing software which employed almost 10,000 persons.

TABLE 3
Information Technology
Firms 1990-1991 (number of firms)

	Quebec	%	Ontario	Others	Canada
Telecommunications Goods and Services Sector					
Telecommunications Equipment	77	27.1	132	75	284
Telecommunications Services	1	50.0	1	0	2
Telephone Services	8	29.0	32	12	62
Sub-total	96	27.6	165	87	348
Computer Goods and Services Sector					
Computer Equipment	103	21.8	274	95	472
Software	—	—	—	—	—
Computer Services	2,419	22.1	5,391	3,114	10,924
Sub-total	2,522	22.1	5,665	3,209	11,396
TOTAL	**2,618**	**22.3**	**5,830**	**3,266**	**11,744**

Source: Industry Canada, Direction des industries de communications et de services, Quebec regional office. Data are from Statistics Canada.

TABLE 4
Information Technology
Relative Importance in the Economy 1990-1991
Revenues / Gross Internal Production (%)

	Quebec %	Ontario %	Others %	Canada %
Telecommunications Goods and Services Sectors				
Telecommunications Equipment	1.19	1.25	0.34	0.91
Telecommunications Services	0.09	0.09	0.09	0.09
Telephone Services	1.88	1.84	2.32	2.02
Sub-total	3.16	3.18	2.75	3.02
Computer Goods and Services Sectors				
Computer Equipment	0.69	1.16	0.18	0.70
Software	0.12	0.18	0.09	0.13
Computer Services	0.81	0.97	0.41	0.73
Sub-total	1.62	2.31	0.68	1.56
TOTAL	**4.78**	**5.49**	**3.43**	**4.59**

Source: Industry Canada, Direction des industries de communications et de services, Quebec regional office. Data are from Statistics Canada.

TABLE 5
Quebec International Exports
(billions of $, Can.)

Five Main Groups of Exported Products	1993	1992	1991
1. Telecommunications Equipment and Materials	3.05	3.19	3.36
2. Newsprint	2.88	2.72	2.73
3. Aluminum and alloys	2.87	2.36	2.23
4. Cars	1.56	0.21	0.69
5. Entire Planes	1.33	0.67	0.86

Source: *La Presse*, based on statistics from the Ministère des Affaires internationales du Québec and Quebec's Bureau of Statistics.

Northern Telecom

Northern Telecom[19] is the largest Canadian manufacturer of telecommunications equipment and one of the ten largest such manufacturers in the world. Like Bell Canada, Northern Telecom is owned by BCE. Many agree that NT is a leading global manufacturer of telecommunications equipment, providing products and services to telephone companies, cable television companies, corporations, governments, universities and other institutions worldwide. Among Northern Telecom's major products are central office switching systems (48% of total revenues in 1993), multimedia communications systems (27 % of revenues), private branch exchanges and key systems, including asynchronous transfer mode (ATM)-based products, digital, high-capacity cellular mobile telecommunications switches and radios, wireless business communications systems, and a complete range of optical fibre transmission and cable products.

TABLE 6
Northern Telecom

	1993	1992	1991
	Millions of US dollars		
Revenues[1]	8,148	8,409	8,183
Net Earning (loss)	(884)	536	497
Capital Expenditures	471	572	514
Research and Development	1,100	1,020	1,010
Revenues from Canada	3,338	3,349	3,170
Revenues from United States	4,842	4,900	4,336
Revenues from Europe	1,693	1,399	1,351
Revenues from Other Countries	441	420	273

1. In Canadian dollars, because of change rate fluctuations, the Northern Telecom revenues have increased steadily in the last three years. They have been respectively $10,550 million (in 1993), $10,222 million (in 1992) and $9,379 million (in 1991).

As shown in Table 6, in 1993 Northern Telecom earned revenues of $8.15 billion (US), and had 60,293 employees and 48 manufacturing facilities worldwide at the year-end, including three in the Montreal area employing some 3,900 people. Total R&D expenses amounted to $1.1 billion (US), which reflected programs for new products, process development and advanced capabilities and services for a broad array of existing products.

---

19.   Information in this section comes from Northern Telecom's 1993 Annual Report.

RESEARCH AND DEVELOPMENT

The Conseil de la science et de la technologie, created by the government of Quebec, highlighted the importance of Research and Development in economic development. In its 1993 report, *Emergency: Technology; for a Bold, Competitive and Prosperous Quebec*, it recognizes that Quebec's economic growth is based less and less on the exports of products related to natural resources, and more and more on exports of high-tech products. With an average annual growth rate of about 14.9% since 1986, exports of high-tech products represented $7.4 billion in 1991, or 28% of Quebec's total exports. For the same period, export of products related to natural resources increased by an average of only 2.7% per year.

In 1992, the Communications and Information Technologies represented approximately 36% or $1.9 billion of the $5.3 billion of Research and Development (R&D) performed by industry in Canada, which is much more than its relative part in the GDP. The communications equipment[20] sector is the leading industrial R&D performer with 21% of all intramural R&D expenditure. Northern Telecom is the number one R&D spender in Canada and accounts for the bulk of R&D spending in the C&IT industry. It spent $1.1 (U.S.) billion worldwide on R&D in 1993, or 13.5% of its revenues. Canadian telecom carriers spent a much smaller proportion of their revenues on R&D. Bell Canada[21] spent $132 million (Can.) on R&D in 1991, or 1.7% of its revenues, while Teleglobe and Telesat spent respectively 2.3% and 2.1% of their revenues on R&D in the same year.

The Fonds de développement technologique (FDT) is the main Quebec government tool for stimulating industrial R&D. Since its creation in 1989, it has invested $150 million (Can.) in industrial R&D of information technologies.

In 1991, some 125 enterprises in Quebec, employing a total of 5,560 employees, were performing R&D in the area of information technologies. This represents almost half Quebec's industrial R&D activity.

There is a general consensus that technological advances will continue to drive the evolution of the telecommunications sector, which may have important impacts on the industry and on public policies. For instance, the cost of providing satellite computerized switching services has been reduced by over 100 times in real terms during the past 25 years. The major reductions in cost impact on both supply (it becomes possible for smaller companies to challenge large traditional monopolies) and demand (increased accessibility).

---

20. Communications equipment is composed of telecommunications equipment ($764 million) and other equipment ($343 million) manufacturers.

21. Here is an international comparison of R&D for major telecom carriers (% of revenues spent on R&D in 1991): DBP Telekom (1.1%), Bell Canada (1.7%), British Telecom (1.8%), Swedish Telecom GRP (3.6%), France Telecom (3.9%, in 1990), Ntt (4.4%), and AT&T (7%). AT&T is both a carrier and an equipment manufacturer. Source: Data compiled by Industry Canada from annual reports.

In June 1993, the federal government, in partnership with the private sector, announced the creation of the Canadian Network for the Advancement of Research, Industry and Education (CANARIE). The objective is to connect researchers and educational communities across Canada by 1999 with a high-speed broadband highway and to upgrade the gateway to the Internet and international network. Another objective is to accelerate the development of new network products, applications and services through joint funding of innovative projects. A third objective is to establish a high-speed experimental test network. Total investment for phase I, to be completed by March 1995, is $115 million (Can.), with the government contributing $26 million and the private sector $89 million. CANARIE Inc., a non-profit corporation, has been established to manage this project. Five of the fourteen projects accepted as part of phase I are from Quebec. The federal government announced in November 1994 that it will support CANARIE's business plan to speed the development of key parts of the information highway in Canada by investing $80 million over four years, matched with an estimated $396 million from the private sector and the provinces.[22] Plans for phase II foresee over 300 firms coming into the CANARIE consortium.

SchoolNet, a joint federal, provincial, and territorial initiative, is providing Canadian teachers and students with electronic services to stimulate the skills needed in the global information economy. SchoolNet is not a network in its own right. Rather, it is a set of learning resources provided in a user-friendly educationally-oriented menu structure to schools with access to Internet. Over 4,000 of Canada's 16,500 schools are already electronically connected to the information highway through SchoolNet. The federal government will invest a further $13 million over the next four years to expand SchoolNet.

The National Research Centre (NRC), the Communications Research Centre (CRC), both located in the National Capital Region (Ontario) and the Centre for Information Technology Innovation (CITI), located in Laval, near Montreal (Quebec), are examples of federal government laboratories. Their R&D activities focus on the elements that expand the main backbone network structure, for example: integration of wireless networks and satellite, integration of cable TV and telephone networks, enabling technologies that maximize the use of networks, user-friendly delivery of applications in multi-media/multi-modal environments and development of government service applications. CITI research aims to deliver enabling applications at the tail-end of the information technology value-added chain.

In Quebec, Bell-Northern Research (BNR) is the main private research centre on telecommunications with 400 employees, including 300 researchers. BNR is the largest R&D institution in Canada; it is 70%-owned by Northern

---

22.   Industry Canada, *Agenda: Jobs and Growth, Building a More Innovative Economy,* November 1994, page 56.

Telecom and at 30% by Bell Canada. The development of switches to interconnect telephones is generally recognized to be as important as the invention of the telephone itself, and switching technology has always been the subject of extensive research. Northern Telecom made a major advance in switching technology in the 1970s by designing the DMS series of digital switches. This reinforced the strength of Canada's strong telecommunications equipment industry. BNR is the largest private industrial R&D organization in Canada.

The Canadian Space Agency was established on March 1, 1989. It is responsible for federally funded activities in research, development and applications in space sciences and technology, for overall coordination of the space policies and programs of the Government of Canada, for promoting the transfer and diffusion of space technology to Canadian industry, and for encouraging commercial exploitation of space capabilities, technology, facilities and systems. The Agency is located in St-Hubert, close to Montreal, in Quebec. Given that Canada is only a mid-size player in world space activities, and in order to optimize value for money from investments, the Agency undertakes most major initiatives in partnership with other countries, especially the United States (NASA) and European countries (European Space Agency).

Spectrum Management

The radio frequency spectrum is that portion of the electromagnetic spectrum used for all communications through the airwaves. It is divided into bands of frequencies which are allocated for use by various radiocommunication services. It is a vital resource, essential to such services as broadcasting, mobile radio, satellite, cellular, telecommunications and public safety, and a basic element of the telecommunications and broadcasting infrastructure.

There are several reasons for government involvement in spectrum management. The primary reasons have to do with the physical nature of the spectrum (i.e., the potential for interference and other externalities) and the large number of international commitments required to manage it (radio emissions cannot be confined within borders and there is a need to coordinate large numbers and varieties of radio spectrum uses internationally). Also, the radio spectrum is important for strategic and national defence, public safety, cultural activities and education. Radio frequency spectrum is universally managed by governments, outside the market. In Canada, the federal Department of Industry is responsible for the allocation and management of the civil radio frequency spectrum to ensure that high quality and efficient radio communications services are available to as many users of the radio spectrum as possible with a minimum of interference. All telecommunications service providers must renew their licences through Industry Canada.

International agreements are aimed at ensuring that Canada has sufficient access to the international radio frequency spectrum. Domestic access and compliance are achieved through the development of legislation, standards and engineering rules affecting broadcast and non-broadcast radio stations and licence-exempt radio devices, the approval of radio equipment, licensing of applicants and enforcement of regulations through inspections.

A key dimension of the spectrum management program is its radio station licensing function. In 1992-1993, more than 850,000 radio station licences as well as 5,900 (AM/FM/TV/Cable) broadcasting certificates were in effect. The annual growth rate of the licence population is approximately 6%, which translates to over 57,000 applications to be processed every year. Approximately 62,000 radio station applications for single or multiple radio station installations were processed and over 8,000 examinations for radio operator certificates and approximately 9,000 radio interference investigations were carried out.

In 1992-1993, $105.4 million in revenue was collected from radio licence fees and $2.4 million in revenue from radio equipment and terminal attachment certification programs. In addition, the CRTC recovered approximately $13 million from its broadcasting licence fees on behalf of the spectrum management as part of its broadcasting regulatory function. Total expenditure on spectrum management was estimated at $58.6 million.

Spectrum allocation decisions are made available in Spectrum Utilization Policy Documents which are announced or published in the *Canada Gazette, Part I.*

Table 7 provides more detailed information on these activities.

TABLE 7
Spectrum Management Activities

	Estimates 1994-1995	Forecast 1993-1994	Actual 1992-1993
	Volume	Volume	Volume
Radio licences	87,390	86,120	84,871
Broadcast applications, certificates and notifications	5,340	4,660	4,720
Radio operators examined*	7,160	7,611	8,091
Bilateral proposals and international notifications	118,173	104,900	87,235
Radio equipment approvals	1,025	975	927
Inspections/investigations at public request	9,083	9,624	10,199
Directed investigations/surveys	4,149	4,550	4,998
Financial resources (thousands of Can. dollars)	$27,269	$27,269	$27,270

* Program staff also oversee the examination of over 22,000 candidates by delegated examiners

Sources: Industry Canada, 1994-95 Estimates, Part III, Expenditure Plan and Annual Managements Reports of Communications Canada.

CONCLUSION

Telecommunications and information technology – as recognized by the Quebec government in its industrial strategy based on the notion of industrial cluster – is already a key economic sector whose impact goes beyond its major direct economic impact in terms of revenues generated and employment. Its relative importance is growing in a global market environment, as new technologies are developed and adopted.

In fact, advances in technology are transforming the world of telecommunications. Fibre optics vastly increase transmission capacity. Optical fibre transmissions deliver telecommunications at the speed of light. The advent of cellular telephones is attaching communications to people rather than places. At this pace, one can easily imagine a situation where it would be possible to reach individuals anywhere in the world using a personal telephone number.

In this context, the evolution of the telecommunications sector will depend, to a large extent, on technological developments and on the merger of the telecommunications, informatics, broadcasting and cable worlds. As telecommunications technology converges with computers and cable television, technological developments will also lead to the development of a new media industry in Canada. These new media will allow individuals to take advantage of new technologies to complete their work in a more efficient, creative, flexible manner, with more accuracy and with homes and offices interconnected with interactive video, data, image and voice services. The information will circulate on the highway, probably over a hybrid network of optical fibre cable, coaxial cable, copper wire and wireless radio systems. The electronic highway system has the potential to provide a market environment that will enable Canadian industry to produce and distribute new media learning materials to a variety of institutions and individuals users. Again, Quebec is positioned to be a leader in the development of this industry, with its computer firms and research capability in the area.

Furthermore, Quebec can count on the support of the Quebec government, which published a new industrial development policy in 1993 aimed at accelerating the transition from its traditionally resource-based economy to an added-value economy and encouraging business to increase its competitiveness over the medium and long terms. The strategy relies on the notion of industrial cluster. For the Quebec government, Information Technology Products represent one of the five competitive clusters encompassing firms of international calibre that are competitive on the world market. Also, access by companies to an ultra-modern telecommunications infrastructure and services is a key asset for Quebec's economic development.

As a result of convergence, traditional barriers among telecommunications, broadcasting, cable and information industries are becoming increasingly irrelevant. These changes have led to a worldwide reorganization of the industry, characterized by mergers, acquisitions and strategic alliances. Canada and Quebec also face the same situation. For instance, the Montreal-based company Astral Communications Inc. has formed a partnership with other major telecom companies (BCE Inc., les Communications par satellite canadien Inc. (Cancom), Labatt Communications, Electroniques Tee-Comm, Western International Communications (WIC)) in a $120-to-$150-million project to offer all Canadians a DTA (Direct to Home) television service using satellites.

This situation is creating opportunities and challenges. In terms of public policy, the government will have to use policy and regulatory tolls to permit new services and new infrastructures to be offered at a lower cost. The government should provide an environment that allows the private sector to build and provide applications for the information highway in response to demand. At the end of the day, the information highway must offer the type and level of services required by customers. As a user of the highway, government can also stimulate the demand and participate in the construction and operation of the highway. For instance, the federal government's Chief Information Officer is engaged in a significant re-engineering exercise, depending heavily on electronic delivery of government services.

Moving to an information society also has social policy implications pertaining to personal and corporate privacy and access to services at affordable rates. Canada must maintain the key competitive advantage provided by its state-of-the-art telecommunications system and remain a major centre for innovation in telecommunications and information technology. Presently, Canada has one of the most advanced integrated telecommunications networks in the world. Canada's long-distance network, based on Northern Telecom DMS switches, is entirely digital and virtually all Bell Canada's local network will be digitally served by the end of 1994.

The year 1993 started a new area in the telecommunications service industry with the coming into force of the *Telecommunications Act* on October 25, 1993. The CRTC decisions regarding its regulatory framework, forbearance and exemption of certain competitive services and service providers will have an impact on the present level of regulation.[23] It is a clear signal that competition must be the driving force in telecommunications. As specific regulation diminishes, general policies, laws and regulation may increasingly be relied upon to address key policy issues. In this context, one can expect that the movement toward a more open and free market will continue.

In this business, the real market is the international scene. In the Canadian telecommunications sector, there are two leaders in their respective areas, BCE and Northern Telecom (a subsidiary of BCE). These giants have to com-

---

23. But the CRTC decision will not impact on the level of jurisdiction.

pete internationally – especially Northern Telecom, which has a very strong presence in Quebec. So far, it is under the leadership of these two large enterprises that Canada has been able to develop a solid basic telecommunications infrastructure and provides customers with access to good quality services at reasonable prices. The regulator now faces the challenge of permitting healthy competition from smaller firms without threatening what has been built in previous years. It must implement the right regulatory and policy framework.

Demand for international telecommunications services is vigourous, with an annual growth in the order of 15% to 20%. The services Teleglobe provides are essential and, in the context of Canada's increased focus on external trade, these services take on ever greater economic importance. In providing links to the rest of the world, Teleglobe also plays an important societal role. Again, Quebec is well positioned with Teleglobe Canada, located in Montreal, a world leader in the field of intercontinental telecommunications.

REFERENCES AND FURTHER READING

ADDY, George N., *The Competition Act and the Canadian Telecommunications Industry*, speech by the Director of Investigation and Research under the Competition Act to the Institute for International Research Telecommunications Conference, Toronto, March 1994 (and Montreal, March 1994), 15 pages.

BELL CANADA ENTERPRISES, *Annual Report 1993: Leadership in Telecommunications*, Montreal, 1994, 80 pages.

CANADIAN RADIO-TELEVISION AND TELECOMMUNICATIONS COMMISSION (CRTC), *1994-95 Estimates, Part III, Expenditure Plan*, 1994, 55 pages.

CANADIAN RADIO-TELEVISION AND TELECOMMUNICATIONS COMMISSION (CRTC), *Telecom Decision CRTC 94-19*, Ottawa, September 16, 1994, 165 pages.

CANADIAN SPACE AGENCY, *1994-95 Estimates, Part III, Expenditure Plan*, 1994, 38 pages.

COMMUNICATIONS CANADA, *1990-91 Annual Management Report, Summary of Program and Administrative Performance*, May 1991, 18 pages.

COMMUNICATIONS CANADA, *1991-1992 Annual Management Report*, May 1992, 154 pages.

COMMUNICATIONS CANADA, *1992-1993 Annual Management Report*, May 1992, 124 pages.

COMMUNICATIONS CANADA, *Evaluation Report for the Radio Frequency Spectrum Management Program*, Program Evaluation Division, February 1991, 54 pages.

COMMUNICATIONS CANADA, *Overview of Telecommunications Policy Developments*, April 1994, 19 pages.

COMMUNICATIONS CANADA, *Radio Frequency Spectrum Management Program Evaluation, Economic Nature of the Spectrum; A Review of the Literature*, Program Evaluation Division, March 1989, 38 pages.

COMMUNICATIONS CANADA, *Supporting Documentation to the 1990-91 Annual Management Report,* May 1991, 96 pages.

CONSEIL DE LA RECHERCHE ET DE LA TECHNOLOGIE, *Emergency: Technology, for a Bold, Competitive and Prosperous Quebec,* Summary and recommendations, Government of Quebec, ISBN: 2-550-27485-7, April 1993, 53 pages.

CONSEIL DE LA RECHERCHE ET DE LA TECHNOLOGIE, *Science et technologie, région de Montréal,* Gouvernement du Québec, ISBN: 2-550-27079-7, 1992, 184 pages.

CONSEIL DE LA SCIENCE ET DE LA TECHNOLOGIE, *Urgence technologique: pour un Québec audacieux, compétitif et prospère,* Gouvernement du Québec, ISBN: 2-550-27482-2, April 1993, 194 pages.

GIBBENS, Robert, "Teleglobe Poised for Growth," Toronto, October 16, 1993.

GOVERNMENT OF CANADA, *16 – Information Technologies: Canada's International Trade Business Plan 1994-1995; An Integrated Plan for Trade, Investment and Technology Development,* Minister of Supply and Services, Cat. No. C2-226/16-1994E, ISBN: 0-662-22082-X, 1994, 12 pages.

INDUSTRY CANADA, *Statistiques économiques sur la production des industries canadiennes des communications 1990-1991,* Direction du développement technologique, Direction générale des communications et de la culture, Montreal, March 1994, 63 pages.

INDUSTRY CANADA, *Agenda: Jobs and Growth, Building a More Innovative Economy,* Communications Branch, Minister of Supply and Services Canada, Cat. No. C2-254/1994, ISBN 0-662-61481-X, PU 0036-94-03, Ottawa, November 1994, 66 pages.

INDUSTRY CANADA, *1994-95 Estimates, Part III, Expenditure Plan,* 1994, 134 pages.

INDUSTRY CANADA, *Information Technologies – Statistical Review 1993,* Information Technologies Industry Branch, Ottawa, 1993, 191 pages.

INDUSTRY CANADA, *Phone Rate Increase Set Aside Pending Further Study on Costs,* News Release, Communication Branch, Ottawa, December 13, 1994, 2 pages.

INDUSTRY CANADA, *Telecommunications Infrastructure and Regulatory Environment, Questions & Answers, Response Provided by Canada to APEC,* Fall 1993, 35 pages.

INDUSTRY CANADA, *Telecommunications in Canada: Toward a Competitive, Integrated National Market,* Telecommunications Policy Branch, not published, March 1994.

INDUSTRY CANADA, *The Canadian Information Highway: Building Canada's Information and Communications Infrastructure,* Spectrum, Information Technologies and Telecommunications Sector, Minister of Supply and Services Canada, Cat. No. C2-229/1994E, ISBN 0-662-22189-3, April 1994, 33 pages.

MARTIN, André, *Autoroute électronique: portrait régional, Québec,* Direction des industries de communications et de services, Industry Canada, Montreal, March 1994, 30 pages.

MINISTÈRE DE L'INDUSTRIE, DU COMMERCE ET DE LA TECHNOLOGIE, *Industrial Clusters*, Published by the Direction des communications, ISBN 2-550-28048-2, Gouvernement du Québec, 1993, 37 pages.

MOZES, Dora, and LACROIX, Lise, *The Canadian Telecommunications Carriers: Overview, Economic and Financial Analysis, 1991*, Financial and Regulatory Policy, Telecommunications Policy Branch, Communications Canada, 1991, 34 pages.

MOZES, Dora, and LACROIX, Lise, *The Canadian Telecommunications Service Industry: Market Segments 1987-1994*, Financial and Regulatory Policy Division, Telecommunications Policy Branch, Industry Canada, January 1994, 100 pages.

MOZES, Dora, and LACROIX, Lise, *The Canadian Telecommunications Service Industry: Market Segments: Investments, Revenues and Expenses 1987-1994 (supplement to working document)*, Financial and Regulatory Policy Division, Telecommunications Policy Branch, Industry Canada, January 1994, 100 pages.

NATIONAL ADVISORY BOARD ON SCIENCE AND TECHNOLOGY, *Committee on Federal Science and Technology Priorities: Phase II; Spending Smarter*, February 1994, 67 pages.

NORTHERN TELECOM, *1993 Annual Report,* 1994, 56 pages.

RENS, Jean-Guy, *L'empire invisible: l'histoire des télécommunications au Canada de 1846 à 1956,* Volume 1, Presses de l'Université du Québec, Quebec, 1993, 572 pages.

RENS, Jean-Guy, *L'empire invisible: l'histoire des télécommunications au Canada de 1956 à nos jours,* Volume 2, Presses de l'Université du Québec, Quebec, 1993, 570 pages.

TELEGLOBE, *Rapport annuel 1992*, 1993, 60 pages.

TIGER, Michael, *NAFTA'S New Code Book For The World's Largest Market*, IIC conference, 1993.

Appendix

Bill 51:
An Act Respecting the Implementation of International Trade Agreements

WHEREAS Québec subscribes to the principles and rules established by the North American Free Trade Agreement, the North American Agreement on Environmental Cooperation, the North American Agreement on Labor Cooperation and the Agreement Establishing the World Trade Organization; and

Whereas the aforesaid agreements contain certain provisions falling within the constitutional jurisdiction of Québec and whereas Québec alone is competent to implement those agreements in each field coming under its jurisdiction;

THE PARLIAMENT OF QUÉBEC ENACTS AS FOLLOWS:

1.   In this Act,

"Agreements Establishing the World Trade Organization" means the Agreement Establishing the World Trade Organization, including the agreements set out in the annexes to that Agreement to which Canada is a party, all forming an integral part of the Final Act Embodying The Results Of The Uruguay Round Of Multilateral Trade Negotiations, signed at Marrakesh on 15 April 1994;

"Environmental Cooperation Agreement" means the North American Agreement on Environmental Cooperation entered into by the Government of Canada, the Government of the United States of America and the Government of the United Mexican States, and signed on 14 September 1993;

"Labor Cooperation Agreement" means the North American Agreement on Labor Cooperation entered into by the Government of Canada, the Government of the United States of America and the Government of the United Mexican States, and signed on 14 September 1993;

"North American Free Trade Agreement" means the North American Free Trade Agreement entered into by the Government of Canada, the Government of the United States and the Government of the United Mexican States, and ratified on 1 January 1994;

"Secretariat of Labor" means the Secretariat of the Commission for Labor Cooperation established under Article 8 of the Labor Cooperation Agreement;

"Secretariat of the Environment" means the Secretariat of the Commission for Environmental Cooperation established under Article 8 of the Environmental Cooperation Agreement.

2.   The following agreements are hereby approved:
  - the North American Free Trade Agreement;
  - the Environmental Cooperation Agreement;
  - the Labor Cooperation Agreement;
  - the Agreement Establishing the World Trade Organization.

3.   The commitments and reservations of Québec which are to appear in the Schedules of Canada annexed to the North American Free Trade Agreement shall be the commitments and reservations set out in the list established by the Gouvernement du Québec.

The list shall be transmitted to the authorities concerned by the Minister of International Affairs, Immigration and Cultural Communities.

4.   The commitments, reservations, measures and programs of Québec which are to appear in the Schedules of Canada annexed to the agreements forming part of the Agreement Establishing the World Trade Organization shall be the commitments, reservations, measures and programs set out in the list established by the Gouvernement du Québec.

The list shall be transmitted to the authorities concerned by the Minister.

5.   The Minister may propose that the Government take any measure he considers necessary for the purpose of implementing the measures taken by Canada under Article 2019 of the North American Free Trade Agreement.

6.   Except for the dispute settlement mechanisms available to investors under Section B of Chapter Eleven of the North American Free Trade Agreement,

no person has any cause of action based on the application of any of sections 2 to 5 of this Act or any order made thereunder.

7.   Only the Minister or the Deputy Minister of International Affairs, Immigration and Cultural Communities may appoint a person to be the representative of the Gouvernement du Québec on the committees and working groups established under the North American Free Trade Agreement and the Agreement Establishing the World Trade Organization. The representative shall be appointed after consultation, where applicable, with the minister concerned.

In the case of the Environmental Cooperation Agreement and the Labor Cooperation Agreement, the Minister or Deputy Minister, jointly with the Minister or Deputy Minister of the Environment and Wildlife, or the Minister or Deputy Minister of Labour, as the case may be, may appoint a person to be the representative of the Gouvernement du Québec on the committees and working groups established under the said Agreements.

8.   The Commission for Environmental Cooperation or the Commission for Labor Cooperation, as the case may be, may file at the office of the Superior Court a certified copy of any determination by an arbitral panel that is a panel determination described in Annex 36A of the Environmental Cooperation Agreement or in Annex 41A of the Labor Cooperation Agreement which imposes on Québec, upon failure by Québec to fully implement an action plan in such matters, full implementation of the action plan or a monetary enforcement assessment. The filing shall be made in the circumstances provided for in the aforesaid annexes.

When filed, a panel determination has all the effect of a final judgment of the Superior Court against the Gouvernement du Québec, and is not subject to appeal.

9.   No civil, administrative or penal proceedings may be instituted against an employee or the Executive Director of the Secretariat of the Environment or the Secretariat of Labor by reason of any performed in the exercise of his functions.

Such immunity cannot be waived except in the circumstances provided for in the rules of international law.

10.   The Minister of International Affairs, Immigration and Cultural Communities is responsible for the administration of this Act.

11.   The provisions of this Act will come into force on the date or dates to be fixed by the Government.

Glossary

Acid rain:

The common term for acidic deposition, caused by emissions of sulfur dioxide and nitrogen oxides from anthropogenic sources. Acid rain may result in regional-scale damages to freshwater ecosystems, forests, materials, and visibility.

Agenda setting:

Influencing the priorities of concerns.

Air Quality Agreement (Canada – U.S.)

An agreement signed by the governments of Canada and the United States in 1991 to address problems on the issue of transboundary air pollution.

Arm's length administration:

A mode of public management in which an autonomous agency is created to independently administer a policy. Quebec's council on the arts and letters (the Conseil des arts et des lettres) was established in 1992 as such a vehicle for allocating grants to artists and arts organizations.

Bloc québécois (BQ):

A recent political formation, presenting sovereigntist candidates in federal elections.

CANARIE:

CANARIE stands for Canadian Network for the Advancement of Research, Industry and Education. It is a government-private sector partnership with the objective of connecting researchers and educational communities across Canada by 1999 through a high-speed broadband highway.

Centrale de l'enseignement du Quebec (CEQ)	Major teachers' union, representing all Francophone elementary and secondary teachers, and a section of the college teachers.
Competition Act:	A law of general application, which pertains equally to all industries, except where specific exemptions exist either within the Act or in other legislation. The Bureau of Competition Policy – an arm's length organization under the responsibility of Industry Canada since June 1993 – is principally an investigative agency, charged with enforcing the Act.
Common market:	A zone where all duties and quotas on goods and services have been eliminated. Members have a common external tariff. There is also free mobility of production (labour and capital).
Confédération des syndicats nationaux (CSN):	A central whose member unions are virtually confined to Quebec employees in the private and especially the public sectors, the successor organization to the Confédération des travailleurs catholiques du Canada. [English name: Confederation of National Trade Unions (CNTU)].
Conseil des arts et lettres: du Québec	The autonomous administrative entity established in 1992 to allocate grants to artists and arts organizations and to represent the concerns of the artistic milieu to the Ministère de la Culture.
Conseil du patronat du Québec (CPQ):	The major employers' grouping in Quebec, representing the big multinational, Canadian and Quebec companies operating in the province.
CRTC:	The Canadian Radio-television and Telecommunications Commission is an administrative tribunal constituted under the CRTC Act (R.S.C. 1985, c. C-22) as amended by the Broadcasting Act (S.C. 1991, c. 11). It is vested with the administrative and quasi-judicial authority to licence and regulate telecommunications common carriers that fall under federal jurisdiction.
Culture mondiale:	Places an emphasis on Quebec creating artistic and literary products that can compete in the international cultural market.
Democracy:	Literally, "rule of the many." The modern meaning implies widespread participation in government typically through voting in periodic elections presenting a meaningful choice of candidates.
Dispute settlement:	The institutional provisions in a trade mechanism agreement that provide the means by which differences of view between parties can be settled.

Double chapeau:	The "two hats" worn by the head of the Conseil des arts et des lettres as its chief administrative officer (directeur général) and chief executive officer (president).
Economic dependency:	A situation in which a significant proportion of a province's economy is controlled by foreign interests.
Economic union:	A common market with the added element of harmonization of economic policies with a central authority administering these policies.
Efficiency cost:	Loss incurred by consumers and not captured by producers. Also called deadweight loss.
Effluent charges:	Charges to be paid by sources for discharges into the environment, based on the quantity and/or quality of discharged pollutants.
Elite:	Small group of people possessing power within a specific sphere of activity.
Environmental Impact (NAFTA):	The environmental impact of trade-related economic growth resulting from the reduction of trade barriers with NAFTA.
Environmental Protection Act (Quebec):	The framework environmental protection legislation in Quebec, originally approved in 1972, which sets limits on air and water emissions and standards for sewage treatment and hazardous wastes.
Environmental side agreement (NAFTA):	An agreement between the governments of Canada, Mexico and the United States addressing environmental concerns related to increased North American economic integration.
Factor endowments:	Availability of factors of production (e.g., labour, land, capital).
Fédération des travailleurs et des travailleuses du Québec (FTQ):	A central that includes the unions affiliated to the international unions (AFL-CIO) and Canadian unions, primarily in the private sector. The FTQ is the Quebec affiliate of the *Canadian Labour Congress* (CLC). [English name: Quebec Federation of Labour (QFL)].
Formal agenda:	The ranking of the top issues in policy-making circles.
Free trade area:	A cooperative arrangement among two or more countries which agree to remove substantially all tariff and non-tariff barriers to trade with each other, while each maintains its differing schedule of tariffs applying to all other nations.
Government:	Institution in a country that has the primary right to exercise political authority.
High-salience periods:	The time when an issue is at its highest salience.

Import-substitution policy:	Substitution of domestic production for imports of manufactures.
Industry Canada:	Industry Canada, as a key economic department, is mandated to make Canada more competitive by fostering the development of Canadian business, by promoting a fair and efficient Canadian marketplace and by protecting, assisting and supporting consumer interests. As the flagship microeconomic federal department, it has the lead role in setting policy agenda within the federal system.
Information Highway:	The term "information highway" is used to designate an advanced information and communications infrastructure which will become a network of networks, linking Canadian homes, businesses, government and institutions to a wide range of information-based services from entertainment, education, cultural products, and social services to data banks, computers, electronic commerce, banking and business services. Its enabling effects will be felt in all industry sectors.
Information Technologies:	With the convergence of telephone, cable, broadcast, wireless and computer technologies, it is becoming increasingly important to consider the telecommunications sector not only alone but as a subset of the larger class of the industry of information technologies goods and services.
International efficiency:	A situation where the market prices of goods traded internationally fully reflect the social costs of their production, including any transfrontier environmental costs.
Issue abstractness:	The condition of an issue that is not easily comprehended or visualized.
Issue cycle:	The rise and fall of an issue's ranking on an agenda.
Issue obtrusiveness:	The condition of an issue that pertains to personal experience.
Labour centrals:	The name by which the major trade union federations are commonly known in Quebec.
Marketable emissions allowances:	Pollution sources are allowed to emit a certain amount of a pollutant and hold allowances which specify the allowable emissions. The allowances are freely transferable.
Ministère de la Culture:	A cabinet-level department of the government of Quebec that was created in 1960 with responsibility for supporting culutral organizations, encouraging artistic excellence, preserving the cultural heritage and promoting the French language.
Mobilizing effect:	Influence on opinion when an issue is highly salient.

New Democratic Party (NDP): A pan-Canadian party created in 1961 with the direct participation of the trade union movement; has never really established itself in Quebec.

Non-committed respondents: The sum of respondents in a public opinion poll who were either unable or unwilling to respond.

Non-tariff barriers: Government measures or policies other than tariffs that restrict or distort international trade.

North American Environmental Commission (CEC): A trilateral agency to monitor North American environmental conditions and investigate and settle environmental disputes among NAFTA member countries.

Opinion polls: Scientific attempts to measure public attitudes by surveying a sample of people about opinions.

Parti québécois (PQ): A party formed in 1968, advocating the political sovereignty of Quebec.

Patrimoine: Refers to Quebec's culutral heritage which, in arts policy, typically involves an emphasis on preserving historic sites, promoting local artistic activity and encouraging French-Canadian traditions.

Policy instruments: The differents means available to governments to implement their policies, such as state enterprise subsidies, regulation, etc.

Politique culturelle: An official expression of the governments' policy concerning cultural affairs. As formulated by the Ministère de la Culture in *Notre Culture, Notre Avenir* in 1991, the goals were to: (1) emphasize the French language; (2) support artistic excellence; (3) promote accessibility to culture.

Privatization: Full ou partial transfer of ownership from the state to the private sector

Province-building: The increased capacity of a provincial government to act in favour of regional or provincial interests

Public agenda: The ranking of the top issues in the public mind.

Public opinion: An aggregate of individual attitudes and beliefs about political phenomena.

Quiet Revolution: The "quiet revolution" of the 1960s initiated by the Liberal government of Jean Lesage and associated with a resurgence of Quebecois nationalism and the blossoming of French-Canadian cultural identity.

Radio Frequency Spectrum: The portion of the electromagnetic spectrum used for all communications through the airwaves. It is a wireless medium through which various forms of information are generated, transmitted and received between distant points.

Salience:	The public's ranking of the relative importance of an issue.
Sample:	A smaller number of elements selected from a large group in order to try to gauge the entire group based on the characteristics of the sample.
Semi-periphery:	A situation of economic dependency where a country or a province is partly in control of its economic development – whereas countries in the periphery of the economic world-system are highly dependent.
State enterprise:	A commercial enterprise owned by the government which nominates the chief executive officier and the members of the board of directors. State enterprises are economic policy instruments used for various social and economic development. In many cases, they provide services that could be delivered by the private sector.
Stentor:	One of the major networks in Canada. It is an association of eleven companies (the major telephones companies in each province and Telesat Canada) and provides satellite link across the country.
Sub-national state:	A generic term to designate non-national states such as the Canadian provinces.
Subsidy:	An economic benefit granted by a government to producers of goods – often to strengthen their competitive position.
Survivance:	The survival of Québécois culture and French-Canadian national identity during the period from the fall of Quebec (1759) to the start of the Quiet Revolution in 1960.
Telecommunications:	Communication at a distance, especially by means of a system using electromagnetic impulses, as in radio, radar, telegraphy, or television.
Transfrontier pollution:	Pollution that occurs in one legal jurisdiction as a result of emissions from another. The flow of pollutants can be either reciprocal or unidirectional but the term usually refers to pollution that crosses international borders.
U.S. Clean Air Act:	The primary U.S. law for air pollution control, originally passed in 1963, which sets standards for emissions of sulfur dioxide, nitrogen oxides, carbon monoxide, and other "criteria" pollutants.

The Authors

Luc BERNIER. Ph.D. (Political Science). A Northwestern graduate (1988), he is associate professor of public policy at the École nationale d'administration publique (affiliated with the Université du Québec). He is the author of *From Paris to Washington: Quebec's Foreign Policy in a Changing World*. He is co-author, with Guy Lachapelle, Gérald Bernier and Daniel Salée, of *The Quebec Democracy* (McGraw-Hill Ryerson, 1993) and also, with Carolle Simard, of *L'administration publique* (Boréal, 1992). He has written several articles and chapters on the use of state enterprises as policy instruments, on privatization and in administrative reform in Quebec. He has also worked on the subject of political parties and their impact on public policy.

Anne-Marie COTTER. J.D. Ph.D. candidate (Political Science). She earned a bachelor's degree in Political Science from McGill University. Later, she pursued a graduate diploma in Community Politics and the Law, a Master's degree in Public Policy and Public Administration, and a graduate teaching certificate in Teaching French as a second language to adults, from Concordia University. She earned a Juris Doctor degree from Howard University School of Law in Washington, D.C., and is an Attorney member of the Washington State Bar Association. She has published a bilingual pamphlet entitled *Montreal's Disarmament and Peace Groups*, and was an organizer of a Symposium on the International Law of Human Rights in Washington, D.C. She is presently a doctoral student in the Department of Political Science at Concordia University, researching the impact of NAFTA on pay equity in Quebec, Canada, the United States and Mexico.

Serge DENIS. Ph.D. (Political Science). He is professor of political science and Associate Dean and Secretary of the Faculty of Art & Science at the University of Ottawa. He is the author of *Un syndicalisme pur et simple* (1986), co-author, with C. Andrew, C. Archibald and F. Caloren, of *Une communauté en colère* (1987), author of *Le long malentendu* (1992) and co-author, with Roch Denis, of *Les syndicats face au pouvoir* (1992). He has conducted extensive comparative research on labour organizations, their support to political parties and their relationships with the state.

Rock DENIS. Ph.D. (Political Science). He is full professor of political science at the Université du Québec à Montréal (UQAM). He is currently president of the Quebec Association of University Professors (Fédération québécoise des professeurs et professeures d'université). He is the author of *Luttes de classes et question nationale au Québec* (1979), *Québec, fin de l'indépendantisme?* (1987), *Québec, dix ans de crise constitutionnelle* (1990), and co-author, with Serge Denis, of *Les syndicats face au pouvoir* (1992). His scholarly writing has focused on political change in Quebec's society, nationalism and the political role of labour unions in Quebec and Canada.

Hervé DÉRY. M.Sc. (Economics). He has a B.Sc., and an M.Sc. in Economics from the Université de Montréal. He has twelve years' experience in the Canadian federal public service in the areas of economic research, policy analysis and program evaluation. He has worked for several Government Departments, including Fisheries and Oceans and the Office of the Comptroller General (Treasury Board of Canada). He was working for the Department of Communications when the reorganization of federal departments took place in June 1993. He now works for the Management Consulting Branch of Industry Canada. Hervé Déry is a specialist in the government decision-making process. He has published and made presentations on the subject of program evaluation and methods for evaluating public programs and policies. He is also a past president of the Canadian Evaluation Society (National Capital Chapter) and a member of the Board of Directors of the Quebec Association of Economists (Outaouais Section).

Gilles DURUFLÉ. Ph.D. (Director, Strategic Studies – Caisse de dépôt et placement du Québec). He has a doctorate in mathematics from the Université de Paris and a diploma from the Centre d'études des programmes économiques (Paris). He has worked as an economic consultant in France, Africa and Canada and published serveral books and articles on economic development, regional development and the construction of commercial blocks in Europe and North America. He is presently Director of Strategic Studies at the Caisse de dépôt et placement du Québec.

Pierre-André JULIEN. Ph.D. (Economics). He has a degree from the Université catholique de Louvain (Belgium) and a Diploma in Management Science from Université Laval (Quebec). He is director of the Bombardier Chair in the Management of New Technologies for Small Firms at the Université du Québec à Trois-Rivières and Editor of the *Revue Internationale PME*. He has been visiting fellow at several foreign universities (Sussex (England), Wharton School (United States), École des Hautes Études en Sciences Sociales (France), Universités de Dijon and Montpellier (France), McGill University and Université de Montréal (Quebec), etc.). He has worked for the FAST Project of the European Economic Commission in Brussels and for the Industrial Districts Project of the International Institute for Labour Studies in Geneva. He is currently a consultant for small businesses and globalization studies for the Industry and Science Committee of the Organization for Economic Co-operation and Development (OECD). He has published more than three hundred scientific articles and government reports in French, English, German, Spanish, Italian and Finnish. He is the author or co-author of 16 books on subjects in the areas of economic prospects and small businesses economics.

Guy LACHAPELLE. Ph.D. (Political Science). He is associate professor in the Department of Political Science at Concordia University. He is co-author, with Jean Crête and Louis M. Imbeau, of *Politiques provinciales comparées* (1994). With Gérald Bernier, Daniel Salée and Luc Bernier, he published *Quebec Democracy: Structures, Processes, and Policies* (1993). He is the author a study (#16) for the Royal Commission on Political Parties and Party Financing (Lortie Commission): *Polls and the Media in Canadian Elections: Taking the Pulse* (1991). He is also co-editor of *Québec: un pays incertain – réflexion sur le Québec post-référendaire* (1980). His publications include contributions to the *Canadian Journal of Political Science*, the *Revue québécoise de science politique*, *Quebec Studies* and the *Canadian Journal of Program Evaluation*. His recent work has focused on public opinion theory, comparative voting behaviour and Quebec public policy.

Frederic C. MENZ. Ph.D. (Economics). He received his Ph.D. from the University of Virginia in 1970. He is professor of economics and director of the Center for Canadian-U.S. Business Studies at Clarkson University in Postdam, New York. He is co-editor (with Sarah A. Stevens) of *Economic Opportunities in Freer U.S. Trade with Canada* (State University Press, New York, 1991). His recent research has focused on environmental policy, particularly on issues involving Canada and the United States. Recent publications include "Transboundary Acid Rain: A Canadian-U.S. Problem Requiring a Joint Solution," in Jonathan Lemco (editor), *Tensions at the Border: Energy and Environmental Concerns in Canada and the United States* (Praeger, 1992: 45-60); "Minimizing Acidic Deposition Control Costs through Transboundary Emissions Trading," *American Review of Canadian Studies* (Summer, 1993:

247-66); "The North American Environment: Economic and Public Policy Issues," *North American Outlook* (March 1994: 3-22); "The Great Whale Hydroelectric Project: Some Economic and Environmental Issues," *Quebec Studies* (December 1994). His research in environmental economics has been supported by the U.S. Environmental Protection Agency, the U.S. Department of Commerce and the U.S. Department of Interior.

Kevin V. MULCAHY. Ph.D. (Political Science). He received his Ph.D. from Brown University in 1976 and is professor of political science at Louisiana State University in Baton Rouge, where he has taught since 1980. Prior to this, he taught at Queens College in the City University of New York and Claremont-McKenna College. He specializes in the study of public policy with special interests in cultural policy-making and presidential administration of American national security. He is co-editor of *America Votes* (Prentice-Hall, 1976; Japanese edition, 1978); *Public Policy and the Arts* (Westview, 1982): *Presidents and the Administration of Foreign Policy: FDR to Reagan* (Louisiana State University, 1986); *The Challenge to Reform Arts Education* (American Council on the Arts, 1989); and *American National Security: A Presidential Perspective* (Brooks/Cole, 1990). He has written numerous articles for professional publications. In 1990, he testified as an expert witness before the Independent Commission on the Arts appointed by President George Bush. He has been the recipient of several teaching awards including the Amoco Foundation Award for Distinguished Undergraduate Teaching.

Benoît M. PAPILLON. Ph.D. (Economics). He is currently associate professor in the Department of Administration and Economics at the Université du Québec à Trois-Rivières. He served previously as senior economist on two economic inquiries by the Canadian International Trade Tribunal in the field of agriculture: the Competitiveness of the Cattle and Beef Industry in North America and the Allocation of Import Quotas. Prior to that, he served as economist on a number of projects of the Economic Council of Canada in the areas of trade and adjustment, financial markets and regulation. He holds a Ph.D. in economics and a B.Sc. in mathematics (statistics) from Université Laval. His recent publications and research concern to the performance of the distribution sector (retail trade and wholesale trade) and the measurement of non-tariff barriers in agriculture.

Andrea M.L. PERRELLA. M.A. (Political Science). He earned a bachelor's degree in political science (Honours) from Concordia University. Later he obtained a graduate diploma in journalism, also from Concordia, which led him to an internship with the *Toronto Sun* and various freelance jobs, as well as a full-time position as a reporter and photographer with an Ottawa Valley community newspaper. His experience in journalism inspired a deeper curiosity in politics from an analytical perspective, which led him to pursue graduate work in political science. He is currently completing a Master's degree at the Université de Montréal, where he is doing work on political behaviour.

Pierre-Paul PROULX. Ph.D. (Economics). He is currently professor of economics at the Université de Montréal. He studied economics at the Universities of Ottawa, Toronto and Princeton. He is a former Assistant Deputy Minister – Policy and Small Business – in the Canadian Department of Regional Industrial Expansion. His current research and publications are in the area of economic integration, with special attention to international and interregional (cross-border) trade flows, the location of economic activity, sharing of power between levels of government, the growth and decline of the regions, the FTA, NAFTA, and development policies at the sub-national level. His recent publications in these areas include: *L'espace économique extérieur du Québec et de trois de ses régions, sous l'effet de l'intégration économique*, co-authored with C. Manzagal and F. Amesse (Ministère du Conseil exécutif du Québec, 1994); "Quebec in North America: From a Borderlands to a Borderless Economy," *Quebec Studies* (16: 1993); "Conceptual Framework and Theory Related to the Location of Economic Activities: The Case of International Cities," *Canadian Journal of Regional Science* (14: 2, Summer 1991). Forthcoming in P. Kred, "Determinants of the Growth and Decline of Cities in North America" (Sage Publications).

Jean-François PRUD'HOMME. Ph.D. candidate (Political Science). He is a political scientist specialized in Mexican studies. He is currently a Ph.D. candidate at York University (Toronto). He has taught in graduate programs at various universities and research centres in Mexico, where he has been living for the past ten years. He is currently a researcher in the Division of Political Studies at the Centre for Research and Teaching in Economics (CIDE). Author of various articles on the Mexican political system, his most recent publications include: "Elecciones, partidos y democracia" in *La construcción de la democracía en México* (Siglo XXI Editores, Mexico, 1994); and "Acción colectiva y lucha por la democracía en México y Chile" in *Transformaciones sociales y acciones colectivas: America Latina en el contexto internacional de los noventa* (El Colegio de Mexico, Mexico, 1994). He is a member of the editorial board of the magazine *Voz y Voto* and editor of *Politica y Gobierno*.

Maryse ROBERT. Ph.D. (International Relations). A trained economist, she studied applied and international economics at the École des Hautes Études commerciales (HEC) of the Université de Montréal (B.B.A. 1982, M.Sc. 1985) and holds a Ph.D. (1995) from The Fletcher School of Law and Diplomacy (Tufts University). Her thesis was concerned with "The determinants of negotiation outcome and Canada's performance in NAFTA." Her fields of expertise are: international trade, macroeconomics, development economics and international political economy. From 1987 to 1989, she was deputy director of the Centre for International Affairs at the École nationale d'administration publique (Université du Québec) in Montreal. She has also worked for the World Bank, the United Nations, two consulting firms and two research centres. She has taught economics at both the undergraduate and graduate levels.

Maria Isabel STUDER. Ph.D. candidate (International Relations). She is studying in International Relations at the Paul H. Nitze School of Advanced International Studies (SAIS) at the Johns Hopkins University (Washington, D.C.). She is currently a researcher at the Centre for Research and Teaching in Economics (CIDE) in Mexico City. Her Master's degree (from SAIS) is in International Relations and Canadian Studies, and she also holds a Licenciate in International Relations from El Colegio de Mexico (Mexico City). She is a Galo Plaza Fellow of the Inter-American Dialogue (Washington, D.C.). She has published several articles on Canadian constitutional reform, NAFTA and the U.S. decision-making process, and on the North American automobile industry.

Benoît TÉTRAULT. M.Sc. Finance (Analyst, Strategic Affairs – Caisse de dépôt et placement du Québec). He obtained a Bachelor's degree in economics from the Université de Montréal and a Master's degree in Finance from the École des Hautes Études commerciales in Montreal. He has also completed the first-level requirements of the Chartered Financial Analyst program. He joined the Caisse de dépôt et placement du Québec in 1993 as a member of Strategic Affairs. Since then, he has worked on different studies in the areas of structural economy, corporate analysis and international trade. His fields of interests are macroeconomics, public choice theory, corporate finance, investment strategies, management, technologies and fiscal policies.

André TURCOTTE. Ph.D. candidate (Political Behaviour). He is currently studying at the University of Toronto and is senior research analyst at Insight Canada Research. Prior to this, he was the co-editor of the Gallup Report, published in ten newspapers across Canada. In his work, he specializes in the study of voting behaviour, public opinion research and public policy analysis.